Italian
Cinema

FROM NEOREALISM
TO THE PRESENT

Italian Cinema

FROM NEOREALISM
TO THE PRESENT

NEW EXPANDED EDITION

Peter Bondanella

ROUNDHOUSE PUBLISHING

FOR MARIO LONGARDI,
FRANCESCA PIERI, AND ALDO TASSONE

1999

Roundhouse Publishing Ltd.
Millstone
Limers Lane, Northam,
North Devon EX39 2RG, UK

Published by arrangement with The Continuum Publishing Company.

Printed in the United States of America

ISBN: 1-85710-079-4

A CIP catalogue record for this title is available from the British Library.

Preface to the Second Edition

This second edition of *Italian Cinema: From Neorealism to the Present* incorporates substantial changes. The original ten chapters have been revised. A greatly expanded bibliography testifying to the explosion of scholarly commentary during the past decade has been compiled. And the footnotes of the original edition have been completely updated in order to offer the reader a clearer guide through such an imposing mass of critical literature. The rental information, originally limited to available 16-mm prints, has been enlarged to incorporate videocassettes currently available for purchase or rental in both the United States and in Italy. The reader or researcher should be aware of the fact that Italian videocassettes are manufactured for the PAL video format. While viewing them in the United States will require a video recorder capable of reading the PAL format, such machines are becoming increasingly more accessible in universities and large research libraries. Finally and most importantly, a new eleventh chapter has been written to cover the history of the Italian cinema during the present decade.

Since the publication of the first edition of this book, while I have continued to enjoy the friendship and help of a number of people whose efforts were acknowledged in the original preface, I have been assisted in my labors by an additional group of generous colleagues, editors, archivists, photographers, and filmmakers. The following list cannot begin to measure the debt I owe to all of them: Gianfranco Angelucci; Pupi Avati; Bernardo Bertolucci; Antonio Breschi; Bill Cagle; Liliana Cavani; Zeno Collantoni; Masolino d'Amico; Caterina d'Amico de Carvalho; Evelyn Ehrlich; Sergio Ercolessi; Federico Fellini; Harry Geduld; Norma Giacchero; Manuela Gieri; Giovanni Grazzini; Guy Hennebelle; Joanna Hitchcock; Daniel Keel; Tullio Kezich; Gianna Landucci; Michael Leach; Sergio Leone; Mario Longardi; Denis Mack Smith; Millicent Marcus; Franco Mariotti; Gaetana Marrone-Puglia; Maureen Mazzaoui; Umberto Montiroli; Nanni Moretti; Mark Musa; Tullio Pinelli; Fiammetta Profili; Bruno Rondi; Ettore Scola; Emilio Vesperini; John Welle; Dario Zanelli; and Bernardino Zapponi. A number of grants from various sources (the American Council of Learned Societies; the Lilly Foundation; Indiana University's Office for Research and Graduate Development and its West European Studies Center) have afforded me time in Italy to complete my work or funding to procure illustrations for this book. For all of this support, both financial and personal, I am deeply grateful.

Rome, 1988

Preface to the First Edition

This book, the first comprehensive English treatment of the contemporary Italian cinema in many years, is the fruit of some ten years of teaching and research in the area. One of the major goals of this study has been to rescue the study of Italian cinema from the monolingual bias of most English and American critics, who rarely possess an adequate knowledge of the language these films speak or the culture they reflect. I hope that the ample footnotes and bibliography contained within this book will suggest the richness and variety of work on the Italian cinema published abroad and may serve to spur critics on this side of the Atlantic to pay more attention to it.

I have tried to analyze the major trends in this sometimes overwhelming mass of material, sifting out those films or directors that constitute, in my personal opinion, the most important artistic achievements of the postwar period. Since films made in Italy have always been characterized by a close link to Italian literature or current social problems, I have attempted to point out such relationships wherever possible. And in discussing such topics, I have tried to temper the too often ideological tone of Italian film scholarship by what I hope is a more detached and dispassionate assessment of the Italian cinema's many, many achievements and sometimes spectacular failures. While I have striven to provide an accurate picture of general economic trends within the industry, this book is primarily about Italian cinema as an art form, with the director playing the key role. I realize only too well the pitfalls of overemphasis on the director, and whenever possible, I have also attempted to discuss at least briefly the place of the studio system, as well as the contributions of scriptwriters, musicians, cameramen, and actors. However, a single book on this vast topic can only hope to accomplish so much, and I have been constrained to limit my remarks.

I would be less than honest if I did not admit to a preference for Italian films above those produced anywhere else in the world, as well as to an admiration for the many brilliant and unfailingly generous people who work in the Italian industry. While it is my hope that my critical judgment has not been misled by my enthusiasm, I should be disappointed if the reader did not detect in this study my passionate interest in its subject matter. A completely analytical study of Italian cinema would not only make boring reading but would betray the spirit of the material itself. One book will not exhaust this rich field, but it is my hope that the present work will stimulate a reconsideration of already acknowledged classics, help to increase interest in films and directors not so well known outside of Italy, and contribute something of value to the history of a national art form second only to that of Hollywood in importance to world cinema since the end of World War II.

My debt to other scholars or critics has, I trust, been amply documented in the notes and bibliography. Stanley Hochman was a perfect editor, always generous in his support and advice. Mary Corliss of the Film Stills Archive at the Museum of Modern Art in New York and Alfredo Baldi of the Centro Sperimentale di Cinematografia in Rome, were most helpful in providing illustrations. My good friend Ben Lawton, one of the brightest lights in American scholarship on the Italian cinema, supplied many helpful suggestions and corrective criticism, as did Bruce Cole. Indiana University provided funds for the preparation of the final manuscript, ably typed by Deb Munson, as well as for the illustrations. Several research grants from the National Endowment for the Humanities (admittedly given for quite different projects!) permitted two lengthy stays in Italy and Paris which made possible the completion of the book. My greatest debt is owed to three good Italian friends, to whom this book is dedicated, and without whose generosity and cordial welcome in Italy I should have never begun this task. In addition, a number of people in the

Italian film industry assisted me by allowing me to observe their work on location, stimulating my own ideas with their suggestions, inviting me to participate in the Venice Film Festival, giving me permission to do vital research at the Centro Sperimentale, and setting up special screenings of hard-to-locate prints: they include Federico Fellini, Carlo Lizzani, Lina Wertmüller, Adriano Aprà, Guido Cincotti, Gideon Bachmann, Carlo Bersani, Guido Fink, Francesco Rosi, and the Taviani brothers.

Rome — Florence — Bloomington

1

Background:
The Silent Era and the Fascist Period

Given its unsurpassed contribution to the development of the plastic arts in Western Europe from the time of Giotto to the present, it would be remarkable indeed if Italy had not made a major addition to the art of the early cinema.[1] Much of its claim to artistic hegemony on the European continent for a number of centuries rested upon not only a steady succession of artists of genius but also upon the resolution of certain technical problems, such as the study of perspective, which would eventually raise similar problems and demand equally ingenious artistic and technical solutions in the realm of photography. The first major step forward occurs in November 11, 1895, when Filoteo Alberini applied for a patent on an early device for the production of motion pictures, the Alberini Kinetograph. One of the first films produced for commercial use in Italy appeared the next year, Vittorio Calcina's *King Umberto and Margherita of Savoy Strolling in the Park* (*Umberto e Margherita di Savoia a passeggio per il parco*), a brief documentary which also has the honor of being the first Italian film to which admission was charged. We have a number of such brief documentaries from this period, memorable not only for the slice of life from Italy's *belle époque* that still lives through them but also because they reveal the Italian cinema's first infantile steps towards a film language beyond still photography—early panoramic shots of crowds, camera placed on moving automobiles to capture the finish of a bicycle race, and so forth. In many respects, this early documentary cinema was indebted to the example of the Lumières in France; Calcina was, in fact, the Italian representative for their company. Alberini produced the first feature film with a complex plot in 1905—*The Taking of Rome (La presa di Roma)*—a brief work celebrating the patriotic theme of the breaching of the Porta Pia by Italian troops in 1870 and the annexation of the Eternal City to the fledging republic. Perhaps more crucial to the future development of this new medium was the formation in 1906 of a major production company, Cines, which helped to set the new industry on a rational economic basis and permitted it, within only a decade, to capture and dominate the world market for a brief period, what Pierre Leprohon has termed Italy's cinematic "golden age" (1909–1916).

The early silent cinema in Italy was not, as many cursory treatments of it imply, completely dominated by the historical film and the costume drama, although such works were to represent its most popular and profitable product. There existed a variety of topics—ranging from the celebrated Roman epics to filmed theatrical works, dramas inspired by Italian *verismo* or regional naturalism, adventure films in episodes or in series, comic works, and several experimental films produced by the Italian artistic avant-garde. All of these genres contributed something to the evolution of Italian film art, although it is ultimately the historical film which must be given special attention. The appearance of *The Taking of Rome* marked one major step forward from the brief work designed for intermissions in music or concert halls to the much longer feature film. The continued interest in historical topics helped to create the need for an artistic director, in addition to the cameraman and the producer, whose task it was to coordinate the necessary historical research, the construction of sets and costumes, and the increasingly central role of the often temperamental actors and actresses who would soon replace the man in the street of the early documentary. The wealth of ruins and grandiose monuments, as well as the favorable climate and natural light of the peninsula, encouraged feature films shot on location, and the relatively inexpensive cost of Italian labor made possible the huge crowd scenes that characterize historical works of the period. Much of the artistic value these early works possess lies in their treatment of such crowds and the spectacular sets they made necessary. The period's greatest directors were Giovanni Pastrone (1883–1959) and Enrico Guazzoni (1876–1949). In *The Fall of Troy* (*La caduta di Troia*, 1910), an early work of 600 meters, Pastrone develops the aesthetic possibilities of the long shot, opening up with his camera a sense of boundless space populated by large crowds and magnificent sets that stand in sharp contrast to the opera-like, one-dimensional sets of earlier historical works. *Agnes Visconti* (*Agnese Visconti*, 1910) by Pastrone reveals his mastery of creating suspense through careful editing, as parallel actions involving different characters are developed skillfully toward a forceful conclusion.

Giovanni Pastrone's *Cabiria* (*Cabiria*, 1914) is the acknowledged masterpiece of the Italian silent costume film. A work of some 4,500 meters, it embodies a number of artistic and technical innovations which guaranteed it a market all over the world and placed the Italian film industry momentarily ahead of its competitors. Pastrone's film on the Second Punic War followed closely upon two costume films of Roman inspiration—*The Last Days of Pompeii* (*Gli ultimi giorni di Pompeii*, 1913) by Mario Caserini (1895–1981), and Guazzoni's *Quo vadis?* (*Quo Vadis?*, 1913). Caserini's film derived from the novel by Bulwer-Lytton, and Guazzoni's was based upon that of Henryk Sienkiewicz; and while *The Last Days of Pompeii* helped to establish the popularity of the Roman costume film and may justly be termed the ancestor of the hundreds of such films produced in Italy and abroad during the cinema's history, Guazzoni's work was more innovative in its continuation of the aesthetic exploration of cinematic space begun earlier by Pastrone and in its exemplary treatment of crowd scenes and spectacular sets. But it was *Cabiria* which established a level of craftsmanship that few works of the silent era could surpass. A stickler for accuracy and historical reconstruction, Pastrone spent a great deal of time at the Louvre researching the sets and costumes. The seven-month production cost one million lire (a tremendous sum at that time), including 50,000 lire in gold paid to Gabriele D'Annunzio (then the world's most popular novelist) for the use of his magic name[2] and for intertitles. The premiere in Milan featured specially commissioned symphonic music by Ildebrando Pizzetti performed by an orchestra of one hundred. The fact that some 20,000 meters of film were shot for a three-hour feature film clearly demonstrates the importance of artistic editing to the director. Pastrone invented the *carrello* or dolly in order to track in and out of his enormous sets. The aesthetic effect of moving from an extremely long shot to a medium close-up or close-up was particularly successful in establishing a sense of space and grandeur; increased attention to close-ups underscored the facial expressions and heroic gestures of his actors. Several dream sequences employ superimpositions most effectively. In addition, sequences of the film were tinted by hand, giving parts of *Cabiria* the effect of a color film. His use of artificial lighting (twelve 100-amp spotlights equipped with individual reflectors) for interiors in the Turin studio—particularly for the scene in which the heroine Cabiria ("born from fire") is about to be sacrificed to the Carthaginian god Moloch—produced effects that are still miraculous today. His on-location work (which included shooting in both Tunisia and Sicily) included footage of Hannibal crossing the Alps with elephants, which were somehow transported to the snowy peaks to satisfy Pastrone's scrupulous insistence on historical detail. Finally, his use of special effects, process shots, and scale models in two memorable scenes—the eruption of Mt. Etna and the burning of the Roman fleet by Archimedes's mirrors at the siege of Syracuse—represents a most valuable and original contribution to the language of the silent cinema.

The epic battle of two great civilizations, Rome and Carthage, immortalized by Livy's histories and a score of lesser works, thus came to life on the screen for the first time; however, it was not merely Pastrone's technical virtuosity that appealed to the average filmgoer, although this is clearly what attracted D. W. Griffith to imitate the film in the Babylonian sequence and the conclusion of *Intolerance* (1916). Vast historical themes often fail to achieve an emotional impact upon an audience unless this historical atmosphere is filtered through the lives of more mundane characters, and so Pastrone focused the plot of *Cabiria* around not Livian figures but, instead, purely fictitious characters of his own invention: Cabiria, a girl from Catania

Giovanni Pastrone's *Cabiria* (1914). Maciste (Bartolomeo Pagano) rescues Cabiria from sacrifice to the Carthaginian god Moloch.
(Photo courtesy of the Museum of Modern Art)

captured by pirates and sold into Carthaginian slavery; Fulvius Axilla, a Roman spy who falls in love with Cabiria and eventually marries her; and his slave, Maciste, played by a non-professional actor named Bartolomeo Pagano whose muscular exploits turned him overnight from a Genoa dock worker into a star. The Maciste figure also established an enduring Italian tradition of musclebound historical films (labeled "neomythological" works by French critics) that is very much alive today and which in the 1960s produced hundreds of works treating characters such as Hercules, Ursus, and Maciste once again.[3]

After World War I, a severe economic crisis struck the Italian cinema industry just when its products had captured a major share of the world market, including that in America. Yet, historical extravaganzas continued to be produced. Guazzoni's postwar films, usually featuring his favorite actor, Amleto Novelli, attempt to move away from the historicism of Pastrone to a more fanciful and poetic view of past history: *Fabiola* (*Fabiola*, 1917) reflects the beginning of psychological introspection in a treatment of the martyrdoms of Saints Agnes and Sebastian; his *Jerusalem Delivered* (*Gerusalemme liberata*, 1918) reflects the triumph of fantasy over archaeology—the location of Torquato Tasso's baroque epic is placed in Rome among the ancient ruins of the Eternal City rather than in the Holy Land. The religious impulse encouraged a growing simplicity in the historical film, most apparent in Giulio Antamoro's *Christ* (*Christus*, 1915) where the simple narrative style and the focus upon the drama of Christ contrast sharply with the grandiose historical sets of contemporary Roman films, or in his *Brother Francis* (*Frate Francesco*, 1926), a portrayal of the life of St. Francis wherein the influence of primitive Italian painters is particularly apparent in the stigmata sequence. Guazzoni produced a monumental work entitled *Messalina* (*Messalina*, 1923), in which for a spectacular chariot race he created a set of the Circus Maximus. Unequaled at the time in vastness and historical accuracy, it was subsequently copied in the several American versions of *Ben Hur*.

Immediately before the outbreak of the Great War, a phenomenon which later came to be known as the star system ("divismo"), first arose in Italy even before a similar development occurred in Hollywood. A number of new faces in the entertainment industry profited from the initial reluctance of established theatrical actors to enter the new film medium, and as the movies grew in popularity by leaps and bounds, their role as an attraction to the public and their importance to the economic success of a work steadily grew. Lydia Borelli's gestures and her languid style came, in such works as Mario Caserini's *Love Everlasting* (*Ma l'amore mio non muore*, 1913), to epitomize the melodramatic genre which she helped to create. A number of such female stars or *dive* ("goddesses") emerged, creating an image of the *femme fatale* in the early Italian cinema that reflects, as Pierre Leprohon has justly put it, "the self-portrait, willed or not, of an era, a world as devoted to extravagance and cynicism as ours is to eroticism and violence . . . paradoxically enough, it is the basis of reality in the masquerade of the upper-class drama that gives it its historical value."[4] Francesca Bertini added passion to languid manner, and the sexual symbolism of a work such as Roberto Roberti's *The Serpent* (*Il serpente*, 1919), wherein a love affair's development is interspersed with shots showing a snake devouring a meek rabbit, is remarkable. Set in the midst of Liberty drawing rooms and an *art-nouveau* ambience of passionate love and fatal affairs, this melodramatic mode required an increased attention to close-up shots and a sometimes too declamatory acting style. Besides Borelli and Bertini, other important *dive* included Hesperia, whose renown depended on her unique personality, as she was no beauty; Pina Menichelli, who abandoned the declamatory gestures of other female leads for a wider and more contemporary range of feminine images; Maria Jacobini, Diana Karenne, and Anna Fougez. Few male actors in Italy, with the possible exception of Amleto Novelli and Bartolomeo Pagano, ever achieved the same degree of popular appeal in the silent era. The star system encouraged by the melodramatic mode of film making had another technical consequence which become even more important with the advent of the sound film: film making moved primarily inside the studios and employed artificial lighting. This was a departure from the on-location shooting and the natural lighting which were dominant features of the historical costume cinema.

Most Italian film historians, until recently, have viewed the silent cinema and film during the Fascist period from the perspective of neorealism and have often criticized both the melodramatic works with their *dive* and the Roman films as proof that Italian cinema lost its initial economic advantage in the industry because it failed to keep up with the technical advances that produced new aesthetic effects and—more seriously—because it failed to explore the kinds of human themes that would so clearly characterize the early works of Visconti, De Sica, Rossellini, and others of the post-World War II generation. No less an authority than Carlo Lizzani pronounced historical films such as *Cabiria* a "dead end"; the obsession with an "unreal" subject matter located in the distant past, the economic burdens imposed by the new star system, and the influence of D'Annunzianism in Italian culture, primarily seen in film melodramas, have all been declared overwhelming obstacles to a cinematic realism in the silent era.[5] There is, of course, some truth to these allegations. Yet the star system and the costume film arose in America and did not create such disastrous effects. It is important to realize, moreover, that the realist current in Italian cinema has always been less popular than other forms of film making, even though it consistently receives the plaudits of the critics and scholars. In most cases, the Italian public simply preferred the gestures of a Lydia Borelli or the muscle flexing of Maciste, as well as the episodic adventure films of Emilio Ghione, the comic shorts of Leopoldo Fregoli, and the fifty "clown" films by Polidor—not to mention the many imported works in a variety of genres—to the films usually cited as early examples of silent "realism." Two such films, however, deserve mention here. Gustavo Serena's *Assunta Spina* (*Assunta Spina*, 1915), a Salvatore Di Giacomo play set in a realistic Neapolitan setting with Francesca Bertini in the lead role, managed to transfer a crude, documentary, photographic style to the cinema. Another interesting work—regrettably lost in the wreckage of World War II except for some surviving still photographs—is Nino Martoglio's *Lost in the Dark* (*Sperduti nel buio*, 1914), an adaptation of a play by Roberto Bracco. The film's melodramatic plot treats a girl of the people born out of wedlock and abandoned by her upperclass father. Martoglio's skillful editing, cutting back and forth from the sunlit Neapolitan slums of the girl's world to the palatial splendor of her father's world, moved a number of influential critics who had been privileged to see it (including Georges Sadoul, Henri Langlois, and Umberto Barbaro) to pronounce it a masterpiece, worthy of inclusion in the artistic traditions leading to *Rome, Open City* (*Roma, città aperta*, 1945) or *The Bicycle Thief* (*Ladri di biciclette*, 1948).

Mention should be made of the attention paid to cinema by the Italian Futurist movement, which exploded upon the European cultural scene with an iconoclastic manifesto published by its founder, Filippo Tommaso Marinetti (1876–1944), and a number of his associates on February 20, 1909, in the Parisian newspaper *Le Figaro*. Futurism's many revolutionary views on poetry, art, and culture have until recently been consistently overlooked because of the movement's nationalistic flavor and its compromising accommodation with Mussolini's Fascism. Yet, the Futurist penchant for modern technology, machines, and the interplay of speed, light, and space, as well as its violent opposition to tradition in the arts, certainly recommended the cinema to the movement as the prototypical modern art form for those who claimed to prefer the aesthetic qualities of a racing motor car to the "Winged Victory" in the Louvre. Their most lasting and influential contribution was an early manifesto entitled "The Futurist Cinema," dated September 11, 1916. The document is one of the first and most persuasive attacks against imposing outmoded and traditional art forms upon the revolutionary medium of modern cinema:

> The cinema is an autonomous art. The cinema must therefore never copy the stage. The cinema, being essentially visual, must above all fulfill the evolution of painting, detach itself from reality, from photography, from the graceful and solemn. It must become antigraceful, deforming, impressionistic, synthetic, dynamic, free-wording.[6]

The manifesto also suggests concrete techniques and themes for this new cinema. Reality should be presented directly, employing cinematic analogies—a view later advanced within the context of contemporary semiotics by Pier Paolo Pasolini in a number of essays. For example, rather than developing various phases of the anguish of a character's suffering, it would be sufficient to show a jagged, cavernous mountain to suggest the emotion's equivalent in a single image. Moreover, the manifesto recommends filmed dramas of abstract objects, dramatized states of mind captured on film, and filmed words-in-freedom, the cinematic equivalent of Futurist poetry based upon this alogical technique. In the history of film theory, this manifesto must be considered one of the earliest considerations of cinema's right to an existence that is no longer dependent upon its sister art forms. In practice, the movement produced few works and the most famous of these—Arnaldo Ginna's *Futurist Life* (*Vita futurista*, 1916), and Anton Giulio Bragaglia's *The Wicked Enchantment* (*Il perfido incanto*, 1916)—survive today only in scattered still photographs. From contemporary descriptions, however, it is clear that both works employed innovative techniques (hand coloring or tinting of black-and-white film, split screen techniques, double exposures, the use of mirrors to distort images); *Futurist Life* consciously rejects any traditional narrative plot and employs an essentially abstract structure. In the absence of copies for detailed examination, little more can be said of them. However, it should be pointed out that some claims in the manifesto cannot be substantiated. Marinetti's view that the cinema had embodied only outmoded literary or theatrical techniques fails, for instance, to take into consideration the numerous aesthetic innovations achieved in a work such as Pastrone's *Cabiria*, which was based on exactly the kind of literary or historical theme Futurists rejected as being incapable of cinematic innovation. Moreover, there is every likelihood that some of the ideas the Futurists outline in their manifesto only seem avant-garde and ahead of their time when contrasted with contemporary film theories. In reality, these ideas may have been derived from films of the period. For example, though the Futurist admonition to dramatize objects first found concrete expression in Marinetti's brief play *Feet* (*Le basi*, 1915)—in which the alogical events on stage evolve through a view of only the actors' feet which must express a wide variety of modes and expressions—this kind of drama was actually suggested by an early Italian avant-garde film by Marcel Fabre entitled *Love on Foot* (*Amor pedestre*, 1914), which provides proof that even in the silent era cinematic practice in Italy was often in advance of the theorists and historians.

The early Italian cinema never lacked directors, actors, or technicians of genius. Economic and political factors, and not merely artistic deficiencies, explain much of the industry's rapid decline after its unparalleled initial successes. A single fundamental feature of the Italian film market has remained constant from the end of World War I to the present day: the total percentage of Italian-made films distributed within the country at any one time has never risen above approximately one-third of the total number of films in circulation. The results have been predictable: the Italian cinema has never dominated its own home market, even in those years when the quality as well as the quantity of its product have been most favorably received abroad. Moreover, the competition of the American film industry has been a factor of primary importance from the first boycotts against Italian imports into the American market around 1911 until the present day. In addition, unlike their American counterparts, the men in control of the Italian cinema at any given point in its development were comparatively poor businessmen and often failed to create a profitable infrastructure of theater chains and rental agencies which might have established the distribution of their product upon sounder business practices. The Italian state was slow to realize the foreign threat to a major Italian industry; when the first censorship regulations were passed beginning in 1913, for example, the effect of the laws was to allow foreign works practically free access to the Italian market while, at the same time, making it relatively more difficult for Italian-made films to be distributed.[7]

There was some effort to meet the American challenge. In 1919, a group known as L'Unione Cinematografica Italiana (UCI) was established, and included the major Italian production companies: Cines, Ambrosio-Film, Caesar-Film, and Tiber-Film. Its purpose was to retain control of the Italian market, but bad planning and excessive expenditures for poorly conceived projects resulted in its bankruptcy in 1927. The industry's economic problems were further complicated in 1923 by the arrival in Rome of an American company set to produce *Ben Hur*, a colossal costume film which challenged the Italians in the very film genre that had made their industry successful abroad. Although the film was eventually completed in America by director Fred Niblo with Ramon Novarro and Francis X. Bushman in lead roles, the company's presence in Rome and its relatively inexhaustible source of funding tied up studios and prevented progress on other Italian films. By the time the shooting was moved from Rome, the Italian film industry was virtually destroyed. The figures speak for themselves: from some 220 Italian films produced in 1920, the figures drop dramatically to 100 (1921), 50 (1922), 20–30 (1923), 15–20 (1924), around 15 (1925–26), and less than a dozen between 1927 and 1928. During this period, the over 3,000 movie theatres in Italy could procure only imported films—and this in a nation whose official policy under Fascism was national autonomy (*autarchia*)![8]

The lamentable state of the Italian film industry cannot be explained solely in terms of an inferior product but must, instead, take into consideration deadly foreign competition, primarily from America. Given the circumstances, massive state intervention would have eventually occurred under any type of government. Mussolini's regime was actually rather late in moving to assist Italian film makers, and it was not until 1934 that it began such active support. One earlier but only partially effective private initiative should be remembered. An entrepreneur named Stefano Pittaluga began a career as a renter of films, then bought some 150 movie theaters and controlled many others; in 1926 he founded the S.A.S.P. (Società Anonima Stefano Pittaluga), which bought up a number of failing film companies (Cines, Itala, Palatina). As a result, Pittaluga was in virtual control of whatever was left of the Italian film industry. Furthermore, in 1927 Mussolini's government granted Pittaluga's company the distribution of documentaries and newsreels produced by L'Unione Cinematografica Educativa (LUCE), a move which represented the first major cooperative effort between private industry and the Fascist state. Pittaluga offered hope for a more rationally organized market which might successfully meet foreign competition, but his death in 1932 cut short any such potential development. The most progressive force in the film industry at this point, he was instrumental in introducing the first Italian sound film—Gennaro Righelli's *Song of Love* (*La canzone dell'amore*, 1930)—through his newly reorganized Cines-Pittaluga company. Cines-Pittaluga would eventually form the basis of the Ente Nazionale Industrie Cinematografiche (ENIC) which the Italian government formed in 1935 to direct the entire industry.

After the disappearance of Pittaluga, governmental intervention increased dramatically. In 1934, the Direzione Generale per la Cinematografia was created with Luigi Freddi (1895-1977), a strong supporter of the Fascist movement, as its head; Freddi would later hold important positions at Cinecittà, Cines, and ENIC until the fall of the regime. The Direzione Generale formed part of the Ministero per la Cultura Popolare (commonly referred to as "Minculpop"). In 1935, a special fund for the production of Italian films was created at the Banca Nazionale del Lavoro (the "Sezione autonomo per il credito cinematografico"), while two years earlier Count Galeazzo Ciano, first Undersecretary, then Minister for Press and Propaganda (and Mussolini's son-in-law) encouraged the creation of "cinegufs," or Fascist cinema clubs formed within the Gioventù Universitaria Fascista (G.U.F.). In 1934, film was added to the arts festival in Venice, and the Venice Film Festival subsequently became a showcase for the Italian film industry. The important school for training in film, the Centro Sperimentale di Cinematografia, opened in 1935 with Luigi Chiarini as its director, and its well deserved reputation for excellence has continued until the present day. After the Cines studios burned in 1935, one of the world's great film complexes—Cinecittà ("Cinema City")—was inaugurated by Mussolini himself on April 21, 1937, the choice of the date—the mythical anniversary of the founding of Rome—underlining the importance the regime now attributed to film. (Mussolini's son Vittorio headed an important film periodical, *Cinema*, after 1937.) Cinecittà still stands today, across the street from the Centro, and is the site for the production of many Italian and foreign films.

In 1937, the Centro began the publication of *Bianco e Nero* ("Black and White"), which remains one of Italy's most prestigious academic journals. In 1938, ENIC received the monopoly of all film imports, and the ensuing policies set up by the government caused the Hollywood Big Four (20th Century-Fox, Paramount, MGM, and Warner Brothers) to withdraw completely from the Italian market. Ultimately, this served to increase national film production: in 1937, 33 Italian films competed with 290 imports (most from Hollywood); the next year the proportion changed, with 45 Italian works and 230 imports.

Italian production rose fairly rapidly and was remarkably high even during the war years: 77 (1939), 86 (1940), 71 (1941), 96 (1942), 66 (1943), and 37 (1944).

Italy was ruled by a Fascist government from 1922 until 1943. The advent of the talkies during this period, as well as a number of important cultural and artistic developments, set the stage for the appearance of neorealism and Italy's move to preeminence among European film-producing nations in the postwar period.[9] Two individuals—Alessandro Blasetti (1900–87) and Mario Camerini (1895–1981)—dominated the Italian cinema during these years. Each made his first important film in the year preceding the advent of the Italian sound film. Blasetti's *Sun* (*Sole*, 1929), destroyed during the war except for surviving still photographs, treats land reclamation in the Pontine marshes, a subject at least outwardly favorable to the Fascist regime's grandiose public works projects. But the film is no mere propaganda piece: its authentic exterior locations combine with the appeal of its contemporary social theme to produce a convincing sense of realism. Camerini's *Rails* (*Rotaie*, 1929), to which a sound track was later added, struck an entirely different chord: it is a psychological study of the complex interrelationships between two fugitive lovers which reflects the influence of German silent cinema. The lengthy and cinematically eloquent sequence in which the two contemplate suicide in a lonely hotel room uses only images and masterful editing to convey the essence of their solitude without recourse to printed titles.

From *Sun* Blasetti moved to make *Palio* (*Palio*, 1932), a costume film combining a romantic plot with the spectacle of the medieval festival in Siena; like *Sun*, *Palio* aimed at the recreation of an authentically and uniquely Italian environment on film. It was followed in 1934 by *1860*, usually considered to be Blasetti's masterpiece, a film which blends two tendencies typical of the director and many of his contemporaries: the historical drama, a genre which comprises the largest proportion of works produced during the Fascist period, and an interest in regional naturalism, a less common phenomenon during the period but one which was always present. Against the background of Garibaldi's invasion of Sicily and his first major battle, Blasetti examines the impact of such a momentous historical event upon the lives of simple, ordinary people. Making use of non-professional, Sicilian-speaking characters, he shows an attention to linguistic detail that will be continued in a number of postwar neorealist works. In addition, the complex battle scenes he organizes demonstrate his great technical skill in handling large numbers of actors. It was common for the regime to associate the Fascist revolution with Garibaldi, and while Blasetti's original ending of *1860* concluded with a sequence set in Mussolini's Rome (a scene Blasetti cut after the war!), the bulk of the film is a work of art motivated by nationalistic sentiments rather than Fascist ideology. This same patriotic tone, concentrating upon moments of history illustrative of Italian greatness, would be continued in several of Blasetti's works he set in the Italian Renaissance, an era when Italy could boast of cultural hegemony over all Europe: *Ettore Fieramosca* (*Ettore Fieramosca*, 1939), an adaptation of the nineteenth-century historical novel by Marchese Massimo D'Azeglio; and *The Jester's Supper* (*La cena delle beffe*, 1941), derived from a Renaissance *novella* and a twentieth-century adaptation of it for the stage by Sem Benelli. At least one of Blasetti's major films, *The Old Guard* (*Vecchia guardia*, 1935), had clear political overtones and could be correctly labeled a Fascist film. Set in the rough-and-tumble atmosphere of 1922 when bands of Fascist *squadristi* battled in the streets with their leftist opponents, Blasetti's film portrays Mussolini's supporters in an heroic light and concludes with a celebration of the March on Rome. In spite of the work's subject matter, Blasetti's realistic portrayal of this dramatic moment in Italian history employs a documentary style that would later find favor during the postwar period. The most unusual of Blasetti's films, perhaps the most unusual of all the almost seven hundred works produced during this period, is *The Iron Crown* (*La corona di ferro*, 1941), a pseudohistorical fairy tale which may be compared to Marcel Carné's *The Devil's Own Envoy* (*Les Visiteurs du soir*, 1942) in its hermetic symbolism and its evocative, fanciful style. The theme of *The Iron Crown* concerns the journey of a sacred crown to Rome and the rise of a chosen leader who will lead his people into an era of peace and prosperity. The sumptuous and very expensive sets produced for the work at Cinecittà testify to the technical virtuosity attained at Italy's major studio in spite of the economic restrictions imposed by the outbreak of the war. *The Iron Crown* is an ambiguous work: while its message underlines a common sentiment among Italians, the desire for peace and the cessation of hostilities, the symbolic implications of the search for a charismatic leader who will restore a magic crown to its rightful place in Rome may also point to Mussolini, Il Duce of a newly revived Rome. Whatever political meaning Blasetti intended, *The Iron Crown* certainly revives the perennial Italian treatment of heroic mythology that was born in the silent era with Pastrone's *Cabiria*. Blasetti's last important film before the end of the war, *A Stroll in the Clouds* (*Quattro passi fra le nuvole*, 1942), represents an abrupt shift to an infinitely more simple storyline, one which may be said to prefigure the neorealist plots of Vittorio De Sica and his scriptwriter Cesare Zavattini: a traveling salesman meets a young unmarried girl who is pregnant; feeling compassion for her, he unsuccessfully poses as her husband when she visits her family; as the girl is about to be driven out of the house, the man urges her family to forgive her and to have compassion for her tragedy. Zavattini's contribution to the script may have influenced Blasetti to move from the baroque complexities of *The Iron Crown* to the discovery of the cinematographic potential inherent in the simple events of everyday life. At any rate, *A Stroll in the Clouds* provides proof that even before the fall of the Fascist regime or the experience of the Resistance and Allied occupation, Italian cinema was already moving towards an interest in simple, but eloquent, human situations and a realistic appraisal of Italian daily life.

The films of Mario Camerini, the second important director of the period, are less varied in theme and style. His works are typically sentimental, romantic comedies with highly complex plots and characterization, indebted to and comparable with the best works of the French director René Clair. In most cases these comedies are by no means frivolous and provide an ironic and critical view of the polite society of middle-class Italy. The demands made upon the individual by society and the roles characters are forced to play in their relationships with others constitute Camerini's favorite theme. This interest in role playing and the interconnection of illusion and reality

Alessandro Blasetti's *The Iron Crown* (1941). Ornately stylized sets testify to the technical prowess of Cinecittà's craftsmen.
(Photo courtesy of the Museum of Modern Art)

had already been explored in the greatest dramatic works written during the Fascist period, the many plays by Luigi Pirandello. *I'd Give a Million* (*Darò un milione*, 1935) brings together for the first time Vittorio De Sica (in a leading role) and Cesare Zavattini (as a scriptwriter). The story concerns a rich man who disguises himself in order to discover someone worthy of receiving his wealth, and the film thus examines an aspect of role-playing in society. Camerini's *Mr. Max* (*Il signor Max*, 1937) casts De Sica in a similar performance: in a satirical portrait of fashionable society, De Sica plays a newsstand dealer posing as a *bon vivant* in the fashionable circles of Rome, the stylish Signor Max. Over twenty years later, Roberto Rossellini was to recall Camerini's film by casting De Sica in another such role, a swindler posing as a Resistance hero fighting the Nazis in *General Della Rovere* (*Il*

Generale Della Rovere, 1959). Thus, while Blasetti's films gradually
moved toward a realist interpretation of Italian life, Camerini's many
comedies explored Italian social values in a more light-hearted manner. Both the realistic tradition and the tradition of comic satire reflected by Blasetti and Camerini were to find important expressions
in the immediate postwar period. The lessons learned from these two
masters would be retained by the next generation of neorealist directors, for neorealist cinema would be characterized not only by the
realism of Rossellini's *Paisan* (*Paisà*, 1946) or De Sica's *The Bicycle
Thief* but also by the comic vision of society exemplified in De Sica's
Miracle in Milan (*Miracolo a Milano*, 1950), Rossellini's *The Machine
to Kill Bad People* (*La macchina ammazzacattivi*, 1948), or Renato Castellani's *Two Cents' Worth of Hope* (*Due soldi di speranza*, 1952).

In spite of the regime's theoretical interest in influencing all levels
of Italian society, its impact upon the Italian film industry was somewhat less pervasive; indeed, only a small percentage of the over seven
hundred films produced during the Fascist period can truly be termed
Fascist or propaganda films, although it is impossible to determine
the degree to which Italian directors might have turned to social criticism and less oblique attacks upon Italian institutions or values if the
government had been more permissive. It is certainly not accurate to
describe every work with a nationalistic flavor produced during this
period as a Fascist film, even though films of this sort obviously could
be used by the regime to bolster many of their claims for Italy's cultural
preeminence. Nevertheless, a number of films, primarily among those
produced during the second half of the regime's twenty-two-year
reign, can be accurately described as films which supported the values
and the policies of Mussolini's government. Most of these films treated
colonial wars or moments of Italian imperial glory, either under Mussolini or in a more distant past. The African wars attracted several
important pro-Fascist directors: Augusto Genina's (1892–1957) *The
White Squadron* (*Lo squadrone bianco*, 1936), filmed on location in
Libya, contains some very beautiful sequences underlining the vastness and solemnity of the African desert; Goffredo Alessandrini
(1904–1978) produced a film on the Ethiopian War, *Luciano Serra,
Pilot* (*Luciano Serra pilota*, 1938), starring the very popular actor Ame-

deo Nazzari in a production supervised by Vittorio Mussolini, Il Duce's son. It was also scripted in part by the young Roberto Rossellini. Alessandro Blasetti's *The Old Guard* and the impact of its innovative documentary style have already been mentioned. Genina produced another work of some merit devoted to the Spanish Civil War, *The Siege of the Alcazar* (*L'assedio dell'Alcazar*, 1940). This film combined interior sets designed by Cinecittà with on-location shooting among the ruins of Toledo's Alcazar, the citadel which Franco's soldiers defended against an overwhelming republican army. The battle scenes, all designed to glorify the heroes of this Fascist victory, are remarkable cinematic achievements. Perhaps most famous of all the works that clearly follow the regime's ideology was a spectacular historical film on the Second Punic War by Carmine Gallone (1886–1973). Entitled *Scipio Africanus* (*Scipione l'Africano*, 1937), it consciously returned to subject matter once popularized by the Italian silent cinema but now employed in an attempt to bolster the imperial designs of the Fascist government's African policy. Some seven thousand people were said to be involved in its grandiose battle scenes on both land and sea, including an ambitious reconstruction of the climatic battle of Zama complete with elephants. Not surprisingly, the work was awarded the Mussolini Cup at the Venice Film Festival of 1937 for the best Italian film of that year.

Though such pro-Fascist and pro-war films emphasized the ideology of the regime, they nevertheless reflected contemporary themes of importance—the colonial wars and the Italian role in Africa and Spain—and thus cannot be fairly characterized as merely escapist entertainment. And, in general, there was a very noticeable trend toward a realistic style during the years preceding the advent of the first neorealist works. The German director Walter Ruttmann produced an excellent film on two steelworkers in love with the same woman in *Steel* (*Accaio*, 1933), a free adaptation of a script by Luigi Pirandello on which Mario Soldati was the assistant director. The scenes shot inside the steel mills of Terni are masterful examples of rhythmic editing within a semi-documentary style. Francesco Pasinetti's (1911–1949) *The Canal of the Angels* (*Il canale degli angeli*, 1943), the story of a sailor who falls in love with a married woman in Venice whose

Carmine Gallone's *Scipio Africanus* (1937). Romans giving the Roman (Fascist?) salute implicitly link Mussolini's imperialistic policies in Africa to the heritage of the Roman Empire.
(Photo courtesy of the Museum of Modern Art)

child becomes seriously ill, presents a more melancholy and less romanticized vision of daily Italian life than was the norm. Amleto Palermi's (1889–1941) *Rustic Chivalry* (*Cavalleria rusticana*, 1939) transfers Giovanni Verga's (1840–1922) short story and one-act play to the screen, and while Pietro Mascagni refused to allow his opera score based on the same material to be used in the film, the work presents a realistic portrayal of local Sicilian customs, dress, and folk music.

A number of directors turned between 1940 and 1943 to adaptations of late nineteenth—or early twentieth-century—naturalist fiction. The most important of these were Renato Castellani (1913–85), Mario Soldati (now best known as a novelist, 1906–), Luigi Chiarini (1900–1975), and Alberto Lattuada (1914–). Perhaps the best of these adaptations was Castellani's *A Pistol Shot* (*Un colpo di*

pistola, 1942), taken from a story by Pushkin. Chiarini, the influential
director of the Centro Sperimentale di Cinematografia in Rome until
1943 and an editor of *Bianco e nero*, turned for inspiration to a story
by the Neapolitan realist Matilde Serao (1857–1927) for *Five Moons
Street* (*Via delle Cinque Lune*, 1941). Soldati, who had visited the
United States in 1929 and again in 1932–33 and whose description
of that country in *America, First Love* (*America, primo amore*, 1935)
would provide an important interpretation of America during the Fascist period, produced two versions of novels by Antonio Fogazzaro
(1842–1911): *The Little World of the Past* (*Piccolo mondo antico*, 1941)
and *Malombra* (*Malombra*, 1942). Lattuada directed *Giacomo The Ide-
alist* (*Giacomo l'idealista*, 1943), taken from a novel by Emilio De
Marchi (1851–1901). Ferdinando Maria Poggioli's *Jealousy* (*Gelosia*,
1942) and *The Priest's Hat* (*Il cappello da prete*, 1944) derive respectively from the naturalist masterpiece *The Marquis of Roccaverdina* (*Il
marchese di Roccaverdina*, 1901) by Luigi Capuana (1839–1915), the
contemporary of Giovanni Verga, and from Emilio De Marchi's *The
Priest's Hat* (*Il cappello del prete*, 1888). Since many of these directors
also worked on each other's films as assistants or script writers, a
certain similarity of style among these adaptations can be detected.
Italian film historians have generally defined these works by the label
"calligraphy," and their directors with the term "calligraphers," underlining their interest in formalism, style, and, by implication, their
choice of themes from past history or literature rather than from contemporary Italian culture. The implicit criticism contained in the terms
"calligraphy" and "calligraphers" is perhaps unwarranted. If an interest
in current events were the only prerequisite of cinematic realism, then
the war films produced under the regime or works of overly political
intent could be so classified. While it may be true that these "calligraphers" evaded contemporary issues in their adaptations of novels
from the realist and naturalist periods, such literary inspiration would
nevertheless be an important factor in neorealist films praised by these
same critics. An encounter with major novelists, even from a past era,
would slowly but surely direct Italian cinema toward social problems
and the more complex relationships between individuals or classes
characteristic of the realist school of Italian and European fiction.
Moreover, a number of scriptwriters, technicians, actors, and assistant

directors later associated with neorealist cinema or postwar Italian culture—for example: Sergio Amidei (1904–1980), Vitaliano Brancati (1907-1954), Giacomo Debenedetti (1901–1967), Nino Rota (1911–1979) and Dino De Laurentiis (1919–   )—gained invaluable technical training working on these adaptations, training that would prepare them for their more remarkable contributions to Italian cinema immediately after the end of the war.

The events which preceded the flowering of the Italian neorealist cinema with Rossellini's *Rome, Open City* in 1945 are connected to major changes in both cinematic and literary Italian culture, and, paradoxically, to stylistic shifts within the cinema produced by the Fascist regime itself. The changes in works produced by the government are associated with Francesco De Robertis (1902–1959), the head of the Centro Cinematografico del Ministero della Marina, a department of the Navy charged with making documentaries. In *Men on the Bottom* (*Uomini sul fondo*, 1941), De Robertis produced a documentary on the techniques developed by the Italian navy in the rescuing of men trapped beneath the surface of the ocean. As it appeared before the outbreak of the war, it lacked the strident, propagandistic intent of later similar films produced by the government. In it, De Robertis skillfully employs nonprofessionals in a plot shorn of anything but the barest narrative elements to render an exciting account of a rescue necessitated by an accident during naval exercises. The film's most important episode involves the crash of a submarine and its subsequent sinking highlighted by the suspense developed through the director's masterful editing. De Robertis's documentary realism had a profound influence upon the young Roberto Rossellini, who made *The White Ship* (*La nave bianca*, 1941) under his supervision. Like De Robertis, Rossellini employed only nonprofessional actors—the actual troops and sailors from the hospital ship *Arno* and an Italian warship—and produced his entire film on these locations. This realistic technique is combined with real footage of a naval battle in a marriage of drama and documentary that was later to reappear in the three works of Rossellini's war trilogy immediately following the end of the war. There are also several clear allusions to Eisenstein's *Potemkin* in Rossellini's work. De Robertis was committed to the Fascist cause, and with the fall of Mussolini's regime in 1943, he moved north to supervise the film industry associated with Mussolini's Republic of Salò, a fate other younger men, such as Rossellini or De Sica, managed to avoid. This close association with the fallen regime naturally limited his immediate postwar career, although he did manage to produce several minor works at that time. Rossellini continued making films for the government, producing *A Pilot Returns* (*Un pilota ritorna*, 1942) and *The Man of the Cross* (*L'uomo della croce*, 1943). While both of these films are more clearly propaganda pieces, each attempts to combine a fictional plot with attention to a realistic depiction of the war. *A Pilot Returns*, partially scripted by Michelangelo Antonioni and made under the supervision of Vittorio Mussolini, moves away from the use of nonprofessionals as practiced by De Robertis and employed by Rossellini with such success in *The White Ship*. In fact, Rossellini casts Massimo Girotti, a well-known actor who starred in Blasetti's *The Iron Crown*, in the lead role of an Italian airman who manages to escape from a prison camp in Greece. With *The Man of the Cross*, Rossellini produces a work which focuses upon the Italian expeditionary forces on the Eastern Front and upon a Catholic chaplain representative of Italy's religious majority. The end-title of the film informs the audience that the work is dedicated to the memory of military chaplains who died in the "crusade" against the "godless" enemy in Russia. Though the principal character's humanity and sacrifice seem to prefigure the good-natured priest of *Rome, Open City* who works with leftist Resistance leaders, and in spite of the fact that in several scenes Rossellini underlines the common humanity in Fascist and Bolshevik alike, it would be inaccurate to claim, as one critic has done, that the ultimate meaning of the film is to be found in several lyrical panning shots following the flight of birds or running horses on the battlefield which underline the "common theme of liberty" in all of Rossellini's works.[10] It is, quite simply, a very able film in the service of an ideology which Rossellini was to reject in his postwar trilogy but accepted, at least in part, in his earlier "Fascist" trilogy before the war's end. And in *The Man of the Cross*, Rossellini not only continues his use of professional actors but also employs the sophisticated technical resources of Cinecittà. After the war these features of his early style would sometimes be rejected along with the Fascist political content of the films.

The early work of De Robertis or Rossellini in the service of the regime constitutes an important step towards the realism of the post-war decade. But its contribution was primarily a stylistic one which uncovered the dramatic possibilities of combining documentary with fictional narratives and the expressive potential of nonprofessional actors. The more significant changes in perspective which made possible the rise of what has been termed "neorealism" in postwar Italian culture would also owe a great deal to a creative encounter with a number of foreign cultures. Under the influence of Umberto Barbaro (1902–1959) and Luigi Chiarini (1900–1975) at the Centro Sperimentale di Cinematografia,[11] translations of the theoretical works on cinema by Eisenstein, Pudovkin, Balázs, and others were read and discussed, and while there is little reason to believe that Soviet cinema itself was a major influence upon this young generation of Italians, Russian film theory certainly helped to move the focus of Italian film-makers toward a penchant for realism. It was the French cinema of such directors as Jean Renoir, Marcel Carné, or René Clair, however, which had the most appeal to Italians, especially after works from Hollywood were less frequently imported into the country during the Fascist period. A number of Italians enjoyed connections with French artists or sought to emulate their works. Vittorio De Sica admired Clair and would eventually imitate his surrealist comic style. Michelangelo Antonioni served as Carné's assistant in the making of *The Devil's Own Envoy*. Luchino Visconti worked with Renoir on *A Day in the Country* (*Une Partie de Campagne*, 1936) and *The Lower Depths* (*Les Bas-Fonds*, 1936), as well as *Tosca* (*La Tosca*, 1940), a film based on Sardou and Puccini that Renoir began in Italy but which, with the outbreak of the war, was completed by Carl Koch. Perhaps Visconti's greatest debt to Renoir was a copy of a French translation of James M. Cain's *The Postman Always Rings Twice* that Renoir gave him in 1940, a work upon which he would base *Obsession* (*Ossessione*, 1942) a few years later.[12] The term "neorealism" was in fact first applied not to postwar Italian cinema but, instead, to the French films of the thirties in an article written by Umberto Barbaro in 1943; this usage was echoed again in 1945 by Guido Aristarco, who was soon to become Italy's leading Marxist film historian and the editor of the influential periodical *Cinema nuovo*.[13]

Visconti's heuristic encounter with Cain's novel underscores a major influence upon Italian culture at this time, as American fiction was to prove a decisive external stimulus to the rise of neorealism. English-speaking audiences familiar only with the masterpieces of postwar Italian cinema too often overlook the fact that "neorealism" is a term which has come to characterize not only a given moment in cinematic history but also a significant trend in Italian literature of the same period.[14] In spite of official government disapproval, during the Fascist period the popularity of American fiction among the younger generation of soon-to-be-published writers was never greater. Cesare Pavese (1908–1950) defended a thesis on Walt Whitman in 1930, translated Melville's *Moby Dick* in 1932, and produced versions of various works by Sinclair Lewis, Edgar Lee Masters, William Faulkner, John Dos Passos, and Sherwood Anderson. His first important novel, *The Harvesters* (*Paesi tuoi*, 1941), a study of rural violence, is deeply indebted to American models in its combination of naturalism and poetic suggestiveness. Pavese's masterpiece, *The Moon and the Bonfires*, (*La luna e i falò*, 1950), relates an Italian's voyage to America and his return, an event narrated against a background of Partisan resistance to the Fascists. Elio Vittorini (1908–1966), the self-taught worker who learned English by translating *Robinson Crusoe*, went on to translate Steinbeck and Faulkner, edited an important anthology of American literature, and was profoundly influenced by the prose style of Hemingway and Steinbeck in his neorealist masterpiece *In Sicily* (*Conversazione in Sicilia*, 1941). American fiction thus became a counterculture phenomenon among neorealist writers such as Pavese, Vittorini, or Italo Calvino (1923–85), all of whom opposed its effortless realism with symbolic overtones to what they considered the inauthentic and bombastic rhetoric of official Fascist culture. Pavese best expressed the sentiments typical of his generation in a retrospective essay published in 1947 by *L'Unità*, the newspaper of the Communist Party.

> Around 1930, when Fascism was beginning to be "the hope of the world," some young Italians happened to discover in their books

America—an America thoughtful and barbaric, happy and truculent, dissolute, fecund, heavy with all the past of the world, and at the same time young, innocent. For several years these young people read, translated, and wrote with a joy of discovery and of revolt that infuriated the official culture; but the success was so great that it constrained the regime to tolerate it, in order to save face.[15]

The encounter with American prose had also moved the best and most perceptive writers and critics to reevaluate Italy's greatest naturalist novelist: Giovanni Verga.

Visconti's *Obsession* occupies a pivotal position in the history of Italian cinema precisely because it simultaneously reflects the convergence of so many of these different cultural and intellectual experiences, and establishes itself as great art rather than as an ideological manifesto. Visconti's cinematic style was first formed under the influence of Renoir; back in Italy, he was associated with a number of young intellectuals and filmmakers around the journal *Cinema*, edited by Mussolini's son Vittorio, and in that journal he published his first theoretical essays on film, including a blast at the Italian commercial films of the past ("Cadavers") and another eloquent plea for a cinema made to human measure in which "the most humble gesture of a man, his face, his hesitations and his impulses, impart poetry and life to the things which surround him and to the setting in which they take place" ("Anthropomorphic Cinema").[16]

Always a sensitive observer of the trends within Italian culture, Visconti had originally intended to make a film of "Gramigna's Lover" ("L'amante di Gramigna"), one of Verga's best short stories; however, when Alessandro Pavolini, then Minister of Popular Culture, saw the proposed script, he rejected it because of its subject matter. Sicilian bandits were apparently not suitable subject matter for Fascist cinema. Therefore, after considering a number of literary works for adaptation, including Melville's *Billy Budd*, Visconti turned back to the French translation of Cain's *The Postman Always Rings Twice* which Renoir had given him years earlier. With a group of young friends associated with the Centro Sperimentale and *Cinema*—Giuseppe De Santis (later to become an important neorealist director), Gianni Puccini, Mario Alicata, Antonio Pietrangeli, and Alberto Moravia (whose name did

Luchino Visconti's *Obsession* (1942). The debilitating effects of their tawdry love affair can be seen in the faces of Gino (Massimo Girotti) and Giovanna (Clara Calamai).
(Photo courtesy of the Museum of Modern Art)

not appear on the eventual credits)—Visconti set about placing Cain's "tough-guy" novel in an Italian ambience. In the book—a crisp, hard-boiled, first-person novel narrated from the perspective of the main character as he awaits execution in prison—a tramp named Frank meets Cora, the wife of Nick, a Greek-American restaurant owner, has an affair with her, and is led to murder her husband. The world these characters inhabit is both tawdry and absurd, a quality which explains why the book influenced *The Stranger* by Camus. Irony abounds, for while Frank and Cora murder Nick in a fake accident and escape punishment, Frank will be executed for murder when an authentic accident kills Cora but is considered a homocide. Cain refuses to moralize or to inject into the work any sense of tragedy or melodrama; there are rare descriptive passages, and the bulk of the novel consists of staccato dialogue, so sparsely written that many critics have seen the novel as itself a cinematic mode of fiction akin to the scenario.

As a work of art, Visconti's interpretation of Cain's novel is vastly superior to either the American version of 1946 by Tay Garnett (*The Postman Always Rings Twice*) or an earlier French adaptation by Pierre Chenal (*The Last Turn* [*Le dernier tournant*], 1939), and it represents a radical transformation of the original text. Frank, Cora, and Nick are retained as Gino, Giovanna, and Bragana (although the greasy restaurant owner is now made more complicated, if no less loathsome to his wife, by virtue of his interest in Verdi's opera), but Cain's emphasis upon Sackett, the District Attorney, and Katz, Frank's lawyer, is totally eliminated. Instead, Visconti introduces into the plot a very ambiguous character, a homosexual nicknamed "Lo Spagnolo" ("The Spaniard"), who will function as an alternative to Gino's sensual obsession with Giovanna—an obsession that constitutes the Italian director's main focus. The novel's first-person subjective narrative is eliminated for a more omniscient and objective camera style which is, however, as obsessed with the highly formal compositions it photographs as the characters are by their passions. In the pages of *Cinema*, Michelangelo Antonioni and Giuseppe De Santis had earlier argued for a more authentic use of landscape in Italian cinema;[17] with the example of Renoir behind him and the admonitions of such men in the back of his mind, Visconti achieved in *Obsession* a magnificent linkage between his tragic protagonists and their environment—their tawdry living quarters, the provincial inn, the streets of Ancona or Ferrara, the sandbanks of the Po River. Extremely lengthy medium shots, a typical feature of Visconti's mature style, allow the director to follow Gino and Giovanna (played brilliantly by Massimo Girotti and Clara Calamai) as their destinies unfold and become shaped by their surroundings. Simple gestures, glances, or even the lack of any significant action at all, impart to the work a poetic sense that Visconti recommended in "Anthropomorphic Cinema." Vanished is Cain's emphasis upon dialogue. In fact, the most memorable parts of the film lack any dialogue whatsoever. (In the next decade, this technique was to be even further developed in Antonioni's films.) When, for instance, Visconti shoots past Gino shaving at the inn and his hand holding a straight razor appears in the same frame with a view in the background of Giovanna massaging her husband's corpulent body, we are prepared for the husband's eventual death, especially since Bragana is at that precise moment discussing insurance. Even more remarkable is the famous scene that takes place after Bragana's murder: a world-weary Giovanna enters her squalid kitchen, takes a bowl of pasta, tries to eat it while she reads the newspaper, but falls asleep from exhaustion. It is a moment in which the director captures perfectly Giovanna's growing desperation and loneliness, and it is achieved by matching film time and real time. It is this characteristic of Visconti's film style that postwar critics, André Bazin in particular, were to regard as a fundamental aspect of neorealist aesthetics. By emphasizing the close interrelationship of the film's protagonists to their surroundings, Visconti transforms the ironic and often absurd world he found in Cain's novel into a world of genuine tragedy, a world in which the role of destiny within the plot seems inexorable and determined entirely by the logic of the situation. The fatal obsession and sensuality drive Gino and Giovanna first to murder, then to disagreement, and finally to a hopeful reconciliation just before their dreams are shattered by the automobile accident in which Giovanna (and the child she is expecting) is killed and Gino's fate sealed forever.

Obsession was received as an act of provocation by censors and government officials. Mussolini himself examined the work but allowed it to be distributed. His son Vittorio, however, expressed the sentiments of Italian officialdom when he stormed out of the film's first public screening, exclaiming "This is not Italy!" It was certainly not the Italy that had come to be familiar to audiences during the Fascist period, for the picturesque Italian landscape had been transformed into a stage for violent passions and burning sensuality presented with a tragic intensity that had almost been forgotten on the Italian screen. *Obsession* is thus a turning point in the history of the Italian cinema. Though the Fascists destroyed the original negative when much of the official film industry was transferred north to Mussolini's Republic of Salò, luckily Visconti managed to retain a dupe negative. While it is

neither a film about wartime experiences, partisans, or social problems, nor one in which nonprofessional actors and a documentarylike
style are employed—traits often considered to be central to any neorealist film—it prepared Italian filmmakers, if not the Italian public
or the critics, for an entirely different intellectual and aesthetic climate
in which to work.

2

The Masters of Neorealism: Rossellini, De Sica, and Visconti

There is a general agreement among critics and film scholars that the moment in Italian cinematic history known as "neorealism" was a crucial watershed in the evolution of the seventh art. However, it is rare indeed to discover any unanimity in specific definitions of what this phenomenon represents. The label itself is confusing, for it limits the parameters of any critical debate to concern with the connection between the films produced and the society or culture which produced them. And, indeed, the traditional view of Italian neorealism reflects this emphasis on social realism, as can be seen from one very typical list of its general characteristics: realistic treatment, popular setting, social content, historical actuality, and political commitment.[1] The most sensitive critic of the era, André Bazin, called neorealism a cinema of "fact" and "reconstituted reportage" which contained a message of fundamental human solidarity fostered by the anti-Fascist Resistance within which most of the greatest Italian directors came of age. In his view, such works often embodied a rejection of both traditional dramatic and cinematic conventions, most often employed on-location shooting rather than studio sets, and made original use of nonprofessional actors or documentary effects. Bazin defined the aesthetics of neorealism as akin to a separate and differently motivated evolution in the *mise-en-scène* techniques of Welles or Renoir with their penchant for deep-focus photography, which he contrasted sharply (and approvingly) to the montage of Eisenstein and its ideologically inspired juxtaposition of images and shots. Thus, the neorealists in principle "respected" the ontological wholeness of the reality they filmed, just as the rhythm of their narrated screen time often "respected" the actual duration of time within the story; neorealist aesthetics thus opposed the manipulation of reality in the cutting room.[2]

The vexing problem posed by any comprehensive definition of neorealism derives ultimately from its almost universal association with the traditions of realism in both literature and film, an association which quite naturally moves critics to emphasize its use of nonprofessionals, the documentary quality of its photography, or its social content. And yet, with the exception of several too-frequently cited statements by Cesare Zavattini, an important scriptwriter and collaborator with De Sica but never a major director, the remarks of the artists themselves sound an entirely different note. Only Zavattini advocates the most elementary, even banal storylines Bazin prefers, and only he stresses the need to focus upon the actual "duration" of real time.[3] By contrast, while such figures as Rossellini, De Sica, or Fellini sympathize with Zavattini's reverance for everyday reality, what he terms an "unlimited trust in things, facts, and people," rarely if ever do they equate their artistic intentions with traditional realism. Fellini, for example, who worked on a number of neorealist productions in various capacities before beginning his own career as a director in 1950, declared simply that "neorealism is a way of seeing reality without prejudice, without conventions coming between it and myself—facing it without preconceptions, looking at it in an honest way—whatever reality is, not just social reality but all that there is within a man."[4] Rossellini remarked that realism was "simply the artistic form of the truth,"[5] linking neorealism most often to a moral position similar to Fellini's rather than to any preconceived set of techniques or ideological positions, and De Sica stated that his work reflected "reality transposed into the realm of poetry."[6] In an obvious reference to the origins of the cinema in the early dichotomy between the documentaries of the Lumières and Méliès's fantasies, Rossellini has asserted that film must respect two diametrically opposed human tendencies:

"that of concreteness and that of imagination. Today we tend to suppress brutally the second one . . . by forgetting the imaginative tendency, as I was saying, we tend to kill in ourselves every feeling of humanity and to create the robotman who thinks in only one way and tends toward the concrete."[7] And while even the best interpretations of neorealism provided by Armes or Bazin note at least in passing that it is a cinema quite involved with artifice and with the establishment of its own cinematic conventions, it is still unfortunately true that most critical discussion of neorealism emphasizes its relationship to Italian social problems and minimizes its cinematic artifice.[8]

If film historians had approached their subject matter from a broader perspective, this overemphasis on the "realism" of films in the immediate postwar period might well have been avoided. Certainly, they should have recognized that the major works of neorealist fiction which appeared almost contemporaneously with the most important films embodied an entirely different aesthetic. Novels such as Elio Vittorini's *In Sicily* (1941), Carlo Levi's *Christ Stopped at Eboli* (*Christo si è fermato a Eboli,* 1945), Italo Calvino's *The Path to the Nest of Spiders* (*Il sentiero dei nidi di ragno,* 1947), and Cesare Pavese's *The Moon and the Bonfires* (1951), to mention only the most important works, all deal with social reality in a symbolic or mythical fashion, and all employ unreliable and subjective narrators, thereby embracing a clearly antinaturalistic narrative stance quite contrary to the canons of literary realism established by the masters of the nineteenth century. Calvino's retrospective preface added in 1964 to *The Path to the Nest of Spiders* makes this quite clear, for he declares that neorealists "knew all too well that what counted was the music and not the libretto . . . there were never more dogged formalists than we; and never were lyric poets as effusive as those objective reporters we were supposed to be."[9] Pavese strikes a similar note in his assessment of how American fiction influenced the culture of the neorealist generation:

> the expressive wealth of that people was born not so much from an obvious search for scandalous and ultimately superficial social assumptions, but from a severe and already century-old desire to compress ordinary experience in language, without there being anything

left over. From this motive sprang their continuing effort to readjust language to the new reality of the world, in order to create, in effect, a *new* language, down-to-earth and symbolic, that would justify itself solely in terms of itself and not in terms of any traditional complacency.[10]

Italian novelists and directors were not concerned only with social realism in their works. On the contrary, they were seeking a new literary and cinematographic language which would enable them to deal poetically with the pressing problems of their times. As Pavese notes, they wanted to view their world afresh and from a new perspective, thereby creating a "new reality" through an artistic means. They knew, as Calvino asserts, that the music was always more significant than the lyrics, form more crucial to innovation in language than content.

Certainly the cinema neorealists turned to the pressing problems of the time—the war, the Resistance and the Partisan struggle, unemployment, poverty, social injustice, and the like—but there was never a programmatic approach to these questions or any preconceived method of rendering them on celluloid. And the phenomenon was clearly unlike other avant-garde movements in the sense that it never adhered to a governing manifesto or ever felt one was even necessary. In short, neorealism was not a "movement" in the strictest sense of the term. The controlling fiction of neorealist films, or at least the majority of them, was that they dealt with actual problems, that they employed contemporary stories, and that they focused on believable characters taken most frequently from Italian daily life. But the greatest neorealist directors never forgot that the world they projected upon the silver screen was one produced by cinematic conventions rather than an ontological experience, and they were never so naive as to deny that the demands of an artistic medium such as film might be just as pressing as those from the world around them. In fact, in many of their films they underlined the relationship of illusion and reality, fiction and fact, so as to emphasize their understanding of the role both played in their art. Thus, any discussion of Italian neorealism must be broad enough to encompass a wide diversity of cinematic styles, themes, and attitudes. No single or specific approach was taken and, therefore, much of the discussion which arose in the next decade over the "crisis" of neorealism or its "betrayal" by various directors was essentially groundless and founded upon ideological disagreements between various critics rather than any abrupt change on the part of the filmmakers themselves. Directors we label today as neorealists were a crucial part of a more general postwar cultural revolution which was characterized by a number of aesthetic and philosophical perspectives, all united only by the common aspiration to view Italy without preconceptions and to develop a more honest, ethical, but no less poetic cinematic language.

Setting aside the traditional overemphasis upon social realism in neorealist cinema, there are other and perhaps even more pernicious myths concerning the period from Rossellini's *Rome, Open City* to the middle of the next decade, by which time Italian film had definitely moved into a new phase. The most surprising statistic that emerges from an analysis of the style or content of the some 822 films produced in Italy between 1945 and 1953 is that only about 90 (or slightly over 10%) could ever be called neorealist films, and the percentage does not change drastically if we limit our sample to those 224 films produced between 1945 and 1948. Thus, it is even misleading to identify postwar film production in Italy with neorealism. To do so is to make an aesthetic judgement, one shared by all film historians or critics, which stresses the quality of the works in question, not the economic structure of the industry as a whole. But it is even more remarkable to discover that the great masterpieces of this era were rarely among the most popular films distributed. While *Rome, Open City* achieved first place at the box office in 1945–46, in spite of the relative commercial success of Rossellini's *Paisan* (ninth place in 1946–47), Pietro Germi's *In the Name of the Law, (In nome della legge,* third place in 1948–49), De Sica's *The Bicycle Thief* (eleventh place in 1948–49), and De Sanctis's *Bitter Rice* (*Riso amaro,* fifth place in 1949–50), the majority of these ninety films, including many of the best, were dismal box office failures and many were critical failures as well.[11] They were often praised more abroad than at home, and the small but important export market for the best films enabled the beleaguered directors to sustain their work in the face of opposition within their own industry. Paradoxically, while the greatest films of the time set out to project a more authentic image of Italy in as honest a cinematic language as they could create, neorealism always remained primarily an "art" cinema, never capturing the mass public it always tried to gain. In most respects, the generally enthusiastic reception of these works within a limited circle of perceptive critics and cosmopolitan film enthusiasts abroad was no exception to the Italian experience, for a large commercial market for neorealist films was never achieved in either the domestic or the export market. With the deluge of Hollywood films in Italy following the end of the war, most Italians simply preferred the Hollywood products or native Italian farces and historical dramas. And while Italian film production gradually rose above the relatively low figures of the war years under the Fascist regime, the Italian market was virtually dominated by imports from America, which controlled between two thirds and three fourths of the Italian market in 1945–50. Furthermore, the economic and political priorities of the Italian government, allied closely with the United States at the time, made any immediate changes in this situation extremely unlikely. Only in 1951, with an accord between ANICA (the Associazione Nazionale Industrie Cinematografiche ed Affine) and the American Motion Picture Export Association, would the government attempt to curb the flood of American films at around 225 films per year. In principle, this agreement was as much designed to open up the American market to Italian exports as it was to limit imports. Before the accord was signed, 178 Italian films had been exported to America between 1946 to 1950, while 1,662 Hollywood products had been shown in Italy.

Yet, after the agreement Italian films exported to America had only increased to a total of 220 films between 1951 and 1955, while 1,149 works were imported from America into the peninsula for distribution.[12] Even the Italian Communist Party could not have invented a more disturbing illustration of American economic hegemony in postwar Italy! Directors and producers were unable to find relief in the supposedly inexpensive production costs of neorealist works, given their substantially lower rate of return at the box office and the fact that films made on location rather than in the traditional studios effected only a minimal savings, which usually evaporated with the more lengthy and costly shooting time they required.

The limitations of traditional interpretations of Italian neorealism are immediately apparent from a close examination of the universally acclaimed masterpieces of the period: Rossellini's so-called war trilogy —*Rome, Open City* (1945), *Paisan* (1946), *Germany Year Zero* (*Germania anno zero,* 1947); Vittorio De Sica's touching portraits of postwar life in *Shoeshine* (*Sciuscià,* 1946), *The Bicycle Thief* (1948), or *Umberto D.* (*Umberto D.,* 1951); and Luchino Visconti's synthesis of Antonio Gramsci's Marxist theories with the *verismo* of Giovanni Verga in *The Earth Trembles* (*La terra trema,* 1948). These seven works do not by any means exhaust the wealth of neorealism, but neorealism's contribution to the evolution of cinema must in large measure be ultimately judged by their achievements.

Rossellini's *Rome, Open City* represents the landmark film of this group. It so completely reflected the moral and psychological atmosphere of this historical moment that it alerted both the public and the critics to a new direction in Italian film. The conditions of its production (relatively little shooting in the studio, film stock bought on the black market and developed without the normal viewing of daily rushes, postsynchronization of sound to avoid laboratory expenses, limited financial backing) did much to create many of the myths concerning neorealism. With a daring combination of styles and moods ranging from use of documentary footage to the most blatant melodrama, Rossellini almost effortlessly captured forever the tension and the tragedy of Italian experiences during the German occupation and the Partisan struggle against the Nazi invaders. Its plot is an intriguing reflection of the contradictions inherent in that struggle and focuses upon a few dramatic episodes in the lives of a handful of simple characters: Don Pietro (Aldo Fabrizi), a Partisan priest, joins with a leftist Partisan leader named Manfredi to combat the Nazis; Manfredi's former mistress Marina eventually betrays him to the diabolic Gestapo officer, Major Bergmann; a working-class woman named Pina (Anna Magnani), is engaged to be married to a typesetter named Francesco, a friend of Manfredi's, and she is already expecting his child. These people are strongly stereotyped into good and evil categories, depending upon their attitude toward the Resistance struggle. In fact, it is not enough for Rossellini that Bergmann is a monster; he is also pictured as an effeminate homosexual, while his assistant Ingrid is a viperlike lesbian who seduces Marina with expensive presents and drugs in order to obtain information about Manfredi. Since Rossellini cares most about how the tragedy of warfare affects common people, he concentrates the action around the impending marriage of Francesco and Pina, intertwining it skillfully with the narration of the Gestapo's brutal search for Manfredi and his collaborators. As a result, Rossellini creates a narrative incorporating both fact and fiction, reality and artistic invention. While he fuses Catholic and Communist elements of the Resistance into a coherent storyline, he never avoids the hints of tension between the two major sources of anti-Fascism which will later oppose each other when the struggle has ended. Manfredi, for example, expresses mild disapproval of Pina's religious marriage but admits it is better to be joined in wedlock by a Partisan priest than by a Fascist official at city hall; in spite of Don Pietro's obvious good intentions, a leftist printer tells him sharply that everyone cannot be lucky enough to hide from the Germans in monasteries; when Bergmann arrests Manfredi and Don Pietro, he tries unsuccessfully to move the priest to betray Manfredi by arguing that the Communists are the sworn enemies of the Church, but Don Pietro declares that all men who fight for justice and liberty walk in the pathways of the Lord.

The tone of the work is thus far more indebted to Rossellini's message of Christian humanism than it is to any programmatic attempt at cinematic realism. The good characters are set sharply apart from the corrupt ones by their belief in what Francesco calls an impending "springtime" in Italy and a better tomorrow: Marina is corrupted by Ingrid not because of political convictions but because she lacks faith in herself and is therefore incapable of loving others. Marxists and Christians alike adhere to Rossellini's credo embodied in Don Pietro's last words before he faces a firing squad at the close of the film: "Oh, it's not hard to die well. It's hard to live well."[13] Beneath the surface of the work, which often seems to possess the texture of a documentary and frequently seems closer to a newsreel than to fictional narrative, there is a profoundly tragicomic vision of life which juxtaposes melodramatic moments or instances of comic relief and dark humor with the most tragic of human experiences which reconstruct the reality of a moment in Italian history. When Fascist soldiers arrive at the workers' apartments near the Via Casilina to look for concealed Partisans, Manfredi and others manage to escape because the troops are preoccupied with trying to peer up the women's skirts on a staircase; a sympathetic Italian policeman looks on while Pina and others loot a bakery, and rather than doing his duty, he only remarks sadly that it is too bad he is in uniform; when German soldiers enter a restaurant where Manfredi is eating, we immediately fear he is about to be captured, but this suspense is undercut by our discovery that the Germans have only come to butcher a live lamb and to eat it, and our fear (as well as Manfredi's) is dissolved by the humorous quip of the restaurant owner Flavio—he had forgotten that Germans were specialists in butchering!

The entire film revolves around Rossellini's shifting perspective from a comic to a tragic tone, and nowhere is this more evident than in the film's most famous sequence, the search of Pina's apartment building which results in her death in the street, mercilessly machine-gunned by German soldiers as she races towards Francesco, her fiancé now captured and about to be taken away to a work camp. This is the day when Pina and Francesco plan to be married: the promise of a better tomorrow for her and her family will thus end in despair. But this tragedy is preceded by a comic introduction; just before her death, Don Pietro and Marcello (Pina's son) arrive at the apartment building supposedly to give the last rites to Pina's father but actually to locate and conceal weapons and bombs kept there by Romoletto ("little Romulus"), the crippled leader of a group of Partisan children who humorously repeats Marxist slogans without understanding their significance. In spite of Rossellini's often cited aversion to dramatic editing,[14] he skillfully creates a moment of suspense as he cuts back and forth between the priest's search for the weapons and his subsequent descent to the dying man's room, on the one hand, and the menacing ascent of the suspicious Fascist officer on the other. When the Fascists enter the room, Don Pietro is peacefully administering the last rites to a man who appears to be sleeping. Only after they leave and the priest frantically attempts to revive the moribund sleeper do we realize that to keep him quiet Don Pietro has knocked the old man unconscious with a bent frying pan and then concealed the contraband munitions under his bed. But this slapstick comedy routine immediately shifts to the darkest of tragedy as in defiance of the soldiers around her Pina runs after the truck taking Francesco away. We hear a burst of machine-gun fire, Marcello races toward his mother screaming and Pina is shown lying in the street, face down with her right leg bared to the garter belt, an image underlining the obscenity of her unnecessary death. Ironically enough, and Rossellini never misses the opportunity to underline the paradoxes in the world of history, in the next sequence Francesco's truck is ambushed by Partisans and he is rescued. Pina's death, like so many others in wartime, was pointless.

Roberto Rossellini's *Rome, Open City* (1945). Pina (Anna Magnani) is shot to death by the Nazis.
(Photo courtesy of the Museum of Modern Art)

The scene at Gestapo Headquarters in the Via Tasso is justly famous, and it, too, is constructed around the juxtaposition of different moods and techniques. But in this sequence, Rossellini arranges this juxtaposition around the very structure of the set itself. Two doors lead out from the office in which Bergmann interrogates both Manfredi and Don Pietro: one door opens into a torture chamber inhabited by ghoulish soldiers whose fingers are stained with blood and who light cigarettes from the very torch they use on Manfredi with complete indifference to his suffering; another opens into a parlor where Gestapo officers play cards, listen to piano music, and drink comfortably, oblivious to the human misery on the other side of the wall. Bergmann moves effortlessly between these three locations, and his physical movements (viewed most often from Don Pietro's perspective, who remains in the central room and peers through each door) underline the emotional distance between their separate worlds. Manfredi's torture is one of the most horrifying of many such scenes in the history of filmmaking; yet, Rossellini achieves this startling effect on the viewer not by showing us merely the reality of the torture with minute attention to detailed close-up shots but, rather, by exploiting the power of our imaginations and focusing upon the reactions of Don Pietro. We see Don Pietro's anguished face while voice-overs convey the screams from the other room; our revulsion at this sound is further increased by masterful touches of black humor. While Don Pietro is moved to tears, a German soldier quietly sharpens his pencil and awaits Bergmann's orders. When Manfredi dies without betraying his cause, Rossellini frames this Communist Partisan leader as if he were photographing the crucified Christ, employing the traditional iconography familiar to us all from numerous works of religious art.

During Manfredi's torture, a drunken Nazi officer (Major Hartmann) listening to the piano in the salon had argued against Bergmann's view that since the Germans were a master race—else the war had no meaning—the Italian would end by betraying his friend. Yet, on the morning Don Pietro is led to his execution, the same Hartmann who, inebriated, seemed sympathetic to the thirst for liberty typical of opponents of Nazi tyranny, now soberly commands the firing squad. It is the final irony Rossellini injects into this story, but his last shots accentuate the religious tone of the entire film: Romoletto, Marcello,

Roberto Rossellini's *Rome, Open City* (1945). Major Bergmann (Harry Feist) observes the torture of Manfredi (Marcello Pagliero) at Gestapo Headquarters.
(Photo courtesy of the Museum of Modern Art)

and the other children walk away from Don Pietro's execution and are followed by the panning camera which sets them, Italy's future, against the backdrop of the dome of St. Peter's Cathedral. Out of a moment of tragic despair, Rossellini has created a vision of hope from the first of the many symbolic images associated with children that will characterize almost all of the great neorealist classics.

While *Rome, Open City* employs a melodramatic plot to overwhelm the viewer with a sense of tragedy and moves freely from moments of documentary realism to others of theatrical intensity, *Paisan* reflects to a far greater extent the conventions of the newsreel documentary, even though it, too, goes beyond the mere statement of facts or depiction of events. Its episodic organization presents a step-by-step narrative of the Allied invasion of Italy, beginning with the early landing in Sicily, and moving successively to the occupation of Naples; to a moment six months after the liberation of Rome; to the struggle between Partisans and Fascists for control of Florence; to the visit of three American chaplains to a monastery in the Apennines; and finally to the capture of Italian Partisans and their Allied advisers in the Po River Valley. The film exploits many of the conventions of the wartime documentary. Pincer movements on a map, an authoritative narrative voice-over, and actual newsreel footage introduce each of the separate episodes as if the work were an army training film. Made when the rubble of the destruction was still visible in Italian cities, much of the photography retains the grainy quality and the immediacy of subject matter we associate with newsreels. Yet, Rossellini's subject is not merely a realistic view of the Allied invasion. Instead, he aims at a more philosophical theme—the encounter of two alien cultures, Italian and American. The results of this fateful juncture in history are shown in brief, individual vignettes set against a backdrop of the Italian landscape, which itself becomes one of the main protagonists of the film. The meeting of two different worlds involves a variety of problems subtly treated by Rossellini, such as linguistic communication or its frequent breakdown, as well as empathy or antipathy between alien cultures and peoples. The film's title, *Paisà,* a colloquial form of the word *paesano*—countryman, neighbor, kinsman, even friend—was typically used by Italians and American soldiers as a friendly greeting, and the implications of its deeper meanings provide the basis for Rossellini's exploration of the Italian-American encounter.

As the film opens in Sicily, there is little to indicate that any basis of comradeship is possible: the Sicilians are suspicious of the GI's, even though one American's parents are from Gela, a nearby town; the Americans are justly dubious of the Italians' intentions (at this point Italy and Germany are still allies), calling them "Eyeties." One of the townspeople, a young girl named Carmela, nevertheless volunteers to lead the Americans through a minefield. Most of the sequence concerns an incomprehensible conversation between Carmela, who speaks no English, and an American who cannot speak or understand Italian (not to mention Sicilian dialect) who calls himself Joe from Jersey. In spite of this linguistic comedy of errors, they establish an understanding that transcends linguistic barriers, but when Joe uses a cigarette lighter to show Carmela a photograph of his sister, the flame attracts a German sniper's bullet and he is mortally wounded. Carmela seizes Joe's carbine and in a series of scenes characterized by puzzling, uncertain camera locations shot in the dark from a series of different perspectives, Rossellini perfectly captures the sense of disorientation associated with night combat. Joe's friends return and find his corpse; unaware that Carmela has attacked his killers, they mistakenly blame his death on the girl ("Why, that dirty little Eyetie!"). As Carmela is cursed by Joe's comrades, the final shot of the episode shows her dead body sprawled on a rocky cliff. Rossellini's first vignette of an attempt to cross cultural boundaries in the conversation between Joe and Carmela ultimately results in the deaths of both the Italian and the American.

With the Naples sequence, Rossellini portrays the disastrous effects of the war upon the Neapolitan through the perspective of a black soldier and a young boy named Pasquale who "buys" the Negro while he is drunk in order to steal whatever he can from him (apparently a common occurrence in wartime Naples). Irony rather than realism is once again Rossellini's vehicle as he shows an Italian buying a black, the descendant of former slaves who has paradoxically been sent to liberate the very Neapolitans who now purchase him; the irony shifts to a comic tone when Joe and Pasquale enter a puppet show featuring the traditional Christian knights (white men) and their enemies, the Moors (black men), an entertainment familiar to every Italian but probably not a common sight to most American soldiers. In his drunken state, mistaking this theatrical show for reality, Joe leaps upon the stage and tries to assist the Moorish puppet against its white opponents and is ejected from the theatre for his foolish confusion of illusion and reality. While Joe fails grotesquely to sort out these two vastly different realms of human experience, Rossellini also implicitly reminds us that the story he is telling is composed of equal elements

Roberto Rossellini's *Paisan* (1946). Joe (Dots Johnson) confuses illusion and reality and attacks the white knight in the Neapolitan puppet show. (Photo courtesy of the Centro Sperimentale Cinematografico, Rome)

from both fact and fiction and we would do well, as intelligent spectators, not to forget this.[15]

Soon afterward, the black GI dreams of a triumphant return to America as a successful hero complete with ticker-tape parades, but as he becomes more and more sober, his joy turns into tragic despair, for he begins to understand that as a black man in America, he is little better off than the street urchins of Naples ("Goin' home! Goin' home? I don't want to go home! My house is an old shack with tin cans at the doors!"). As he falls asleep, Pasquale steals his boots. We immediately fade out to a moment three days later: driving his jeep, Joe, a military policeman, runs into Pasquale, picks him up for stealing Allied goods, and only later recognizes him as the boy who took his boots. He forces the child to go home to recover them: he soon discovers that Pasquale's home is actually a filthy cave teeming with poverty-stricken Neapolitans; moreover, his parents have been killed in Allied bombing raids. The black GI, astonished at such misery and obviously moved by the human suffering he witnesses, drops the shoes and turns away. The subjective shots of this scene from Joe's perspective tell the story of his empathy for his fellow sufferers more eloquently than any elaborate commentary; Joe has taken the first step, that of understanding, toward becoming Pasquale's *paisà*.

The Rome sequence opens with a number of documentary clips showing the departure of German troops from Rome and the entry of the Allied army, but history quickly yields to Rossellini's fictional narrative as the camera dissolves to a moment six months later: a prostitute named Francesca picks up a drunken American soldier named Fred who knows a bit of Italian, just as she has rudimentary knowledge of English; when she takes him to bed, his cynical remark that "Rome's full of girls like you" leads him to recall the more innocent days during the liberation of Rome, when everything seemed possible and when "girls were all happy and laughing and fresh, full of color, beautiful . . . And now it's all different. You should've seen the one I knew—her name was Francesca . . ." With this remark, Rossellini dissolves to a flashback which shows how Fred and Francesca met earlier. However, the economic deprivation following the liberation has forced Francesca onto the streets. The camera again dissolves back to the bedroom; while Fred is sleeping, Francesca leaves her address with the madam and hurries home to prepare for the renewal of the hope in the future she feels will result from a reunion between them when she is transformed from a prostitute back into Francesca, the innocent young girl of Fred's memory. While she waits for him in the rain, Fred awakens sober; unaware that his lost ideal is within his grasp, he tosses her address away, remarking bitterly that it is only the address of a whore. The entire sequence is an ironic commentary upon the hope and optimism contained in *Rome, Open City* of only a year earlier; yet, its melodramatic plot based upon the perennial male fantasy of the whore with the heart of gold—as well as the uncharacteristic flashback undercutting the documentary style opening the sequence—plays upon the conventions of fiction rather than realism to achieve a deeply moving portrayal of the corruption and unhappiness that follows in the wake of military triumph.

The failure of a love story to reach its fulfillment in Rome is sharply contrasted to the story contained in the Florentine episode. Whereas Fred spoke only broken Italian and his efforts to bridge the gap between his culture and that of Italy ended disastrously, the American nurse Harriet of this fourth episode had previously spent several years in Florence, speaks Italian well, and was apparently in love with a painter named Guido Lombardi, now a Partisan leader named Lupo ("Wolf"). Hearing that he may be wounded, Harriet races away from

Roberto Rossellini's *Paisan* (1946). Fred (Gar Moore) fails to recognize Francesca (Maria Michi), who has become a prostitute in the Roman sequence.
(Photo courtesy of the Centro Sperimentale Cinematografico, Rome)

her hospital and with another Partisan crosses the Arno River through the Vasarian corridor leading from the Palazzo Pitti to the Uffizi in search of her former lover. Nowhere else in *Paisan* does Rossellini's camera capture so perfectly the sense of a historical event. The three earlier episodes clearly juxtaposed the main storyline of their episodes to the newsreel clips preceding them, but here with his highly mobile camera and the grainy film stock he uses, everything seems to be filmed as if it were actually unfolding before us as historical and film time merge completely. After braving German bullets, Harriet reaches her destination only to learn that Lupo has already died. Her pain and commitment are sharply contrasted to the aloofness demonstrated by two British officers who sit on a hill peering through binoculars at Giotto's tower, both oblivious to the human suffering all around them. Once again, an attempt to bridge the gap between two people from two different cultures ends in death and unhappiness.

The fifth episode set within a monastery in northern Italy represents an interlude from the war raging all around: three chaplains—a Catholic, a Protestant, and a Jew—visit a spot which seems to have remained unchanged since the discovery of America. When the monks discover that Captain Martin, the Catholic chaplain, has yet to convert his two friends to the true faith, they begin to fast in order that God may provide salvation for these two "lost souls"! Martin, who speaks Italian well, does not react in a way we might expect when he learns of this. He delivers to the monks a brief Italian speech incomprehensible to his friends and no doubt puzzling to the average non-Italian:

> I want to tell you that what you've given me is such a great gift that I feel I'll always be in your debt. I've found here that peace of mind I'd lost in the horrors and the trials of the war, a beautiful, moving lesson of humility, simplicity, and pure faith.

The irony is completely intentional: are the monks providing a lesson in pure faith or, rather, one of religious intolerance and bigotry? We must remember that this particular episode was suggested to Rossellini and scripted in large measure by Federico Fellini, whose contribution as both scriptwriter and male lead for Rossellini's later meditation on the meaning of Christian faith in the controversial episode of *The Ways of Love* (*L'amore*, 1948) entitled *The Miracle* (*Il miracolo*), would create a scandal only two years later. Rather than reflecting a moment of comprehension and understanding, the episode underlines the vast intellectual distance between the two cultures represented by the fasting monks and their American guests. And yet Martin accepts their act of faith as a genuine one, while most non-Italian viewers lacking his training or experience with Italian culture will undoubtedly overlook Rossellini's characteristic belief that true religious feeling cannot be explained by the rules of logic. The world of facts filmed dispassionately by Rossellini reveals itself to be ambiguous and as puzzling as the world of fiction.

The final Po Valley episode brings together a number of elements from the other five episodes: here Dale, an American liaison officer, is directly involved in the daily no-quarter-given struggle of the Partisans and the Germans, his command of the language testifying to his complete integration in the effort. Rossellini's highly mobile camera is employed brilliantly to portray the circumscribed world of the Partisans from a completely subjective viewpoint: landscape plays a dominant role here, as the camera embodies the Partisan perspective, never peering above the thin row of reeds in the marshy river basin that provides the only cover available to these harried men. As we view the sequence through this tightly controlled point of view, we share, in Bazin's words, the "exact equivalent, under conditions imposed by the screen, of the inner feeling men experience who are living between the sky and the water and whose lives are at the mercy of an infinitesimal shift of angle in relation to the horizon."[16] Rarely has such a simple cinematic technique so movingly rendered a subjective human emotion. The story concludes on a note of desperation and despair rather than hope: the Partisans are rounded up by the Germans as if they were animals and are separated from their Allied advisers by the Nazis, who intend to observe the Geneva Conventions with the regular soldiers but to execute the Partisans mercilessly. Hands tied behind them, the Partisans are pushed into the water by the Germans, who thrust a sign reading "Partisan" into the life jackets that will keep the bodies afloat without saving the men from drowning;

their fate is a warning to anyone who opposes the Nazis. Dale rushes forward to protest and is shot down. The last image we see, a floating Partisan, is similar to the one that opened the episode; a voice-over informs us: "This happened in the winter of 1944. At the beginning of spring, the war was over."

Rossellini has provided us with the "facts" of the Allied invasion—the brutality, the dreams, the corruption, and the compassion. But the facts alone do not explain the film's greatness. The confrontation of two alien cultures, that of the Old World and the New, has been marked by errors, failures of understanding, ambiguity, and—ultimately—tragedy. And yet from this pessimistic narrative he makes a moving testament to the human spirit: in the beginning Joe from Jersey died on Sicilian soil almost by accident, unable to understand the people for whom he was sacrificing his life; at the conclusion of the film, Dale sacrifices his own life for his Italian comrades and becomes one of them, a *paisà* who is a kinsman to all those who struggle and suffer for a better world. He belongs to the same moral universe as Don Pietro, for he demonstrates that the value of a man's life presupposes love for one's fellows, a Christian notion which transcends all the feeble intellectual attempts to comprehend or to communicate by rational means alone. Ultimately, linguistic barriers, so brilliantly portrayed in *Paisan*, give way in the face of moral commitment.

Germany Year Zero, shot amidst the rubble of postwar Berlin, followed the death of Rossellini's first son Romano in 1946. The work is dedicated to Rossellini's son and his death explains why Rossellini would turn to a young protagonist, a feature more typical of De Sica's greatest works. The film opens with a epigraph title (absent from the print distributed in America) which announces the moralistic perspective of the film: "When an ideology strays from the eternal laws of morality and of Christian charity which form the basis of men's lives, it must end as criminal madness . . ."; this is immediately followed by a fade-out to a long tracking shot of the bombed-out German buildings accompanied by a newsreel-like voice-over announcing that the film is "intended to be simply an objective, true-to-life picture of this enormous, half-destroyed city . . . It is simply a presentation of the facts. But if anyone who has seen the story of Edmund Koeler comes to realize that something must be done . . . that German children must be taught to love life again, then the efforts of those who made this film will have been amply rewarded." Yet from the moment the director's purpose is announced, his objectivity is in open contrast to his moralistic message.

The plot represents a return to the more structured storyline typical of *Rome, Open City* and a move away from the episodic collection of cinematic short stories held together by geographical location and theme in *Paisan*. Edmund, a young boy of fifteen, lives with his sick father, his sister, Eva (who consorts with Allied soldiers for money), and his brother, Karl Heinz, a former Nazi soldier, in hiding for fear of imprisonment. Edmund lacks any real friends or an authentic relationship to his family (we learn he even denounced his father to the authorities for trying to keep him out of the Hitler Youth). A former Nazi schoolteacher and an obvious pederast, Herr Enning, uses Edmund to sell souvenir records of Hitler's speeches to Allied soldiers. The unreconstructed Nazi ideology he still preaches to Edmund—that the weak must die while only the strong should survive—prompts Edmund to poison his sick father in a perverted act of mercy. Lacking any sort of effective moral code, as the epigraph title suggests at the outset, Edmund thus resorts to murder and is only afterward dimly conscious of the gravity of his act. He then commits suicide by throwing himself off the roof of a building.

Rossellini hovers in this work between objective documentary and the depiction of a moralistic horror story. His camera is much more mobile than in the other parts of the war trilogy, and its characteristic movement in the work is a long—almost obsessively long—tracking shot following Edmund through the rubble and debris of the desolate city landscape. Thus, Rossellini portrays the moral emptiness of his youthful protagonist by purely external means without recourse to more subjective techniques. His ethical message once again moves him to construct stereotypical characters, a return to the practice of *Rome, Open City*: dressed in short pants and with carefully combed, straight blond hair, Edmund represents the prototype of Hitler's Aryan race. His stiff, cadenced manner of walking and erect posture remind the viewer more of a soldier than of a young boy of fifteen.

The diabolic message his former teacher inculcates is linked to his sexual perversity, just as in *Open City* Bergmann and Ingrid were both ethical and sexual deviants. Edmund's tragedy stems not only from the evil effects of the moral climate which produced Nazi Germany but also from his tragic failure to find an appropriate paternal authority figure—neither his father, nor Herr Enning, nor Hitler, nor the Church has provided him with a workable moral code. Perhaps the most chilling moment in the film is created through the simple juxtaposition of sound track and photography: selling an old recording of Hitler's speeches to Allied soldiers for Herr Enning, Edmund demonstrates his wares on a wind-up Victrola, and as Hitler's voice booms out accompanied by the delirious cheers of his followers, Rossellini shows the rubble of the Reichschancellory building. For a moment, it seems that an evil spirit has returned to haunt Berlin again. And the legacy of that spirit lives on in Edmund's mind. In *Germany Year Zero* there is no note of hope such as that symbolized by the Italian children of *Rome, Open City* who witness Don Pietro's execution.

I have devoted a relatively lengthy section of this chapter to Rossellini's war trilogy not only because of its historical and aesthetic importance in the rise of neorealism but also because such careful attention reveals conclusively that these seminal works are hardly exhausted by what traditional criticism of them views as their realistic perspective. Certainly they bear an interesting and suggestive relationship to the world they depict, but they are primarily works of art with their own order of priorities. And when Rossellini's three films are compared to three major works by Vittorio De Sica within the neorealist tradition, it becomes abundantly clear that there was no single aesthetic or programmatic approach to society in their works. As André Bazin perceptively wrote years ago, "Rossellini's style is a way of seeing, while De Sica's is primarily a way of feeling."[17]

Rossellini's style can be more easily described as a method, while De Sica more frequently injects innovative stylistic touches into what are often rather traditional storylines. Rossellini's background in the cinema was in the documentary film; De Sica began his career as a popular actor in comic roles and turned to direction in 1940, producing four interesting works before he began his fruitful collaboration with Cesare Zavattini in 1942 with *The Children Are Watching Us*, (*I bambini ci guardano*). His best films in the neorealist vein were all to be scripted by Zavattini, whose theoretical ideas on the direction neorealism should take in the postwar period were only partially embodied in De Sica's films.[18] *The Children Are Watching Us* represents the key to De Sica's postwar works, for its relatively literary and elaborate script allows less improvisation than is common in Rossellini's or Visconti's works, employs studio locations more frequently, and uses a child's perspective to obtain a sentimental response from the viewer. Its plot, a rather conventional story of a wife's adulterous affair which drives her husband to suicide and destroys her son's affection, is presented, as its title suggested, from the child's point of view, a simple but effective technique exploited even more eloquently only a few years later by Calvino's important neorealist narration of the Partisan struggle, *The Path to the Nest of Spiders*. And it is De Sica's sentimentality in his dealings with his young protagonists in all his neorealist classics which ultimately sets his work far apart from that of Rossellini.

Shoeshine is almost an ironic commentary on the note of hope sounded by the conclusion of *Rome, Open City*, for in it De Sica dramatizes the tragedy of childish innocence corrupted by the adult world. Two shoeshine boys, Pasquale and Giuseppe, use their hard-earned wages to buy a horse; however, they become involved in a blackmarket scheme because of Giuseppe's older brother and are sent to a reformatory prison for juvenile offenders, where their friendship is gradually destroyed by the social injustice usually associated with the adult world and authority figures. After an escape, Giuseppe's accidental death (which will be blamed on Pasquale) concludes De Sica's exploration of the tragic impact of the adult world on youthful friendship. Within this elaborately plotted film, De Sica's camera style incorporates a profound understanding of the aesthetic possibilities of *mise-en-scène* editing, which is obviously indebted to the French masters of the preceding generation. He constantly uses camera angles or shot placements to underline the progressive limits imposed upon the freedom of the two children. The credits of the work are imposed over the set of the children's prison, an ominous hint of future disaster.

Vittorio De Sica's *Shoeshine* (1946). The faces of Giuseppe (Rinaldo Smordoni) and Pasquale (Franco Interlenghi) reveal the corruption of youthful innocence by the adult world.
(Photo courtesy of the Museum of Modern Art)

The opening scene of the film, shot outside on location, is a view of the gallopping horse which will represent the ideal of freedom in the work, a gauge against which the rest of the film should be measured. While on horseback, the children are shot from a low-angle perspective which ennobles their character and gives them the appearance, as Bazin noted, of an equestrian statue; however, when they pursue their trade, the same low-angle shot from their perspective underlines their humble status in the world; the sense of confinement continues as a number of shots through cell windows place the boys in a tight, claustrophobic atmosphere and restrict their movement. However, the climactic scene of the film—that set outside the prison and staged not on location, as was the opening shot of the horse but, instead, inside a studio—concludes the sense of confinement as the aesthetic qualities of the photography merge perfectly with Pasquale's tragedy. Like Renoir or Welles, De Sica frequently exploits the possibilities of the *mise-en-scène* technique to pack a great deal of visual information into a single shot. Typical is his treatment of a prison riot, in which three visual planes act to delineate the human drama only implicit in the plot: in the background in deep focus are the rioting children, the middle plane contains the boy who will act as a peacemaker between the two shoeshine boys, Pasquale and Giuseppe stand in the foreground.

Visual complexity combines with complexity of plot. The story begins and ends with a vision of the horse, a free spirit whose final escape symbolizes the end of a friendship. Pasquale betrays Giuseppe in prison, revealing the details of the blackmarket operation only because the prison guards lead him to believe they are beating Giuseppe with a leather strap (in fact, another boy pretends to scream while a guard feigns the sound of a whipping). In revenge, Giuseppe arranges for the prison director to search Pasquale's cell, where the discovery of a planted file leads to an actual whipping with the leather belt; when Giuseppe escapes and goes to recover their horse, Pasquale follows, purposely betrays him to the guards, and beats him with yet another leather strap. Trying to avoid the belt, Giuseppe falls over the bridge to his death. Even the design of the prison set contributes to the exposition of the plot, for parallel rows of cells, upon which the two boys separately walk, underline their similar but ultimately different fates.

In all of his early neorealist films, De Sica is even more conscious than Rossellini of the fact that his filmed "reality" is a product of cinematic illusion, and he takes great pleasure in revealing this to the careful viewer. Inside the prison, an American documentary film reminiscent of the "Why We Fight" series and ironically titled "News of the Free World" is screened, but it is interrupted by a freak accident as the director humorously but unmistakably rejects the view that cinema must necessarily reflect the outside world of social reality. Earlier, the prisoners in the courtyard mimic grand opera just before the dramatic confrontation between Giuseppe and Pasquale, warning the viewer of the melodramatic qualities of what will follow. In spite of the fact that authority figures are carefully photographed to underline their sinister role (the approach of a policeman, for instance, shows only his disembodied and advancing legs), there is often a note of wry humor in De Sica's work. The authoritarian director of the reformatory once slips and uses the obligatory Fascist form of address to an underling ("Voi, anzi Lei"), revealing his true nature, and an old man who works in the kitchen forgets that the year is 1946 when he instinctively gives the Roman salute to the director as he makes his inspection tour of the premises.

And yet De Sica accomplishes this marvelous work of art employing nonprofessional children in the principal roles, a reminder that the most complicated artifice can be combined with inexperienced actors by a skillful director. De Sica has stated that his method of direction is "being faithful to the character," which involves a reversal of Hollywood techniques:

> It is not the actor who lends the character a face which, however versatile he may be, is necessarily his own, but the character who reveals himself, sooner or later, in "that" particular face and in no other . . . their ignorance is an advantage, not a handicap. The man in the street, particularly if he is directed by someone who is himself an actor, is raw material that can be molded at will. It is sufficient to explain to him those few tricks of the trade which may be useful to him from time to time; to show him the technical and, in the best sense of the term, of course, the histrionic means of expression at his disposal. It is difficult—perhaps impossible—for a fully trained actor to forget his profession. It is far easier to teach it, to hand on just the little that is needed, just what will suffice for the purpose at hand.[19]

A great actor himself, De Sica is suspicious of the ease with which professionals seem to be able to leap from one emotion to another.

De Sica's absolute faith in the expressive powers of ordinary people achieved perfect artistic form in his masterpiece, *The Bicycle Thief*, in which two nonprofessionals filling the leading roles of the father and his son produce performances that could never be surpassed by even the most experienced of theatrical actors. David Selznick offered to finance the film if only he would cast Cary Grant in the leading role, an offer De Sica wisely refused! This film continues the *mise-en-scène* style of *Shoeshine*, combining a number of realistic elements (non-professionals, on-location shooting, social themes) with an extremely complex plot aimed at moving the sympathies of the audience. Once again, De Sica focuses upon the relationship of children and adults. Antonio Ricci, unemployed for two years, is finally offered a job as a bill-poster, but he must own a bicycle to keep the job; when this bicyle is stolen, he and his son Bruno search all over Rome for it but are unsuccessful, although the thief is located immediately after they consult a fortune teller, Signora Santona; in despair, Ricci attempts to steal another bicycle, is captured, humiliated in front of his terrified son, and then released by an angry crowd.

The realistic texture of the work was produced not by improvisation or a documentary approach to the plot but, instead, by careful planning. The film's budget was a relatively large one, due primarily to the expensive preparations De Sica insisted upon at each stage of the work. All the crowd scenes were carefully choreographed (forty market vendors were hired for a single scene, and the Roman fire brigade drenched the set to simulate a rain storm). The nonprofessional actors playing Ricci and Bruno were carefully selected because of particular mannerisms in their walk and their facial expressions. In the sequence where Ricci's bicycle is actually stolen, De Sica employed six different cameras from a number of various angles. Thus, there was nothing amateurish about this or any of De Sica's films, and there are often subtle but unmistakable hints within his works that they should be construed primarily as works of art—illusions of reality—rather than as mere reflections of Italian society. For example, the scene preceding the theft of Ricci's bicycle, as artistically contrived a sequence as one can imagine, shows Ricci posting a Rita Hayworth film poster, the director's pointed reference to the careful viewer that he is watching a film, not reality.

We should remember De Sica's remarks concerning transposing reality to the realm of poetry, for this perspective is precisely what lies at the root of his aesthetics in all of his neorealist films. While

Vittorio De Sica's *The Bicycle Thief* (1948). De Sica's casting for the role of Bruno (Enzo Staiola), the son of the unemployed worker, guaranteed an emotional response from his audience.
(Photo from the author's private collection)

The Bicycle Thief certainly does treat the many pressing social problems of postwar Italian reconstruction, it is not merely a film on unemployment, nor will André Bazin's famous remarks about the film—that it is the "only valid Communist film of the whole past decade" or that it represents pure cinema with no more actors, sets, or storyline—bear close scrutiny in spite of the fact that no other critic ever wrote so sympathetically on De Sica's films.[20] De Sica's careful instructions to the nonprofessionals in the film produced a level of acting competence far surpassing the self-conscious nervousness of the nonprofessionals in the works of Rossellini or Visconti. His scrupulous organization of the on-location shooting differs drastically from a documentary approach to his material. And the complexity of its plot negates Bazin's view that storyline has disappeared in the work. The mythic structure of the story—a traditional quest—as well as its strange and suggestive sound track and the crucial role of chance or fortune in the film all depart from a strictly realist approach to the subject matter and constitute the very elements of the film which make it a great work of art.

The meaning of *The Bicycle Thief* is problematic indeed. The traditional view construes the work as a political film which combines a presentation of pressing social problems with an implicit denunciation of a particular socioeconomic system. Closer analysis, however, reveals this view to be only one of several plausible interpretations, for the film may also be seen as a pessimistic and fatalistic view of the human condition, as well as a philosophical parable on absurdity, solitude, and loneliness. Antonio Ricci emerges in the opening shot from a crowd at an employment agency; in the moving closing shot, he merges back into the crowd at a soccer match with his small son and disappears. Crowds and masses of people outside Ricci's immediate family are always threatening rather than reassuring forces in the film, hardly the proper iconography for a work depicting proletarian solidarity or class consciousness. When Ricci receives his job, his fellow unemployed are more than eager to take it from him; when he comes to the union hall to seek assistance for his stolen bicycle, vague offers of aid are forthcoming but no real understanding of his personal tragedy emerges from a gathering that understands only collective action; he is threatened by crowds waiting for buses, and the final destruction of his self-respect before the eyes of his son occurs within the hostile crowd that captures him after his attempted theft. This act of a hostile crowd is in direct contrast to the complete lack of assistance Ricci receives from another crowd when he tries to prevent the theft of his own vehicle. Of course, De Sica shows us bureaucrats, police officials, and pious churchgoers who do not understand Ricci's plight either, but the fact that members of his own class are no more sympathetic to him than they are is even more devastating. In De Sica's universe, economic solutions are ultimately ineffective in curing what is a meaningless, absurd, human predicament.

De Sica's carefully contrived visual effects underline the hopelessness of Ricci's struggle, not merely the economic or political aspects of Italian society which have supposedly produced his dilemma. A long, slow tilt of his camera reveals an incredible number of packages of bed linens at the pawn broker's when Ricci goes to sell these materials and to redeem his bicycle—obviously the hopes of countless others have already been dashed before. At the police station, he shows us an equally infinite number of police dossiers—all unsolved cases such as Ricci's. Even more depressing is the masterful sequence at Rome's open market where stolen items are resold to their victimized former owners: the almost endless tracking shot of countless bicycle parts, intercut with the shots of the anxious faces of Ricci or Bruno, lends their efforts a meaninglessness and futility worthy of a Kafka novel.[21] Extreme depth of field shots accentuate Ricci's isolation: when he searches the thief's home for traces of his stolen bicycle, for example, we see in the background most clearly a neighbor closing her window, as if to cut off all possibility of communication between Ricci and the thief's neighbors. The plot itself, as well as the evocative quality of the sound track, underscores the illogical character of Ricci's world. Characters appear, drop out of sight, and reappear again as if by magic: the thief vanishes with Ricci's vehicle into thin air rather than actually escaping; an old man who knows where the thief lives seems to dematerialize once outside a church; Ricci mysteriously bumps into the actual thief when he leaves the fortune teller's home; and finally, the man who apprehends Ricci when he turns to steal another bicycle appears unexpectedly almost as if the director had called him out by magic. While the music sometimes accentuates our sentimental response to the film, in other cases its mysterious, suggestive tunes, particularly when Ricci unsuccessfully tries to chase the thief at the market place, imply that an event is explained only by illogical, mysterious circumstances.

Most of such antirealistic elements in De Sica's storyline are associated with the figure of Signora Santona, a fortune teller visited at the opening of the film by Ricci's wife to pay her for having predicted that Ricci would find a job. At that time, Ricci scoffed at his wife, claiming he alone located his employment. Thus, at the outset the question of destiny is clearly posed—is Ricci really in command of his life or are sinister forces at work? Time and again before the theft of his bicycle, Ricci leaves his bicycle leaning against various buildings, and since the Italian title of the film is *Bicycle Thieves*, not *The Bicycle Thief*, we should be prepared for the impending disaster. Cyclical events abound in a film about cycles, and the pun is intentional: Ricci first refuses to believe Signora Santona's predictions, then in despair returns to her for assistance in locating his bicycle, receiving the cryptic prophecy that "either you will find it immediately or you will never find it." This prediction, too, proves accurate, for as he steps outside her home, he encounters the thief. The film time that elapses progresses from Friday to Sunday, a cycle of time with particular resonance for Italian culture, referring ironically not only to the death and resurrection of Christ but also to Dante's journey through Hell, Purgatory, and Paradise towards salvation. Ricci's bicycle is a brand called Fides (Faith), and his failure to locate such an item is intentionally ironic. The ultimately fatalistic, absurd cycle in the work concerns Ricci himself: a man who having lost his own bicycle becomes a bicycle thief himself, and an unsuccessful one at that! But this primarily pessimistic subplot is combined with another, more complicated one: while Ricci progressively becomes a thief, his relationship to Bruno is gradually transformed from one of the son's dependence upon his father to the father's eventual dependence upon his son.

Social reform may transform the immediate situation De Sica described in 1948. Economic development will indeed change a society in which a stolen bicycle may signify hunger and deprivation. But no amount of social engineering or even revolution, De Sica seems to imply, will alter the basic facts of life—solitude, loneliness, and alienation of the individual within the amorphous and unsympathetic body of humanity. The only remedy De Sica suggests, one typical of an Italian, is the support and love Ricci receives from his family, for no amount of determinism or fatalism can destroy the special relationship between Bruno and his father. Psychologically, De Sica's story has only one resolution—the love between father and son. On the level of dramatic plotting, the film achieves a resolution when Ricci's tragedy is linked to Bruno's touching gesture of support, offering his father his hand before they both disappear into the alien crowd at the conclusion of the film. All the technical expertise De Sica can muster, which is considerable, underscores these themes. But seldom has any film of supposedly realistic pretensions been characterized by a more problematic, ambivalent conclusion. On a positive note, Ricci puts his faith in an object, a Fides bicycle, loses it and only then realizes that his real wealth lies in his son's love, a human emotion; the question of social change is begged, at best. Viewed from a pessimistic perspective, however, Bruno's affection resolves nothing, life remains tragic and absurd, in spite of it, and Ricci's frantic odyssey through Rome looking for his bicycle ends in the triumph of fate and chance without the possibility of social change being suggested at all.

Umberto D. may be said to complete De Sica's neorealist trilogy of solitude (*Miracle in Milan*, filmed before *Umberto D.*, represents a special critical problem treated elsewhere). It was De Sica's favorite work, produced with his own money, and its disastrous record at the box office was due in some measure to the fact that few sentimental concessions to public tastes were allowed. Yet, André Bazin's view that the work was a masterpiece in the face of bitter critical opposition when it first appeared in Paris has now been generally accepted. The film portrays a brief and traumatic period in the life of a retired pensioner (Umberto Domenico Ferrari), as well as his complex relationship to a pet dog and the young maid in his apartment building. Once again, De Sica's choice and direction of nonprofessional actors is brilliant: Umberto D. was portrayed by a professor from Florence whose facial expressions and general appearance capture perfectly the mannerisms and the moral values of the older generation. While the film deals courageously with the problem of the aged in modern society, it steadfastly refuses an overly sentimental perspective. Umberto D. is purposely characterized as cross, irritable, and grouchy, for De Sica wanted him to have an untidy, unpleasant disposition, since the aged are considered a nuisance to others and sometimes even to themselves.

Umberto's position in Italian society is even more tragic than the plight of the characters in De Sica's earlier films: he lacks the protection Ricci enjoyed from his family, and most of his few friends are now dead; there remains only his mongrel dog and Maria, a pitiful young maid whose life is even more desperate than his, for she is an unwed mother who will lose her job as soon as the bigoted landlady notices her condition. Because Umberto is part of the middle class, his life often revolves around the protection of outward appearances— a clean shirt, proper behavior, good manners—what the Italians call a *bella figura* in public. As inflation and illness erode his meager pension, he is almost more afraid of losing face, of appearing poor, than of poverty itself. Once again, De Sica poses a dilemma similar to that in *The Bicycle Thief*: will Umberto's problems be resolved with a mere increment to his pension, or is social reform incapable of curing human solitude? While exterior locations are important, the bulk of the work was shot in the studios of Cinecittà. Thus, *Umberto D.* is one of the first neorealist masterpieces to depend as much on the resources of a professional studio as it does on authentic locations. As a result, De Sica's camera style and editing technique reach a level of complexity uncommon for neorealism. The camera is increasingly mobile: instead of the earlier process shots simulating travel in moving vehicles, De Sica now brings his camera into city trolleys and taxi cabs; he uses a variety of odd camera angles to underline Umberto's disorientation; he frequently shoots through keyholes and at reflections on mirrors for sophisticated visual effects.

Even more remarkable are the aesthetic effects achieved through extensive use of deep-focus photography both within studio interiors and outside on location. Umberto's insignificance in Italian society is underlined right from De Sica's first scene, an extremely high-angle shot down on a crowd of demonstrating pensioners. The position of the camera accentuates their insignificance and vulnerability; as police cars sweep them effortlessly off the street because they lack a parade permit, we are reminded of insects being brushed aside, a visual hint that is later reinforced when the maid scatters a swarm of ants in her kitchen. Older people are as expendable as insects in this society. In four locations crucial to the film's meaning, the depth of field in the photography goes beyond simple representation of any "real" spatial distribution of objects to produce a visual correlative of the loneliness and solitude felt by Umberto. The long, empty hall of his apartment projects a sterile, hostile, foreboding environment. The many rows of hungry men eating in the charity soup kitchen he frequents, similar to the endless rows of pawned linens in *The Bicycle Thief*, inform us that Umberto is no isolated case but only one tragic character out of thousands. The long halls of the hospital with their endless lines of elderly patients suggest the desperation people in De Sica's universe must feel. Finally, the endless rows of trees interspersed with playing children that close the film after Umberto's unsuccessful suicide attempt allow the main characters—the old man and his dog—gradually to merge into the background and out of our vision in a lyrical ending reminiscent of the disappearance of Ricci and Bruno into the soccer crowd.

Perhaps in no other film made during the neorealist period would Zavattini's views on film time find a more eloquent expression. Zavattini's notion of realism involved a complete respect for actual time or duration: ninety minutes in a character's life should require ninety minutes of screen time; a film about the purchase of a pair of shoes should possess as much dramatic potential as the account of a war. Bazin's famous essays on this film quite rightly point to two scenes, Umberto's retirement to bed, and more importantly, the maid's awakening in the morning and her work in the kitchen, which embody Zavattini's concept of duration where "the real time of the narrative is not that of the drama but the concrete duration of the character . . . the film is identical with what the actor is doing and with this alone."[22] In the latter sequence, there is a perfect coincidence between narrative film time and that of the protagonist: the director refuses to give any dramatic structure to her mundane activity, respecting every intimate detail of reality equally and making no hierarchical choices between them. The sense of time's duration weighs upon the

Vittorio De Sica's *Umberto D.* (1951). The servant girl (Maria Pia Casilio) visits Umberto (Carlo Battisti) in the hospital.
(Photo courtesy of the Museum of Modern Art)

viewer just as it does upon the maid, and her simple, yet eloquent, gestures require no dialogue whatsoever to tell us all we need to know about the tragedy of her life.

De Sica's reliance upon the sound track to advance the story of *Umberto D.* represents a step beyond *The Bicycle Thief.* His landlady, once kept alive by her old boarder's surplus ration coupons during the war, now wants to evict him, and she even rents his room by the hour to prostitutes and adulterers; yet, she is so hypocritical she will doubtless fire Maria when she learns of her pregnancy. The decor of the apartment, her lover, and her friends all show her selfishness, superficiality, and venality, and the immoral qualities she exhibits are underscored by the sound track, which almost always associates her with opera heard on a record. She views operatic music not as an expression of genuine emotions, which she could appreciate neither in art nor in life, but as a means of confirming her social status. Opera, with its refined control of emotion and its theatrical or melodramatic overtones, is posed by De Sica as a counterpoint to the genuine, elemental, and truly pathetic human suffering experienced by both the maid and Umberto but ignored by the landlady.

De Sica's complex plot has affinities to his two films previously examined. Most obvious is the role of Umberto's dog, reminiscent of the symbolic qualities of *Shoeshine*'s horse or the bicycle in *The Bicycle Thief*. This animal represents a burden willingly assumed by Umberto, his only link to life and ultimately the thing which prevents his suicide. No doubt De Sica was aware of the fact that the presence of such an innocent and vulnerable creature would guarantee a sentimental response to the film, just as he often employs children to play upon our emotions. And as in his earlier works, both of which employed parallel subplots (the lives of Giuseppe and Pasquale; the progressive changes in Ricci and Bruno), De Sica again delineates character by playing Umberto's tragedy off against that of Maria, the maid. Throughout the film, she is his counterpart in suffering, but Umberto rarely understands how similar their lives actually are, just as no one understands his suffering. When Maria's negligence allows the dog to escape, Umberto scolds her for her carelessness immediately after she has told her boyfriend about her pregnancy and has been abandoned by him. Umberto is concerned for his dog and is completely unconscious of her pain, yet he expects others to be sensitive to his problems. Human loneliness thus fails to produce a sense of empathy in us, and as the film ends, Umberto is left alone with his pet—his problems and especially his solitude still unresolved. Bazin has cleverly remarked that "the cinema has rarely gone such a long way toward making us aware of what it is to be a man. (And also, for that matter, of what it is to be a dog.)"[23] De Sica has also shown us in no uncertain terms that there is very little difference between the two.

Luchino Visconti's role in the birth of a neorealist cinema stems from dramatic political choices as well as artistic motives. After making *Obsession*, Visconti became directly involved in the Resistance movement, aiding escaped Allied prisoners behind German lines and concealing Partisans in his Roman villa. Attacks on German troops in Rome led to bloody reprisals—the massacre of three hundred and thirty-five Italian hostages at the Fosse Ardeatine in March of 1944—and a subsequent roundup of anti-Fascists included Visconti, who was eventually sentenced to death after lengthy interrogations. Fortunately, he escaped from prison with the aid of his guards. In the following year, he returned to work in the theater until an American psychologial warfare group requested Visconti to film the trials and executions of Pietro Koch and Pietro Caruso, the former being the very man who interrogated him in prison. His work became part of a collective documentary on the Resistance and Italy's liberation. Directed by Mario Serandrei, the film was entitled *Days of Glory (Giorni di gloria*, 1945). But the young aristocrat had not forgotten his earlier association with the intellectuals of *Cinema*, nor had he completely ignored the advice contained in an early essay by Mario Alicata and Giuseppe De Santis which *Cinema* had published in 1941. Entitled "Truth and Poetry: Verga and the Italian Cinema," the essay called for a return to the best realist traditions of Italian culture:

> Our argument leads us necessarily to one name: Giovanni Verga. Not only did he create a great body of poetry, but he created a country as well, an epoch, a society. Since we believe in an art which above all creates truth, the Homeric, legendary Sicily of *I malavoglia, Maestro Don Gesualdo, L'Amante di Gramigna*, and *Jeli il pastore* offers us both the human experience and a concrete atmosphere. Miraculously stark and real, it could give inspiration to the imagination of our cinema which looks for things in the space-time of reality to redeem itself from the easy suggestions of a moribund bourgeois state.[24]

Visconti was also interested in Antonio Gramsci (1891–1937), the Marxist theoretician who focused much of his writing on the problems of Italy's *Mezzogiorno* or southern region. Thus, with initial financial backing from the Italian Communist Party, Visconti arrived at the Sicilian fishing village of Aci Trezza, the setting for Verga's *The House by the Medlar Tree (I Malavoglia)* with the intention of filming a trilogy on a prospective revolution in the South brought about by a union of fishermen, miners, and peasants, the kind of national-popular alliance

Gramsci envisioned between southern agricultural peasants and northern workers. The film he actually made, still retaining the subtitle "The Sea Episode" ("Episodio del mare"), was only the first part of the planned work.[25]

In many respects, *The Earth Trembles* (*La terra trema*, 1948) fits many of the traditional definitions of Italian neorealism better than any other work of the period. Absolutely no studio sets or sound stages were employed, and special lighting effects were used only during certain difficult night scenes at sea. Aci Trezza provided the entire cast of the work: each morning, Visconti would explain the day's shooting to the villagers, describing the events to be filmed, and soliciting their opinions as to how they would respond in similar situations. Their spontaneous reactions were then incorporated into the script, which thus evolved as the film progressed. Unlike so many other Italian films during and since the neorealist period, the popular technique of shooting without synchronized sound and dubbing the sound afterward during editing was rejected, as Visconti insisted upon the authentic voices and sounds of the Sicilian environment. In this, he took a revolutionary cultural stance, refusing standard Italian (as well as the official culture it symbolized) for the dialect of the simple people he filmed, believing that the authentic expression of the people's emotions could only be achieved using their own language. Because this dialect was incomprehensible to some Italian audiences, he then chose to employ a voice-over, an objective narrative voice in Italian to provide an often ironic commentary to the storyline. He was also forced to employ Italian subtitles in order to translate the Sicilian dialogue for nothern audiences. His two young assistants, Francesco Rosi (1922–   ) and Franco Zeffirelli (1923–   ), later became directors themselves.

Verga's novel had emphasized the pessimism and fatality of peasant society and did not necessarily see room for social reform in such a timeless world. Visconti modifies the book considerably, moving the focus from the father of the fishing family to his young son Antonio ('Ntoni), who rejects traditional ways, seeks to better himself, and opposes the corrupt middlemen who exploit the fishermen by paying very little for their catch. At 'Ntoni's insistence, the Valastros mortgage the family home to purchase their own boat in order to avoid working for others, but the need to pay the mortgage forces them to fish in bad weather, and a storm destroys the boat, resulting in foreclosure on all their property. The family's attempts to oppose the harsh economic system fail totally, and 'Ntoni is forced to humiliate himself by begging the middlemen for a job as a day laborer on the boats of others.

Such a pessimistic conclusion is obviously closer to Greek tragedy than to the revolutionary conclusion of the projected Marxist trilogy, which ended in the rise of class consciousness and proletarian unity among peasants, mine workers, and fishermen. While the film did receive some backing from the Communist Party, Visconti's aesthetic sensibilities, perhaps too aristocratic ever to produce a mere propaganda piece, had altered the story considerably. Moreover, in spite of the realistic attention to authentic locations, dialect, and the use of nonprofessionals, Visconti's emerging cinematic style sometimes contrasts sharply with any purely political message.

The world of Aci Trezza is circumscribed completely by the two huge rocks in the harbor, the *faraglioni* which, according to classical mythology, represent the rocks Polyphemus the Cyclops hurled toward the fleeing Odysseus. The spot seems outside of time or history, except for 'Ntoni's disastrous attempts to bring change to it. The plot structure reveals a similarity to the classical theater Visconti knew so well, for it may easily be divided into five discernible sections with the tragic reversal and downfall of the principal character occuring in the conventional place: (1) 'Ntoni first challenges traditional ways of living; (2) he then turns to direct action, casting the fish merchants' scales into the ocean and creating a riot, leading to his imprisonment and subsequent release when the middlemen discover that they need the fishermen to survive; this new knowledge leads 'Ntoni to persuade the family to purchase a new boat but the action also sets them apart from the rest of the village; (3) a brief moment of happiness ensues, as the seemingly prosperous family salts anchovies together; (4) disaster strikes at sea, the boat is destroyed, and the family's fish are sold for almost nothing; the family disintegrates—a brother leaves home, a sister is dishonored, and 'Ntoni becomes a drunkard; (5)

Luchino Visconti's *The Earth Trembles* (1948). Statuesque fishermen's wives await the return of their husbands from the storm at sea.
(Photo courtesy of the Centro Sperimentale Cinematografico, Rome)

'Ntoni encounters a young girl by his now abandoned boat, realizes his fatal error in basing his hopes on the traditional family rather than on a new sense of class consciousness and unity, but remains hopeful for the future; 'Ntoni returns to the sea as the Valastros have always done, receiving his mother's traditional blessing.

Many of the film's stylistic characteristics stress the cyclical, timeless quality of life in Aci Trezza rather than any ideological plan of future reform. Visconti's cinematic signature, his typically slow panning shots with a stationary camera, or his long, static shots of motionless objects, produces a formalism which is infrequent in documentary work. Characters enter into and exit from a carefully controlled frame, the pure aesthetic qualities of which once moved Orson Welles to complain that Visconti photographed fishermen as if they were *Vogue* fashion models![26] But this strange objection, which would deny beauty to poverty and restrict realism to distasteful topics, has no place in Visconti's homage to the mythical dimensions of the fishermen's daily struggle to survive. In no other Italian film does the photography capture the inherent nobility of its subject matter so well as in his unforgettable images of the women, black shawls wrapped about them and beating in the wind, waiting motionlessly for their men to return from the storm at sea.

Visconti's careful framing of each shot embodies the same *mise-en-scène* techniques already examined in De Sica's best work, but more than any other neorealist director, Visconti employed extreme depth of field in both exterior and interior shots. As a result, he achieves a marvelous sense of open space as he shows us the Valastros' world. One brilliant shot combines the exterior world of the men with the interior female world, as the camera is placed within the dark house with the women but shoots past them through the doorway into a brightly lit exterior. Another shows us the three Valastro men washing and talking in two separate rooms, as the women carry on their activities in different locations; outside, the depth of field allows Visconti to capture a rooftop conversation which includes the entire neighborhood. But Visconti's photography serves various purposes: a deep-focus shot during the first part of the film will capture the family's solidarity and unity, whereas toward the end of the work it can just as easily emphasize their alienation and separation not only from the other villagers but from each other as well.

One central problem in analyzing *The Earth Trembles* must be found in Visconti's character. A nobleman and a member of one of Italy's most distinguished families, Visconti displays a "progressive," if not Marxist, ideology in his works which often seems to conflict with his obvious love for the beauty he discovers in the very society he condemns. This is true not only in *The Earth Trembles* but in *Senso (Senso,* 1954), *The Leopard (Il gattopardo,* 1963) and in his last work, *The Innocent (L'innocente,* 1976) as well. Even as 'Ntoni delivers his moving speech concerning the need for united collective action ("We have to learn to stick up for each other, to stick together. Then we can go forward . . ."),[27] his tone of self-sacrificial martyrdom is closer to Christian than to Marxist precepts. It is no accident that when he

Luchino Visconti's *The Earth Trembles* (1948). Visconti's depth of field un-
ites interior and exterior worlds in his depiction of the timeless society of
his fishermen.
(Photo courtesy of the Centro Sperimentale Cinematografico, Rome)

returns to work, his sister puts the family portrait photograph back next to that of the Sacred heart. Christian and Marxist ideas seem equally appropriate in this timeless world: 'Ntoni casts a pair of "Judas" scales into the sea to protest prices paid for fish; behind the grinning middlemen can be seen barely erased slogans from Mussolini's Fascist regime.

The artist in Visconti triumphs over the party ideologue, for the film's storyline and its cinematic style accentuate the cyclical, archetypal quality of life in a mythical, ahistorical world much like that chronicled by Carlo Levi's *Christ Stopped at Eboli* a few years earlier. The film opens and closes with shots of fishing boats gliding over a glassy sea; they are framed between the gigantic rocks which form the symbolic boundary between Aci Trezza and the world of history. Daily activities in the fishing village—eating, mending nets, family conversation, courtships, the mother's blessing before work—all become part of a timeless ritual, the character of which is accentuated by the extreme length of Visconti's shots, many of which last three to five minutes without a cut. Even the narrative voice-over serves to reinforce the sense of stoic pessimism which pervades the film. Rather than a Marxist fable about the necessity of class struggle, Visconti presents an archetypal drama within the structure of the nuclear family, as old, timeless, and compelling a tale as any Homeric ballad.[28]

3

Exploring the Boundaries of Neorealism

The films examined in the preceding chapter may be accurately described as films by *auteurs,* i.e., films bearing the unmistakable signature of a single director's individual stylistic or thematic preoccupations. At the same time, by capturing the spirit of postwar Italian culture, these films established Italian neorealism as a vital force in Italy and abroad. Not reflecting any programmatic or coherent group style, such works are united by a common moral purpose and a deep-seated faith in the dignity of their subject matter. While they represent the greatest cinematic achievements of a brief but eventful decade, other films produced during the same time have an important but secondary role to play in the history of neorealism. Like the films of Rossellini, De Sica, or Visconti, many of them examine a number of pressing problems within Italian society—the effects of the war, poverty, labor unrest, migration from Sicily, the Mafia, the heavy burden of Italian history—but some lack the artistic concentration typical of such classic works and may include a mixture of styles or film genres. Others drift away from a cinema of realism, actual or apparent, toward a more traditional commercial cinema, the very kind of cinema neo-realist theoreticians such as Zavattini sought to avoid at all costs. Even when the characters in such works or their surroundings seem recognizably neorealist, they may be developed within the film genres more traditionally identified with Hollywood than with Rome. A few even question the relationship between fact and fiction, illusion and reality, which was at the heart of much critical debate on neorealist aesthetics. Some of these films were quite popular and generated a respectable cash flow at the box office. It would be impossible to assess neorealism's impact upon Italian cinema without reference to these interesting works, for they bear witness to the incredible variety and richness of expression typical of Italian cinema in the immediate post-war period.[1]

Michelangelo Antonioni served as a scriptwriter with a number of neorealist directors—with Rossellini on *A Pilot Returns* (1942), and later with Giuseppe De Santis on *Tragic Pursuit* (*Caccia tragica,* 1947). Before the war, he was closely associated with the young intellectuals on the staff of *Cinema,* and an article he published in that periodical in 1939, "Concerning a Film on the River Po," led to his first documentary, *The People of the Po* (*Gente del Po,* 1943), but much of this work was damaged during the war and was only partially salvaged for release in 1947. Between 1947 and 1950, Antonioni produced five brief documentary shorts, but *Sanitation Department* (*Nettezza urbana,* 1948), a brief, eleven-minute treatment of Roman *spazzini* or street-cleaners, is perhaps his finest early documentary film. Judging from its plot or its genre, *Sanitation Department* would seem to have its immediate origins in the neorealist interest in capturing current events and exploring the drama in the lives of ordinary people. A summary of its plot—the depiction of the ordinary, even banal events in a single working day of these humble city employees—seems to follow Zavattini's prescriptions for cinematic realism. But whereas De Sica or Zavattini would uncover drama or even tragedy underneath the mundane affairs of the *spazzini,* Antonioni's style dedramatizes their lives by the abstract quality of his photography. The brief, terse, voice-over that introduces the work only informs the viewer that Rome's street-cleaners are hardly noticed by their fellow citizens. After this comment, there is no further dialogue. This is far removed from the rhetorical flourishes or the ideological statements contained in the voice-overs of Rossellini's *Paisan* or Visconti's *The Earth Trembles.* The only other commentary from the sound track is provided by the musical accompaniment, juxtaposing modern jazz by Giovanni Fusco with Bach, and its function is generally to underline the sense of solitude captured by the camera. The camera dispassionately follows the *spaz-zini* from the time they awaken in the morning until they complete their work and return home, and the film resolutely refuses to evolve any sort of narrative storyline or semblance of plot from the material it treats. Antonioni simply records the disconnected occurrences in these humble lives without comment, creating with the rhythm of his editing and the mood of his music a tone poem on loneliness, an abstract photographic vision of a world divided between two categories of people—those who pick up trash and those who throw it away. Antonioni's style, in particular his long shots capturing the "dead time" in the lives of the streetcleaners, seems partially indebted to Visconti's *The Earth Trembles.* But the cool, dispassionate treatment of the subject matter already sets Antonioni far apart from most neo-realist films of the period and announces, in this beautiful and brilliant work, his evolution beyond realistic documentary toward complex and more abstract works, such as *The Eclipse (L'eclisse,* 1962) or *The Red Desert (Il deserto rosso,* 1964), which relate characters so integrally to their landscapes.[2]

Luigi Zampa's popular film, *To Live in Peace (Vivere in pace,* 1946), is in an entirely different vein. Awarded the New York Film Critics' Award for the Best Foreign Feature of 1947, the film chronicles the tranquil life of a remote Italian mountain village and how the desire of its inhabitants to "live in peace" is disturbed by the appearance of two escaped American prisoners of war: Ronald, a journalist (who hopes eventually to write a "true" account of events which take place in the town); and a black GI named, predictably enough, Joe. Uncle Tigna, a kindly peasant, assists the two Americans, as well as an Italian deserter named Franco, who will eventually marry Tigna's daughter Silvia. The effects of the war seem far away, and all goes well until the single German soldier in the village, a simple peasant like Tigna, drops by the farmhouse while the group is eating, forcing the Americans and the deserter to hide. The German drinks too much wine and becomes inebriated, while downstairs in the wine cellar, Joe does the same. He becomes violent, breaks down the cellar door, and in a magnificent scene of comic relief confronts the drunken German: instead of shooting at each other, they stare, then embrace, and everyone dances the "boogie woogie" to Joe's jazz trumpet solo. Afterward, Joe and the German stagger out arm in arm and announce to the entire village that the war is over, shooting out streetlights and touching off a wild celebration. When everyone recovers the next morning, however, they all realize that the war is indeed not yet over. The German remembers having seen escaped Allied prisoners, calls his superiors on the telephone, then has a change of heart and begs Uncle Tigna to help him desert; as he is taking civilian clothing from Tigna's clothesline, other Germans appear and shoot them both. As Tigna dies in his bed, surrounded by friends and relatives, Joe arrives with the advancing Allied troops to announce that the war is truly over for the tiny village.

Except for its wartime theme and its location shooting, *To Live in Peace* is closer in style to a traditional comedy than to any of the masterpieces of neorealism; Zampa turns the same thematic material Rossellini had treated in a tragicomic manner in *Rome, Open City* and *Paisan* into a burlesque farce. Rossellini's Bergmann was an evil genius engaged in a life-and-death struggle with valiant men; Zampa's German soldier is a stock character from the *commedia dell'arte* tradition of the braggart soldier, his dignity undercut every time he appears on the screen by the musical accompaniment of the first bars of "Deutschland über alles." And although the narrative voice-over that introduces and closes the work insists the events depicted actually occurred and were not invented, Zampa's comic style avoids any documentary realism. Nevertheless, the influence of Rossellini is still present: Uncle Tigna embodies many of the best qualities of Rossellini's partisan priest Don Pietro (he is even played by the same actor, Aldo Fabrizi), and the black soldier seems borrowed from *Paisan's* Neapolitan episode. The fundamental message of human brotherhood André Bazin found to be characteristic of all neorealist works is certainly present in the absurd view of warfare Zampa portrays and in his forthright stance against its brutality and senseless killing, but there is little in the film's style, except for its theme, to set it apart from any number of good, commercial comedies produced before or after the war.

A number of interesting minor works of this period turned from

Luigi Zampa's *To Live in Peace* (1946). Drunken enemies celebrate what they think is the end of the war.
(Photo courtesy of the Museum of Modern Art)

the war and the Resistance to treat the pressing social or economic problems that followed in their wake. Three of these films—Alberto Lattuada's (1914–   ) *Without Pity* (*Senza pietà*, 1948); Giuseppe De Santis's (1917–   ) *Bitter Rice;* and Pietro Germi's (1914–1974) *The Path of Hope* (*Il cammino della speranza*, 1950)—are typical of this shift of thematic material from the war to its impact upon postwar society, best expressed in the neorealist masterpieces made by De Sica and Zavattini. However, the three films are important for other reasons, for they reveal a gradual move closer to conventional and even typically American themes or film genres. Alberto Lattuada's first postwar film, *The Bandit* (*Il bandito,* 1946), dealt with the role violence played in a society where men are compelled to fight for their very existence; it portrays the plight of a returned Italian prisoner-of-war who learns his sister has become a prostitute and finds that he, too, must turn to a life of crime to survive.[3] The film's violence, gun battles, and car chases are indebted more to Hollywood models (*film noir,* gangster films) than to the canons of realism, and this focus upon criminality is continued in *Without Pity.* The cast and crew of *Without Pity* bring together many of the same people later identified with the works of Fellini: Fellini himself scripted the film with Tullio Pinelli; music was provided by Nino Rota; the cast included Lattuada's wife, Carla del Poggio, and Fellini's wife, Giulietta Masina, both of whom were to reappear again together in *Variety Lights* (*Luci del varietà,* 1950). Its plot is a daring one for the times—the story of an interracial love affair between Jerry, a black American soldier, and Angela, an Italian prostitute. The film is set against a realistic depiction of life in postwar Livorno (Leghorn), a major depot for American supplies as well as for Italian smuggling or blackmarketeering, but the opening information title underlines the melodramatic rather than documentary mood of the film:

> This is a story not of two races but of two people who met in Italy after the war. Men and women had forgotten compassion and abandoned tenderness in their desperate struggle for survival. But there was pity and devotion in the heart of one G.I. This is his story.

By focusing upon an interracial love affair, Lattuada is able to contrast American racism with Angela's affection while, at the same time, he can underline how the American influence on postwar Italy has been a corruptive force. Angela first meets Jerry in a boxcar after he has been wounded in the line of duty as a military policeman. Although she obtains medical assistance for him, other American policemen take her for the gunman's accomplice, arrest her, and send her off with a truckload of prostitutes even after they learn of her innocence, merely because they do not wish to bother with the necessary paperwork to clear her name and keep her from being branded as a criminal. Livorno's underworld feeds on the corruption in the wake of the Allied army. The criminal activities there are controlled by a sinister character named Pier Luigi, whose effeminate mannerisms and pure white linen suits (as well as his initials) associate him clearly with many similar roles played by Peter Lorre in the American *films noirs* Lattuada admired so much. Pier Luigi exploits Jerry's love for Angela, convinces him she needs someone to protect her, and brings him into his organization. Jerry is eventually arrested, giving Lattuada the opportunity to expose the racism in the court system of the occupation army. Jerry is beaten by his white guards, and most of the prisoners in the stockade are blacks, whose spirituals composer Nino Rota works into the sound track of the film as emblematic not just of the suffering of their oppressed race but of all oppressed people.

A number of the film's most important sequences point toward the traditional gangster film, a genre not usually associated with neorealism: these include several gun battles; car chases with automobiles careening around city corners, pistols blazing; a melodramatic prison breakout by Jerry and a black friend, who is mortally wounded but begs Jerry to go on without him; and night club parties, complete with American jazz, presided over by a criminal mastermind club owner (Pier Luigi). In a desperate effort to escape Pier Luigi's clutches, Jerry and Angela rob him and attempt to flee, but their plan fails: Angela steps in front of Jerry to receive a bullet meant for him and dies. Jerry vows never to abandon her, leaps into his truck to the sound of a crescendo of black spirituals, and drives off a pier into the ocean. As the military police arrive on the scene, we see only a spinning truck wheel with a parting shot of Angela's head and other arm clutching Jerry. At last, the pair is united in death.

Alberto Lattuada's *Without Pity* (1948). Jerry (John Kitzmiller) confronts Pier Luigi (Pierre Claudé) in a story of an interracial love affair in postwar Livorno.
(Photo courtesy of the Museum of Modern Art)

Without Pity reflects a typically neorealist message of human brotherhood which, in this particular film, transcends not only national but also racial boundaries. In its emphasis upon the conditions in postwar Livorno, it remains within familiar neorealist territory. But it is of interest primarily for its marriage, an uneasy one in parts, between such neorealist material and the older, more familiar Hollywood gangster film. There is little of the complex cinematic artifice we discovered in the works of Rossellini, De Sica, or Visconti, but the novelty of its storyline and its generic code make it still worthy of viewing.

Giuseppe De Santis was closely associated with Antonioni and Visconti on *Cinema* and had previously worked with Visconti on *Obsession* and on Serandrei's *Days of Glory,* the Resistance documentary. His first major work was *Tragic Pursuit* (*Caccia tragica*, 1947), a film produced by the ANPI, an Italian Partisan organization of leftist leanings. In this work, De Santis sets the struggle of a collective farm within the framework of the traditional gangster film, much as Lattuada did in *Without Pity:* bandits steal the collective's funds, and the film chronicles the pursuit of the gang by the farmers as well as the final redemption and reintegration of one of the criminals back into the group. The dichotomy between men and women who work together for the betterment of their class, on the one hand, and those outlaws from society who exploit the poverty of others, on the other, is continued in *Bitter Rice* as is De Santis's use of a popular Hollywood genre. In *Bitter Rice,* however, the director presents a broader condemnation of American values and the results of the cultural confrontation of Italy and America that Rossellini had celebrated in *Paisan* and Lattuada had criticized in *Without Pity.*[4]

The plot of *Bitter Rice* is indebted to that of *Obsession.* Its melodramatic storyline treats the disastrous effects of violent love on the relationships of two couples: Francesca (Doris Dowling) and Walter (Vittorio Gassman), fleeing from a jewel robbery, join a train carrying women to work the rice fields of the Po Valley. There, Francesca falls in love with Marco (Raf Vallone), an Italian soldier. Walter jilts Francesca for a star-struck rice worker named Silvana (Silvana Mangano), whom he uses to help him steal the rice harvest. In a dramatic climax, Francesca and Marco thwart Walter's plans, Silvana shoots Walter when she learns that the necklace he has given her is only worthless costume jewelry and then commits suicide. De Santis's original intention was to provide a realistic study of the women rice workers (the *mondine*), who labor an entire harvest season under miserable working conditions for only a sack of rice and 40,000 lire, and to condemn the corruptive influences of American popular culture upon working-class values. Such a goal would have reflected De Santis's Marxist convictions, but the style of the film that was actually made represents an uneasy compromise between ideology and the impact of American cinema and its typical genres (the gangster film, the musical, the Western), as well as De Santis's admiration for the works of John Ford and King Vidor, or the acting style of Joan Crawford. As a result, Silvana Mangano paradoxically emerged from *Bitter Rice* as an international pin-up model and a box-office sensation, the very essence of the shallow fascination with movie stars, mass media, and beauty queens De Santis set out to condemn in the film. Social commentary is thus combined with, or rather is overwhelmed by, eroticism: an information title prefacing the film stresses not only its theme of "hard work requiring delicate hands," but perhaps more significantly, "their long, long nights" as well. Silvana, photographed whenever possible in tightly fitting sweaters revealing her ample cleavage and in tight short pants underscoring her sensual body, is completely dominated by the facile myths of wealth and success associated by De Santis with America. In one famous scene, there is a brief glimpse of her nude breast, a daring shot for the time. (It was so unusual that by the time the film played in provincial theatres, projectionists had cut out this section of the work for souvenir pin-ups!) She constantly chews gum, dances the "boogie woogie" whenever possible, reads pulp magazines (*Grand Hotel*) which present, in photographs, stories typical of *True Romance* magazine; and she hopes to make her fortune by going to America, where she believes "everything is electric." Marco, the symbol of proletarian solidarity and good, common sense, tells her pointedly that everything *is* electric in America, even the electric chair—characteristically, he dreams of going to South America, not North America, to set up a traditional family and to find honest employment.

Bitter Rice was one of neorealism's few commercial successes, and its production was a far cry from that of a typically low-budget picture made with limited technical resources. One Italian critic has even defined it as a "neorealist colossal."[5] It necessitated seventy-five days of shooting on location with a huge cast of actors and technicians (totalling almost 12,000 working days); to obtain the effects of a highly mobile camera in the slippery rice fields, De Santis had constructed a wooden dolly that allowed the camera to move over the soft terrain; he also employed a crane throughout the film, a type of shot usually avoided by neorealist directors, and used this technique quite effectively to obtain a sense of epic proportion and grandeur. The famous boogie-woogie sequence danced by Silvana and Walter, which leads

Giuseppe De Santis's *Bitter Rice* (1949). Hollywood sex appeal is set within the proletarian world of the rice workers as Silvana (Silvana Mangano) embraces the corrupting values of America.
(Photo courtesy of the Museum of Modern Art)

to the first of the violent confrontations between Walter and Marco, was choreographed down to the last detail by De Santis, who claimed that editing the episode required two full months. As photographed from a crane, the scenes of the *mondine,* their skirts pulled up to their thighs, consciously make reference to scenes from American films showing blacks working in antebellum cotton fields. The fact that the girls were not permitted to speak with each other on the job allowed De Santis to stage a sequence typical of American musicals: the girls communicate with each other by singing in the rain. A climactic gunfight and showdown typical of the American Western, previously employed in *Tragic Pursuit,* reappear in the splendid finale of the work, where the two couples meet in a slaughterhouse and Walter is shot repeatedly. De Santis satirizes the mania for beauty queens and contests—imported from America in the postwar period—linking Silvana's corruption by foreign values to her election as "Miss Mondina 1948" ("Miss Rice Worker, 1948"). Following the rescue of the rice harvest and her killing of Walter, she is reincorporated—after her suicide—into the society of her fellow *mondine*. The film closes with a highly symbolic sequence redolent of peasant folklore. As her body lies on the ground, the *mondine* file silently past, sprinkling a handful of their hardearned rice on Silvana, while De Santis's camera shifts to a crane shot of the entire group, thus underlining the collective nature of the workers' struggle. *Bitter Rice* is a powerful film, but one which reflects a hybrid style and reveals the presence of a number of genres. It proved conclusively that eroticism as well as social protest could become grist for a neorealist director's mill and that cheesecake added to the box-office attraction of even a Marxist-inspired work of art. While some leftist critics preferred to view the work as a betrayal of the social realism they prescribed as the norm, De Santis cleverly employed the very conventions he was most intent upon undermining to make a powerful statement about the disastrous effects of embracing a foreign culture rather than remaining true to the best traditions of the Italian working class. *Bitter Rice* rejects the more optimistic vision of Italian-American relationships found in Rossellini's *Paisan* and goes far beyond the criticism of the American way of life in Lattuada's *Without Pity,* but it is, paradoxically, the neorealist film most obviously indebted to the American cinema and its rich generic traditions.

Germi's *The Path of Hope* owes more to the influences of Visconti's *The Earth Trembles* than to his *Obsession*. It is also, as Roy Armes observed, a stylized Italian adaptation of the narrative patterns found in the classic Westerns of John Ford, a director Germi admired, and whom he had imitated in his first major work, *In the Name of the Law* (*In nome della legge,* 1948), a film about the Sicilian Mafia.[6] Germi shares Visconti's sympathy for the lower classes of Sicily, in this case a group of exploited sulfur miners, but he combines this perspective with a typically American Western plot—the workers' epic trek across

Italy to find a better life in France. He focuses the action of the film around the relationships of characters who are recognizable types from the Western: Saro (Raf Vallone), a widower with three children who is the stalwart leader of the band of workers; Barbara (Elena Varzi), a prostitute who joins the group and who is eventually revealed to have a heart of gold; and Vanni, Barbara's criminal lover (Franco Navarra). Thus, the theme of the quest for a better life is combined with that of a developing confrontation between a noble hero and a villain, Vanni, with Barbara's love as the victor's reward. The gunfight required in a Western to settle this dramatic tension is transformed into a traditional Sicilian knife fight, a transposition of the Western's code of behavior to traditional Sicilian *cavalleria rusticana,* Verga's "rustic chivalry." And, as in the Western, Saro's victory is never in doubt for a moment. An epic tone, also typical of the best American Westerns, is injected into its rather melodramatic storyline by Germi's photography, indebted again to Visconti. Shots of statuesque Sicilian women, dressed completely in black and waiting silently for their men to emerge from the deep-pit mines, juxtaposed beautifully against the stark white Sicilian landscape at the opening of the film, recall sequences in *The Earth Trembles;* as the workers reach their goal and cross the French Alps, they are again beautifully captured in a long shot, their black garments now set off against a completely white snowscape, reversing the symbolic connotations of the opening sequence (despair) to that of hope for the future.

Even the most serious of neorealist classics were never totally devoid of humor or comic episodes, but they were also unquestionably devoted to serious contemporary problems and inevitably called attention to injustice and the need for social reform (if not revolution) in Italy. But the political climate had changed since 1945; on April 18, 1948, the Christian Democrats gained an absolute majority in an election marked by Cold War tensions; on January 6, 1949, De Gasperi asked for Italy's admission into NATO; on July 13 of the same year, the Vatican excommunicated Communist voters, sympathizers, and their allies. Strikes and political violence were becoming more and more common (Palmiro Togliatti, head of the Italian Communist Party, was seriously wounded in 1948). As a result, films with strong social statements became increasingly risky investments, since government subsidies might be withdrawn from a work that was deemed unacceptable, and it might even be sequestered by the censors when it finally appeared. An economic crisis in the film industry coincided with this change in mood, as the total production in Italy fell from 65 films in 1946 and 67 in 1947 to 49 in 1948. Giulio Andreotti, Undersecretary of Public Entertainment (and De Gasperi's protégé), guided the ministry concerned with cinema until 1953, and his open letter to De Sica, criticizing the picture of Italy in *Umberto D.* as a disservice to a nation which could boast of very progressive social legislation, strongly suggested that Italian directors should embrace a more optimistic, healthy, and constructive attitude. The atmosphere during the late forties and early fifties may be accurately gauged by the fact that distinguished journalists or critics such as Guido Aristarco or Renzo Renzi could be arrested and tried by a military (not a civil) tribunal in 1953 for "defaming the armed forces" by suggesting that a film on the Italian occupation of Greece be made, or by the fact that the American Ambassador to Italy, Clare Boothe Luce, could exert pressure on the Venice Film Festival to block the presentation of an entry directed by Richard Brooks on the grounds that it was offensive to American prestige.[7] Political pressure was thus added to the threat of foreign competition to control the content of Italian cinema, while the public's consistent preference for melodrama, historical epics, or comedies provided economic incentives for moving the cinema toward a more popular and less uncompromising social stance during the decade of the fifties. Popular works such as *Chains* (*Catene,* 1949), *Torment* (*Tormento,* 1950), and *Nobody's Children* (*I figli di nessuno,* 1951) by Raffaello Matarazzo (1909–1966), usually despised by the critics, were in fact box-office sensations in Italy, reaching respectively the first, second, and third place in three successive years. Yet, most of Matarazzo's popular works were never exported. Simultaneous commercial phenomena were the successful comedies serving as vehicles for the acting talents of Erminio Macario (1902–1980), including a trilogy of films directed by Carlo Borghesio (1905–83): *How I Lost the War* (*Come persi la guerra,* 1947, first in box-office receipts that year); *The Hero of the Street* (*L'eroe della strada,*

1948, eighth in popularity); and *How I Discovered America* (*Come sco-persi l'America,* 1949). Another great comic actor, Totò (1898–1967), in an age before television became a serious competitor to films in Italy, was unquestionably the most popular actor in the country. His comic style combined elements from the classic silent comedies as well as the native *commedia dell'arte* and Neapolitan theatrical tradi-tions. The darling of the less advantaged classes in the provinces and in the improverished South, Totò placed at least one of his works in the ten top films between 1948 and 1957, and by 1963 he had ap-peared in more than 90 works, sometimes averaging six per year! Typical of his many, many films, still undistributed abroad, is *Totò Looks for a House* (*Totò cerca casa,* 1949), codirected by Mario Monicelli (1915–88) and Stefano Vanzina (known as Steno, 1915–88), which was second in box-office receipts for that year. Many of Totò's films were made within a few days and often reflected current events in much the same manner as the classic works of De Sica dealt with pressing social problems. Yet, the farcical quest of Totò for a home in the bombed-out rubble of postwar urban Italy, and the perennial Italian penchant to laugh at rather than resolve social prob-lems his comic mask suggested, made a far greater impact upon the Italian public than did *Umberto D.* or even the relatively successful *The Bicycle Thief.*[8] Yet, Totò was practically unknown outside Italy until Pier Paolo Pasolini employed his comic talents in a political allegory, *Hawks and Sparrows* (*Uccellacci e uccellini,* 1966), which was favorably received by critics at home and abroad.

Given the particular economic and political situation, as well as the public's constant demand for *commedia all'italiana,* it was no wonder that a comic vein in neorealism—*neorealismo rosa*—emerged and found favor with the general public just as predictably as it was attacked by leftist critics. Typical of this type of film are the pleasant works of Renato Castellani (1913–85), the "calligrapher" of the Fascist period: *Under the Sun of Rome* (*Sotto il sole di Roma,* 1948); *It is Spring* (*È pri-mavera,* 1949); and *Two Cents' Worth of Hope* (*Due soldi di speranza,* 1952). *Two Cents' Worth of Hope,* perhaps Castellani's best and most popular film, focuses upon postwar poverty and unemployment in Naples, but the only real link to the neorealist tradition to be found in it is the director's authentic locations and his interest in retaining the flavor of regional dialect. Based upon endless episodes employing comic gags and local color, the film offers as its hero an unemployed ex-soldier named Antonio Catalano, who is finally able to marry his sweetheart, Carmela. In a wonderful scene that parodies the departure of St. Francis from his parents, before marrying Carmela, Antonio strips her of the clothes belonging to her family, tosses them at her irate father, grabs a dress from a streetside peddler (on credit!), then receives donations of shoes, stockings, and a silk shirt from happy bystanders. In the concluding sequence, Antonio delivers the "message" of the film, one calculated to infuriate critics intent upon turning the Italian cinema toward revolutionary goals: "He who has created us is not poor. If He wants us to live, He must feed us. If not, what are we doing here?" It is a measure of how different the climate had become in Europe that this work was awarded the Grand Prize at Cannes. Even more popular in Italy, although not as well distributed abroad as the works by Castellani, were the series of comedies directed by Luigi Comencini (1916–   ) and Dino Risi, (1916–   ) usually labeled the *Bread and Love* series. These included Comencini's *Bread, Love and Fantasy (Pane, amore e fantasia*, 1953), and *Bread, Love and Jealousy (Pane, amore e gelosia*, 1954), and Risi's *Bread, Love and . . . (Pane, amore e . . .*, 1955), and *Poor But Beautiful (Poveri ma belli*, 1956). Such works dealt with the question of poverty in a comic fashion and were important in establishing an international public for the *commedia all'italiana* which has continued to be a staple product of the Italian cinema industry until the present day. Just as De Santis, Lattuada, and Germi had initially attracted audiences by employing elements of traditional Hollywood genres (the musical, the Western, the *film noir,* the gangster film) within a compromised neorealist style, so the directors of comic films broadened the appeal of their films by treating very serious social or political issues in a completely comic vein.

Traditional criticism of Italian neorealism has consistently viewed such departures from social realism as part of the so-called crisis of neorealism, but this view is, at best, shortsighted. The works discussed in this chapter, as well as the early films of Fellini or those made by Rossellini and Antonioni in the first years of the Fifties, cannot be said to constitute a "betrayal" of realist principles, since such principles were never accepted as governing norms by the directors themselves. This "crisis" is more accurately described as a crisis in the history of neorealist criticism which reflected the often opposed views of men such as Guido Aristarco, André Bazin, and Cesare Zavattini.[9] Yet, comic works such as Rossellini's *The Machine to Kill Bad People* (1948) and De Sica's *Miracle in Milan* (1950) deviate from a purely realist aesthetic precisely in order to illuminate issues crucial to any treatment of realism in the cinema. Both films are highly self-conscious treatments of the interplay between reality and appearance, and do not provide evidence, as many critics would have it, that a political and economic crisis in Italian society was systematically ignored in the cinema on account of political or financial pressure on directors or producers, who supposedly displayed a cowardly willingness to make films for escapist entertainment rather than for progressive social change.[10]

Rossellini and De Sica explicitly rejected a strictly realist aesthetic during this period. De Sica remarked that he made *Miracle in Milan* to resolve problems of "form and style."[11] In 1952, Rossellini defined realism as "simply the artistic form of truth,"[12] and stated that he had made *The Machine to Kill Bad People* in order to shift his work toward the traditional Italian *commedia dell'arte*. Despite the marked differences between the earlier works of Rossellini and De Sica, *The Machine to Kill Bad People* and *Miracle in Milan* share a remarkable number of stylistic and thematic similarities. Both employ frequent comic gags that betray obvious debts to silent film comedy (Chaplin and René Clair) or to the regional dialect theatre of Naples (Rossellini's subject was suggested by Eduardo De Filippo); Rossellini's work even opens with a traditional prologue in verse and a stage full of characters set up by the hand of a puppeteer or *capocomico,* and it closes with a rhymed epilogue and a moral. Because of this link to similar dramatic and cinematographic conventions, both films reveal a similar approach to characterization. Neither director is principally preoccupied with the subtle psychological nuances achieved in such works as *Germany Year Zero, The Bicycle Thief,* or *Umberto D.* Instead, characters are almost without exception motivated by a single force—greed and self-interest on the one hand, or pure goodness on the other—and their actions identify them as traditional comic types. The storyline of each film is equally simple and represents what may best be described as an allegory or a fable involving the relationship of the rich to the poor, the evil to the good. Although Rossellini's film is perhaps simpler from a technical point of view, containing fewer special photographic effects while De Sica's work exploits surrealist comic effects in the manner of René Clair, it is also more richly plotted, with subplots parodying both the story of Romeo and Juliet and Rossellini's own film *Paisan* (in particular, the arrival of the Americans in Italy). While the thematic content continues what is usually considered a typical neorealist preoccupation with social justice and socioeconomic problems in postwar Italy, it is precisely their attention to style which makes these works significant. In Rossellini, there is an extended treatment of the very nature of photography, while in De Sica the conventions usually associated with neorealism are called into question. In so doing, each director provides the viewer with a clearer idea of the boundaries of neorealist aesthetics.

With *The Machine to Kill Bad People*, Rossellini presents an extended meditation, albeit in a comic vein, on the relationship between photography—or artistic reality—and the equally noble reality of ethics and moral conduct. A demon grants to Celestino Esposito, a professional photographer, the miraculous power of causing evildoers to disappear from the face of the earth by means of his camera (*la macchina* of the original Italian title). A good man consumed by moral indignation, Celestino takes his weapon and turns it upon those in his village who exploit the poor and act only from self-interest. Soon, several of the town's most illustrious citizens (Donna Amalia, the loan shark; the mayor; the policeman; the owner of a fleet of fishing boats and trucks) suffer the same comic fate: once Celestino photographs a previous picture of them, they are frozen in that pose and pass to their reward. As the film progresses, Celestino becomes impatient with all the inhabitants of his village. The poor, themselves no better than the rich, have exactly the same greedy motives alluded to in the prologue, where we have already been warned that "In the end, nice or not/they resemble each other a lot." Rapidly demoralized by this discovery, Celestino embarks upon a plan to destroy everyone, since all are imperfect, and in the very act of doing so he murders the good town doctor who has been trying to stop him from photographing another picture of the entire village. Driven by remorse, Celestino decides to punish himself with his magic camera, but only after he eliminates the demon who granted him this miraculous power. Before he can succeed, however, the demon reappears, is converted after Celestino makes the sign of the cross, and restores Celestino's victims to life as if nothing had ever happened. A final moral is delivered in the epilogue: "Do good but don't overdo it!/Avoid evil for your own sake./Don't be hasty in judging others./Think twice before punishing."

Rossellini is chiefly concerned with the symbolic importance of the camera and, by extension, the nature of photography itself. In a good neorealist fashion that recalls statements made by such important figures as Cesare Zavattini, Celestino views the camera as a means of separating reality from illusion, good from evil, substance from appearance. Photography is, for him, a metaphor for a way of knowing, for a means of apprehending essential moral and ethical facts; it enables him, so he believes, to penetrate the surface of events to the bedrock of reality and to fulfill a godlike role in his small village (a role not unlike that of a film director on the set). Interestingly enough, Celestino does not perform this miraculous feat with a direct duplication on film of objects in the "real" world. Instead, he must first take a photograph of another photograph to accomplish this. As any good Platonist knows, he is two steps removed from the world of tangible objects or sensory reality by the time he takes the second picture and is engaged in the essentially self-reflexive act of producing a work of art from another work of art, not from reality itself. While creating an elaborate joke with Celestino's self-delusory activity, Rossellini emphasizes a fundamental characteristic of filmic art. In a comic manner, he tells us emphatically that photography (and by extension, the cinema as a branch of this art form) is incapable of separating good from evil or of readily distinguishing reality from appearance. Celestino mistakes a demon for the patron saint of the town, and when he attacks the rich to help the poor, he learns that some of the wealthy are not entirely evil (Donna Amalia's will leaves her money to the three poorest people in the village), and that the poor share the selfish vices of the rich. Nowhere is there any clear distinction between diametrically opposed metaphysical or ethical positions. The camera, viewed as a means of acquiring knowledge of social reality by overly optimistic neorealist theorists, has been reduced to a fallible and neutral instrument which reflects not reality but human subjectivity and error.

The main character of De Sica's *Miracle in Milan,* Totò (not to be confused with the famous comic actor of the same name), is as concerned with good and evil as is Celestino. Yet, he is infinitely more innocent and naive, without a malicious thought in his heart. A white dove given to him by his foster mother, Lolotta, enables him to fulfill the wishes of every poor person living in the shantytown outside Milan. When it is taken away from him, he and his friends are forced to escape their wicked oppressors by flying on broomsticks over the cathedral of Milan! Here, we are clearly in the realm of fantasy, of the fairy tale or the fable, in spite of the often-cited remark of the scriptwriter, Cesare Zavattini, that "the true function of the cinema is not to tell fables."[13] The film attacks the very definition of neorealism canonized in the essays of André Bazin. Although the storyline of this fable echoes the social concerns characteristic of neorealist works, De Sica's style departs even more radically than that of Rossellini in *The Machine to Kill Bad People* from the traditional definitions of neorealism. Chronological time is rejected, as is duration or ontological wholeness; commonsense logic is abandoned as well, and the usual cause and effect relationships between objects in the "real" world are replaced by absurd, even surreal events (the sunlight shines in only one spot at a time; angels or magic spirits visit earth; people are granted any wish they desire). The fantastic is bodied forth by a number of special effects foreign to neorealist works: people fly over the cathedral of Milan on broomsticks, thanks to process shots; images are superimposed upon other images; smoke appears to reverse its course; rapid editing makes it seem that hats chase a character out of the camera's vision.

De Sica goes beyond Rossellini's suggestive treatment of the camera's relationship to reality and concentrates upon the place of the

Vittorio De Sica's *Miracle in Milan* (1950). Edwige (Brunella Bovo) and
Totò (Francesco Golisano) escape the confines of their poverty by flying
over the Cathedral of Milan on a magic broomstick.
(Photo courtesy of the Museum of Modern Art)

imagination itself (which may, as in *Miracle in Milan,* employ the
camera as a means of expression). The entire film is thus an extended
metaphor, a hymn to the role of illusion and fantasy in art, as well as
in life; however, it is not merely a frivolous entertainment. De Sica
tells us that the human impulse to creativity in the work of art, like
the broomsticks which carry the poor over the church steeples of
Milan, is capable of transcending social problems but not of resolving
them. Filmic art can only offer the consolation of beauty and the hope
that its images and ideas may move the spectator to social action that
will change the world.

Rossellini's film questions the cognitive potential of the camera and
undermines the belief that good and evil are easily distinguished. De

Sica's work affirms Rossellini's doubts that the poor or downtrodden of the world are morally superior to the wealthy or their exploiters (indeed, the poor in the shantytown of *Miracle in Milan* aspire only to become wealthy themselves and are equally selfish), but it makes an even more positive statement about the place of the imagination in both filmic art and life. While Rossellini limits the camera's power to discover reality, De Sica demonstrates that the camera can uncover new dimensions of experience through the poetry of the creative fantasy. Seen from this perspective, each work reveals itself to be not merely a comic fable about the rich and the poor but also a significant treatment of the relationship between reality and illusion. The distance traveled by Rossellini or De Sica since *Paisan* or *Shoeshine* is not so far as most critics believe and is more a change of degree than of kind. *The Machine to Kill Bad People* and *Miracle in Milan* clearly mark the outer boundaries of the Italian neorealist movement, since they push the dialectic of realism and illusion almost to the breaking point.

In dealing with the relationship of fact and fiction, Rossellini and De Sica moved away from the recognizable historical world of postwar Italy toward the realm of fable and imagination. Equally important, however, in neorealism's quest to explore a number of contemporary problems was the burden of Italian history, the relation of the past to the present. This topic was pursued with vigor in two important films made in 1954: Carlo Lizzani's (1922–   ) *Tales of Poor Lovers* (*Cronache di poveri amanti*) and Visconti's *Senso* (*Senso*). Both were adaptations of literary texts. Lizzani's film was a version of a novel by Vasco Pratolini (1913–   ), entitled in translation *A Tale of Poor Lovers*. It appeared in 1947 and was one of the very few masterpieces of neorealist fiction that followed the canons of traditional literary realism. In the novel, Pratolini employs the word *cronaca* in his title in a deliberate reference to the work of the medieval historian Dino Compagni (circa 1255–1324). He believes that Fascism imposed its grip upon the people of the Via del Corno in the Santa Croce district of Florence much as the Guelphs gained power over the Ghibellines centuries earlier—by terror and violence. His work presents an historical analysis of Florence from the year 1925 with a group of over fifty characters, revealing the complex social and personal relationships of the inhabitants of this poor street near the Palazzo Vecchio. The protagonist of the work is a heroic proletarian figure named Corrado, called "Maciste" by his friends, recalling the legendary strongman of the Italian silent cinema. His death during one of the Fascist "punitive expeditions" against the working class results in the birth of a sense of class consciousness in Ugo Poggioli, a fruit vendor who inherits Maciste's anti-Fascist ideals and eventually becomes a member of the Communist Party. Visconti's source is a famous short story entitled in translation "A Thing Apart" ("Senso," 1882) by Camillo Boito (1836–1914)—brother of Arrigo Boito, Verdi's celebrated libretti composer—and reflects the Bohemian movement in late nineteenth-century Italian literature known as *scapigliatura*. It tells the tale of a Venetian noblewoman and her Austrian lover, Lieutenant Remigio Ruz, who uses his mistress to procure a certificate exempting him from combat. When the Countess learns of Ruz's infidelity, she denounces him to the Austrian authorities, who execute him by a firing squad and invite the woman to witness his death. The tale is set against the backdrop of the Risorgimento, the Italian struggle for national independence against Austria.[14]

Lizzani's film is as faithful to its literary source as possible; Pratolini's social realism finds its cinematic equivalent in an authoritative narrative voice-over in the film. There are no spectacular stylistic effects, as Lizzani attempts to render Pratolini's gift of presenting all the small, seemingly insignificant details of daily life in a single street in Florence, viewed as a microcosm of all of Italy. The rise of Fascism is shown indirectly through its effects upon the simple inhabitants of the city, and the director's condemnation of this political ideology is muted, yet effective. Lizzani's technique is to follow as closely as possible his literary model, trusting in the expressive power of the novelist's complicated web of interpersonal relationships to explain an important and controversial historical period in Italian life.

Lizzani approaches history as chronicle, as a mass of diverse facts which, taken together, explain broader historical trends, such as the rise of a particular ideology or the birth of class consciousness in a particular social group. Visconti's approach to Italian history is substantially different: his aim in adapting a literary text (as we have already seen in *Obsession* or *The Earth Trembles*) is generally to transform the original source into something closer to his own sensibility or ideology. Rather than accumulate historical data, Visconti aims at what one critic has termed a "demystification" of history, uncovering not only the actual events of the Risorgimento but also less obvious ideological contradictions and their connection to Italy's future development.[15] *Senso* opens with the performance from Act III of Verdi's *Il trovatore* in Venice's La Fenice Opera in the spring of 1866: as Manrico sings the famous lines "Di quella pira . . ." and the chorus joins in with the call to arms ("All'armi, all' armi . . ."), the audience, composed of Austrian officers or government officials as well as Italian civilians, is startled by the outbreak of a patriotic demonstration. Tricolor Italian flags are displayed, the Austrians are taunted, and cries of "Viva Verdi!" ring out (Verdi's initials provided nationalist patriots with a thinly disguised cheer for the House of Savoy—"Viva *Vittorio Emmanuele, Re d'Italia!*"). In the orchestra, the leader of the demonstration, Roberto Ussoni (Massimo Girotti), challenges a young Austrian officer, Franz Mahler (Farley Granger), to a duel for a disparaging reference to Italian cowardice. In a box overlooking this scene, Countess Livia Serpieri (Alida Valli) and her husband are seated with high-ranking Austrian officials, a mark of the Count's collaboration with the decadent foreign regime, soon to lose its grip on Venice and Northern Italy as a result of Austria's defeat by Prussia at the battle of Sadowa. In an effort to save her cousin Ussoni (an important revolutionary leader) from becoming embroiled in such a meaningless duel, Livia speaks with Mahler and tells him that while she loves opera, she does not care for it offstage, or for people who act like melodramatic heroes without considering the consequences of their impulsive gestures. The duel does not take place, but the melodrama of Verdi's opening sequence is transposed from the stage into the film's plot. Livia and Franz become lovers; Livia employs monies collected by her cousin Ussoni for the uprising against the Austrians to buy Franz's safety with a forged medical examination; her discovery that the Austrian lieutenant has been unfaithful to her, her subsequent betrayal of his cowardice to the Austrian authorities, and his execution are thus juxtaposed to scenes depicting the Italian defeat by the Austrians at the disastrous battle of Custoza (where Ussoni is wounded.)

With *Senso,* Visconti intended to present the cinematographic equivalent of a great nineteenth-century novel after the fashion of Tolstoy's *War and Peace,* using the lives of private individuals to analyze historical developments of moment. Thus, his use of the opening scene from Verdi is not a concession to mere spectacle but embodies a very authentic aspect of the popular culture of the Risorgimento which saw in Verdi's music, more than in any single individual literary work, the best expression of Italian patriotism and nationalism. True to his aristocratic origins, Visconti loves the decadent world of Mahler and the Serpieris, although he realizes it is doomed to pass away, and the meticulous historical recreations of period costumes or decor lend the film a certain sterile splendor which, as André Bazin once remarked, caused viewers to appreciate the work more with their intellect than with their emotions; we admire the art of Visconti while finding it difficult to participate in the world it portrays.[16] And yet, beneath the facade of sumptuous uniforms and bejeweled women, Visconti conceals a devastating critique of the Italian Risorgimento which he will continue more successfully in *The Leopard.* Leftist critics were quick to see the film in this light, just as their opponents attacked it for what they saw as a slanderous travesty of glorious past history. The young Vittorio Taviani (1929–)—better known as an organizer of film clubs in Pisa when *Senso* appeared than as the brilliant young director he was to become—grasped quite clearly Visconti's use of past history as a vehicle for analyzing contemporary political problems:

> More than a month after its presentation, *Senso* continues to be at the center of the cultural debate in our city. Visconti's latest film seems to us the most coherent consequence of the premises of neorealism. If our postwar cinema was born from the Resistance—as above all a resistance to Fascism—it was inevitable that after turning its gaze on the present, it would seek to reach the roots of political and social phenomena: that is, that it would confront the Risorgimento as the historical moment which signals the birth of Italy as a modern nation. And it was also inevitable that with such an attentive

analysis, conducted along the lines of the most illuminating results from current historiography led by Gramsci, Gobetti, and Salvatorelli, the bourgeois revolution would reveal its fundamental characteristic as an incomplete revolution.[17]

Such, indeed, was Visconti's original intention when he began the film, and while the splendid sequence at the Venetian opera does capture the popular nature of Italian patriotism, the rest of the film underlines the ambiguities and the equivocal motives behind the events of 1866. Count Serpieri first aids the Austrians, then turns to Ussoni when it is clear that Austria will eventually be defeated and Venice liberated, as he is concerned only for his wealth and property and not for the goals of national unity. The patriots led by Ussoni were as much an embarrassment to the troops of the regular Italian army as were Garibaldi's Redshirts, and a crucial scene which shows Ussoni's offer of volunteer troops being refused by regular officers before the battle of Custoza makes it clear that a much different outcome might have been expected if Italy's ascendant middle class had harnessed the energies of the entire population during the Risorgimento. The Risorgimento was betrayed not so much by passionate women like Livia Serpieri as by others of her class who twisted the noble aspirations of Italian patriots to ignoble, class-oriented ends. The parallel between the failure of the Risorgimento and that of the anti-Fascist Resistance was also evidently intended by Visconti. However, after the film was released at the Venice Festival, the Ministry of Defense intervened and forced Visconti to eliminate a crucial sequence from the film which confused Visconti's original comparison of the Risorgimento and the Resistance, thus weakening much of the film's political impact upon its public.

The film thus made a splendid and beautiful attempt to marry spectacle and melodrama with a critical realism worthy of the best historical novel, broadening the horizons of neorealism from the immediate facts of daily life to more complex problems of historical development. It was to set the pattern Visconti would follow in his greatest films still to come. And yet, beneath the historical setting and the ideological issues Visconti treats in *Senso,* we can still discern a pattern of passionate love leading to tragic conclusions, melodrama in the best sense of the term (Verdi's) that Visconti employed so brilliantly in *Obsession*.

A few other facts related to the film are of some historical importance. *Senso* was the first color film directed by a major Italian artist, some ten years before Antonioni and Fellini turned away from black-and-white to color in *The Red Desert (Il deserto rosso,* 1964) and *Juliet of the Spirits (Giulietta degli spiriti,* 1965). Visconti's spectacular results, particularly in the night sequences set in the tiny streets and canals of Venice, and in his sumptuous re-creations of lavish interiors, provided proof that Italian directors could move not only to more commercial subjects (broad historical spectacles), but that they could also match their foreign competition in a new and increasingly important technology.

This commercial consideration was of some import. *Senso* marked an important initial step toward the dependence of Italian film production upon foreign capital, the effects of which are still being felt today. Since American monies bankrolled the production, Farley Granger was imposed upon Visconti by his American backers (Visconti originally wanted to cast Marlon Brando and Ingrid Bergman), and Tennessee Williams worked on the dialogue of the English version. However, because English-speaking audiences lacked familiarity with Italian history, the film had only a limited success with them. (Similarly, the English version of *The Leopard,* with Burt Lancaster in the lead role, was a commercial failure outside the European market.)

The diversity of cinematic styles that had evolved within the boundaries of neorealist cinema during the decade since the appearance of *Obsession* and *Rome, Open City* had thus ultimately burst the boundaries of a naive view of realism. In spite of Zavattini's insistence upon turning Italian film toward everyday reality, avoiding the "spectacular" or the "intervention of fantasy or artifice," many of the best works in this period did exactly the opposite. They moved closer to traditional commercial Hollywood genres and away from the close connection between documentary and fiction that was at least partially responsible for the appeal of some of the early classic films by Rossellini or Visconti. Rather than focusing exclusively upon contemporary events, directors began to employ the cinema for historical investigations of crucial moments in Italian history. One particular film, *Love in the City* (*Amore in città,* 1953), underlines clearly and quite accidentally how far removed Italian film actually was from Zavattini's own guiding principles. Zavattini had intended *Love in the City* to initiate a series of cinema news magazines in which directors would be reporters. Impatient even with scripted stories, such as his own works for De Sica in which nonprofessional actors nevertheless portrayed fictional characters in fictional works, Zavattini wished to create a new style close to *cinéma-vérité,* and he called this the "film inquiry" ("film inchiesta"). He enlisted the services of six directors for six different episodes: Dino Risi's "Invitation to Love" ("Paradiso per tre ore"); Antonioni's "When Love Fails" ("Tentato suicidio"); Fellini's "Love Cheerfully Arranged" ("Un'agenzia matrimoniale"); Lattuada's "Italy Turns Around" ("Gli italiani si voltano"); his own "The Love of a Mother" ("La storia di Caterina"), which he codirected with Francesco Maselli (1930–   ); and Carlo Lizzani's "Paid Love" ("L'amore che si paga"), censored from the original American version by the Italian government because of its shocking revelation that prostitution existed in Italy! While Zavattini's intentions were realistic in the extreme, bordering on cinema journalism (the opening credits, for example, are listed on the turning pages of a magazine), and the narrative voice-over introducing the work informs the viewer that only the most unusual and poignant stories were selected in consultation with the people who actually experienced the events in the film, there is little in the work to suggest either a coherent sense of realism or even a harmony of directing styles. Zavattini's sequence, recreating the tragedy of an unwed Sicilian girl who was abandoned by her lover in Rome, is the only part of the film with recognizable links to classic neorealist masterpieces. Lattuada's sequence employs a "candid camera" technique: close-ups of thighs, breasts, and buttocks are intercut with the lecherous and leering stares of Italian men as they peer at some twenty gorgeous women on the street. Antonioni's investigation of the causes behind the suicide attempts of several women points not backward to neorealist techniques but forward to his highly abstract psychological analyses of love affairs in his greatest works. Fellini's sequence

involves the preposterous premise, one apparently accepted by Zavattini as factual, that a client might contact a marriage bureau to locate
a woman willing to marry a man who thinks he is a werewolf. Its
lyricism reveals the surreal and symbolic universe of Fellini's early
works rather than a truly documentary approach to daily events. Little
can be learned from the film about unwed mothers, prostitution, suicide, or the "reality" of love in Italy or elsewhere, and its use of
actual locations, actual people, and actual stories leads the viewer no
farther than the compilation of facts in the daily newspaper. Zavattini
may have ingenuously considered *Love in the City* as a form of factual
reporting, but it is evident the other five directors did not accept his
facile assumption that description or information would automatically
lead to interpretation, understanding, and a more profound sense of
the reality of Italian life. The Italian cinema, led by the makers of the
two most unusual and original sequences in the film—Federico Fellini
and Michelangelo Antonioni—was about to embark on an entirely
different cinematic journey.

The Break with Neorealism: Rossellini in Transition, Early Antonioni and Fellini

The artistic achievements of Italian neorealism made it extremely difficult for directors with different visions to discard a concern for social realism or the semidocumentary techniques which such themes seemed to demand. And yet, only a few years after the appearance of the major neorealist films, newer and different forces were changing the direction of Italian cinema. Federico Fellini (1920–) and Michelangelo Antonioni (1912–) were primarily responsible for this shift in direction, although the contribution of Rossellini, the father of neorealism, cannot be ignored. The attitude of these three men toward neorealism was an ambivalent one. All three played an important role in scripting or directing neorealist works, but they all felt continued critical association with the implicit goals or techniques of neorealism to be increasingly confining.

During the year that Rossellini made *The Machine to Kill Bad People*, he also completed *The Ways of Love* (*L'amore*, 1948), a film in two episodes which displayed the acting talents of Anna Magnani, the star of *Rome, Open City*. Like many of the films from the Fifties he made with Ingrid Bergman (whom he married in 1950 after a widely publicized love affair), *The Ways of Love* depends upon the sensitive talents of a professional actress, and Rossellini's increasing reliance upon professionals, as opposed to his earlier predilection for amateurs, may be explained by his desire to explore more psychologically complex themes than the nonprofessionals of many neorealist works were capable of portraying. *The Ways of Love*'s first episode, *A Human Voice* (*Una voce umana*) is derived from a play by Jean Cocteau; the second part, *The Miracle* (*Il miracolo*), was written by Fellini, who plays the male lead. *A Human Voice* requires a virtuoso performance, as it consists entirely of a monologue by a woman speaking on the telephone to a lover who has left her for another woman. While the acting is somewhat melodramatic by today's standards, Rossellini's increasingly characteristic *plan-séquence* shooting, which organizes actions normally shot in a sequence by a single complex take, concentrates the entire force of the episode upon a single actress, her facial expressions, and her solitude and suffering (no response from her lover is ever revealed by the sound track). *The Miracle* is a curious companion piece, for its plot parodies the love between Joseph and Mary, the parents of Christ: a demented peasant girl (Magnani) meets a man whom she takes to be Saint Joseph (Fellini); when she discovers afterward she is pregnant by this mysterous stranger, she declares it to be a miraculous conception, but the peasants in her village scoff at her and force her to run away to a deserted sanctuary to deliver her baby. Neither the mysterious Joseph nor the lover on the other end of the telephone ever utters a word, nor does either offer any solace to the suffering and loneliness of the two very different women. In *The Miracle*, Magnani's talents are used to portray the nature of sainthood in a secularized and unbelieving world, as Rossellini underlines his belief that modern civilization has no understanding of what the religious experience behind Christ's birth actually represents. It is no accident that the careers of Fellini and Rossellini would be linked together again with this script: Fellini had also scripted the ambiguous monastery episode of *Paisan*; Rossellini himself would examine the theme of the "saintly fool" in *Francesco, Jongleur of God* (*Francesco, giullare di dio*, 1950), just as Fellini would do in two of his greatest early films, *La Strada* (*La Strada*, 1954) and *The Nights of Cabiria* (*Le notti di Cabiria*, 1957). Both directors were moved to explore dimensions of human life unrelated to social, economic, or political concerns and which were deemed unsuitable by many to neorealist treatment.

Rossellini's changing perspective is obvious in a series of films completed over the next few years as vehicles for Ingrid Bergman: *Stromboli* (*Stromboli, terra di dio*, 1949); *Europe '51* (*Europa '51*, 1952); *Voyage in Italy* (*Viaggio in Italia*, 1953); *Joan of Arc at the Stake* (*Giovanna d'Arco al rogo*, 1954); and *Fear* (*La paura*, 1954). Most of these films examine the dimensions of contemporary marriage, emotional alienation, and personal despair. They were generally failures at the box office, although the young critics and intellectuals associated with the French journal *Cahiers du Cinéma* greeted them as an original and revolutionary force in film, one which transcended neorealism. In an interview given to this periodical in 1954, Rossellini hesitates to be linked forever with his neorealist past:

> One can't help being interested in other subjects and problems and trying new directions; one can't forever shoot films in bombed cities. We all too often make the mistake of letting ourselves be hypnotized by a certain milieu, by the atmosphere of a certain moment. But life has changed, the war is over, the cities have been reconstructed. What we needed was a cinema of the Reconstruction.[1]

Furthermore, Rossellini asserted that the lack of "cinematic effects" noted by his interviewers constituted the very essence of his newer style:

> I always try to remain impassive; it seems to me that what is so astonishing, so extraordinary, so moving in human reality is precisely the fact that noble acts and momentous events happen in the same way and produce the same impression as the ordinary facts of everyday life; I therefore attempt to convey both in the same manner.[2]

Voyage in Italy is perhaps the most important work from this period; though it is infrequently shown today, in 1958 the critics of *Cahiers du Cinéma* considered it one of the twelve greatest films of all time. Partially indebted to James Joyce's "The Dead," it deals with a visit to Naples by an English couple, Alexander and Katherine Joyce (George Sanders and Ingrid Bergman), where they must dispose of property inherited from their Uncle Homer. While in Italy, their stodgy English mentalities are assaulted by the Italian gusto for both life and death, and their reactions drive them to the brink of divorce.

The Joyces have none of the close, personal connections to the past, to history, or to natural forces that the seemingly vulgar Italians enjoy, a fact underlined by their desire to sell Homer's villa, their only link to this past, as soon as they can; the film's loose plot centers around a number of excursions they take in the surrounding area. Katherine's first trip is to the National Museum of Naples, where Rossellini reverses the typical documentary techniques of museum photography, focusing upon Katherine's shocked reactions to the nude statues of the Farnese collection rather than upon the works of art themselves. Her second visit is to the ancient site of the Cumean Sibyl, where an insinuating Italian guide embarrasses her by placing her in the same spot that the Saracens once used to sacrifice women (again, Mediterranean sensuality overwhelms her Anglo-Saxon temperament). As she makes a third trip to visit the nearby lava fields, she is assaulted by more images of strolling lovers and pregnant women; another guide demonstrates the mystery of ionization near the lava beds, where any source of fire, such as a cigarette, produces an eruption of steam everywhere. The very Italian soil seems to have a mysterious sense of harmony with sexual energy. Yet when Alexander visits Capri, the site of the legendary sexual exploits of Tiberius and Caligula, his encounter with an attractive woman there leads nowhere. Later, Katherine visits a church where Italians preserve the skeletons of their dear departed relatives; again observing pregnant women everywhere (six on one street!), she learns that the lust for life in Italy also includes the acceptance of its counterpart, death. Finally, the Joyces make their first excursion together to the Pompeii excavations just in time to witness the discovery of the remains of a married couple who were trapped in the Vesuvian eruption and eternally frozen in each other's arms. No single image could be in greater contrast to the sterility and unhappiness of their own marriage. This final scene provokes not only a morbid reaction from Katherine but also a decision to obtain a divorce from Alexander. As the couple returns to the city, they are swept up by a religious procession honoring a town's patron saint, and a miraculous reconciliation takes place between them.

The scandalous press Rossellini received in the English-speaking world during his affair with Ingrid Bergman may explain his denun-

Roberto Rossellini's *Voyage in Italy* (1953). Katherine (Ingrid Bergman) and Alexander Joyce (George Sanders) achieve a miraculous reconciliation at the religious festival.
(Photo courtesy of the Museum of Modern Art)

ciation of English morality in *Voyage in Italy*, which for whatever reasons aroused little critical interest outside France. Rossellini's impassivity, his technique of revealing only the outer surfaces of reality, forcing the viewer to confront his seemingly inconsequential and undramatic style without obvious clues as to how the film must be interpreted, could never gain a broad appeal, nor could his *mise-en-scène* technique relying upon the long take seem anything but boring to the average moviegoer. Nevertheless, the understated, simple images from everyday existence reveal intellectual profundity and emotional complexity. In only a few years after the appearance of *Rome, Open City*, Rossellini had shifted the focus of Italian neorealism perceptively toward psychological analysis or emotional behavior and away from themes directly associated with the war.

Michelangelo Antonioni's major works in the Fifties are closest to Rossellini's middle period in tone, if not in style. *Sanitation Department* had already anticipated Rossellini's evolution toward a cinema of solitude and alienation characterized by unusually long takes. Like Rossellini, Antonioni was increasingly impatient with neorealist aesthetics or themes, and he, too, desired to create a cinema of the Reconstruction period:

> The neorealism of the postwar period, when reality itself was so searing and immediate, attracted attention to the relationship existing between the character and surrounding reality. It was precisely this relationship which was important and which created an appropriate cinema. Now, however, when for better or for worse reality has been normalized once again, it seems to me more interesting to examine what remains in the characters from their past experiences. This is why it no longer seems to me important to make a film about a man who has had his bicycle stolen. That is to say, about a man whose importance resides (primarily and exclusively) in the fact that he has his bicycle stolen. . . . Now that we have eliminated the problem of the bicycle (I am speaking metaphorically), it is important to see what there is in the mind and in the heart of this man who has had his bicycle stolen, how he has adapted himself, what remains in him of his past experiences, of the war, of the period after the war, of everything that has happened to him in our country—a country which, like so many others, has emerged from an important and grave adventure.[3]

In particular, Antonioni had already become dissatisfied with traditional narrative devices embodied in even the best neorealist works or documentaries. As a reaction against a technique based upon blocks of logically connected sequences, in *Sanitation Department* he had already tried to evolve "a montage that would be absolutely free, poetically free," and a storyline liberated from logic, lacking a clear-cut beginning and ending. Instead, he preferred to juxtapose isolated shots or sequences, rendering (rather than merely relating) the essence of his vision of the *spazzini*'s world. And in his first feature film, *Story of a Love Affair* (*Cronaca di un amore*, 1950), he employed what would eventually come to be recognized in his greatest works as a distinctive personal cinematic style—characteristically long shots, tracks and pans following the actors without interruption, especially after they have delivered the lines in their written scripts—in order to capture the "intensely dramatic scene" when the actor is left "alone by himself to face the after-effects of that particular scene and its traumatic moments."[4] More than any other Italian director, Antonioni consciously aimed to produce a modernist cinema, a cinema which was tied to "the truth rather than to logic" and which responded to the rhythm of life in its daily routine, "not so much concerned with externals as it is with those forces that move us to act in a certain way and not in another."[5] This cinema would become increasingly abstract and cerebral during the course of Antonioni's evolution from *Story of a Love Affair* to such masterpieces as *The Eclipse* and *The Red Desert*, which embodied many of the philosophical concerns usually associated with European existentialism.

Story of a Love Affair evinces obvious affinities to Visconti's *Obsession* and that film's source, Cain's novel: it employs a traditional plot and theme, one common to American crime films of the Forties, but its original treatment marks it with the director's personal vision. A plot summary only conceals its originality: Enrico Fontana (Ferdinando Sarmi), a wealthy Milanese engineer, hires a private investigator to look into the murky past of his young wife, Paola (Lucia Bosè); the detective learns that some years earlier, Paola's girl friend was killed in Ferrara by a fall into an elevator shaft under mysterious circumstances and that Guido (Massimo Girotti), her fiancé (also Paola's lover) had vanished shortly afterward; Guido learns of this investigation, and returns to Milan to see Paola again, and their meeting initiates a chain of events leading to the rekindling of their love affair and Enrico's death. Outlined in this fashion, *Story of a Love Affair* seems to possess a conventional plot based upon dramatic suspense and an affair which drives a pair of lovers toward a crime of passion. But Antonioni's actual narrative techniques reject any such traditional form. He refuses to unfold the information we seek in any logical order; chance plays a greater role than cause and effect; and the true drama resides not in the plot's unfolding but in the complex emotional reactions to what are often unexplained events. The selection of Mas-

Michelangelo Antonioni's *Story of a Love Affair* (1950). Incongruous and disturbing images reflect Antonioni's new photographic style. (Photo from the author's private collection)

simo Girotti, the male protagonist of *Obsession*, to play the role of Guido is a conscious reference to Visconti, but Antonioni's focus shifts from the tawdry provincial atmosphere of *Obsession* to an upper-class environment. The luxurious costumes and the elegant Milanese locations in *Story of a Love Affair* are emblematic of the director's change of perspective, for Milan is the capital of postwar Italy and the forthcoming "Economic Miracle," the habitat of the new middle-class protagonist so central to the best of Antonioni's films in the decade to come. Guilty passion dominates Paola and Guido: past guilt haunts them, for they knew Guido's fiancée was walking toward a faulty elevator shaft but said nothing; now their guilty love leads them to consider killing Enrico. Only fate spares the couple from the commission of a crime. Enrico's death occurs just before he crosses a bridge where Guido is waiting for him in the shadows with a loaded pistol, and we are never quite certain whether it was the result of suicide or an automobile accident. For Antonioni, mental processes are more important than actions, however, and the tragic results of this death are the same as if Enrico had actually been murdered. When the police come to Paola's home to tell her of the accidental death before Guido has had the opportunity to report what really occurred, she runs from the house; when she finally does confront Guido, she blames him (rather than herself) for planning what she thinks is a murder. Their guilt and remorse have destroyed their love, and Guido leaves Milan without Paola.

Rarely has a first feature film been so attentive to formal details. *Story of a Love Affair* already reveals the masterful photography of Antonioni's greatest films, his careful framing of individual shots coupled with a suggestive and rhythmic editing. One memorable shot juxtaposes two enormous bottles of vermouth placed on either side of a deserted country road where Guido (posing as a car dealer) makes love to Paola in his car while his partner demonstrates a powerful Maserati to Enrico. The incongruity of this abstract image reflects the disequilibrium found not only in the lives of these guilt-ridden adulterers but in the wealthy society they inhabit as well. Desolate landscapes (an empty soccer stadium, rain-drenched urban streets) provide poetically appropriate backdrops for the anguish of the suffering protagonists, who are always presented in carefully composed frames within such locations. Irony abounds, undercutting any logical development in the plot: when Paola discovers her husband is having her investigated, she discusses this with Guido in a spot fraught with memories from their past—near an elevator shaft. The elevator that caused the accident which once separated them now provides the impulse for their resolve to commit murder. Yet, no murder is ever committed, although the effects of their mental resolve to commit murder are equally real. The tone of American crime films is absent, for Antonioni, true to his modernist predilection, resolutely avoids any sense of dramatic development through a crescendo of suspense.

Antonioni completed a number of interesting films following *Story of a Love Affair*—including *The Vanquished* (*I vinti*, 1952), a three-part episodic work set in England, France, and Italy; *The Girl Friends* (*Le amiche*, 1955), an adaptation of a novel by Cesare Pavese; and the episode devoted to suicides in Zavattini's *Love in the City*. He then made *The Cry* (*Il grido*, 1957), a film which embodies in a pure form for the first time his characteristic method of narrative—what a perceptive study of his works has termed "the emotional progresssion and its physical counterpart, the journey"—which was perfectly adapted for treating the slow, often illogical unfolding of psychological processes or emotions in a manner that traditional film plotting made impossible with its accent upon suspense and dramatic tension.[6]

The Cry follows the wanderings of Aldo (Steve Cochran), a worker at a sugar refinery, after he discovers his love has disintegrated. We receive our first glimpse of Aldo as Irma, his mistress (Alida Valli), hurries to the factory to deliver his lunch; the shot is photographed from a high angle from atop the tall tower on which Aldo is working. She brings him both good news (that her husband is officially dead, thereby making a marriage between them possible) and bad news (after an affair of eight years, she loves another man!). This shattering revelation destroys Aldo, who quits his job and taking Rosina (Mirna Girardi), his daughter by a previous marriage, with him leaves, thus cutting himself off from his hometown and his future hopes. As the film's picaresque and almost plotless structure unfolds, Aldo encounters an old girl friend, Elvia (Betsy Blair), who still loves him; he takes up with Virginia (Dorian Gray), a sensual woman who operates a gas station in the provinces and sends Rosina back to Irma; and he has a brief relationship with a prostitute named Andreina (Lynn Shaw). None of these relationships can overcome his alienation and despair over the loss of Irma. When he eventually returns home to witness a contented Rosina and Irma changing the diapers of a new child, in the midst of a strike called at the factory by his former coworkers with whom he no longer has any connection, Aldo climbs the tower that opened the film, apparently faints, and plunges to his death. We see not his fall but the terrified expression on Irma's face, and the concluding shot of the film is a long shot from the tower of the couple in the courtyard, Irma kneeling beside Aldo's body.

The emotional impact of this work is achieved by completely understated methods. Very little musical accompaniment is employed and dialogue is often sparse or elliptical; silence rather than words accompanies the director's stark images of alienation. A characteristic shot in the film involves a stroll by the muddy banks of the Po River. Aldo is accompanied by one of his female lovers, but the deserted landscapes and the careful stationing of the figures apart in the midst of this terrain always underline Aldo's solitude. The result is an existential portrait of despair buttressed by a poetic evocation of the Po landscape always so important to Antonioni's view of the world. Nor is there any resolution of Aldo's tragedy (he simply gives up his effort to live) or any injection of facile optimism. Little occurs in the film, but the viewer comes away from it with unforgettable memories of the flat, misty landscapes Antonioni photographs, where people alone stand out in sharp relief—solitary and sad figures whose tragedies seem reflected by their environment. In a retrospective look at the film almost two decades later, one critic quite correctly realized that Antonioni was less interested in Aldo than in the landscape: "The *subject* of those sequences was in fact the desolate autumnal wastes, the oppressive horizon. These were the things that inspired Antonioni, and the plot of the film—including Aldo's state of soul—was an expression, so to speak, of the landscape, not the other way around."[7]

Federico Fellini's evolution beyond his neorealist origins began with the same dissatisfaction over the confines of a critical label felt by

Rossellini or Antonioni. While he never directed a film that could be termed a neorealist work, he had been actively involved with assisting the directors or writing the scripts of many of the important works of Rossellini (*Rome, Open City; Paisan; The Miracle; Europe '51*), Pietro Germi (*In the Name of the Law; The Path of Hope*), and Lattuada (*Without Pity; The Mill on the Po*). Fellini has always viewed neorealism as a moral position rather than a true movement, more a way of viewing reality without preconceptions or prejudices—any reality, not just social themes—and he was dissatisfied with neorealist insistence upon certain specific themes or techniques. As he put it, "it sometimes seemed as if the neorealists thought they could make a film only if they put a shabby man in front of the camera."[8] Moreover, he insisted upon the director's control over his material and the role of fantasy and imagination, as opposed to documentary and fact, drawing no real dividing line between imagination and reality. Commenting upon Rossellini's conviction that neorealism represented an act of humility toward life, Fellini set his approach to film clearly apart from those neorealist theoreticians, such as Zavattini, who insisted upon forcing cinema to reflect only the "reality" before the camera:

> Yes, an act of humility towards life, but *not* towards the camera, there I *don't* agree. . . . once you're in front of the camera, you ought to abandon this humility completely; on the contrary, you ought to be arrogant, tyrannical, you ought to become a sort of god, in total command not only of the actors, but also the objects and the lights. This is why, in my view, the confusion created by neorealism was a very serious matter, because if you have an attitude of humility not only towards life but towards the camera as well, carrying the idea to its logical conclusion, you wouldn't need a director at all. The camera can work by itself; all you need to do is set it up and make things happen in front of it.[9]

Fellini's break with his past was less abrupt than that of either Rossellini or Antonioni, for it was first apparent not in his choice of subject matter, as he continued to share the somewhat vague belief in human solidarity and honesty typical of neorealism, nor in any technique he employed in his early films. Rather, his earliest innovations lie in his conception of film character, a shift in perspective which would eventually permit his evolving style to express a completely original and uniquely personal vision or mythology. Neorealist characters were generally defined and limited by their surroundings. Visconti's poor fishermen in *The Earth Trembles*, De Santis's exploited workers in *Bitter Rice*, and De Sica's pensioner in *Umberto D.* or his man in search of his lost bicycle in *The Bicycle Thief* are all "typical" figures in the sense that they reflect specific historical conditions and can be understood, at least in part, by the influence of their environment. Fellini's early works create completely atypical characters who are unique and almost unbelievable and, therefore, more amenable to the personal symbolism and mythology of an *auteur* unrestrained by a social message. They are examined philosophically and psychologically, a necessary step in Fellini's evolution to his increasingly introspective or self-reflexive films.

Fellini's development of a personal interpretation of character parallels and even repeats an operation that his compatriot Luigi Pirandello (1867–1936) undertook some years earlier in his reaction against the conventions of realism in the theater of his day. In each case, a realist conception of character as socially determined, as a reflection of social influence and pressures, was bifurcated by a fundamental philosophical inquiry into the nature of character itself. Both Pirandello and Fellini move from character as a function of some outside factor to a basically subjective attitude, thus defining it both in terms of society's influence—character as "mask"—and as the reflection of the individual's own subconscious aspirations, ideals, and instincts—character as "face." The title of Pirandello's collected works, *Naked Masks*, might well serve as a label for the early works of Fellini. In both instances, the thrust of the works is toward an unmasking operation; the masks worn by the characters as they act in their socially defined roles are torn off to reveal something of the intimate personality underneath. In plays such as *The Rules of the Game* (actually better translated as "The Game of the Roles"), *The Pleasure of Honesty*, and *Right You Are (If You Think You Are)*, Pirandello moved from the realist focus upon a unifed character in conflict with other like individuals to the interplay and clash of mask and face; in other words, the character's internal conflicts with elements of his own personality.

In addition, Pirandello rejected the idea that character could ever be
unified or static or even completely known; it was a flux, an ever-
changing entity beyond the grasp of human reason precisely because
its foundation, the face behind the mask, was composed of raw emotions, instincts, and preconscious feelings which could only be expressed outwardly by actions that seemed irrational and incomprehensible without a knowledge of their inner motivations. This
fundamental redefinition of the nature of dramatic character was the
necessary first step in the intellectual evolution that eventually led
Pirandello to question and examine the nature of dramatic art itself
in his trilogy of the theater. Fellini lacks Pirandello's scholarly ground-
ing in European philosophy and literature and probably would have
little sympathy with Pirandello's desire to establish such ideas on a
programmatic basis; there is no equivalent in Fellini's early works of
the theoretical treatise *On Humor* (1909) which precedes Pirandello's
dramatic works and contains many of the new ideas on art which would
later be developed on the stage. Fellini once declared: "I'm not a man
who approves of definitions. Labels belong on luggage as far as I'm
concerned; they don't mean anything in art."[10] Fellini's ideas about
character in cinema developed largely by trial and error in his early
films, although the example of Pirandello may have been suggestive
even then, as it certainly was to be in *8½ (Otto e mezzo*, 1963), a film
about filmmaking.

   With *Variety Lights* (1950), Fellini plunges us directly into the world
of variety theater, the world of alluring illusion beneath which codirectors Lattuada and Fellini will uncover a tawdry and mundane reality.
The narrative is built upon illusion and its subsequent unmasking in
the person of Checco Dal Monte (Peppino De Filippo), an insignificant
variety show performer with illusions of grandeur, his fiancée Melina
Amour (Giulietta Masina), and Liliana (Carla Del Poggio), a stage-
struck amateur whose ambition to succeed will cause Checco to betray
his fiancée. The plot is circular and static, never revealing any essential change or development in Checco. Besides the now familiar
scenes of abandoned *piazze*, which reflect the unauthentic existence,
loneliness, and solitude of his characters, as well as the frenzied cel-
ebrations by night which are followed by the inevitable moment of

truth at the arrival of dawn, Fellini and Lattuada expand the image of the variety theater as a collection of eccentric individuals into a philosophical abstraction wherein the realms of life and art interpenetrate. Nowhere is this concept clearer than in the dramatic confrontation between Checco and Liliana after she has abandoned him for a more promising theatrical producer and a night on the town in Rome. Checco waits dejectedly for her return, and when he reminds Liliana of what he has done for her and then argues that she is obliged to pay him back by sharing his bed, she demurely agrees without a moment's hesitation. Her acceptance reveals her essential nature, for the first time, and Checco catches a brief glimpse of her true face beneath the mask of innocence she normally wears. In this moment of truth, Checco lets his own pretentious mask fall; the role he has performed until this moment as the worldly actor and man-about-town is set aside and his true identity is revealed to Liliana, who is incapable of appreciating his basic honesty and goodness. He slaps Liliana for agreeing to the very thing he most desires, rejecting her lack of morals and commitment to genuine human emotions. As he leaves her, climbing the stairs toward his hotel, we hear what sounds like applause on the sound track. The poetic necessity of this intrusive commentary by the directors is unassailable, even if it would be out of place in any purely representational treatment of the scene. We have, indeed, witnessed the finest performance of Checco's career, an act which is both genuine and far removed from the ridiculous roles of the variety theater we have seen earlier. He has thrown aside the false mask required by his self-imposed social role and, for a brief moment which will not be repeated, he has allowed his true personality to guide his behavior in the theater of life. The directors applaud him for this and we, as spectators, must agree with their judgment. Suddenly, a tram passes by, and we are now offered the possibility that the applause on the sound track may only be the noise of its passage. However, repeated viewings of this scene fail to pinpoint the exact origin of the applause. Reality and illusion thus blend, as the film reveals its novel conception of character through the dramatic clash between social role (mask) and authentic personality (face). Moreover, Fellini and Lattuada have additionally gone behind the mask of the theater itself as a social institution in *Variety Lights* and have revealed the underside of this medium, underlining the petty jealousies, the irrational causes for success or failure, the economic motives behind the search for a pure artistic form. In an almost imperceptible manner, by concentrating upon the revelation of the nature of one artistic medium, Fellini has begun his long journey which will eventually lead to the examination of the medium of film itself in his later works. And, indeed, there are hints of these self-reflexive masterpieces to come in this work—we are shown the codirector Lattuada as a character who organizes the variety show at the close of the film, and we are given brief glimpses of posters of two earlier films scripted by Fellini, Lattuada's *The Crime of Giovanni Episcopo* and Germi's *In the Name of the Law*.

It would be unfair to Lattuada to bestow all the credit for this film upon Fellini, as some critics do when they detect the familiar Fellinian universe in the picture. They are named as codirectors—a partnership solidified by the fact that their wives, Giulietta Masina and Carla Del Poggio, play the two female leads—and at the time, Lattuada was already an established director with major films to his credit, while Fellini was only a beginner lacking the authority of experience behind him. It is impossible to determine which aspects of the film we should attribute to each man.[11] *Variety Lights*, nevertheless, bridges the gap between the end of the neorealist period and the new cinematic style evolving in Fellini. It is certainly a coherent first effort by a young director which embodies an important and innovative idea of character in cinema, but it is also proof of the fact that Italian neorealists like Lattuada never embraced the simplistic antithesis of illusion and reality accepted by critics and scholars. Instead, neorealists perceived these two realms as inseparably linked together in a mutually illuminating manner by the imagination of the director and the aesthetic forms of art.

While *Variety Lights* introduces us to Fellini's new notion of character in film, *The White Sheik* (*Lo sceicco bianco*, 1952) expands the director's vision of character and examines it in detail. Once again, Fellini sets his work against the background of the world of art—in this instance, the world of the photo-novel or cartoon-romance, such as the *Grand Hotel* read by Silvana in *Bitter Rice*, the pictorial equivalent of the pulp magazine or the television soap opera in our own culture.¹² The title is doubly significant, as it evokes the memory of Rudolph Valentino, the Italian immigrant whose roles in such American films as *The Sheik* and *Son of the Sheik* made him an international celebrity. Fellini builds the film around the visit of a newlywed couple, fresh from the provinces, to Rome. Still concerned with the metaphysical clash of reality and illusion and the tension between mask and face, Fellini uses the fastidious Ivan Cavalli (Leopoldo Trieste) and his wife Wanda (Brunella Bovo) to embody each aspect of this conflict.

Ivan, a typical petit-bourgeois husband from the provinces, is trapped within a life of mechanical forms and conventions and is the antithesis of spontaneity and emotion. From the moment he arrives in Rome, he has every minute of his visit planned down to the obligatory stop at the Vatican, the dutiful homage to the monument of the unknown soldier, and even the consummation of his marriage toward evening. Superficial piety and patriotism characterize Ivan's view of life, and these elements of his personality led some critics to view the film when it first appeared as an authentic neorealist critique of Italian provincial mores. Wanda embodies a rather naive attempt to break out of the provincial forms and her conventional marriage into a world of illusion and fantasy, symbolized for her by the world of the white sheik and the *fotoromanzi*—the world of art—and set apart from the real world of her everyday existence. As Wanda steals away from the hotel to visit the editorial office of *Blue Romance*, leaving her bath water running in the process, the film's structure shifts to follow the two characters in parallel action sequences, employing extensive crosscutting between separate stories—and therefore dividing the twin realms of illusion and reality the characters reflect—in order to comment on them both. As the storyline shifts back and forth from Ivan to Wanda, the transitions are most carefully made, the sequences are tightly edited, and the result is a minor masterpiece which belies the impression of carelessness that a first viewing of the film (or a reading of the superficial comments of the critics) might suggest.

The initial parting of Wanda from Ivan is a typical example of Fellini's attention to detail in this film. As Wanda walks to the editorial office, her path is lined with film posters, all reflecting the illusions that make her character what it is. Moreover, church bells are heard on the sound track as she walks, suggesting that the ultimate source of deception and illusion in Fellini's universe really is the Church. At the editorial office, Wanda declares that illusion is preferable to reality when she agrees with Marilena Alba Velardi, the editor, that "dreams are our true lives."[13] As she leaves the office, she witnesses a strange procession of the characters in the *fotoromanzo*, all dressed in their Arabic costumes, and her fantasy world merges with the real world. In addition, the music on the sound track underlines the point, for it is not a part of the world being filmed but is, rather, music supplied by the director to support the fantastic nature of the procession. In addition, the parade is without any apparent order or structure, reminiscent of figures in a dream.

The transition back to Ivan and the hotel is made by a black African priest who discovers the bath water Wanda has left flowing in the tub; this strange individual who speaks an incomprehensible language is the counterpart in Ivan's real world of the falsely made-up Arab with a dark complexion that Wanda takes for a real Bedouin in the office of *Blue Romance*. In contrast to Wanda's mysterious procession with its evocative music, Ivan encounters an entirely different kind of procession as he searches for Wanda—a highly regimented parade of Italian *bersaglieri* (shock troops). The music accompanying this scene is played by the troops themselves, as if to underline their location in the world of everyday reality. Fellini then crosscuts to the beach at Fregene, where the pictures for the *fotoromanzo* will be shot. Wanda meets her idol the sheik (Alberto Sordi) and is persuaded by him to dress as a harem girl and to play a role in the next issue of the magazine. Unlike the other actors, however, Wanda accepts the illusion of the *fotoromanzo* as reality and actually lives her part. As Wanda becomes a part of this world of the imagination, life and art merge in the hilarious sequence during which the stills for the *fotoromanzo* are made. Here, Fellini reproduces the process of film montage, and the narrative structure of *The White Sheik* as a whole, with its drastic cross-cutting, implicitly rejects one major neorealist approach to editing, Rossellini's in particular, which refuses to "manipulate" reality wit

Federico Fellini's *The White Sheik* (1952). The White Sheik (Alberto Sordi) poses for a still photograph in the production of the *fotoromanzo* at the beach.
(Photo from the author's private collection)

dramatic editing. Early, Wanda had been asked by Marilena in the office of the *Blue Romance* what kind of line might be appropriate for a scene such as the one now being filmed, and she had replied: "Oh . . . I feel so uneasy . . ." At that time, the line had been described as reflecting "the simplicity of life itself." Now, Wanda repeats this line almost unconsciously while the photographs are being taken, as the realms of art and life merge together on the screen.

At this point, the narrative returns to Ivan who is entertaining his relatives at a restaurant. He, too, is playing a role, for he must pretend to speak to his lost wife on the telephone in order to convince his relatives that Wanda actually exists. But Ivan's role is assumed unwillingly, unlike the role Wanda plays in the world of the *fotoromanzo*, and while Wanda breathes life into her part and causes her reality to merge with the world of illusion, Ivan merely assumes a dead form to protect his social mask. Just as Fellini had made the transition from beach to restaurant by having both groups eat lunch, we now return to Wanda with the transition effected by the restaurant music which directs our attention back to the ocean ("O sky, o sun, o sea"). Wanda and her sheik leave the seaside and sail out onto the ocean, where she is gullible enough to accept the sheik's fantastic lie about how he has been tricked into marriage by a woman with a magic potion. Just as he tries to force a kiss from her, he loses control of the boom and is struck several times on the head by it. Fellini immediately cuts to the opera house where the frantic applause of the people around Ivan and his relatives supplies the director's implicit judgment of the sheik's accident; furthermore, the opera being performed is *Don Giovanni*, an ironic contrast to the white sheik's bungling attempts to seduce Wanda.

By this time, both Wanda and Ivan have been frozen in their re-spective roles—Wanda lives a life based upon empty romantic illu-sions which cause her to assume a mask constructed by herself, while Ivan lives a life according to society's demands upon him which causes him to assume a mask constructed for him by others. Neither of the two is really aware of their comic situation, for neither has a sense of self-consciousness. The director provides the viewers of the film with a privileged position, so that we can appreciate the absurdity of their predicament. Our sympathies, and those of Fellini, are clearly with Wanda, however. By this time, each of the characters is considered mad by those around them. When Ivan goes to the police to complain of his wife's disappearance with a white sheik, he is thought to be insane. Returning from the boat to the beach, where his fat, shrewish wife awaits him, the white sheik (now reduced to the status of Fer-nando Rivoli, a mediocre actor in our eyes, but still the white sheik for Wanda) calls Wanda crazy when she accuses his wife of forcing him to marry her by means of her magic potion. Returning to Ivan, we see him meet two prostitutes and go off with one of them, thereby breaking his own code of admittedly conventional ethics and destroying whatever earlier claim he might have had to respectability. While Ivan is playing the truant, Wanda is returned to her hotel by a man whose advances she rejects. Deciding to end her life, and bidding goodbye to her husband, she exclaims: "Dreams are our true life . . . but sometimes dreams plunge us into a fatal abyss . . ." Her suicide attempt ends in a comic failure, as the water level of the River Tiber is sufficient only to dampen her spirits. She is immediately rushed to a mental hospital where Ivan finds her again just a few minutes before they are to meet their relatives in St. Peter's Square to visit the Pope and only a short time after Ivan has returned from his tryst with a lady of the night. The two threads of the narrative, so carefully divided and interrelated throughout the film, have thus been rejoined. Now, before the final scene at St. Peter's Square, Ivan and Wanda are forced to confront each other and their respective illusions in a madhouse. Both have been misguided, for Fellini has demonstrated how a life based upon either social convention or romantic dreams is doomed to disaster.

Standing before the entrance to St. Peter's, Ivan decides to live a lie—that he has not, himself, soiled the family honor—while Wanda now transfers her illusions from the world of the *fotoromanzi* to that of her marriage. In the past, she has pursued a more spontaneous life, one opposed to her provincial marriage, through a fantasy life centered about the romances she read every week. But this reliance upon illusion alone has turned her illusions into dead forms and has destroyed them by bringing them into contact with the world of reality; they are now rendered as meaningless as the empty form of her marriage. Wanda's marriage and her husband represent the encrusted form of convention which has grown over spontaneous life, illusion, and the fantasy world of the imagination. Yet, at the end of the film, Wanda tells Ivan just before they enter the church that *he* is now her white sheik! Her solution is to accept the form of marriage (and the role or mask it entails) as her illusion and, in a sense, to merge the world of illusion and reality. While both Ivan and Wanda vaguely glimpse the true nature of their respective illusions, since her fantasy world and his respectable family life have been undermined, both ultimately reject an awareness of the truth and take refuge in another illusion.

Wanda resolves her search for a dream world by declaring that her reality will suffice as her illusion; Ivan is now transformed into her new white sheik. Ivan, for his part, pretends that the honor of the family is intact, accepts Wanda's purity without confessing his own fall from grace, and thus continues to live out his role of the respectable married man. Now, however, he does so with a guilty conscience. As the couple and their relatives head into the church, their brisk manner of walking recalls the earlier ordered procession of the *bersaglieri*. Here, at the source of the ultimate illusion (or is it the ultimate reality?), a brief shot of an angel's statue provides an ironic benediction for this final but basically unauthentic reconciliation of illusion and reality. A similar shot prefaced Wanda's ridiculous attempt to commit suicide earlier, and its repetition here is a none too subtle declaration that the reconciliation between Ivan's social pretensions and Wanda's romantic dreams within the form of matrimony sanctioned by Holy Mother Church will also end in a dismal failure. *The White Sheik* is therefore no mere light comedy or only a satirical commentary on the shallowness of Italian provincial life from a neorealist perspective. It is, instead, a serious philosophical statement about the nature of character and the roles we are forced to play in life as we contend with the demands of our social forms and the attractions of our personal illusions through the conflict of mask and face.

I Vitelloni (1953) represents a further step in the development of Fellini's concept of character and with it, his interest in the dramatic clash of mask and face.[14] Like *The White Sheik, I Vitelloni* was first interpreted as a simple, satirical critique of provincial life from a neorealistic perspective, but unlike Fellini's earlier film, this one was both a critical and commerical success and was the first of his works to achieve foreign distribution, thus helping to establish his international reputation even before the astounding success of *La Strada* in the following year. Like so many of his later films, *I Vitelloni* draws upon Fellini's childhood memories—or at least upon memories invented from a childhood created in his imagination. Its main characters are five loafers or overgrown adolescents—*vitelloni*, in the slang of Rimini, Fellini's birthplace. The most important is Fausto (Franco Fabrizi), described by the narrator as the "guide and spiritual leader" of the group: his affair with Sandra Rubini (Eleonora Ruffo)—the sister of Moraldo, the most likable of the *vitelloni*—their subsequent forced marriage, and Fausto's failure at his job selling religious articles receives most of Fellini's attention. Alberto (Alberto Sordi) is the most pathetic of the five; a weak and slightly effeminate wastrel, he lives off the wages of his sister Olga, all the while boasting to his friends about how sisters must be supervised in order to protect the family honor. Leopoldo (Leopoldo Trieste) is a would-be poet who wastes his time dreaming of hunting in Africa "like Hemingway," or of the day his pedestrian plays will be performed in the local opera house. The most sensitive of the group, and the one whose departure from the provincial village finally concludes the film, is Moraldo (Franco Interlenghi), a figure often linked to Fellini himself and a trace of whom can be seen in most of the displaced provincials who populate many of his films. The character of Riccardo, played by Fellini's own brother, Riccardo, is poorly developed; he is simply a very pleasant fellow with a melodious voice.

While the twin protagonists of *The White Sheik* reflected each aspect of the theme of illusion and reality and were closely interrelated by frequent crosscutting between their respective storylines, Fellini modifies his narrative structure in *I Vitelloni* in several important ways. To increase the distance between his characters and himself, he inserts an omniscient narrator whose voice-overs tie the rather formless plot together and provide a running commentary, as well as an objective perspective, on the action. We never know the identity of this voice— it may represent Fellini; or, it may reflect the views of a mature Moraldo as he examines his past. This objective element, intended to support the existence of a certain realm of reality, from the perspective of which the illusions of the *vitelloni* are judged and found wanting, is in contrast to his more subjective camera work which reflects not the omniscient perspective of the director but, rather, his characters' more limited points of view.

These technical aspects should not cause us to ignore the fact that the theme of the film remains that of *The White Sheik*. Indeed, the worlds of illusion and reality, and the resulting clash of mask and face, are here more clearly delineated than ever by this combination of an objective narrative voice and a subjective camera. More importantly, however, *I Vitelloni* goes beyond the earlier film and provides some resolution for the dilemma posed, but not resolved, in the compromise Ivan and Wanda Cavalli effect with illusion and reality at the end of *The White Sheik*. The film's plot follows and reveals the different personal crises of each *vitellone*; first, their pretentious social roles are outlined and then, their masks are torn away, forcing them to confront the reality of their faces and the emptiness of their illusions. Three of the group—Fausto, Alberto, and Leopoldo—are studied in detail. Riccardo seems to be purposely slighted. Moraldo, the fifth *vitellone*, observes the crises in the lives of his three friends and he, alone, reaches a measure of self-awareness sufficient to change the course of his life.

Each of the three is placed in a situation where the clash of reality and illusion arises naturally from the setting—a beauty pageant, a carnival ball, a variety theater. Indeed, one of the marks of Fellini's genius is that the smallest, most mundane particular of everday existence or of a milieu can have philosophical import. He has no need to seek out gratuitous philosophical abstractions, for his ideas are intuited by his emotions and embodied in his imagery with ease. We meet Fausto at the beauty contest which opens the film. As Sandra receives the news that she has been selected "Miss Siren of 1953," Fausto is in the act of betraying her by flirting with another woman. The future course of their marriage is immediately apparent. As he had done earlier with the world of theater in *Variety Lights*, Fellini now uncovers the tawdry reality behind the dream world of the beauty pageant; Sandra's fainting spell is a sign to the onlookers that she is pregnant. Here, Fellini shifts from the objective narrator to a more subjective perspective, as the camera re-creates the girl's dizziness and fall as she faints. As a result, we are encouraged to view the sequence from her vantage point, and we must regard her with sympathy and Fausto with disgust. Fausto attempts to escape the burdens of a family and marriage by leaving town. His evasions of responsibility recur throughout the film, for his role as a local Don Juan is incompatible with such adult notions as duty and obligation. Nevertheless, his social mask is progressively destroyed by the director; first he is forced to marry Sandra; then, he is fired from his job because of his attentions to his employer's wife, attentions which are (predictably) rejected; finally, he is abandoned by his wife and child. Reduced by these failures to his true status as a spoiled brat, rather than the provincial Casanova he pretends to be, he is finally whipped by his father like the child that he still is and will always remain.

Alberto's moment of truth occurs in a similar situation during a masked ball at carnival time, an even more obvious arena than a beauty contest for the interplay of reality and illusion, mask and face, to evolve. Fellini presents a typically frenzied celebration with its inevitable reckoning at the break of dawn. Again, his subjective camera work with its rapid movement through a variety of positions and angles, and the suddenly increased tempo and complexity of his editing, give us an insight into Alberto's predicament. We see him lurching

Federico Fellini's *I Vitelloni* (1953). The drunken revelry of Alberto (Alberto Sordi) at the masquerade ball.
(Photo courtesy of the Museum of Modern Art)

about the ballroom in a drunken stupor, dancing with a huge papier-mâché head or mask and dressed in a female costume which underlines the effeminate qualities that set him apart from his strong and self-reliant sister Olga. No other image in Fellini's works visualizes so clearly his interest in the clash of mask and face than this surrealistic dance between a man in drag and an empty mask. In his inebriated state, he asks Moraldo the kind of probing philosophical question he himself would never pose while sober: "Who are you? You're nobody, nobody!" As he staggers about, and as Fellini's camera takes on his perspective to make us feel almost as dizzy as Alberto does, we come to realize that Alberto is really addressing the question to himself and has supplied his own answer. His mask is torn aside and the reality of his miserable life is revealed both to him and to Moraldo. Predictably, the final blow occurs as he returns home at dawn. His sister, upon whom he has depended for so long a time, is leaving with her married lover. Although Alberto is a somewhat sympathetic figure, Fellini judges him as mercilessly as he condemns Fausto. At the same time, we sense the typical Fellinian sense of complicity with his characters that softens somewhat his harsh assessment of their inevitable failures.

With Leopoldo, the confrontation of reality and illusion occurs once again against the background of the theatrical world, in this case the variety show of an aged homosexual actor named Natali. While Leopoldo believes Natali is interested in his talent and might like to stage one of his wretched plays, the old man is, in fact, only concerned with seducing the naive *vitellone*. As Leopoldo accompanies Natali to the seashore, he slowly comes to realize that his literary works are merely the pretext for another, and more sinister, purpose. Racing away from Natali and the menacing shadows with which Fellini envelopes this mysterious character, Leopoldo returns to his home, his maiden aunts, and his comfortable illusions—sadder but surely no wiser.

Each of the *vitelloni* experiences a crisis as his illusions collide with reality. Each is forced by this shock to cast aside his social mask and to confront his more authentic, but infinitely less appealing, face. In all three cases, the truth that emerges from this clash is almost too much for these essentially shallow characters to bear. Their lives move on the surface of reality, and when superficial responses to serious problems are no longer satisfactory, the *vitelloni* lose control and cling to the soothing comfort of their shattered illusions. Moraldo, however, is never forced to undergo the kind of trial the others experience; instead, he is allowed to witness their failures and is permitted to profit from their example. His moment of truth involves a decision to abandon the provinces, and the catalyst for his resolve to do so is his contact with a young boy who works at the train station. He reminds Moraldo of his youth when problems seemed simpler and capable of resolution through facile illusions, but Moraldo realizes that infantile illusions such as the ones his fellow *vitelloni* never abandon are unworthy of a mature individual in the adult world. And so, Moraldo sets out, much as Fellini did years earlier. With a brilliant closing shot, Fellini employs a mobile, subjective camera to let us experience Moraldo's emotion as he departs. As the train pulls away from the station toward Rome and Moraldo bids farewell to his young friend, the camera behaves as if it were on the train sharing Moraldo's thoughts; simultaneously, it moves through each of the *vitelloni*'s bedrooms, passing over each of them in their sleep with a nostalgic caress.

Moraldo has put aside childish things and is the first Fellinian character to have experienced a conversion, an epiphany. The nature of this conversion is a philosophical change, a conscious decision to accept the responsibilities of maturity and to abandon the puerile illusions of the past as the basis for life in this world. It is not, however, a complete rejection of the world of illusion for that of reality, nor is it yet the kind of spiritual conversion that will mark the lives of his characters in his next three feature films. But it is interesting to note that the professional actor playing the role of Moraldo—Franco Interlenghi—began his career in the cinema as the nonprofessional who became famous as De Sica's orphan shoeshine boy in *Shoeshine*. Interlenghi has grown up. Moraldo (Fellini's alter ego) has come of age. And finally, Fellini seems to be telling us, the Italian cinema must do the same. Just as Fellini has retained some of his neorealist past in *I Vitelloni* (in this case, an actor), so, too, the Italian cinema must preserve the best of its neorealist heritage—the honesty, the belief in humanist values, and the sincerity that characterized the masterpieces of neorealism regardless of their political perspectives or cinematic styles. But it must also, like Moraldo and Fellini, evolve with the passage of time and the exigencies of the medium itself. With *Variety Lights, The White Sheik,* and *I Vitelloni,* Fellini absorbed the authentic heritage of neorealism and its message that the demands of film art are superior and more compelling than the profits of its producers, the intellectual quarrels and often pedantic objections of its critics, and even the mercurial favor of its fickle public. With this legacy of artistic integrity incorporated into his own creative vision, Fellini transcended his neorealist origins with his new perspective on the nature of film character and the dramatic possibilities of the clash between social roles and authentic feelings, masks and faces. In so doing, he laid the intellectual foundations for the complicated odyssey his carreer was to take in the future, for all his later works would be shaped, to some degree, by this early interest in the dialectical interplay of illusion and reality.

Variety Lights, The White Sheik, and *I Vitelloni* form a trilogy of character devoted to the clash of illusion and convention, social mask and authentic personality. With his next three films—*La Strada,* 1954), *The Swindle (Il bidone,* 1955), and *The Nights of Cabiria (Le notti di Cabiria,* 1956)—Fellini moves beyond his concern with characters to a new dimension, one motivated by a personal vision and a particular Fellinian mythology. These three works form a trilogy on spiritual poverty and an inquiry into the nature of grace or salvation. Although Fellini is always suspicious of received mythologies or systems of belief, he manages to exploit the already existing mythology of Christianity, and most particularly, the notion of conversion. However, he does so outside a properly Catholic context, employing conversion as a readily understandable metaphor for the personal and existential crises his lonely protagonists suffer.

La Strada is the best known of these three films. Its worldwide popularity won for Fellini an international reputation which has lasted for over two decades, as well as numerous awards, including an Oscar for Best Foreign Picture. It also made an international celebrity of Giulietta Masina, Fellini's wife, as well as the composer Nino Rota, whose theme song became very popular. *La Strada* appeared just as interest in Italian cinema abroad was waning after the reception of the neorealistic classics. Moreover, the work sparked a polemical argument over the direction Italian cinema should take, a debate which counted many of the best critics of the period in Europe among the participants, and which became an important part of what has since become known as the "crisis of neorealism." The film's title—"the road"—underlines the picaresque, antilinear structure of the plot. Fellini's rejection of traditional narrative structures parallels a similar development in Antonioni's works, especially in *The Cry* and afterward; both directors found the journey or quest a most suitable metaphor for the search for meaning in life which occupies most of their characters. Like Antonioni, Fellini is concerned with the failure of communication between human beings and the resultant spiritual poverty in life. Consequently, Fellini's characters in *La Strada* have hardly any verisimilitude and are clearly intended to reflect certain unusual traits or to embody definite symbolic meanings. Gelsomina (Giulietta Masina) plays a slightly retarded girl who is bought from her family to assist a circus strongman, Zampanò, in his act; she is a clown type, her mannerisms indebted to circus performances or Chaplin gags. In spite of her limited mental powers, she has a strange ability to comprehend aspects of life which escape the intellect, and she is associated with water and natural forces in the film. Zampanò (Anthony Quinn) is a brutish, insensitive, cruel man who feels no sympathy for Gelsomina and learns to appreciate her only after she is dead. He is typically associated in the film with the earth. Finally, there is "Il Matto" or "The Madman" (Richard Basehart), a bizarre tightwire walker who seems to be a mixture of angel and devil and who is naturally linked to the air. The loose plot of the work is based upon a journey from one seashore, where Gelsomina is first seen and purchased by Zampanò, to another seashore at the conclusion of the film, after Gelsomina has disappeared and Zampanò finally learns to cry in his solitary anguish on the beach. The literal journey, of course, is less important than the figurative distance the characters travel: Gelsomina moves from childish innocence toward womanhood and an acceptance of her vocation as Zampanò's companion to her final death and apotheosis. Her own death makes it possible for Zampanò to travel a similar road from brutish insensitivity toward a limited sort of self-knowledge—he is finally able to weep over the loss of Gelsomina.

But more than a film based upon a loosely structured metaphor, *La Strada* is a philosophical parable with numerous meanings. Various critics have pointed to the fairy tale structure of Beauty and the Beast (wherein the Beast is transformed); to a familiar literary topos—as old as romance itself—in which the love of a good woman changes a bad man; and to the obviously Christian account of a soul's redemption through sacrifice and suffering.[15] It is most likely the third form of the film's parabolic meaning which Fellini intended. Gelsomina expresses a kind of Franciscan religious sensitivity and naiveté; miracles

Federico Fellini's *La Strada* (1954). Beauty and the Beast: Gelsomina (Giulietta Masina) and Zampanò (Anthony Quinn) are juxtaposed at the dinner table.
(Photo courtesy of the Museum of Modern Art)

happen to her which are denied to more intelligent beings. Through the course of the film Gelsomina becomes a secular saint whose death enables Zampanò to experience a limited conversion to humanity. With her, we are reminded of the biblical dictum that we must become like children to enter the kingdom of heaven. From Il Matto, Gelsomina hears the famous parable of the pebble—that there must be some reason for the existence of both an ordinary pebble and her own wretched life. And it is Zampanò's accidental killing of Il Matto which drives her insane and ultimately causes her death.

It is rare indeed to discover a viewer of *La Strada* left unmoved by the film. And yet, there is very little in terms of cinematic technique to explain its emotional appeal, certainly none of the fantastic effects which Fellini employs in later works. To reduce to discursive terms the emotional appeal of *La Strada* generally makes the work seem simpleminded. Peter Harcourt described the work better than anyone else when he noted that the most moving sequences of the film defy "confident interpretation" and are "essentially dumb"; unless the viewer is attuned to what Harcourt terms "a subliminal level, a level largely of images plus the complex associations of scarcely perceived sound," the work will remain an unsatisfying one.[16] Rarely has a film expressed so completely its director's sense of the wonder, fantasy, surprise, and mystery in the simple lyrical moments of life without recourse to special effects or a completely subjective camera style. As Bazin aptly put it, *La Strada* concerns the "phenomenology of the soul" which is clearly set apart from intellectual or social concerns.[17] Fellini achieves this marvelous sense of mystery by treating the unpredictable, the unexpected, and the extraordinary just as if it were part of everyday reality. A single celebrated sequence in the film is typical of Fellini's procedure. Gelsomina runs away from Zampanò and is shown by the roadside, staring at a bug with the curious, enigmatic smile which made Giulietta Masina's performance unforgettable; as she does so and without any plausible explanation whatsoever, a band of circus musicians appears as if by magic in the field, forming a procession into the nearby town, and Gelsomina follows them. This strange event leads the band into another procession taking place there, a religious celebration replete with traditional Catholic symbols

(Gelsomina is photographed against a wall poster referring to the "Immaculate Madonna" and is thereby associated with the Virgin of the Church ritual.) Like the city piazza at night, in Fellini's universe of symbols the procession often has a particular connotation. It frequently represents the ultimate Fellinian miracle, the magic moment in which mental anguish or rational thought gives way to an acceptance and an embracing of life. It is, quite simply, Fellini's symbol for the renewal of faith in life through grace, the mysterious quality—bestowed without merit—which passes all human understanding.

It is no wonder that the eminent Marxist critic Guido Aristarco attacked *La Strada* for its lack of realism and its "poetry of the solitary man, a poetry in which each story, instead of being reflected, lived within the reality of the narrative, is, through a process of individualization, reabsorbed into itself and nullified as an historical entity only to be converted into a symbolic diagram, a legend, a myth."[18] Although such criticism saw Fellini's use of traditional religious symbolism as a move away from the ground gained by the greatest neorealist classics, Fellini did not betray the cause of neorealism. He had instead, like Antonioni and others, moved to another level of discourse with *La Strada*. As he put it,

> Zampanò and Gelsomina are not exceptions, as people reproach me for creating. There are more Zampanòs in the world than bicycle thieves, and the story of a man who discovers his neighbor is just as important and as real as the story of a strike. What separates us [Fellini versus his critics on the left] is no doubt a materialist or spiritualist vision of the world.[19]

The pattern established by Fellini in *La Strada* is continued in *The Swindle* and *The Nights of Cabiria*. *The Swindle* is a variation on the Christian parable of the good thief; its main character is a confidence man whose characteristic swindle is performed while he is disguised as a priest. With Augusto (a role played by Broderick Crawford but designed originally by Fellini as a vehicle for Humphrey Bogart), Fellini takes a petty crook and uses him, as he had Gelsomina, as a means of exploring the implications of human anguish, solitude, grace, and salvation. By choosing an American actor known for his many roles in Hollywood crime films, Fellini manages to expand this traditional film genre in a philosophical direction: Augusto becomes a kind of existential hero, alienated from authentic meaning in life and feeling remorse for his crimes, yet driven to commit them by some strange compulsion. After a hellish voyage of self-negation, he comes to attain a Fellinian state of grace through suffering. Once again, Fellini narrates this philosophical tale with a minimum of obtrusive cinematic effects; as in *La Strada*, his vehicle is symbolism, and he employs as the basis of his imagery his own particularly mythological universe. Once again, Fellini employs an episodic, loosely constructed plot lacking traditional dramatic structure and following the pattern of the journey or odyssey he had employed in *La Strada*.

Several sequences in *The Swindle* reflect Fellini's peculiar vision of the confidence man as emblematic of the alienation his characters usually experience. One involving the discovery by his daughter, Patrizia, of his true profession recalls a famous sequence from De Sica's *The Bicycle Thief*. As Augusto and Patrizia are seated in a cafe, Patrizia tells her father she needs a large sum of money to post a bond for her new job as a cashier and to pay her way through school; Augusto immediately declares he is willing to provide the money but is interrupted by someone nearby. It is one of his former victims, whose brother almost died from some fake medicine Augusto once sold him in one of his many confidence games. The humiliation the father experiences here as he is arrested and eventually sentenced to a prison term has its obvious source in a similar scene in De Sica's film, where the unemployed worker tries unsuccessfully to steal a bicycle and is humiliated in front of his son. In *The Bicycle Thief* De Sica ended the sequence and the film on an ambivalent but possibly optimistic note—when Bruno extends his hand to his embarrassed father, there is at least some solace in familial affection. Fellini employs a similar scene to underline the ambivalence in Augusto's character: although he feels genuine affection for his daughter, he is the kind of man who is willing to endanger the life of a seriously ill patient in order to carry out his swindles. His public humiliation, however, is only one of many steps along the road to a personal calvary, a moment of ultimate anguish and suffering. Like the director's other major protagonists, he is seriously flawed as a human being; however, Fellini feels compassion for even the most despicable of his characters, and his sense of his own complicity in the flaws he attacks in others produces a special warmth and humanity in his works. More than any other Italian director, he hates the sin but loves the sinner, an attitude which sets his vision of the world sharply apart from ideologically oriented Italian directors.

Thus, Augusto is at the same time both sinner and saint. Nowhere is this ambivalence more apparent than in the unforgettable sequence ending the film with Augusto's last swindle and his death. Disguised as a Catholic prelate and accompanied by his cronies, Augusto sets up his final crime: having buried some old bones and what appears to a gullible peasant family—his intended victims—to be a fortune, Augusto informs them that the man who had stolen these goods wished to make amends for his crime by giving the stolen merchandise to the people owning the land on which he had concealed them—on the condition that they pay 350,000 lire to say masses for his soul. It is a confidence game that Augusto has carried out many times before, but now for the first time he begins to experience doubts and remorse, particularly since the peasant must sell his only ox to raise the cash, and one of his daughters is a victim of polio. Trapped in the role of a priest, Augusto is forced to speak to the young crippled girl in that capacity, and obviously moved by her innocent purity he tells her:

> You don't need me. You're much better off than a lot of other people. Our life . . . the life of so many people I know has nothing beautiful in it. You're not losing much, you don't need me. I have nothing to give you.[20]

In Augusto's conversation with the young girl he speaks of miracles and faith in God, of learning through suffering, but his words of traditional Christian piety conceal a far more troubled spirit than the crippled girl can know.

When Augusto and his accomplices drive off, the swindler's moment of truth is at hand. As they stop by the side of the road to divide their score, Augusto informs them he could not take the family's money because he felt compassion for the girl's condition. His friends refuse to believe him, and it is here that Fellini's genius is most apparent, for after they knock him unconscious and search his clothing, they discover in fact that he did take the money! There is no sentimental or artificial conversion in *The Swindler*; until his last gasp, Augusto remains what he is—a swindler. And yet, at that moment, he achieves an apotheosis into a kind of secular saint, purified by his suffering and anguish. As he painfully crawls up an arid rocky hill, now ironically reduced to the condition of a victim, we hear church bells in the distance on the sound track, and a procession of children passes by, a familiar scene in Fellini's films. But Augusto can no longer join the procession; his drama and his death must take place in complete solitude. As the film ends, the camera slowly draws away from this inverted Christ-figure, and we are reminded of our last view of Zampanò in *La Strada*, anguished and alone on a deserted beach. But here, as one critic aptly put it, the movement of the camera is a benediction, "a short, gentle movement, one only those who have faith can truly comprehend."[21] The precedent for Augusto's miraculous redemption after a life of vice is to be found not in the cinema but in the poetic masterpiece of Catholic literature, Dante's *Divine Comedy*. In the Ante-Purgatory, Dante the Pilgrim encounters Count Buonconte da Montefeltro, one of the souls who delayed their repentance until the last moment, just as Augusto seems to have done. Buonconte was saved from eternal damnation by merely uttering the name of the Virgin Mary in his dying breath. As one of the devils complained who fought over his soul with an angel and lost it, only "a measly tear" (*Purgatory* V, 1. 107) is sufficient for man's salvation.[22] And that "measly tear" is all Augusto needs as well.

With *The Nights of Cabiria*, Fellini combines thematic elements from *La Strada* or *The Swindle* with a picaresque plot that recalls his earlier trilogy of character. As the Chaplinesque little prostitute, Cabiria Ceccarelli (a figure appearing in a brief sequence of *The White Sheik*), Giulietta Masina delivers perhaps her greatest film performance, even more masterful than that of *La Strada*. Fellini's symbolic world is again present—the strange, evocative De Chirico-like landscapes; the wild parties with the same morning emptiness; the deserted *piazze* inhabited by exotic figures. Grace or salvation is still the director's philosophical preoccupation. While the sense of a journey or an odyssey of the soul still dominates the plot structure of *The Nights of Cabiria*, Fellini also re-uses aspects of *I Vitelloni*. In that earlier work, several characters suffered successive soul-rending personal experiences that usually resulted in a sense of disillusionment and despair; only Moraldo has a positive reaction, and it leads him to set off to make his future in the city. With *The Nights of Cabiria*, Fellini increases the emotional concentration upon a single protagonist by forcing her to experience five separate misadventures. Cabiria shares many of Gelsomina's traits—she embodies certain clownlike mannerisms and is innocently open to unusual emotional or spiritual experiences. Yet, she plays a far less symbolic function in Fellini's storyline and is, consequently, a more well-rounded, developed, and believable character.

As the film opens, Fellini presents us with a sentimental, old-fashioned image: Cabiria and her boyfriend Giorgio, seemingly deeply in love, are skipping through a field toward the bank of a river; our previous movie experiences on witnessing such a scene lead us to expect a payoff shot of a kiss, but Fellini deflates our romantic expectations—Giorgio pushes Cabiria into the river after he steals her purse. This pattern of hope and illusion being suddenly transformed into despair occurs over and over again, as the luckless but plucky prostitute struggles to survive in a hostile world. Later Cabiria meets a famous actor (Amadeo Nazzari) who has just had a fight with his girl friend; he picks her up, and for a moment she dreams she has found a man who genuinely cares for her. Just before they are to make love in his sumptuous apartment, the girl friend returns, the couple is reconciled, and Cabiria is forced to hide in the actor's bathroom the entire night as the two make love in the bedroom. Cabiria's third misadventure foreshadows the critique of institutionalized religion in later films and reveals how incorrect leftist critics were when they denounced Fellini's trilogy of conversion for its supposedly Catholic ideology. Hoping to cure the crippled uncle of one of their pimps, Cabiria and her prostitute friends go on a pilgrimage to a church renowned for its miracles. Expecting a miraculous cure, the man throws his crutches aside—and falls flat on his face! In like manner,

Cabiria prays for a change in her life but nothing happens. Grace is a mysterious quality in Fellini's universe, bestowed most generously but only when least expected and only after a trial by suffering.

With Cabiria's fourth misadventure, Fellini incorporates the world of show business from his earlier films into his trilogy of salvation. Wandering about the streets, Cabiria goes to a variety show and is invited to participate in the act of an illusionist; hypnotized and in a trance, she reveals all her hidden desires—her hopes for a new life, marriage, children, and a normal home. She even imagines she has met a man named Oscar, who will marry her, but when she asks if he loves her, the hypnotist breaks the trance, as if to suggest that illusion may allow us to express our secret wishes but cannot bear a confrontation with reality, nor can it supply us with a reality that is permanent. Cabiria, the prostitute who deals in sensual love, thus lacks the emotional or spiritual counterpart to this physical sensation. Immediately after leaving the theater, Cabiria meets a man named Oscar (François Périer) in a Pirandellian sequence wherein reality copies illusion; she falls in love and encounters a Franciscan friar who informs her that the most important thing in life is to be in God's grace, since that is the key to worldly happiness. She even describes her love for Oscar as a "miracle." Yet, this hope, too, is doomed to failure. Oscar embodies the kind of shallow personality typical of Fellini's first films—his social "mask" (symbolized by the dark glasses he wears) conceals his dishonest personality. Just as Cabiria believes she has at last found true love, Oscar steals her hard-earned savings and Cabiria finds herself abandoned beside another riverbank.

Her story might have ended as it had begun, with another and final disillusionment from which there seems to be no hope, no exit, no possibility of redemption. But then, the Fellinian miracle occurs. Cabiria leaves the riverbank and returns to the road, where she encounters a group of people singing, and she is transformed by the music on the sound track in a manner which defies logical explanation. Music thus offers Fellini a metaphor for salvation, for it is completely gratuitous, spontaneous, and unexpected. The film ends with one of Fellini's most brilliant, although most simple and economical, shots: in a close-up of Cabiria's face, her gaze toward the camera crosses that

Federico Fellini's *The Nights of Cabiria* (1956). Oscar (François Périer) meets Cabiria (Giulietta Masina) at the bank of a river just before he betrays her.
(Photo from the author's private collection)

of our own but never really settles on a single spot. As André Bazin so sensitively described it:

> . . . here she is now inviting us, too, with her glance to follow her on the road to which she is about to return. The invitation is chaste, discreet, and indefinite enough that we can pretend to think that she means to be looking at somebody else. At the same time, though, it is definite and direct enough, too, to remove us quite finally from our role of spectator.[23]

Zampanò, Augusto, and Cabiria are each abandoned by their companions, and each must endure an existential crisis in complete solitude. In *La Strada, The Swindle,* and *The Nights of Cabiria,* Fellini has created three extended metaphors, three versions of an individual facing the nothingness of contemporary existence and its poverty of spirituality. A tear transforms Zampanò's brutishness into a more human form, as he feels affection for the first time in his life because he has been touched by Gelsomina's love; a tear moves a swindler to repent and to thirst for salvation; and, most importantly, the smile on a prostitute's face signals to us that grace has finally been received and salvation finally achieved. The process of "salvation" or "redemption" in Fellini's universe is ultimately one of self-revelation. And in this regard, it is evident that his female characters clearly fare better than his male protagonists and are more sympathetically portrayed, a curious fact in view of the frequent feminist attacks on Fellini for his allegedly sexist attitudes. Alone of these three protagonists, Cabiria joins the Fellinian procession that affirms life and continues down the symbolic road we must all travel. Fellini's trilogy of salvation thus celebrates the triumph of the director's lyrical and symbolic vision over a material world that constantly threatens his embattled characters. It is a life-affirming vision, one almost out of place in an age characterized by a philosophy of despair and frustration expressed so eloquently in the early works of Antonioni; one which even Fellini could not sustain in his subsequent films. By the mid-Fifties, it was increasingly clear that the greatest Italian directors had broken out of the neorealist tradition and were busy creating a filmic universe reflecting a personal vision of their own making. And such personal visions would be increasingly less optimistic than that of *The Nights of Cabiria*.

5

A Decisive Decade: *Commedia all'italiana*, Neorealism's Legacy, and a New Generation

The decade between 1958 and 1968 may in retrospect be accurately described as the golden age of Italian cinema, for in no other single period was its artistic quality, its international prestige, or its economic strength so consistently high. A major cause of this felicitous conjunction between artistic and commercial success was a contemporaneous economic crisis in the American film industry, Italy's major competitor in its own national market. This American crisis granted Italian producers and distributors some breathing room. From a high point of 369 American films distributed within the peninsula in 1949 (Italians produced a mere 71 films in the same year), the distribution of American products had dropped by 1957 to a total of only 233 films, as compared with a total domestic production of 137 works.[1] Throughout the period 1958—69, Italian production reached new levels: 141 (1958); 164 (1959); 160 (1960); 205 (1961); 245 (1962); 230 (1963); 290 (1964); 203 (1965); 232 (1966) 247 (1967); and 246 (1968). Production of films by Italian companies continued well above a level of 200 films per year, reaching a high point of 280 films in 1972, until a sudden drop occurred from 237 films in 1976 to 165 in 1977 and to 143 in 1978. During this same period, the number of

American films distributed in Italy dropped from 233 in 1958 to a low of 127 in 1967, never again reaching the high levels of deluge immediately following the end of the war. Perhaps even more important for the health of the domestic industry was a sharp increase in the total box-office receipts earned by Italian works. In 1958, Italian films earned only 30.9% of the total, as compared to 53.1% earned by American products distributed within the domestic market; thereafter, we witness a steady increase from that relatively low percentage until 1972, when Italian products gained 62.5% of the box-office receipts as compared to a mere 15.1% earned by Hollywood films. Only during 1977–78, when a new crisis struck the Italian industry, is there real evidence of a renewed American upsurge.

Three production companies in Italy during this period contributed crucial entrepreneurial skills to the revitalization of the industry: Titanus, controlled by Goffredo Lombardo (1920–); Rizzoli, owned by a major Italian publishing firm; and a company owned by Dino De Laurentiis who often coproduced works with Carlo Ponti (1910–). Traditionally blessed with a relatively large number of high quality "art" films by *auteurs* with a somewhat limited market appeal, as well as numerous potboilers aimed at markets in second-run Italian theatres or for Third World distribution, Italian films had often failed to meet the stronger demand for middle-range entertainment, precisely the market for which Hollywoood products were superbly designed. This fact explains why even in the extensive Italian internal market, American products often garnered the lion's share of the box-office receipts. Thus, in this decade, it was of fundamental importance for the Italian industry that domestic films in a number of specific genres (particularly the comedy and the Western) began to conquer not only large segments of the internal market but a very respectable portion of the international audience as well. Moreover, even works of unquestionable artistic importance, such as Fellini's *La Dolce Vita* (*La dolce vita*, 1959), often earned huge profits, reversing the usual expectations producers held for "art" films. Both critical success and popular appeal at the box office were guaranteed for Italian products by the continuously impressive showing films from Italy made at major film festivals around the world. For a brief and exciting moment, it appeared that

Cinecittà and Via Veneto would challenge Hollywood and Beverly Hills.

The decade 1958–68 was thus of pivotal importance in both the economic and the artistic history of modern Italian cinema. The widespread prestige of Antonioni, Fellini, or Visconti established international audiences for their major works (the subject of the next chapter). In addition, a remarkable group of directors, actors, and scriptwriters helped to create a distinctive *commedia all'italiana*, a tradition within which some of the greatest films of the period were produced. At the same time, led by Roberto Rossellini, there was a reassessment of the achievements of Italian neorealism which coincided with the rise of a new generation of young and highly talented directors, many of whose first films grew out of the Italian cinema's postwar film culture.

Film comedy continues to provide the most popular form of cinematic entertainment in Italy today, and most of the directors or actors who rose to prominence during this period still constitute the backbone of the industry. Best known among these directors are: Mario Monicelli (1915–   ), who had earlier created a number of box-office smashes starring Totò in the immediate postwar period; two directors who were both connected with the earlier *Bread and Love* series, Luigi Comencini (1916–   ) and Dino Risi (1917–   ); several names already mentioned in discussing neorealism, such as Germi and Lattuada; plus Mauro Bolognini (1922–   ) and Lina Wertmüller (1928–   ).[2] The popular appeal of film comedy depended upon a star system, and directors were fortunate to have at their disposal exceptional comic actors and, to a lesser extent, actresses: Vittorio Gassman (1922–   ); Marcello Mastroianni (1923–   ); Ugo Tognazzi (1922–   ); Alberto Sordi (1919–   ); Nino Manfredi (1921–   ); Sophia Loren (1934–   ); Monica Vitti (1931–   ); Claudia Cardinale (1939–   ). The mere presence of one or more of these stars was often sufficient for a film to turn a profit. In addition, the period also produced three scriptwriters of rare talent: Age (Agenore Incrocci, 1919–   ), Furio Scarpelli (1919–   ), and Ettore Scola (1931–   ), who worked in collaboration on many of the best comic films during this period for a variety of different directors.

As Mario Monicelli has remarked, the Italian comic film traditionally united laughter with a sense of desperation, employing a cynical sense of humor which reflects a need to survive in the face of overwhelming obstacles.[3] It is a film genre which continues, in some important respects, the older *commedia dell'arte* theatrical tradition and might be more accurately described as tragicomedy bordering on the grotesque. Flourishing at the height of what has been termed the "Italian economic miracle," the *commedia all'italiana* lays bare an undercurrent of social malaise and the painful contradictions of a culture in rapid transformation. Moreover, the sometimes facile and optimistic humanitarianism typical of neorealist comedy is replaced by a darker, more ironic and cynical vision of Italian life. Consistently undervalued by film critics, especially those on the left who believe that comedy's popularity deflects attention from more "serious" social problems, the Italian comic film nevertheless treated such questions quite courageously and ran afoul of the censors as often as films in a strictly dramatic vein.[4]

Three of Monicelli's works—*Big Deal on Madonna Street (I soliti ignoti,* 1958); *The Great War (La grande guerra,* 1959); and *The Organizer (I compagni,* 1963)—represent classic examples of the *commedia all'italiana* at its best. The first film portrays the futile attempts by a group of incompetent thieves to commit a robbery; a hilarious parody of the typical American gangster film, the work concludes not with the traditional gun battle or wild escape and car chase but with a bittersweet conversation among the would-be robbers over plates of pasta and beans. Monicelli thus achieves a brilliant reversal of the generic expectations usually associated with the gangster film and establishes a pattern which will become typical of the *commedia all'italiana*'s protagonists: a comic character-type portrayed in its various and multifarious aspects by Mastroianni, Gassman, Sordi, Tognazzi, or Manfredi. This type is an inept, self-centered, shallow, yet often lovable individual, the eternal adolescent whose lack of self-awareness sometimes borders upon the grotesque. In *Big Deal on Madonna Street,* Monicelli also reverses his audience's expectations by making unconventional casting decisions—as was frequently done in comic films. For example, he obtains a brilliant comic performance from a young

Gassman, primarily known in Italy until that time as a Shakespearian actor in tragic roles. In addition, both Mastroianni and Cardinale appear in comic roles. Finally, there is the magic presence of Totò, Monicelli's tribute to the older and more traditional comic film with its origins in regional humor and the dialect theater of Naples.

Monicelli's next two films further widened the thematic boundaries of the comic genre by combining the inept but sympathetic comic type of *Big Deal* with controversial social issues. *The Great War* shared the Golden Lion Award at Venice in 1959 with Rossellini's *General Della Rovere* and was greeted with a wave of negative comment from conservative elements in Italian society—especially the military, which had consistently opposed a free and honest discussion of Italy's role in World War I. *The Great War* represents a combination of the conventions of film comedy with those of the historical colossal and the war film: it boasted a large budget, a huge cast, and the use of Cinemascope. Gassman and Sordi portray two unwilling soldiers, Busacca and Jacovacci, who spend their service time trying to avoid dangerous combat. Through their misadventures, Monicelli creates two perfect antiheroes, bungling soldiers who recall his equally incompetent thieves. Comic gags abound: stringing telephone wires at the front, the men cross their wires with those belonging to the enemy, and bring about hilarious dialogue between the opposing sides, each of which fails to comprehend the other's language; when they finally reach the front, in a frenzy of patriotic fervor, they jeer at what they assume to be a group of motley German prisoners, only to realize later that they are their own battered compatriots. Such comic moments are fashioned in order to create a grotesque vision of the war's absurdity, an idiotic and quixotic expedition in which simple working-class Italians are sacrificed to the empty ideals held by the vastly incompetent upper-class officers who lead them into battle. Italy's most disastrous military defeat, the battle of Caporetto, is inserted into an irreverent comic framework. Nevertheless, Monicelli rejects a simple or satisfying comic conclusion to *The Great War*: captured by Germans, who accuse them of being spies because they are out of uniform, Busacca and Jacovacci are goaded from their innate cowardice into a heroic refusal to respond to the questions of an overbearing Prussian martinet who brags that he will soon be eating liver and onions in Venice, and they are summarily shot. The film continues to trace a successful Italian counterattack: as their comrades race by the unde-tected dead bodies of these reluctant heroes, they never learn of their courageous sacrifice; they will be remembered only as cowardly de-serters.

The Great War is a skillful mixture of black humor (which under-mines the patriotic rhetoric still employed to obscure Italy's military deficiencies) with what is a superbly directed war film: battle scenes re-created at great expense stand in sharp contrast to the individual but more eloquent human dramas developing in the actions of Mon-icelli's two antiheroic protagonists. In *The Organizer*, Monicelli con-

Mario Monicelli's *The Organizer* (1963). Professor Sinigaglia (Marcello Mas-troianni), the Socialist activist, stares hungrily at the fashionable café and its sumptuous food.
(Photo courtesy of the Museum of Modern Art)

tinues the successful technique of *The Great War*, judiciously combining black humor with an important historical issue. Here he
analyzes an unsuccessful strike among textile workers in 1890 in
Turin, examining the emergence (as well as the weakness) of class
consciousness among the workers, and fashioning a brilliant performance by Mastroianni as an upper-class intellectual who betrays his
origins to work for the cause of socialism. The character of this Professor Giuseppe Sinigaglia represents a stroke of genius on Monicelli's
part: a threadbare vagrant and traitor to his class, Sinigaglia's sincerity
stands in sharp contrast to his frequent ineptitude; he is clearly not
the typical hero of socialist realism, nor are the workers for whom he
has given up wealth and social position always worthy of his gesture
or cognizant of the political goals he espouses. They are easily tricked
by their employers (who claim that they, too, live on a salary), are
quicker to fight among themselves than to protect the interests of
their class, and they dissipate their collective energies over petty problems.

Monicelli's film contains little of the moral indignation or the systematically defined ideology commonly found in the so-called political films of the early 1970s, but his denunciation of an economic
system which exploited men, women, and small children with a fourteen-hour working day is nevertheless quite effective. His genius for
the authentic evocation of scenes from Italian history, so telling in his
recreation of the horrors of life in the trenches in *The Great War*,
creates a convincing portrait of working-class conditions during a
strike in the last century: troops assigned to protect the rich share
their food with hungry strikers until their officers prohibit this simple
gesture of solidarity; railroad workers look the other way as freezing
strikers gather up stray bits of coal which have fallen from the loco-
motives in the railyards. As always, Monicelli's comic cinema contrasts
the simple dignity and generosity of the common working-class Italian
with the insensitivity and incompetence of their bosses and rulers.
Nowhere is Monicelli's talent for blending moments of comic relief
with great tragedy more moving than in a sequence in which the strikers seek to prevent imported scab laborers from usurping their jobs;
a carefully choreographed comic brawl, reminiscent of a Hollywood

Western, leads unexpectedly to disaster, as one of the strike's leaders is killed by a speeding train coming from nowhere out of the fog. At the height of the crisis, Sinigaglia rallies the weakening strikers with a speech parodying Mark Anthony's funeral oration in Shakespeare's *Julius Caesar*. Nevertheless, as in *The Great War*, Monicelli provides no facile conclusion: the strike fails, a young striker is killed, and the professor is arrested. The only consolation is hope of future success, as one of the workers carries on the professor's struggle. The last shot of the film pictures workers filing back to work. A medium close-up shows the dead boy's brother, the last to enter, on whom the factory gates close as if upon a prison. Failure in Monicelli's tragicomic world does not preclude the acquisition of human dignity.

Another landmark in the comic film's developing maturity is Luigi Comencini's *Everybody Home!* (*Tutti a casa*, 1960)— a title derived from the cheer of Italian soldiers when they learned of the armistice signed between Marshal Badoglio and the Allies on September 8, 1943. Alberto Sordi portrays an Italian officer, Lieutenant Innocenzi, who is blissfully unaware of the moral consequences of his tepid support for the Fascist cause. A comic and antiheroic figure whose interest in warfare consists primarily in ordering his men to sing popular songs while marching, Innocenzi abandons his post with his troops and heads home when he learns of the armistice. During this picaresque journey from comic misadventure to comic misadventure, tragedy always looms over him as he is offered three possibilities: a simple return home which requires no moral choices; continuing to fight alongside the Nazis and their Fascist allies; or joining the Partisan struggle to liberate Italy. On the road, our sunshine patriot is at first unaffected by the sight of deportees heading to Germany in boxcars, nor does his superficial patriotism hinder his participation in the traffic of black-market food staples. After a hungry crowd runs off with the stolen flour he is guarding for a buxom blackmarketeer, one of his indignant soldiers tells him that it is precisely because of leaders such as he that Italy has lost the war. And this, of course, is exactly the point of the film. When German soldiers become suspicious of a girl named Modena (they have been correctly informed that Jewish families often bear names of cities), a grotesque but comic dialogue between the Germans and the ex-soldiers ensues, as the Italians temporarily convince the Nazis that there is no such city in Italy. Eventually, however, the girl is brutally executed. Sheltered in the home of one of his men, where an escaped American soldier is also hiding, Innocenzi is unable to respond to the American's embarrassing question, delivered in a humorous and broken Italian, as to why he has fought a war in which he did not believe.

The soldier's voyage home is composed of many such tragicomic moments, each of which entails personal danger and offers a moral choice, and in every instance Innocenzi (true to the character type Sordi usually portrays) saves his skin and shows himself to be the master of the *arte di arrangiarsi* (the art of getting by). Home, *casa*, traditionally viewed in Italian culture as an ultimate value, is shown by Comencini to be subordinate to other ethical values, some of which involve self-sacrifice and a commitment to the welfare of others. Comencini ends *Everbody Home!* on a weak and overly comfortable note, rejecting Monicelli's more ambivalent and profound conclusions: after witnessing the death of a close friend, Innocenzi experiences a conversion, grasps a weapon, and as martial music is heard on the sound track, he joins the Partisans; he is now content to take orders from the simple workers who battle for Italy's national redemption. Though his abrupt change of mind is contrived, the portrayal of his odyssey from indifference to commitment is not atypical of the experience of thousands of Italians during the armistice, and the film provides a trenchant, though flawed, critique of a way of life sanctified by Italian cultural values.

Pietro Germi's vignettes of Sicilian social customs in *Divorce, Italian Style* (*Divorzio all'italiana*, 1961) and *Seduced and Abandoned* (*Sedotta e abbandonata*, 1964) dissect the senseless and unwritten codes of behavior governing relationships between the sexes in that male-dominated, insular culture. The first film, which was produced before Italy's legal system admitted civil divorces, chronicles the comic attempts of a decadent Sicilian nobleman, Ferdinando Cefalu (Marcello Mastroianni)—Fefé to his friends—to divorce his wife Rosalia (Daniela Rocca); in order to marry Angela (Stefania Sandrelli), the cousin he loves, he must find an ingenious means of driving his wife to commit an act of infidelity so that he can murder her, thereby receiving a light sentence for what Sicilian society considers a necessary "crime of honor." Thus, Germi's plot—and that of most Italian films dealing with social customs—may be described as the *reductio ad absurdum* type, wherein a "social question is magnified, reducing the action to chaos and the social question to absurdity."[5] But *Divorce, Italian Style* is no simple commercial comedy of regional manners. Germi's narrative employs a rather complex structure to develop its storyline. From an opening scene picturing Fefé's return home after serving a brief prison sentence, we flash back to receive his version of how he actually obtained his peculiarly Italian "divorce." A narrative voice-over provides commentary on the action. Fefé himself offers his own biased account of the chronological events leading to his killing of Rosalia, but the director inserts into his monologue a number of imaginary scenes embodying his fantastic murder plots (Rosalia is variously blasted into space, buried in quicksand, stabbed and made into soap, and shot in a public square by a Mafia assassin). Even more effective in its ironic impact is the voice of Fefé's lawyer as Fefé imagines it during his future trial; his summation before the court is humorously juxtaposed to the objective account of events rendered by Germi's camera to underscore the absurdity of Fefé's reliance upon a code of honor to justify a premeditated murder. The disparity between these various narrative perspectives forces the spectator into a viewpoint highly critical of Sicilian life.

Germi also manages to recreate the oppressive atmosphere of the small Sicilian village in which the action is unfolded by a camera moving with masterful rapidity through endless groups of staring, leering townspeople. Peer pressure, voyeurism, and repressed sexuality seem to constitute the basis of Germi's vision of Sicily: men aspire to seduce the women of the town, yet ridicule their friends who become cuckolds; people incessantly watch each other through windows or doors, from balconies and opera boxes, and in the streets; fathers subject their daughters to humiliating physical examinations by midwives to certify their purity; anonymous letters containing accusations of infidelities and betrayals circulate so frequently that they occupy the entire post-office staff. Nor are the women superior to their mates:

Pietro Germi's *Divorce, Italian Style* (1961). Fefé (Marcello Mastroianni)
lures his wife Rosalia (Daniela Rocca) into committing adultery with her
former lover (Leopoldo Trieste).
(Photo courtesy of the Museum of Modern Art)

they accept the dominant sexist views on morality, consider adul-
teresses whores, and seek to avenge their offended honor with violence—often more effectively than do the men. And it is in the detailed
description of Sicilian mannerisms that Germi utilizes a time-honored
comic-film plot, that which Gerald Mast has defined as "riffing" or
"improvised and anomalous gaggery." Germi is a master at running
off a series of gags revolving around the central theme—an "Italian"
divorce. Typical of this technique is his description of Fefé's plot to
capture his wife *in flagrante* with a lover: we first witness his purchase
of a tape recorder, then his fumbling attempts to plant microphones
in the living room, all of which terminate in his failure to capture the

lovers' plans to elope because the machine runs out of tape. He attends a showing of Fellini's *La Dolce Vita*, giving his wife time to compromise herself, but when he confidently returns to murder her in her lover's arms, he discovers that their plan was to elope. Naturally, he misses the train that carries them away. And when he finally discovers their whereabouts and goes to murder them, the wife of Rosalia's lover beats him to the location and kills her adulterous husband first! Rarely has a director been blessed with better performances: Mastroianni's dark sunglasses, cigarette holder, slicked-down hair, and nervous sucking of his lips set a pattern for the comic portrayal of the Sicilian male that was to be repeated over and over in later films (most especially by Giancarlo Giannini in works by Lina Wertmüller).

Although less successful commercially, *Seduced and Abandoned* broadens the critique of Italian divorce legislation to include a wider range of sexual relationships and Sicilian customs. In the process, this film presents a larger number of more developed comic types: the frustrated Northern policeman, who stares at a map of Italy, remarking sadly "That's better" as he covers Sicily with his hand, and wonders if an atomic explosion would improve matters on the island; the poverty-stricken Sicilian aristocrat (Leopoldo Trieste) who is provided by his prospective father-in-law with the false teeth he cannot afford in order to persuade him to marry his daughter Matilde; Vicenzo Ascalone, the stern patriarch and father of Agnese and Matilde (Saro Urzì), more concerned over his honor than his own life or their happiness; Agnese's suitor, Peppino (Aldo Puglisi), who seduces her and then declines to marry her because she is no longer pure, and who eventually abducts her to force her to marry him, with the tacit cooperation of both the police and Agnese's parents; finally the courageous Agnese herself (Stefania Sandrelli), who dares to break the traditional code of *omertà* when she charges Peppino with seducing her, thus bringing down upon her and her family (rather than upon Peppino) the disapproval of the entire neighborhood. Individual rebellion proves useless, however, and the inflexible Sicilian moral code ultimately forces Agnese to marry Peppino against her will, drives Matilde into a convent, breaks her mother's heart, and indirectly leads to her father's death. *Seduced and Abandoned* is thus a grotesque comic *tour de force*, combining the sharp delineation of character typical of the Italian comic film with interesting stylistic effects. Germi frequently employs a dramatic zoom lens to underscore the oppressive peer pressure of Sicilian morality upon Agnese and her family, while a wide-angle lens distorts horribly the faces of these jeering people. In this manner, the director forces the spectator to experience the fierce glances of the townspeople in Agnese's direction. A number of subjective and imaginary images from Agnese's perspective (a technique used to perfection in *Divorce, Italian Style*), as well as a hand-held camera capturing her desperate flight from her neighbors, provide the exact stylistic counterpart for Agnese's emotions as the poor girl is hounded in the town's main square. *Seduced and Abandoned*'s chilling vision of how traditional social values can destroy an individual, especially a woman with a mind of her own, is tempered only by brief moments of undeniable comic relief.

Sicilian sexual mores also preoccupy Mauro Bolognini in his *Bell'Antonio* (*Il bell'Antonio*, 1960), a film based upon the excellent novel by Vitaliano Brancati.[6] Here, Mastroianni is cast in a role somewhat unusual for an actor who had by this time become the prototype of the "Latin lover": Antonio is an extremely handsome man who functions sexually only with prostitutes, and is impotent with women he really loves. Brancati's novel linked *gallismo*, or the Don Giovanni complex characteristic of Southern Italian males, to a Fascist mentality, and Bolognini is faithful to the spirit of his source: Antonio's father, who claims he was made the Fascist *federale* of Catania because he once managed to sleep with nine women, dies in a brothel after he has gone there to prove to the entire town that his son's predicament does not derive from genetic causes. And yet, his machismo is undercut by his wife, who confesses to Antonio's unhappy wife Barbara (Claudia Cardinale) that her husband failed to sleep with her for two entire years after their wedding. As in *Seduced and Abandoned*, personal feelings and emotions must always be sacrificed to public mores and family honor: Antonio's family successfully conceals the truth of his condition by arranging his marriage to their maid who has been impregnated by Antonio's best friend, and they proudly display her condition from their front balcony. This grotesque perversion of the authentic relationship between men and women concludes with a hauntingly moving final close-up of a speechless Antonio, reflected in a mirror, as his friend Edoardo, the natural father of the child he must acknowledge as his own to win society's approval, congratulates him on the "normality" he will enjoy in the future. Besides losing the woman he loves, Antonio has to suffer a loss in social status when he marries beneath him.

The problematic nature of normality and conformity in society, gained at great personal expense by Bolognini's Antonio, is the subject of a number of major comic films by Risi, Lattuada, and Wertmüller. Risi's *The Easy Life* (*Il sorpasso*, 1962) employs a loose, picaresque narrative structure—an automobile drive between Rome and Viareggio—to explore changing Italian values during the brief postwar boom years. Juxtaposing two character types—Bruno (Vittorio Gassman), the superficial extravert obsessed with his car, the symbol of Italy's belated entry into a consumer economy, and Roberto (Jean-Louis Trintignant), a pensive, introverted intellectual—Risi follows the pair in what has accurately been called an Italian equivalent to *Easy Rider*. The film abruptly ends with an automobile crash that leaves Roberto dead. Disaster lurks beneath the surface of the newly found Italian prosperity represented by the automobile. Another excellent comedy by Risi, *The Monsters* (*I mostri*, 1963), is a film composed of twenty brief sketches employing the versatile talents of both Gassman and Ugo Tognazzi. In it, Risi moves from the merely comic to the grotesque, revealing the sure hand of a master caricaturist. By unveiling to the spectator such a wide range of easily recognizable Italian types—the rabid soccer fan, the corrupt deputy in Parliament, the cuckolded husband glued to the television set while his wife betrays him in their own bedroom, and numerous others—Risi draws a rogues' gallery of moral monsters whom he sees running amuck in Italian society, driven by cynicism and self-interest and guided by no other consideration than the immediate gratification of infantile desires. Here, the "norm" has been completely overturned, as abnormality— in the shape of Risi's grotesque caricatures—becomes the rule. Lattuada's excellent *Mafioso* (*Mafioso*, 1962) examines Sicilian emigration in the context of rapid social change: Alberto Sordi portrays a

Sicilian transferred to Milan, where he has become a normal part of a modern industrial community. His complacent normality is shaken during a visit to his native island when he is forced by the Mafia to travel to America, commit a murder, and then return to his family and job in Milan as if nothing had happened. Not unlike Germi's Sicilian comedies, Lattuada's film analyzes the clash between modern customs and a more ancient code of conduct that resists and survives in an era of transition. Lattuada's talents were also skillfully employed during this period in a more traditional comic vein with a filmed version of the classic Renaissance play, *The Mandrake Root* (*La mandragola*, 1965) by Niccolò Machiavelli. Totò plays the role of the rascally priest, Friar Timoteo, and this film must be considered an example of the older comic tradition associated with his previous performances rather than as a product typical of the *commedia all'italiana* that evolved in this decade.

The malaise underlying the sudden prosperity of this decade which the best comic directors described and explored is satirized with skill by Lina Wertmüller in her first feature-length film, *The Lizards* (*I basilischi*, 1963), the title referring to what Wertmüller describes as "the reactionary apathy of some zones of southern Italy in analogy with the typical immobility of lizards in the sun."[7] Unfairly considered by some critics as a mere remake of Fellini's *I Vitelloni*, *The Lizards* offers a political interpretation of Italian provincial life which Fellini's earlier film only implies. We see signs of overt class conflict between landowners, ex-Fascists, and laborers, and the Fellinian juxtaposition of town and province now becomes an economic choice rather than a poetic metaphor for an individual's search for maturity. Wertmüller's vision of the Italian hinterlands is thus much darker: while Fellini's Moraldo eventually leaves his *vitelloni* friends and moved on to Rome for presumably a richer and fuller life, Wertmüller's Antonio is forced to return home from Rome after an unsuccessful attempt to shake his provincial roots. Wertmüller's comic technique is clearly indebted to Fellini's example, as it will continue to be in her later and more popular works: her opening sequences picturing the entire town, including the members of the local Communist Party, asleep in the afternoon like the lizards her title suggests, might easily have been lifted from an anthology of Fellini's early films. Yet, major shifts in perspective distinguish Wertmüller in this first work. Most importantly, the narrative voice is provided by a woman, and the critique of this provincial and reptilian world reflects a feminine, if not a feminist, point of view. The strongest characters in the film are women. The viewer remembers most vividly the outlandishly dressed female who appears in a sportscar with a movie camera and who insults the local ex-Fascist landowners (perhaps Wertmüller's comic view of herself); the wealthy widow; or the female physician whose parents were simple day laborers. Even the old woman who after five years of widow's weeds and mourning for her husband abruptly and shockingly commits suicide may be seen in a positive light, for her desperate act rejects traditional values deeply rooted in Southern culture. These strongly delineated female figures are in sharp contrast with the closing image of the male protagonists playing cards and talking endlessly to no purpose. *The Lizards* announces the arrival of a fresh comic talent, one with a woman's point of view.

Once denigrated as merely a commerical genre unworthy of serious critical study, the *commedia all'italiana* nevertheless provided the film industry with works of undeniable artistic quality that also generated a large percentage of its profits. Moreover, it is clear today that the social criticism in such works as *The Great War*, *Seduced and Abandoned*, and *The Lizards* as well as the relatively honest portrayals of Italian daily life they contained, profoundly influenced Italian culture itself. As Monicelli notes, such comic works helped to modify the mentality of the average Italian and forced a greater awareness of the rapid changes taking place in the nation and of the historical burden which lay so heavily upon it. They attacked age-old prejudices and customs and questioned the functioning of ruling elites and established institutions, uncovering social problems demanding attention, thus opening up Italian culture to a wider range of social and political alternatives.[8] Talented directors were fortunate in possessing comic actors of great genius, whose personal mannerisms and very faces created a recognizably Italian film type as representative of postwar Italy as the regional figures of the *commedia dell'arte* had once been of an Italy long since disappeared. The range of figures portrayed by such actors as Sordi, Gassman, and Mastroianni, to mention only the most successful, subjected common Italian defects—fawning respect for established authority, vilification of subordinates, sexual obsessions, cynicism, intellectual shallowness, skepticism, and emotional immaturity—to pitiless scrutiny.[9] Since the entire human race exhibits these same faults in some measure, these actors were recognized by audiences around the world as not only Italian "types" but as the embodiment of universal comic characteristics as well. Perhaps no other nation's popular culture so consistently dared to display its worst features and to subject them to such hearty laughter. It was ultimately an act of artistic courage, as well as sound business practice, to make such films, and they deserve an honored place in Italian film history alongside the neorealist classics, which at one time had functioned as the cutting edge of progressive thinking in Italian popular culture.

A number of genres evolved during this period, some closely linked to the *commedia all'italiana* and most directed at the same general, middlebrow audience that the film comedy attracted. Others were aimed at an even more popular public. By this time, the Italian film market had become the largest in Europe and was divided into two major sectors. Major urban centers boasted a limited number of exclusive movie theaters (*prima visione*) which premiered the newest works (both Italian and imports) and catered to an educated, relatively well-to-do public. The more numerous secondary theaters (*seconda visione*), which charged as little as one third the admission price required in *prima visione* houses, attracted a predominately working-class audience and usually programmed older films or those of artistically inferior quality and limited cultural significance. Since *seconda visione* theaters featured the same kinds of films that began to appear on Italian television (both the channels of the RAI, the state-owned network, as well as the private stations which sprang up in the 1970s), television would eventually compete most directly with the *seconda visione* network. The social distinctions between first-run American theaters in urban areas or prosperous shopping centers, on the one hand, and the drive-in theater or the older urban theater in a zone of inner-city decay, on the other, may give some sense of this bifurcation of distribution in Italy, even though the sociological and cultural implications of these unique economic structures are quite different.[10]

Directly related to the comedy's appeal was the emergence of the so-called episode film, the origins of which can be traced back to earlier works, such as *Love in the City*, Antonioni's *The Vanquished*, or even to Risi's *The Monsters*. This genre became fashionable with the appearance of *Boccaccio '70* (*Boccaccio '70*, 1962), a work produced by Carlo Ponti whose express purpose was to exploit recent box-office hits by four different directors and some of their stars: Fellini and Anita Ekberg from *La Dolce Vita*; De Sica and Sophia Loren from *Two Women* (*La ciociara*, 1960); Mario Monicelli of *The Great War*; and Luchino Visconti after *Rocco and His Brothers* (*Rocco e i suoi fratelli*, 1960). Producers encouraged such works, done in sections by different directors and combining box-office attractions that would normally be employed in three or four separate films, because of their relatively low cost and their large short-term profit potential. The vogue of the episode film thus clearly reflects the domination of economic imperatives over artistic ones. Some 50 such films appeared between 1961 and 1969, and almost every major director participated in such commercial ventures, sometimes with remarkable success.[11]

Between 1957 and 1964, we also witness the flowering of the so-called "neomythological" or *peplum* film,[12] set vaguely in classical antiquity or in a distant but indeterminate past time and populated by buxom and inarticulate damsels in distress as well as by heroic musclemen protagonists, including Maciste from the silent film era, Ulysses, Ursus, Hercules, and Samson, to mention only the most popular. More than 170 films, approximately 10% of Italian film production between 1957 and 1964, belong to this genre. Aimed primarily at audiences in the *seconda visione* circuit and the Third World but eventually reaching even American television screens on the late shows, such works mixed historical periods and figures with reckless abandon: Maciste, originally a figure from the Carthaginian Wars, appears at the court of the Russian Czars, encounters Ghengis Khan, and confronts Zorro; audiences seemed to express little surprise when they witnessed Samson in the Kingdom of the Incas. Occasionally, and for the same reasons that moved producers to finance episodic comic films, several popular heroes were combined in a single film, matching wits (what little they possessed) and brawn. As the neomythological film began to fade in popularity, another and more important genre began to take its place, the so-called spaghetti Western, which reached its most complete artistic expression in the works of Sergio Leone (1929–89). The Western eventually expanded its generic boundaries to encompass political and comic themes as well as those topics associated with the Hollywood Western. More than three hundred such works appeared between 1964 and 1972, with 66 produced in the year 1967 alone. These Italian Westerns captured a wide popular audience, invaded the *prima visione* circuit, and changed the very nature of the American Western as well. The neomythological film was the ancestor of another popular genre with silent musclemen: the kung-fu martial arts film.

The *peplum*, the Western, and the martial arts type, closely related genres characterized by strong, antiintellectual heroes and violent action, may also be linked to films in the spy genre, a relatively minor but popular group of films in imitation of the James Bond series with its handsome and indestructible Agent 007: between 1965 and 1967, some 50 Italian spy adventures were made, most of which were marked less by any artistic distinction or pretension than by the many ingenious numeric combinations they devised for their various imitations of Sean Connery's code number. Erotic themes, often present in the *peplum* or spy film but relatively less important to the spaghetti Western, become central to the so-called sexy genre, which arose from pseudo-documentary vignettes of nightclubs, nightlife, and international sexual behavior. Such films relied on voyeuristic audiences from a culture steeped in sexual restrictions. The word "sexy" entered the Italian vocabulary with such films as Alessandro Blasetti's *Europe By Night* (*Europa di notte*, 1959)—a documentary visit to risqué nightspots, much of which was actually shot inside a studio—and *Mondo Cane* (*Mondo cane*, 1962) by Gualtiero Jacopetti (1919-   )— a series of titillating and grotesque vignettes laying bare, as it were, unusual sexual practices and customs from around the globe. And while such films merit only brief mention here, their popularity attests to profound changes in the Italian sexual customs that often find more compelling artistic expression in the film comedy. Obviously sensational films made by major directors who dealt more profoundly with sexuality quite often encountered vigorous opposition, censorship, and even confiscation. The "sexy" film heralded the imminent arrival of other, apparently now permanent developments in Italian popular culture: magazines containing softcore and hardcore pornography; special film theaters for pornography (the "luce rossa" or "red light" cinemas); and eventually, with the rise of private television stations that would challenge the state-operated television's monopoly in the 1970s, even the screening of soft and hardcore pornography on late shows.

The existence of faddish film genres created by numerous and rapid imitations of a single and often quite excellent pioneering work, imitations which were generally of lesser quality and which disappeared after the public's interest in or patience with a particular theme had diminished, is a typical characteristic of Italian cinematic culture. It is a function of the particular economic structure of its industry and reflects attempts by producers understandably greedy to reap quick and easy profits without incurring large financial risks. Such a widespread phenomenon also weakened any development of a consistent industrial infrastructure capable of delivering a predictable product for a stable market. And thus, even in a period of great prosperity, the Italian film industry remained an essentially risky, entrepreneurial operation.

It was left for Roberto Rossellini, so seminal a force in the immediate postwar period, to signal renewed attention to Italy's neorealist heritage. With the plot of *General Della Rovere*, we seem to have returned to the melodramatic atmosphere of *Rome, Open City* and its struggle between Partisans, Fascists, and Nazis. An Italian confidence man named Bardone (Vittorio De Sica) is arrested by a German colonel just before an Italian Resistance leader, General Della Rovere, is killed; Colonel Müller (Hannes Messemer) conceals the news of the general's death, hoping in this way to uncover the identity of his Partisan contact, a man named Fabrizio whom Müller unknowingly has in his prison under an assumed name; Müller decides to offer Bardone a choice between impersonating the dead general or facing execution. Rossellini's view of the war had changed considerably since 1945; it was now tinged with an ironic awareness that the sacrifices made during wartime had not led to the springtime his characters dreamed of in *Rome, Open City*. Moreover, following the intervening decades and postwar reconstruction, Rossellini no longer had access to readymade, authentic "sets" composed of wartime buildings and their ruins, the backdrop that gave the texture of his war trilogy its celebrated documentary tone. In fact, when documentary footage of Allied bombing raids is inserted into the fictional narrative of *General Della Rovere*, it stands out so sharply from the rest of the work, which is shot inside studios designed to recreate the atmosphere of Genoa in 1943, that it draws our attention to one of the film's major themes, the contrast of reality and illusion. The implicit comparison between *General Della Rovere* and the earlier war trilogy that Rossellini certainly intends the viewer to make thus assists the director's artistic objectives.

The film's first half provides a sketch of Bardone and introduces the theme of deception and illusion. Aided by Vittorio De Sica's brilliant performance as the swindler, Rossellini concentrates less upon the political implications of the Partisan struggle here than upon the strange transformation in Bardone's character which takes place as the role he performs begins to reshape his personality. First, Bardone calms Italian prisoners during an air raid with an authoritative command; next, he suffers torture with them; soon, he is caught up in the gripping personal dramas of the real general, as he receives letters from his wife and interacts with his fellow prisoners under the constant threat of execution. Gradually, Bardone is transformed from a shallow confidence man into an admirable figure worthy of the role he impersonates: his *persona* eventually dominates his character, and he ultimately becomes the man he only initially pretends to be. Declaring that dying for a just cause is preferable to dying for no cause at all, Bardone refuses to reveal Fabrizio's identity to the Germans when he does discover it and decides to face death with the other patriots. His execution represents his ultimate confidence game, his final and most impressive swindle. And with this portrait of a likable petty criminal who assumes a courageous role, Rossellini presents a brand of heroism

Roberto Rossellini's *General Della Rovere* (1959). Colonel Müller (Hannes Messemer) meets Bardone (Vittorio De Sica), the confidence man. (Photo courtesy of the Centro Sperimentale Cinematografico, Rome)

quite different from that which evolves from the Manichaean struggle between good and evil in *Rome, Open City*. The political achievements of the Resistance are implicitly called into question by such ambivalence: only the act of personal sacrifice Bardone makes seems to have any meaning in Rossellini's reinterpretation of his cinematic origins; the cause for which Bardone dies never really engages our attention. Like the most skillfully drawn figures from the period's comic films, Bardone is a problematic character, an ambivalent antihero more suitable to the uncertainties of a new age than to the immediate postwar period when black-and-white moral choices seemed possible.

Rossellini's contributions during this decade were not limited to this ironic recreation of the Partisan struggle in *General Della Rovere*, or in a subsequent and less interesting film on the Resistance in the following year, *It Was Night in Rome* (*Era notte a Roma*, 1960). Abandoning commercial filmmaking in 1963, he directed a long series of historical documentaries for television, thus becoming the first major Italian artist to work exclusively for an extended period in this relatively novel medium. Before his eventual return to commercial cinema with *Year One* (*Anno uno*, 1974)—a biography of Alcide De Gasperi, the leader of the Christian Democratic Party—and his last film, *The Messiah* (*Il Messia*, 1976), Rossellini completed nine television documentaries, the most important of which was for French television, *The Rise to Power of Louis XIV* (*La Prise de Pouvoir par Louis XIV*, 1966).[13] Here again, Rossellini seems to have returned to one important element from his war trilogy, the dispassionate and documentarylike technique which collects and presents historical facts. But just as *Paisan* proved to be an extremely personal interpretation of the Allied invasion of Italy rather than an historically accurate account of it, so, too, Rossellini's superficially objective portrait of Louis XIV concerns itself primarily with the social masks disguising the exercise of political power rather than with a history of seventeenth-century France. In this respect, *The Rise to Power of Louis XIV* continues to explore the interrelationships between reality and appearance which constituted the dominant theme of *General Della Rovere*.

Louis's portrait emerges from Rossellini's understated juxtaposition of the formalized rituals at court with a number of privileged views of the young monarch's private life. Louis manipulates power by skillfully playing a number of roles, a point Rossellini makes as his documentary opens: when the dying Cardinal Mazarin receives the sovereign whom he has served as regent for many years, he allows Louis to enter his chambers only after he dons rouge and copious makeup. One consummate actor is leaving the political stage to make way for another. Kingship requires symbolic, ritualistic gestures: Louis mumbles his prayers only because respect for religion is expected of his role; his wife claps her hands after Louis leaves her bedroom, signifying publicly that her husband has fulfilled his marital duties; he refuses the offer of a rich legacy from Mazarin, fearing to reveal that the King owes anything to a commoner, while he accepts the same sixteen million francs when he is assured that its source will remain a secret.

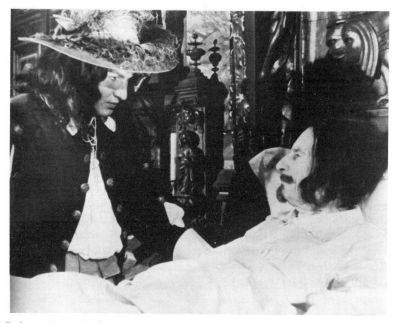

Roberto Rossellini's *The Rise to Power of Louis XIV* (1966). Louis XIV (Jean-Marie Patte) speaks with Cardinal Mazarin (Aldo Silvagni) on his deathbed. (Photo courtesy of the Museum of Modern Art)

Nowhere is Rossellini's preoccupation with the interplay of illusion and reality more striking than in the sequences dealing with Louis's clothes. The Sun King embraces the Machiavellian dictum that men are guided by appearances rather than by the nature of things (a belief he appropriately voices while being fitted by his tailor), and he therefore requires extravagant costumes and elegant wigs in his presence at court, forcing his noblemen to squander their fortunes (and thus their potential to oppose his policies) and to rely on his largesse. Rossellini underlines this same theme in his treatment of courtly meals as Louis's regal dining transforms daily nourishment into a grandiose religious ritual. While Louis eats alone and with his hands on a raised platform, Rossellini's slow zoom onto his figure moves to a lengthy, reverse tracking shot which reveals dozens of courtiers, all dressed in the outlandish costumes they themselves consider ridiculous, arranged in a reverent audience as if they were standing before a cathedral altar.

For Rossellini, Louis has seized power by transforming life into a spectacle, but in the process he has assumed a role essentially devoid of intellectual or moral substance. This is evident from the final, eloquent sequence of the film. Alone at last, Louis slowly removes the many pieces of his elaborate costume, revealing himself to be a diminutive, rather pathetic individual without them; in essence, a man playing a role not unlike that of the confidence man in *General Della Rovere*. And even though the consequences of Louis's role-playing are of more moment than Bardone's masquerade, there is little doubt that in Rossellini's portraits of these two consummate swindlers, he prefers Bardone's performance to Louis's. Each film thus employs elements found in Rossellini's earlier neorealist classics—*General Della Rovere* uses a plot and the historical situation of the war triology, while *The Rise to Power of Louis XIV* continues the use of nonprofessionals and a semidocumentary treatment of subject matter. Yet, Rossellini's cinematic style has clearly advanced beyond neorealism precisely by deepening and broadening ideas which were only implicit in his earlier works. In exploiting this rich heritage as a jumping-off place for works more attractive to a different generation, Rossellini was to set the example for a number of young and highly talented directors, all of whom owed a great debt to his films.

Most of the new directors who rose to prominence in this period continued the interest in current Italian social and political problems typical of neorealism. In some cases, their films would employ a documentary or semidocumentary style with nonprofessional actors, recalling similar works of the previous neorealist generation. Other directors, while profoundly influenced by neorealist themes or style, were nevertheless closer in spirit to their contemporaries of the French New Wave. Intellectuals rather than artisans, they had come to the cinema through a self-conscious artistic choice, often beginning their apprenticeship in film clubs and sometimes attending the Centro Sperimentale as students; many served as assistants to neorealist directors or worked on their scripts.

Bandits of Orgosolo (*Banditi a Orgosolo*, 1961) by Vittorio De Seta (1923–) seems cut from the same cloth as Visconti's *The Earth Trembles*: nonprofessional Sardinian shepherds enact a drama set in their own timeless society, as De Seta contrasts their primitive codes of behavior to modern Italian culture. *Bandits*, like *The Earth Trembles*, demonstrates how economic conditions dictate social behavior, forcing honest men to embrace desperate measures for their survival. The documentary style, simple plot, and the stark, unsentimental narrative all recall neorealist antecedents. Wrongly implicated in the theft of some livestock by the *carabinieri* (always portrayed as an occupation force sent by a distant colonial government from the mainland), an inarticulate but honest shepherd is forced to flee into the hills with his younger brother and their flock; when the animals all perish during their flight, he is forced to become a bandit in earnest, making a living by stealing from other men as poor as he. De Seta's successful portrayal of this primitive Sardinian society moves us precisely because it avoids rhetorical overstatement or patronizing attitudes toward his protagonists; his narrative voice-over intrudes as infrequently as possible, leaving his nonprofessional actors to express themselves more by their slightly stiff gestures than by their dialogue (which has been dubbed from their original dialect into standard Italian). The result is a world not unlike that of De Sica's *The Bicycle Thief*, where theft produces thieves, but De Seta has shorn his plot of anything but the most elemental of narrative techniques, emotions, and plots.

Salvatore Giuliano (*Salvatore Giuliano*, 1962) by Francesco Rosi (1922–) owes little to Visconti's early style, even though Rosi assisted Visconti on *The Earth Trembles* and set his first important work in Sicily. Rosi also avoids the extemely uncomplicated plot De Seta employs, along with the use of nonprofessionals, moving from the simple and evocative presentation of social and economic conditions to a more analytic posture. As he states, it was his aim to effect "not a *documentary* way of making films but a *documented* way."[14] Building upon historical facts the veracity of which could not be denied even by opponents of the leftist political views Rosi holds, the director rejects either a noncommital and documentary presentation of facts, on the one hand, or completely fictionalized narrative on the other.

As he puts it, "you cannot *invent*, in my opinion, but you can *interpret*. There is a big difference . . . this is the important thing for me, the *interpretation* of the facts."[15] Cinema, in Rosi's view, should thus provide an *inchiesta* or investigation into the links between past events and the reality of the present, and such politically oriented works provide a perfect intellectual vehicle for ideological expression in sharp disagreement with official governmental policies or traditional cultural values.

Salvatore Giuliano was a Sicilian bandit who played a brief but violent role in the Sicilian independence movement immediately following World War II. He then turned to political terrorism with an attack upon a group of leftists demonstrating on May Day of 1947, killing eleven people and wounding twenty-seven at Portella della Ginestra. After the 1948 elections produced a Christian Democratic victory, Giuliano returned to regular criminal activities until, according to official police accounts, he was killed by *carabinieri* in 1950. Subsequently, Giuliano's lieutenant, Gaspare Pisciotta, claimed in court that he and not the police had killed Giuliano. Pisciotta himself was mysteriously killed in prison in 1954, and it became clear the official version of Giuliano's death was questionable and that the police had been assisted by members of the Mafia in eliminating a man who had become embarrassing to everyone. In 1960 Benedetto Minasola, the Mafia intermediary between the underworld and the police, was himself murdered.

Rosi's presentation of these "facts" within what seems to be a documentary framework makes it clear that facts do not explain themselves; indeed, they are often only the superficial aspects of a far darker political reality hidden beneath the surface. The figure of Giuliano hardly interests Rosi—he rarely speaks, is shown primarily from distant long shots dressed in a white trench coat surrounded by men in black, and assumes an importance on the screen only in death. Indeed, the most important scene of the film is that which opens the work: an overhead shot of a dead body (Giuliano's) in a courtyard. Here is an indisputable "fact," but Rosi implies that by itself, this fact means nothing. And so Rosi immediately moves to a series of ingenious flashbacks to initiate his interpretation of the historical data. Re-

Francesco Rosi's *Salvatore Giuliano* (1962). An overhead shot of the body of the dead bandit begins the director's documentary study of his career. (Photo courtesy of the Museum of Modern Art)

spect for chronology is completely abandoned, as the period Rosi treats (1945–60) unfolds by a series of disorienting leaps back and forth, from one event to another, woven together not so much to tell a story as to present a legal brief against the political establishment and the underworld figures who manipulate Giuliano to their advantage and then eliminate him when he is no longer of any use. These flashbacks serve not to reveal interior states of mind (as in a work by Germi or Fellini) but to reflect the director's own attempts to reach a satisfactory explanation of why these seemingly disconnected events occurred. Rosi's investigation into the Byzantine interconnections between bandits, the Mafia, the Allied occupation forces, and politicians concludes with a final shot of the murdered Mafia go-between, lying in the same position as Giuliano at the film's opening, as if to conclude that the past corruption is not merely history but is an ever-present aspect of Sicilian life at the time the film was completed. *Salvatore Giuliano* reflects what Rosi has termed a second phase of neorealism, transcending its initial postwar attempt to record reality or to provide an objective witness to social events, and moving gradually toward a critical realism with overt ideological intentions. The decidedly antiestablishment stance Rosi takes in this work was to be continued in *Hands Over the City* (*Le mani sulla città*, 1963), another film of note, which denounces speculation in the building industry and the political corruption which permits it. Both works would be the first of many ideological attacks upon Italy's social system, and their appeal gave rise to a new genre, the so-called "political" film of the late 1960s and 1970s, many of which incorporated Rosi's investigative techniques.

The film of this decade most indebted to neorealist examples, as well as to Rosi's documentary investigations, is *The Battle of Algiers* (*La battaglia di Algeri*, 1966) by Gillo Pontecorvo (1919–   ).[16] Both Rosi and Pontecorvo employed the same writer to produce their screenplays (Franco Solinas). And Pontecorvo's link to neorealism is quite unique: in his own words, while working in Paris as a journalist, he happened to see Rossellini's *Paisan* and was so moved by the experience that he left his job, bought a camera, and began making documentaries, an experience which left a profound influence upon his cinematic style. As Pontecorvo has stated, the ideal director should be three-quarters Rossellini and one-quarter Eisenstein.[17] And, indeed, Pontecorvo's film combines many of the techniques of his Italian model with some of the ideological theories of the Russian master. *The Battle of Algiers* represents another step in the move toward an ideologically oriented cinema in Italy during this period: made with the encouragement of an Algerian producer, Yacef Saadi, who had once been the military commander of the zone of Algiers for the National Liberation Front during the period treated in the film, the film presents a case history of Third World revolution in such vivid and polemical terms that it remained banned from French screens until 1971, even after it had garnered critical acclaim and an award at the Venice Film Festival in 1966.

Pontecorvo's complex plot, which distorts the normal chronology of the events he presents, shows a debt to Rosi and reflects the general move away from continuous narrative time that characterizes many of the greatest films of this decade. The film opens in 1957, as an Arab prisoner has been tortured into revealing to Colonel Mathieu and his paratroops the location of the rebels' last leader, Ali la Pointe. Just before his place of concealment is blown up, Pontecorvo flashes back to 1954 to trace the formation of this Arab revolutionary, the arrival of French paratroops, and the outbreak of a general strike which ends in defeat for the insurgents. Most of the film's action takes place between 1954 and 1957. Finally, Pontecorvo returns to 1957, when Ali la Pointe is killed and the rebellion is apparently destroyed. A brief coda to this central narrative flashes forward to 1960, where we witness massive anti-French demonstrations in the Casbah, after which an offscreen voice informs the viewer that the Algerian nation was born in 1962.

From a technical point of view, *The Battle of Algiers* richly rewards analysis. Pontecorvo's debt to Rossellini's war trilogy is everywhere in evidence: with the exception of an actor (Jean Martin) who plays the French military commander, the cast is all nonprofessional. While there is not a frame of newsreel footage in the work, Pontecorvo and his crew created an absolutely convincing reproduction of newsreel or television reportage through a variety of techniques, conveying to the viewer the actuality and the insistency of history unfolding before his very eyes. Highly mobile, hand-held Arriflex cameras with fast film stock shot in diffused light, as well as the use of a telephoto lens common in television news reporting, and voice-overs or informational titles superimposed over the image, give the work the authenticity of the six-o'clock news. By duplicating the negative of his film in the laboratory, Pontecorvo creates the same grainy, documentary texture characteristic of Rossellini's *Paisan*. A photography indebted to Italian neorealism is combined with editing more typical of the classical Russian cinema: in most cases, the narrative advances not by linking sequences together in a traditional, logical order but by juxtaposing images, sequences, sounds, and ideas.

Central to Pontecorvo's film is the contrast between the French

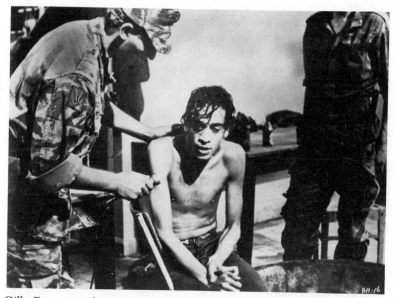

Gillo Pontecorvo's *The Battle of Algiers* (1966). Realistic torture scenes recall Rossellini's *Rome, Open City*.
(Photo from the author's private collection)

colonel and the Arab revolutionary, and the analysis of revolutionary
versus counter-revolutionary violence. Ali la Pointe is an illiterate,
unemployed, ex-draft dodger whose acquisition of a revolutionary
conciousness begins when he witnesses the execution by guillotine of
a fellow Algerian (underlined by Pontecorvo's dramatic zoom into
Ali's eyes to capture his reaction). Mathieu, on the other hand, is a
handsome, urbane, and highly intelligent professional soldier whose
knowledge of the dynamics of Marxist insurrections surpasses even
that of his opponents and who informs inquiring journalists that if
they insist upon keeping Algeria a part of France, then they must
accept the logical consequences of that decision (including torture).
Two logics are therefore set in sharp contrast, both of which spawn
violence and death. While much has been written about the choral

nature of Pontecorvo's film—implying that the Algerian people as a group constitute the real protagonist of the film—there is no doubt that much of the dramatic tension in the film is due to the contrast of two more traditional antagonists, and that the film succeeds precisely because Pontecorvo's ideological preferences do not cause him to picture the French as monsters.

The ambivalence of Pontecorvo's presentation of violence has aroused much criticism; one English critic complained that all of Pontecorvo's "dramatic irony and moral ambivalence is only a romantic humanist's sugaring of the pill for a liberal audience unwilling to stomach the hard facts of revolution."[18] The key sequence in this regard is one which portrays the planting of three bombs by three different Arab women (dressed as Europeans and passing undetected because of their light skins) in three places where only French civilian victims will be killed: a cafeteria where a baby licks an ice-cream cone; a milk bar, where teenagers are dancing to a tune ironically entitled "Until Tomorrow" (tomorrow will never come for them); and the Air France terminal. This massive bombing attack on French civilians was a response to a similar attack on Arab civilians in the Casbah led by the French Chief of Police. And, in both cases, as the Algerians and the French extract their dead from the rubble, Bach's *Mass in B-Minor* is heard on the soundtrack, lending the same tragic dignity to both images. Unlike the ideologues who criticize such scenes, Pontecorvo seems to be asserting that human suffering is always the same, that a bomb recognizes no innocent parties, and that only the verdict of history condemns one side and vindicates another. French bombs are worse than Arab bombs not because traditional morality condemns one and not the other but, rather, because a theory of history (Marxist and anticolonialist) demonstrates that French violence served a lost cause while Arab violence expressed a movement in the vanguard of history.

While Ermanno Olmi (1931-   ) began his career with documentary films, his cinematic style is more indebted to the neorealism of De Sica than of Rossellini or Visconti.[19] *The Sound of Trumpets* (*Il posto*, 1961) is a highly wrought work that examines the anguish and loneliness of a young man, Domenico, as he looks for his first job in

Milan. Olmi employs nonprofessional actors, and his photography and editing style—with its emphasis upon expressive deep-focus shots in office interiors reminiscent of *Umberto D.*, and his concentration upon moments of psychological importance in the protagonist's life where film time coincides with narrative time elapsed (Bazin's duration)— is far more complex than the relatively simple narrative plot of the film would indicate. Like De Sica, Olmi has a genius for expressively employing the simple and seemingly meaningless gestures, glances, and actions gathered from the daily routine of his rather insignificant characters. In depicting Domenico's aptitude test for the position (where giving an incorrect answer means nothing, since the job requires so little intelligence), and his medical examination (consisting of inane questions and meaningless exercises), and his introduction to the office in which he will serve first as an errand boy and later be promoted to clerk upon the death of one of the veterans there, Olmi manages to present a tragi-comical vision of modern labor that underlines its boring, mechanical, and tedious nature. Olmi's rather traditional narrative becomes more complex after introducing us to the clerks, for we cut to brief vignettes of their private lives, and it is here that some notion of the complexity of their personalities is revealed: the nearsighted clerk whose eventual death opens up a position for Domenico spends his spare time in bed writing a novel, hiding his late use of electricity from his avaricious landlady; the clerk who does nothing but cut cigarettes in half is worried over an inheritance; a man who combs his hair constantly is shown having an affair; another man who cleans his desk compulsively is an amateur opera singer; a woman who is often late to work has a ne'er-do-well son who steals money from her purse. The juxtaposition of these compulsive mannerisms at the office to the more spontaneous and natural behavior at home demonstrates the alienating effects of the workplace. And Olmi's vision of Domenico's future is also apparent when he pictures a pensioned clerk who still comes to the office because he is unable to eat lunch without the office bell that arouses his appetite. A brilliant sequence depicts a New Year's Eve office party: Domenico (and others without a date) are given bottles of wine and silly party hats; long shots of an almost empty dance hall produce a depressing sense of loneliness and alienation, and when the gaiety finally does begin (prompted not by spontaneous celebration but by professional revelers hired by the company), it is clear that the frenzied dancing and party costumes conceal but do not eliminate the unhappiness of many there present. An abrupt cut returns the viewer to the office, where an empty desk stands in mute testimony to the clerk-novelist's sudden demise. As each employee moves furtively to occupy a desk one spot further ahead in the office pecking order, and Domenico takes his place at the end of the row, the mechanical and repetitious noise of a duplicating machine grows louder and louder on the sound track as if it were a heart beat, while Olmi's camera holds a close-up on Domenico's vulnerable face for an inordinate length of time, then fades to black. Rarely has such an eloquent portrait of the anguish of daily labor been so successfully depicted on the screen, although Olmi's humor tends to soften the depressing effects. In a subsequent film, *The Fiancées* (*I fidanzati*, 1963), Olmi's narrative technique was to transcend the simple plot structure typical of his neorealist models and move toward a more modernist perspective, freely mixing events out of their normal chronological order in a looser plot structure, much as Rosi and Pontecorvo do.

Like Pontecorvo, Vittorio (1929–   ) and Paolo (1931–   ) Taviani came to the cinema through a chance encounter with Rossellini's *Paisan* when they were playing hooky from school one afternoon; after making documentaries and assisting a number of other directors, they produced their first feature-length film with Valentino Orsini (1926–   ), *A Man for the Killing* (*Un uomo da bruciare*, 1962). Featuring Gian Maria Volonté (1933–   ) in his first starring role, *A Man for the Killing* deals with the return of a political activist named Salvatore to his native Sicily after a prolonged absence from the battle waged by peasants struggling for rights to the lands they work. Salvatore imprudently confronts the local Mafia, urging the peasants not only to occupy the farmlands but also to plow and plant them. However, at a meeting of the peasants' league, Salvatore's policy of confrontation is rejected as too dangerous, and Salvatore is isolated from the political movement. Abandoning the now unprofitable agricultural sector, the Mafia turns to exploiting peasant day laborers in road con-

Ermanno Olmi's *The Sound of Trumpets* (1961). Domenico (Sandro Panzeri) must take his place at the back of the line in the pecking order of the office.
(Photo courtesy of the Museum of Modern Art)

struction work and hires Salvatore as a foreman, thinking to compromise him with a fourteen-hour working day for his men; Salvatore drives his men incessantly, but at the end of eight hours of work, he leaves the job and urges the men to do likewise. This continuous defiance of the Mafia results in his assassination, and the entire town participates in his funeral.[20]

The Tavianis have defined their first work as an act of love toward neorealism, but their affection reflects an ambivalent love-hate relationship, similar to that between father and son[21]. And nowhere is this ambivalence toward their cinematic heritage more apparent than in their treatment of Salvatore. Far removed from the ideological canons of socialist realism, Salvatore is an egotist, bent on exercising power at the head of the peasants even if they reject him and find his

leadership dangerous; intent upon becoming a martyr, he is the antithesis of the simple and pure popular hero of most neorealist films,
and is all in all a more complex and intriguing figure. Obviously somewhat out of touch with the peasants he presumes to lead, at one point
Salvatore addresses them in verse from an opera stage, and his gestures
and actions are comically melodramatic. On viewing a popular film,
the plot of which involves a sailor who must sail or be murdered by
a girl's lover and who eventually falls into a trap and is killed by a
knife-thrower in a variety show, Salvatore experiences a premonition
of his death at the hands of the Mafia. In a dream, his mother asks
him if he believes he is Jesus Christ; melodramatic music is then heard
on the sound track as if to affirm that this is indeed Salvatore's belief;
as he leaves his mother in the dream, he is surrounded by armed men.
About to die, he declaims a speech which parodies the famous "Farewell, mountains" speech of Lucia in Manzoni's classic novel, *The Be-
trothed*. At work the next day, his premonition proves to be true, but
his actual death occurs in a very brief and undramatic scene, set in
stark contrast to the staged and overly literary dream sequence which
reflects Salvatore's exaggerated sense of self-importance.

Irony, the Tavianis have declared, is a constant presence in their
films, expecially insofar as their favorite characters are concerned, for
it enables them to detach themselves from such figures and to remain
true to their own personal poetic vision.[22] Irony dominates not only
their presentation of Salvatore in *A Man for the Killing*, but also *The
Subversives* (*I sovversivi*, 1967), an interesting study of four Communist
Party members during several days before the funeral of Palmiro Togliatti (August 1964), the party's leader throughout the Fascist period,
the Resistance, and postwar reconstruction. Only this common historical event links these four lives, for the individuals never encounter
each other in the film. Rapid and sometimes disconcerting crosscutting
between four separate narratives, however, gradually reveals similar
personal dramas brought to resolution by the pressure of a single
event. Ermanno, a young middle-class intellectual, rejects his class
origins and dedicates his life to photography; Giulia, the wife of a
party official, abandons her hypocrisy and gives in to her Lesbian
tendencies; Ludovico, a director dying of an incurable illness, seeks

to complete a film on an aging Leonardo da Vinci, who abandons his art for direct communication with the masses; Ettore, a Venezuelan revolutionary in exile, breaks up a love affair to return home and take the place of a fallen comrade. Far from being dangerous subversives as the film's title ironically suggests, the four party members presented by the Tavianis are normal human beings with the same personal problems believers in other political ideologies possess. Perhaps Ettore comes closest to the directors' sentiments when he declares to his friends before his return home that utopia is the ultimate goal, but that revolution is not merely development and forward movement; it also entails periods of discontinuity and negation. *The Subversives* concentrates upon one such moment, and as a result the four *compagni* emerge as convincing human characters rather than mere reflections of an ideological position.

Perhaps the most interesting, and certainly the most unusual, young director to emerge during this period was Pier Paolo Pasolini (1922–1975), a poet, novelist, critic, and theorist, whose first experiences in the cinema included scriptwriting for Bolognini and Fellini.[23] Besides the heuristic encounter with Italian neorealism typical of his generation, Pasolini's works reflect a unique and idiosyncratic combination of Gramscian Marxism and linguistic theory. The *Prison Notebooks* of Antonio Gramsci (1891–1937) first appeared after the fall of Fascism. Italian intellectuals were attracted to Gramsci's ideas, considered revisionist when compared to orthodox Leninism or Stalinism, because they rejected a simple, causal relationship between economic substructure and cultural superstructure. Modifying the traditional Marxist view that economic conditions directly determine ideas, Gramsci offered his concept of cultural "hegemony": social classes exercise hegemony over other classes first through the private institutions of civil society (schools, churches, journals, films, books) rather than through those of political society, and they more often obtain this hegemony through reason and common consent than through force. In order for the Communist Party to become a ruling class, the working class it represented would first have to establish its legitimacy as a dominant group by winning cultural hegemony within Italian culture. Only then could the party move to a political victory within the in-

stitutions of political society. Because of the intellectual's crucial role
in this scheme, it is not surprising that young intellectuals such as
Pasolini were attracted to Gramsci's views. Moreover, Gramsci was
expecially interested in the southern peasants of Italy, usually overlooked by classical Marxist theory and dismissed by Northerners as
illiterate and uncultured *cafoni*, (rubes or hillbillies), and Pasolini's
consistent interest in the language, customs, and behavior of what he
terms the "subproletariat"—to distinguish them from members of the
industrial working class and to underline their agrarian and preindustrial origins—owes a deep debt to the Marxist theorist. Representative character types from the subproletarian world were prominent figures in Pasolini's two major novels—*The Ragazzi* (1955) and
A Violent Life (1959)—and would become the protagonists of most
of his early films: *Accattone* (*Accattone*, 1961—the word means "beg-
gar"); *Mamma Roma* (*Mamma Roma*, 1962); the episode entitled *Ricotta*
in *Rogopag*; and *Hawks and Sparrows* (1966). Even *The Gospel According
to Matthew* (*Il Vangelo secondo Matteo*, 1964—Pasolini pointedly
dropped any reference to Matthew's sainthood in his original title)—
reflects Pasolini's fascination with this almost unknown stratum of
Italian society.

Contemporary linguistic and literary theory also greatly influenced
Pasolini, and it was not uncommon for him to cite Leo Spitzer, Roland
Barthes, or Erich Auerbach in discussing specific sequences or shots
in his films. Long before structuralism and semiotics had become
faddish methodologies in the English-speaking world, Pasolini wrote
a number of widely read and hotly debated essays on the semiotics
of the cinema. His basic contention was that the cinema expressed
reality with reality itself (not with separate semiotic codes, symbols,
allegories, or metaphors), and that film's reproduction of physical objects was an essentially poetic and metonymic operation. The poetry
of the cinema conserves not only reality's poetry but also its mysterious, sacred nature; in its most expressive moments, film is simultaneously realistic and antinaturalistic. By communicating reality's
mystery, its *sacralità*, cinema also succeeds in projecting reality's
dreamlike quality, its *oniricità*. From the perspective of the professional semiotician, Pasolini's theories may seem full of contradictions,

but his theoretical speculations on the nature of cinematic language bore fruitful practical results. The intellectual link Pasolini effected between his Marxist ideology and the semiotics of the cinema can be envisioned as early as 1957 in a collection of poetry, *The Ashes of Gramsci*, in which the poet engages Gramsci in an imaginary conversation. He accepts Gramsci's praise of the working class not because of its role as the vanguard of socialist revolution but rather, because a specific part of this class, the subproletariat, has retained a preindustrial, mythical, and religious consciousness, a sense of mystery and awe in the face of physical reality which Pasolini defines as a prehistorical, pre-Christian, and prebourgeois phenomenon. The very nature of cinematic language, as Pasolini defined it, possessed qualities which complemented his views on the characteristics of the subproletariat in Italy and the Third World.

If Marxist and linguistic theory provided Pasolini with his intellectual background, Italian neorealism was the most important influence upon his cinematic culture. Pasolini accepted many of the characteristics of neorealist film with little difficulty: he preferred nonprofessional actors, natural lighting, on-location shooting, and contemporary political themes for much the same reasons they had appealed to his neorealist predecessors. However, like many of the other directors who made their first important films during this period, Pasolini rejected neorealism's hybrid nature which, he claimed, represented an artistic compromise, a mixture of pre-Resistance style with Resistance content and message; in particular he opposed its tendency toward naturalism, since his love for reality was "philosophical and reverential" but "not naturalistic."[24] Along with Rosi and the Taviani brothers, Pasolini defined neorealism as an expression of a past era which ended when the aspirations aroused by the Resistance were destroyed by the reconsolidation of power in the hands of the clergy and the bourgeoisie. The first films Pasolini directed, therefore, pay homage to a cinematic style, but they also assimilate it, rejecting aspects of it, in order to transcend it with a personal vision truer to a very different era.

Pasolini effects this stylistic transformation of his neorealist heritage in his early works by adopting what he calls a "pastiche" construction, mixing the most disparate stylistic and thematic materials in unusual combinations. Thus, in *Accattone* and *The Gospel*, for instance, the most sublime examples of official culture are set against humble elements from popular culture: the music of Bach and Mozart accompanies pimps and beggars; garbage dumps embody images from contemporary art by Italian painters Morandi or Guttuso; faces of subproletarian characters evoke scenes from the early Renaissance masters Giotto, Masaccio, and Piero della Francesca; and so forth. This kind of dramatic juxtaposition forces the viewer into an awareness of the loss sustained from industrial development and the acquisition of self-consciousness—for Pasolini, a bourgeois vice—and it underlines the mythical qualities of life abandoned by modern culture. As Pasolini remarks, "my view of the world is always at bottom of an epical-religious nature: therefore even, in fact above all, in misery-ridden characters, characters who live outside of a historical consciousness and specifically, of a bourgeois consciousness, these epical-religious elements play a very important role."[25]

The plot of *Accattone*, treating the life and death of a thieving pimp living in Rome's poorest district, might well have served for a neorealist critique of Italian economic conditions. But Pasolini modifies this typically naturalist narrative pattern to portray Accattone as an inverted, subproletarian Christ figure: citations from Dante's *Purgatory* (V) opening the film, as well as the use of Bach's *St. Matthew's Passion* on the sound track, point the attentive viewer in this direction, as do the many parallels between Accattone and the Christ of the Gospels. Like Christ, Accattone fulfills prophecy and dies in the company of two thieves; his larceny is termed "divine services," and one of his prostitutes is named Magdalene, a name with clear Biblical connotations. A dream vision Accattone experiences underlines the mysterious element present in subproletarian life (Accattone attends his own funeral but is refused entrance to the cemetery) and foretells the protagonist's eventual death. Pasolini consistently searches for the aesthetic effect in each and every frame depicting this tawdry world, and his narrative technique is willfully erratic and antitraditional. He treats the individual shot as an autonomous unit, the cinematic equivalent of the poetic image, rather than as an integral aspect of a larger

narrative design. This autonomy of the individual image is so pronounced in *Accattone* that some critics first assumed it arose from his
technical incompetence in a new artistic medium. When Accattone
is killed after an attempted robbery, a fellow thief crosses himself in
a strange, backward fashion, underlining Pasolini's view of his protagonist as a Christ-figure in reverse: the subproletarian world of
Rome has been stylistically "contaminated," to use Pasolini's favorite
term, by the iconography and mythology of Christianity.

In *The Gospel According to Matthew*, Pasolini moves in the opposite
direction, "contaminating" the traditional biography of Christ with the
epical-religious qualities he believes the Italian subproletariat retains.
Unable to discover appropriate locations in modern Israel, where Pasolini felt contemporary civilization had erased all trace of the special
characteristics he sought to project, the director turned instead to
underdeveloped regions in southern Italy (Apulia, Lucania, Calabria).
Rather than reconstructing sets of the Biblical world as a Hollywood
or Cinecittà production might have done, Pasolini worked by analogy,
finding parallels and analogues in the present. Thus, he remains faithful to the spirit of the Gospel rather than to its historical letter. Her-
od's soldiers are dressed as if they were Fascist *squadristi*; Roman
soldiers' costumes resemble those of Italian police; the flight of Joseph
and Mary into Egypt recalls photographs of Spanish civilians fleeing
over the Pyranees during the Civil War. Such modern analogies render
the emotion and drama of Christian history far more effectively than
strictly archaeological reconstructions would ever have done. Pasolini's predilection for pastiche is ever present: classical music is juxtaposed to Negro spirituals or the Congolese *Missa Luba*; humble
elements (peasant faces and impoverished locations) are set against
sophisticated cultural references (Botticelli angels, Piero della Francesca costumes, a Rouault Christ). The story of Christ in Pasolini's
version thus embodies an amalgamation of extremely disparate levels
of style and content.

Nothing about *The Gospel* is more striking than its editing and sense
of rhythm, for it is with a continuous process of rapid cutting and the
juxtaposition of often jarring images that Pasolini forces us to experience the life of Christ through a novel perspective. Abrupt changes

Pier Paolo Pasolini's *The Gospel According to Matthew* (1964). Christ (Enrique Irazoqui) receives the kiss from Judas (Otello Sestili) in a scene recalling a Giotto fresco.
(Photo courtesy of the Museum of Modern Art)

of location and time—especially in the scenes evoking Christ's Sermon on the Mount, his selection of his disciples, and a number of miracles—produce an almost demonic and relentlessly dynamic figure. In Matthew's own words, Pasolini's Christ is truly a man come to bring not peace but a sword. Touches of Marxist ideology have been discerned in some of the film's visuals: Satan, as he tempts Christ, is dressed in the manner of a priest; the Messiah indicts the rich and praises the poor as he drives the money changers from the Temple. But Pasolini had no need to insert an ideological message in *The Gospel*, since Matthew's own words are revolutionary enough when construed as literally as they are in the film, and only Italian viewers, very infrequent readers of the Bible, found great disparity between Matthew's text and Pasolini's rendition. A number of different camera styles are employed, ranging from rapidly edited scenes using extremely brief shots to very long takes and to those photographed with a hand-held camera from a subjective perspective, e.g., the trial of Jesus, where the viewpoint is that of a news reporter and probably reflects the vantage point of the traitor Judas. And just as a backward sign of the cross in *Accattone* had underlined Pasolini's indebtedness to Christian mythology and his distance from it, so Pasolini's version of the deposition from the cross reverses the traditional iconography of the event, for the camera is placed not before the cross but behind it. The last images of the resurrection avoid the patently false special techniques often employed by Hollywood versions and which even an atheist such as Pasolini realized were incapable of evoking the mystery of such an event. Instead, Pasolini emphasized the effects of this mysterious and inexplicable phenomenon rather than its actual occurrence, showing the disciples running joyously toward the risen Christ in a burst of visual energy that sweeps the emotions of even the most skeptical spectator along with it.

If *Accattone* and *The Gospel* reflect Pasolini's debt to the figurative arts, *Hawks and Sparrows* marks his parting homage to the ideological and cinematic matrix of his formative years. The film is structured upon a parable within a parable: a father and son, Innocenti Totò and Innocenti Ninetto, wander about in the company of a talking crow, a Marxist intellectual who functions as Pasolini's alter ego. This outer plot encloses another parabolic narrative, one concerning the conversion of hawks and sparrows by two of St. Francis's followers, Brother Ciccillo and Brother Ninetto, played by the same actors who portray father and son (Totò and Ninetto Davoli). The quotations in *Hawks and Sparrows* refer the viewer back to the early works of Rossellini (especially the convent episode of *Paisan*) and to Fellini's trilogy of conversion (especially Fellini's picaresque plot structures). Yet, Pasolini evokes his debt to previous films primarily to underline the fact that Italian neorealism and the ideologies it reflected are now dead and part of history. As the crow remarks, "The age of Brecht and Rossellini is finished." The crow expounds Pasolini's personal theories: the suproletarian pair are pronounced "blessed" since they walk the streets, go into bars with workers, and kiss young girls dressed like angels from Botticelli canvases; by virtue of the fact that the bird, like Pasolini, is an intellectual whose parents are doubt and self-consciousness, the crow is forever excluded form their beatific state.

Because *Hawks and Sparrows* is a parable, it has a moral, often imbodies allegory, and demands exegesis just as scripture does. The seemingly aimless journey the two characters take provides the director with an image of humanity in search of new goals in a post-ideological era. Various alternatives are humorously suggested. One tempting possibility is represented by the Las Vegas Bar, where working-class adolescents dance to American rock-and-roll, as if to suggest that the epical-religious nature of their class may be corrupted by the rise of an Americanized popular culture. (In fact, before his death Pasolini eventually concluded that this had indeed happened, and he was to adjure his faith in the subproletariat in *Salò* [*Salò, o le 120 giornate di Sodoma*, 1975].) The spectacle of the Third World and its exploitation by the West arises with a "Chinese" episode, wherein Innocenti Totò, in the guise of a rapacious landlord, demands an exorbitant rental from an oriental couple, remarking in English that "business is business." The two wanderers then encounter a strange group of show people whose sole act consists of a dramatic childbirth, turning the film's attention to birth control and overpopulation. A brief war over private property breaks out as Innocenti Totò attempts to relieve himself on someone else's land. It is in this explicitly ideological, yet comic, context that the Franciscan parable related by the crow expresses Pasolini's loss of faith in contemporary political ideologies. Brother Ciccillo and Brother Ninetto manage to convert the arrogant hawks after they learn the birds' language. During the process, Pasolini includes a sequence which pays homage to the slapstick comic routines of silent cinema. The humble sparrows are more problematic, since they speak no verbal language and communicate only by hopping about. Each class of bird finally accepts the good news from the two Franciscans, but just as this good news is reported to St. Francis, the converted hawks attack and murder the converted sparrows. As if to underline the point, the sparrows' fate awaits Innocenti Totò: he who had shown no mercy to his Chinese tenants is overcome by an even more rapacious property owner, a hawkish en-

Pier Paolo Pasolini's *Hawks and Sparrows* (1966). Brother Ciccillo (Totò)
prays for divine guidance in his attempts to translate the language of the
sparrows.
(Photo courtesy of the Museum of Modern Art)

gineer. The class struggle between birds and that between men will continue forever, it seems, unless the world is radically changed, as St. Francis remarks (citing Pope John XXIII and not Marx, as some critics thought.)

With the completion of the Franciscan parable about hawks and sparrows, the film's narrative returns to develop the larger parable and the picaresque journey of humanity's twin representatives down the road of life. Pasolini inserts newsreel footage of Palmiro Togliatti's funeral, a technique used by the Taviani brothers in *The Subversives* with much the same elegiac intent, focusing especially upon images of militant Communist Party members giving the clenched-fist salute and crossing themselves at the same time. No more striking and incongruous picture could be presented of contemporary Italy's ideological confusion than this strange mixture of Marxism and Christianity. With the passing of Togliatti, the age of Brecht and Rossellini—that is, the age of neorealism, the Resistance, and postwar reconstruction—had indeed been buried. Incessantly chattering and lecturing, the Marxist crow finally exasperates his two companions, who devour him along the roadside. Marxist ideas and intellectuals such as Pasolini must be digested, assimilated into the popular consciousness, but they must ultimately be transcended and superseded. The cannibalizing of the crow is, of course, a comic version of the traditional Eucharist: the body of Marx, like that of Christ, will provide mystic nourishment for the subproletariat in the future ahead of them on their endless journey. *Hawks and Sparrows* raises interesting problems but provides no definite answers; Pasolini's faith in the subproletariat's epical-religious qualities and his view that this class will serve as the vehicle for social change in Italy and the Third World only provide vague suggestions. But the critical ideological problems contained in the film should not obscure its brilliant comic moments. With the appearance of Ninetto Davoli in his first major role, Pasolini had discovered the perfect visual embodiment of the qualities he admired in the subproletariat. And his use of the legendary comic actor Totò enables Pasolini to incorporate an older and more traditional brand of regional, dialect comedy within a new and idiosyncratic ideological framework.

Pasolini's career began within the framework of neorealism but had transcended this cinematic style in *Hawks and Sparrows*. This same period saw the emergence of two major directors—Bernardo Bertolucci (1941–   )[26] and Marco Bellocchio (1939–   )[27]—whose ideological underpinnings were as far to the left as Pasolini's but whose cinematic culture abandoned neorealism and drew inspiration from foreign directors, professional training, and assiduous visits to film archives and film clubs. Bertolucci was a personal friend of Pasolini, who took him on as an apprentice director in *Accattone* and who provided him with the nucleus of his first script, *The Grim Reaper* (*La commare secca*, 1962). However, the young poet from Parma had previously spent summer vacations in the Cinématèque Française of Paris (he would later declare on numerous occasions that Henri Langlois was the greatest living professor of film history) and had made several short films as a teenager. Bellocchio's career began more formally with a diploma from the Centro Sperimentale di Cinematografia (1962) and a subsequent scholarship at London's Slade School of Fine Arts. Both men thus were to bring to their first major films the broadest possible awareness of contemporary cinema outside Italy—Godard, the New Wave, and the Free Cinema of Great Britain. Precocious young directors, these two figures were to be hailed by foreign critics as the *enfants prodiges* of Italian cinema.

While Bertolucci's *The Grim Reaper* is set within a recognizably Pasolinian environment of Roman squalor, it departs from Pasolini's unique early style by employing the lyrical rhythm and sometimes confusing shifts of narrative time that were to be typical of each of Bertolucci's subsequent works. Its plot—the murder of an aging prostitute and the investigation of various suspects—begins with a long sequence recording the last hours of the woman's life as she awakens during a storm, makes a cup of coffee, and goes off to work and her eventual death; this sequence is interrupted a number of times by the suspects' accounts of their activities, all of which end in the same park where the woman's body is discovered. This first work is thus an ambitious but flawed attempt to join a commercial thriller with a more avant-garde treatment of time and shifting narrative perspectives. *Before the Revolution* (*Prima della rivoluzione*, 1964), also a film with serious structural weaknesses, nevertheless reveals Bertolucci's lyrical style (now completely freed from Pasolini's influence) as well as his intellectual background and autobiographical preoccupations. Based loosely upon Stendhal's *The Charterhouse of Parma* (1838) and replete with numerous citations from literature (Wilde, Shakespeare, Pavese) and the cinema (Rossellini, Godard), *Before the Revolution* explores the contemporary implications of Talleyrand's statement that those who had not lived before the revolution could never realize how sweet life could be. In Fabrizio (Francesco Barilli)—a bourgeois intellectual from Parma who toys with Marxism, has a brief love affair with his strange aunt, Gina (Adriana Asti), and eventually marries Clelia (Cristie Pariset), preferring a safe marriage to either Marxist revolution or an incestuous relationship—Bertolucci projects his own experiences and presents what amounts to a critique of himself and the class to which he belongs. His three main characters parallel those of Stendhal—Fabrice Del Dongo; Gina, the Duchessa Sanseverina; and Clelia Conti (although he omits a figure worthy of comparison to Stendhal's Machiavellian Count Mosca)—and like his novelistic counterpart, Fabrizio has the misfortune to live during an era when his ideological aspirations conflict with his real possibilities. Rejecting his bourgeois origins, yet unable to transcend them, Fabrizio lives in a time *before* the revolution. Like Bertolucci, he suffers from the "nostalgia for the present" typical of the middle class. His inability to challenge society's mores by openly acknowledging his scandalous affair with his aunt parallels his failure to embrace the cause of the working class on anything but a purely intellectual level. Sexuality and politics, Freud and Marx, become uneasy bedfellows here as they do in each of Bertolucci's subsequent films. Fabrizio's eventual marriage to Clelia seals his downfall and represents his ultimate acceptance of his tragic fate as a product of bourgeois culture.

As Pasolini perceptively noted in his essay "The Cinema of Poetry," the dominant spirit of Bertolucci's first work is poetic, subjective, and elegiac.[28] True, some awkward traces of the young director's encounter with the New Wave are evident from the abuse of Godardian citations and coded remarks, as when one pretentious intellectual declares that "one cannot live without Rossellini," or on another occasion, when Fabrizio bitterly criticizes Communists at a workers' celebration as being more concerned with Marilyn Monroe's suicide than with bringing about the revolution and for elevating cinema over ideology. But where the young intellectual ideologue sometimes stumbles in directing his work, the precocious lyrical poet maintains a steadier hand, producing sequences of great emotional intensity. One such passage is a memorable farewell to the River Po and the Lombard marshes delivered by a ruined aristocratic friend of Fabrizio's named Puck (the Shakespearean reference is intentional); in it the director's marriage of classical music and soaring camera movements eulogizes the disappearance of a way of life and a social class to which he, like his protagonist, belongs. Ambivalence is a constant factor in Bertolucci's cinema: while the intellectual condemns the nostalgic vision of life before the revolution, declaring that there is no escape for the descendants of the bourgeoisie, the poet captures this way of life in lyrical images. Verdi's music and the city of Parma are never far removed from Bertolucci's works. And the most important sequence of *Before the Revolution* evolves from a performance of Verdi's *Macbeth* at the Parma Opera Theatre. As the various characters in this provincial melodrama enter the building, they seat thenselves according to their divergent social origins. While the majestic musical tragedy unfolds on stage, Fabrizio's private tragedy develops in the balcony as he rejects Gina and enters Clelia's box after deciding to play to the bitter end his role as a disillusioned son of the decadent middle class. "Fabrizio accepts everything now," his mother remarks. And with this ambivalent and complex figure, Bertolucci represents his own personal drama: both he and Fabrizio are destined to live before the revolution, condemned by their origins to remain outside the course of history, set off emotionally from a struggle which they have embraced intellectually.

While Bertolucci examines his provincial origins with a sense of lyrical nostalgia, Bellocchio, a native of Piacenza, sets his first two films among the small, prosperous nothern towns of the same region which contain a strong and conservative middle class. His artistic perspective is angry and provocatory rather than elegiac, however. With his marriage, Bertolucci's Fabrizio retreats into the comforting womb of the family, but Bellocchio's characters participate in a devastating

Bernardo Bertolucci's *Before the Revolution* (1964). At the opera, Fabrizio (Francesco Barilli) joins his fiancée Clelia (Cristie Pariset) and her family, finally accepting his bourgeois status and rejecting revolution.
(Photo from the author's private collection)

attack upon the very concept of the family itself, as well as all its traditional values and myths. As it analyzes a completely decadent bourgeois family whose physical handicaps underline moral defects, *Fists in the Pocket* (*I pugni in tasca*, 1965) is closer to the spirit of Faulkner or Tennessee Williams than to traditional images of the family in Italian cinema. The mother (Liliana Gerace) is blind; her daughter Giulia (Paola Pitagora), is emotionally unstable, immature, and afflicted with epilepsy; her brother Leone (Pierlugi Troglio) is a mental deficient; the most complex member of the family, Alessandro (Lou Castel), is full of strange plans and energy but is even more desperately epileptic than the others; only the oldest son Augusto (Marino Masé) seems to be a normal, functioning part of society with a job and a fiancée in town. Bellocchio's wrath reaches a bitter apogee when he pictures this family around the dinner table, the focus of Italian middle-class life: here, he presents a grotesque synthesis of the entire range of bourgeois customs and the concern with appearances, social standing, tradition, and banal ideas. Yet, there lurks beneath the conventional surface a wide range of uncontrolled emotions and even madness: Alessandro plays with Giulia's legs under the table, suggesting an incestuous relationship similar to that in *Before the Revolution*; a cat climbs upon the mother's plate and eats her food while her sightless eyes ignore both this theft and the moral corruption around her; none of the characters can resist staring fixedly into their mirrored reflections, so caught up are they in their narcissism; fits of irrational anger break out without warning and verge upon open violence.

Epilepsy seems to incapacitate the entire family (except for the "normal" Augusto). Alessandro, therefore, decides he must rid the family of everything which is no longer useful; he therefore murders both his mother and his younger brother Leone and is about to suffocate Giulia when a violent epileptic attack cuts short his project of purification. His death, one of the most powerful sequences of the film, takes place against the background of a moving aria from Verdi's *La traviata*: as Alessandro mouths the lines "Sempre libera degg'io, folleggiar di goia in goia," the attack destroys him. The most trenchant critique of the family in *Fists in the Pocket* arises from Bellocchio's comparison of Augusto and Alessandro. While the "abnormal" younger brother's actions can partially be explained by his illness, he possesses a positive driving force, a creative energy which lacks only a proper goal; the "normal" Augusto is actually more monstrous, for he is fully aware of what Alessandro is doing but does or says nothing to prevent it, since these crimes serve his own selfish purposes, assisting him in his acquisition of middle-class respectability. Bellocchio's forceful portrait of this angry young man whose rage is misdirected was to strike a responsive cord in a generation of young Italians about to explode after 1968 in a cataclysm of anger against the very fabric of Italian society—its values, and its institutions.

Fists in the Pocket is a virtuoso first performance, a far more perfect film than *Before the Revolution* which explores some of the same themes. It was produced on a shoestring budget (in part borrowed from the director's brother), shot on Bellocchio's family property, and employed two of the director's ex-classmates from the Centro Sperimentale. The film's narrow focus upon the private life of a decadent provincial family was imposed by economics rather than design, and the original script had included a political dimension—a link between Alessandro and an extreme-left student group.

The connection between the family and the wider political universe emerges clearly from Bellocchio's second and even more important film, *China is Near* (*La Cina è vicina*, 1967), a masterpiece which manages the almost impossible task of using a group of thoroughly dislikable characters to produce a brilliant political comedy. During election time in an era of center-left coalitions, the Socialist Party of Imola decides to run as its candidate for city councilman one Count Vittorio Gordini (Glauco Mauri), an opportunist aristocrat and high-school teacher. His candidacy blocks the aspirations for this post held by an enterprising and working-class accountant and long-time party member named Carlo (Paolo Graziosi), who is subsequently named as Vittorio's campaign manager. The Count's sexually rapacious sister, Elena (Elda Tattoli), has remained unmarried to avoid sharing her wealth with a poorer husband. Camillo (Pierluigi Aprà), their younger brother, heads a group of Maoist students in an expensive church school for the well-born, and he alternates between serving at Mass and playing the piano for the priest, and sabotaging his brother's election campaign by means of smoke bombs, disruptions of his speeches with attack dogs, and painted slogans on the party headquarters (which serves more as a trysting place for Carlo and his comrades than as a serious center for political organization).

Set against this grotesque and ideologically incoherent Italian provincial family are Carlo and his mistress, a working-class woman named Giovanna (Daniela Surina), who works in the Count's home as his secretary. Joseph Losey's *The Servant* (1964) influenced Bellocchio, and *China is Near* analyzes how Carlo and Giovanna cynically insinuate themselves into, first, the aristocrats' beds thanks to their proletarian sexual prowess, and then, into the Gordini family itself. As a result of a calculated scheme hatched by the two proletarian lovers, Elena is impregnated by Carlo and Giovanna by Vittorio. And much of the wry humor of Bellocchio's otherwise embittered critique derives from his portrait of Italian *trasformismo* within the confines of the family structure. Yet, Bellocchio intends this political satire and its confusion of sexuality and ideology to reflect a more general situation in contemporary Italian politics—the equally cynical compromise between Italy's Christian Democrats and the Socialists. And while the proletarian couple manages to outsmart their aristocratic lovers, in the process they are corrupted and become assimilated into the class they loathe. The political allegory may escape non-Italian viewers of the film, but Bellochio's razor-sharp satire remains effective. The figure of Vittorio is perhaps the best drawn in the film: his ridiculous sense of self-importance, his political opportunism, and his pretension are all revealed in a brilliant first shot of him seated in a small cubicle, as he gazes toward the ceiling and exclaims: "Lord, Lord, why hast thou forsaken me?" A moment later, he emerges from an ornately decorated antique cabinet hiding a toilet, and we discover him to be the kind of man who would cite Christ's words on the cross over a simple case of constipation. An equally successful example of Bellocchio's black humor occurs when Carlo uses a parish priest to foil Elena's attempted abortion, since only if she bears his child can he hope to gain entrance into the wealthy circles she frequents. As Elena lies on the operating table with her legs awkwardly spread the priest rushes into the room to save the innocent life of the fetus, and the hypocritical surgeon undergoes a Pauline conversion, declaring gratefully to the prelate that his intervention "was my road to Damascus." The surgeon's substantial donation to the parish calms the priest, but fails to convince Carlo, who demands a refund of Elena's fee.

Bellocchio was later to regret the image of the puerile Maoist students who alternated between their Sinophilia and their upper-class comforts, declaring that he should not have portrayed them in the same ludicrous manner he employed in his comic portrait of this provincial *compromesso storico* between the left and the right. But the ideological problems common to a new and more radical generation to which both he and Bertolucci belonged, as well as the fresh, personal cinematic styles their early films embody, reflected important changes in Italian culture. As elsewhere in Western Europe, 1968 marked the beginning of an era of violent social upheavals which began with the waves of protest in the United States over civil rights issues and the Vietnamese War. Since Italian culture was probably the most conservative culture on the continent, it was not surprising that some of the most violent of these reactions would occur in Italy, including the political terrorism which continues to plague the nation. At least a fraction of the intellectual, cultural, and political ferment that took place in Italy during the late Sixties and early Seventies owed something to the novel images of Italy projected by the cinema during the preceding period. The best films of the era, whether made by directors as politically uninvolved as Fellini or by those like Pontecorvo, Bellocchio, and the Tavianis, who were engaged in radical politics, called attention to pressing problems, undermined traditional values, and at times legitimized discontent even when they stopped short of calling for active protest or revolution.

6

The Mature *Auteurs:*
New Dimensions in Film
Narrative
with Visconti, Antonioni, and
Fellini

Much of the Italian film industry's economic success after the neo-realist era was indebted to the popular appeal of genre films aimed at a wide, general audience. However, the international prestige of Italian cinema during these years depended primarily upon a series of important works directed by Visconti, Antonioni, and Fellini, all of whom by this time had transcended their neorealist origins to develop highly personal cinematic styles. Frequently victorious at international film festivals and (what is more surprising) often profitable at the box office, their works seemed to hold out the promise of a dream come true for the industry—the combination of great art with maximum profits.

Of Luchino Visconti's major works during this period—*Rocco and His Brothers* (*Rocco e i suoi fratelli,* 1960); *The Leopard* (*Il gattopardo,* 1963); *The Stranger* (*Lo straniero,* 1967); *The Damned* (*La caduta degli dei,* 1969); *Death in Venice* (*Morte a Venezia,* 1971); and *Ludwig* (*Ludwig,* 1973)—only *The Damned* lacks an immediate literary or historical source.[1] Since Visconti always aimed at establishing links, however tenuous, between his films and their historical context, he quite naturally found support in novels reflecting great historical upheavals or signaling shifts in cultural values. Around such ready-made plots, he erected idiosyncratic interpretations of the texts he adopted, infusing them with a distinctive Viscontian style of set design, costuming, and photography. *Rocco and His Brothers* is, in some respects, a sequel to *The Earth Trembles*. Focusing upon the migration of southern Italians to northern industrial areas, the film's portrayal of the Parondi family's struggle to survive in Milan might well have constituted a continuation of the saga of the Valastro family (in fact, one of the Valastros does leave Sicily for the "continent," as the mainland is called by islanders, to seek employment). As in *The Earth Trembles,* in *Rocco* Visconti concentrates upon the dramatic clash of differing value systems—that of the traditional southern peasant family and its archaic code of honor and family loyalty, on the one hand, and a more individualistic and contemporary morality reflecting industrial society, on the other. By telescoping within the confines of a single family the complex problems associated with Italy's rapid postwar industrialization, Visconti achieves a certain economy of historical explanation.

Rosaria (Katina Paxinou), the matriarchal ruler of the Parondi clan, arrives at the Milan train station with her four sons—Simone, Rocco, Ciro, and Luca—where she is met by her eldest boy, Vincenzo (Spiros Focas), already established in the city with steady employment and a fiancée. Each of her sons represents a possible response to immigrant problems. Vincenzo's efforts to bridge the old ways and the new are immediately undermined by his mother, whose old-fashioned and family-centered views cause him to lose his job and threaten his relationship with Ginetta (Claudia Cardinale), his fiancée. Simone (Renato Salvatori), a handsome but brutish lout, becomes a boxer—the traditional route for advancement among many minority groups even today—but his promising career is ruined by his lack of discipline, his chauvinist mentality, and his stormy love affair with Nadia (Annie Girardot), an immigrant turned prostitute. Rocco (Alain Delon), the kindest and gentlest of the brothers, is somewhat of a saint, constantly sacrificing his own interests for the welfare of the clan, but he, too, cannot escape the burden of the family. When he also falls in love with Nadia, Simone's views of traditional sexuality come into conflict with Rocco's genuine love and respect for Nadia: under Rocco's very eyes Simone rapes Nadia, reasserting his "property rights," and then gives Rocco a severe beating. As a result, Rocco abandons Nadia to the tender mercies of Simone, at whose hands she ultimately dies. Rocco's subservience to the family reaches an apex when he explains to Nadia, in a melodramatic scene shot atop Milan's cathedral, that she must return to Simone because he needs her; he then becomes a prizefighter so that he can earn enough money to cover Simone's growing debts. Rocco is a strange martyr figure, a transitional character set in sharp contrast to Ciro (Max Cartier), who rejects the traditional code of morality that has destroyed his older brothers. When Simone murders Nadia and both Rocco and his mother persist in protecting him from the authorities, Ciro turns his brother into the police, choosing modern justice and his future as a technician in the Alfa-Romeo factory over clan loyalty. Luca, still a small child, cannot understand the drama taking place about him.

Though Vincenzo, Ciro, and Luca remain abstract personifications of alternative responses to immigrant problems, Simone and Rocco become fully realized characters whose fates are closely intertwined through their quite different love for Nadia. By ending their triangular affair on an unhappy note, Visconti manages to link the larger historical problem of cultural and economic change to its melodramatic manifestation in a tale of family tragedy. As in all Visconti's works, the director's point of view is ambivalent: in Nowell-Smith's words, there is a "constant tension in Visconti's work between an intellectual belief in the cause of progress and an emotional nostalgia for the past world that is being destroyed."[2] Visconti's intellectual nostalgia finds a stylistic counterpart in his penchant for operatic cinema. In Italy, his critical reputation has been as firmly based upon his operatic or theatrical productions as on his work in the cinema. Melodrama is never far from Visconti's world, as *Senso* demonstrated, and it has an impact even upon *Rocco*. In fact, the atmosphere established by the triangle of Rocco, Simone, and Nadia is much closer to the spirit of nineteenth-century opera than to that of a naturalist novel or a neorealist film.

Rocco omits much of what a historian or a sociologist would consider essential to a discussion of urban migration in Milan: unions, strikes, racism, crime, and so forth. Instead, it concentrates exclusively on the effects of rapid cultural change upon the ancient values of traditional southern Italian families. Visconti's choices, here as well as in other films, reflect artistic priorities rather than ideological or historical ones. Nowhere is this penchant for melodrama clearer than in the dramatic scenes which cut back and forth between Rocco's fight against a superior opponent in the ring and Simone's killing of Nadia, who meets her fate as if on the stage of La Scala—with outstretched arms, embracing her former lover Simone and his knife.[3]

Visconti's fascination with the dramatic potential of the family finds greater artistic expression in *The Leopard* and *The Damned* which integrate family histories into broad panoramic accounts of the Italian Risorgimento, in the first case, and the rise of National Socialism, in the second. Both films display Visconti's increasing interest in re-creating lavish, carefully designed costumes and period sets, props intended to evoke the spirit of eras which have forever vanished. *The Leopard* opens as Garibaldi's red-shirted volunteers have invaded Sicily in an attempt to annex the island to the Kingdom of Italy. The landed aristocrats, remnants of a feudal era, must now honor their obligations to the Bourbons or come to an accommodation with the victorious middle class. Don Fabrizio, Prince of Salina (the "leopard" of the title, played brilliantly by Burt Lancaster) represents the cream of the old aristocracy: culture, learning, grace, and style. He nevertheless allows his nephew Tancredi (Alain Delon), an impulsive and calculating but likable young man, to join the revolutionaries, a decision which eventually associates the House of Salina with the victors and ensures their survival in the new order. While the older aristocratic families struggle to survive, manipulating whenever possible the course of events, an equally self-serving group of middle-class merchants and liberal politicians emerges to divide the spoils from the political upheaval they have engineered. This class is personified in the film by Don Calogero Sedara (Paolo Stoppa), a comic figure whose power derives from the ecclesiastical properties he purchased after their confiscation, and whose manners provide the House of Salina with a constant source of amusement. Yet, Don Fabrizio amazes his retainers and allows the inevitable marriage of new wealth and ancient title: Tancredi marries Don Calogero's beautiful daughter Angelica (Claudia Cardinale), thus ensuring the family a place in the future. This sordid picture of a classic instance of Italian *trasformismo* concludes with a magnificent ballroom sequence in which the prince contemplates his own demise, his nephew's future, and overhears the sound of an execution at dawn signaling the final destruction of any revolutionary threat to the now established bourgeois regime.

The Leopard thus continues *Senso*'s view of the Risorgimento as a flawed and betrayed revolution. But it is more than an extremely meticulous and lavish recreation of an excellent historical novel. It is also a meditation on death, historical change, and the demise of a social class to which the director also belongs. Visconti's point of view is almost completely identified with that of Don Fabrizio, the Leopard. A passionate astronomer, the Sicilian Prince gazes upon the course of history swirling about him with an air of bemused detachment and slight contempt for the vulgarity of it all, just as Visconti's slow camera movements and long takes caress his subject matter in an elegiac fashion. Unlike his nephew Tancredi, Don Fabrizio takes no delight in the hypocrisy required for survival. Tancredi's credo is expressed in a remark to his uncle when he joins the Garabaldini that "things have to change in order to remain the same." The Prince is more concerned with the passing of an era and his own inevitable death, and Visconti's camera reflects his preoccupation in the beautiful sequence which describes the family's arrival at Donnafugata, their summer palace: as the village band plays "Noi siam le zingarelle" from Verdi's *La traviata* and the family's faithful organist, Don Ciccio, plays "Amami Alfredo" from the same work, the family takes its traditional place at the front of the cathedral. Visconti's camera slowly tilts down from the Baroque ceilings and the sumptuous statuary to the priests and the omnipresent smoke of incense, which it then follows to pan slowly and tenderly over the entire family. The actors have been made up with a bluish colored mascara and are covered with inordinate amounts of travel dust, sitting motionless, as if they were statues. It is a beautiful image of an era about to pass away, and it evokes the thought of death and decay. The Prince's obsession with death appears again when he is visited by a representative of the House of Savoy, Cavalier Chevalley, who asks him to take part in the new government. Don Fabrizio refuses and proceeds to explain his reasoning in an argument taken almost verbatim from the novel. No government has ever succeeded in changing Sicily, because the island's physical squalor and misery reflect Sicily's obsession with death, as does the desire for voluptuous immobility, sleep, sensuality, and violence typical of Sicilians; Sicilians do not desire improvement, for they feel themselves to be perfect, and their vanity is stronger than their misery. The Prince declares that eventually all will only change for the worst, no real progress will be made; whereas the older ruling classes were leopards and lions, the era of jackals and sheep has now begun.

Such a pessimistic view of the Italian Risorgimento is quite typical of a Marxist intellectual such as Visconti. Certainly he sympathizes with the Prince's sense of sorrow when, during the sumptuously re-created ballroom scene (mutilated by severe cutting in foreign distribution), he wanders from room to room and eventually examines a painting by Greuse ("The Death of the Just Man") in the palace library. The painting moves him to imagine his own death, and this morbidity is juxtaposed to the vitality of the beautiful Angelica, who dances with the Prince and arouses in him a sense of passion and desire: the burden of nostalgia for the past causes him eventually to shed one single tear. Meanwhile, Tancredi observes that the "new administration requires order, legality and order," and is pleased that those who deserted from the regular army to the Garibaldian forces trying to effect a true revolution—a short-lived attempt that ended with Garibaldi's defeat at the battle of Aspromonte—will be executed at dawn. As the Prince walks slowly home at dawn, he encounters a priest going to administer the last rites to a dying man and wonders wearily when death will come to him. While the firing squad's volleys marking the end of the rebellion are heard on the sound track, we see a yawning Don Calogero who remarks, "No more to worry about!" The concluding sequence of *The Leopard* is a damning indictment of the political compromises underlying Italian unification. Visconti, the critical Marxist, provides the viewer with a historical context from which to judge the

Luchino Visconti's *The Leopard* (1963). The prince (Burt Lancaster) and his family enter the cathedral at Donnafugata.
(Photo courtesy of the Museum of Modern Art)

events he presents, yet the nostalgia he feels for the past, and the identification he feels with the main character, almost overwhelm the political message of the film, just as they had done in Tomasi di Lampedusa's original novel. And the epic sweep of the film's sets and costumes threatens at every moment to overshadow his historical message.

With *The Damned, Death in Venice,* and *Ludwig,* Visconti moves from analyses of Italian society in the post-Risorgimento or postwar periods to consider a broader view of European culture and politics in what has been termed his "German" trilogy.[4] In these three films, Visconti examines the rise of National Socialism in Weimar Germany through its disastrous effects upon an aristocratic family; he presents a portrait of chilling beauty and decadence in an adaptation of Thomas Mann's novella; and he explores the psyche of Ludwig II of Bavaria, the "mad" king and Richard Wagner's eccentric patron. Each of these films becomes progressively more mannered in the evolution of a personal style that seems far from that of *The Earth Trembles.* They emphasize lavish sets and costumes, sensuous lighting, painstakingly slow camera work, and a penchant for imagery reflecting subjective states or symbolic values. Critics frequently speak of Visconti's "decadent" period as if this were an obvious defect. But Visconti, himself the descendant of Milanese aristocrats born in the midst of a period he treats so sympathetically, makes no apology for his style:

> . . . if you wish to tell a story about a certain society, it is necessary then to tell it in the context of the atmosphere in which that society lived, don't you think? . . . European society until the First World War was that which contained the greatest contrasts and the best aesthetic results. The contemporary world, instead, is so leveled out, so gray, so tasteless.[5]

Elsewhere, Visconti remarked:

> I tell these stories about the self-destruction and dissolution of families as if I were recounting a Requiem . . . I have a very high opinion of "decadence," just as, for example, Thomas Mann did. I have been imbued with this spirit: Mann was a decadent of German culture, I of Italian formation. What has always interested me is the analysis of a sick society.[6]

The Damned and *Death in Venice* were box-office successes, but for each of them Visconti also received violently hostile reviews based on the mistaken notion that the representation of decadence on the screen was synonymous with a recommendation for its continuance.[7]

The Damned has a highly baroque, not to say confusing, plot: it chronicles the dissolution of the von Essenbeck family—modeled upon the Krupp munitions makers—as it is caught up in the Germany of the Thirties. The family is a collection of misfits, power seekers, and perverts. The old Baron Joachim is murdered by the executive director of the steel works, Friedrich Bruckmann (Dirk Bogarde), who is the lover of the widowed Baroness Sophie von Essenbeck (Ingrid Thulin). Sophie's son Martin (Helmut Berger), the Baron's heir, is manipulated by his mother and lover in a plot to rearm Nazi Germany by means of his inheritance, the steel works. Eventually a distant cousin in the S.S. named Aschenbach seeks to set Martin against the pair of conspirators when they prove too weak to fit into his ruthless schemes. The Baron's elder son, Konstantin, is a highly-placed officer in Roehm's S. A. who opposes the power over the family business exerted by Hitler and his S.S. men; with Friedrich's help, Konstantin is murdered by the Gestapo during the Night of the Long Knives. Eventually, Martin rejects the guilt aroused by his various perversities and embraces his cousin's Nazi ideology completely. After raping his mother, he forces Friedrich and Sophie into a grotesque marriage and then into a double suicide. A number of somewhat confusing cultural and literary sources inform the work. The opening scene of the family gathered around a banquet table seems borrowed directly from the opening chapter of Mann's *Buddenbrooks;* the complicated emotional relationships of Sophie, Martin, and Friedrich show the influence of Greek tragedy, Shakespeare's *Macbeth,* and Wilhelm Reich's views on the relationship of Fascism and homosexuality; and, finally, the film's subtitle—*Götterdämmerung,* or *Twilight of the Gods*—points toward the atmosphere of Wagnerian opera and melodrama. In the words of one perceptive reviewer, *The Damned* presents "the Krupp family history as Verdi might have envisaged it."[8]

During the period under discussion, homosexuality in the Italian cinema emerges from the closet largely thanks to the example of Vis-

Luchino Visconti's *The Damned* (1969). The drunken revelry of the S. A. troops which precedes their extermination during the Night of the Long Knives.
(Photo courtesy of the Museum of Modern Art)

conti's "German trilogy," Pasolini's *Theorem* (*Teorema,* 1968), and Bertolucci's *The Conformist* (*Il conformista,* 1970). *The Damned* set a pattern, frequently repeated in the next decade, linking Nazis or Fascists to homosexuality. This completely gratuitous connection, one first made by Rossellini's war trilogy and encouraged by Wilhelm Reich's somewhat discredited theories, would be broken up by Ettore Scola in his poignant *A Special Day* (*Una giornata speciale,* 1977), which presents a sympathetic homosexual, an *anti-Fascist* intellectual. But for Visconti, homosexuality becomes a metaphor embodying both negative qualities (the thirst for power in *The Damned*) as well as more positive intellectual and artistic endeavors (as in *Death in Venice* or *Ludwig*). Nor should *The Damned* be taken as a serious sociological or psychological analysis of German culture in Weimar Germany—

something Visconti certainly did not intend. It is more accurate to consider the film a powerful visual metaphor for the infernal nature of Nazi moral degradation, a pathological case history bordering on the Grand Guignol. The nightmarish quality of this society is immediately set by the film's titles, shot against a fiery red blast furnace. This violent and hellish color is constantly picked up throughout the visuals of the film—in the Nazi flag and banners; in interiors lit by the menacing glow of fireplaces; in scenes of book burning; in the gory sequence literally dripping with blood and shot in a diffused red light depicting the execution of the S.A. troops by the Gestapo; and finally, in the red draperies serving as a backdrop for the ghoulish double suicide ending the film. Color itself becomes a major theme of *The Damned,* as it will in Antonioni's *Red Desert* and Fellini's *Juliet of the Spirits.* And in Visconti's hands, its use uncovers a hyperbolic and horrifying vision of a family embodying a corrupt culture that willfully pulls the world down around its ears.

Death in Venice, too often discussed solely in terms of its relationship to Thomas Mann's novella, avoids much of the confusing narrative structure of *The Damned.* In this work, the director's characteristically lavish use of period costumes and meticulously recreated sets remains controlled by the more coherent vision of a simpler storyline. Visconti's adaptation transforms Mann's writer into a composer reminiscent of Gustav Mahler; indeed, Mahler's music on the sound track of the film frequently threatens to overwhelm the narrative with its ominous, foreboding tones. Visconti now relies, somewhat too insistently, upon flashbacks to clarify the artistic issues that intrigue him in the personality of Gustav von Aschenbach (Dirk Bogarde), his bourgeois protagonist. As the director's effete symbol of the *mal du siècle,* Aschenbach has artistic sensibilities that are at war with the sensual temptations aroused by his unsettling vision of a beautiful boy, Tadzio (Björn Andresen). The film emphasizes, perhaps too clearly, the subtler undercurrent of homosexuality in the original text. The composer's inner thoughts—revealed to us through flashbacks—reflect an intellectual dilemma: Aschenbach's friend Alfried constantly argues for the important role of ambiguity, sensuality, and physical reality in artistic creativity, while the stuffy Aschenbach contends that beauty has a pure, cerebral quality that should function as an example of clarity. In one flashback, we witness a violent rejection of the composer's music by critics and audiences; in another—one underlining Aschenbach's inability to unify intellect and flesh—we move from a shot of Tadzio playing the piano (Beethoven's "Für Elise") in the hotel to a flashback of Aschenbach's earlier visit to a brothel where the same music is being played; in both instances, the artist is unable to consummate his physical desire.

While the artistic issues personified in the character of Aschenbach make interesting subjects for argument, *Death in Venice* is most successful when it abandons philosophical problems and concentrates upon a portrait of *fin-de-siècle* society inside the luxurious Hotel des Bains at the Lido of Venice. In a sensuous and nostalgic farewell to an aristocratic world about to disappear in the cataclysm of World War I, over and over again the director slowly pans his camera around salons, dining rooms, and parlors filled with richly furnished decors, formally dressed guests, and luxurious flowers or foods. Aschenbach's infatuation with Tadzio is meant to represent more than an old man's flirtation with homosexuality; it becomes a graphic image for the composer's confrontation with intellectual sterility and old age. And Visconti, a product of the same "decadent" world he depicts in the film, seems to have identified Aschenbach's dilemma with his own. The diabolic and symbolic figures in Mann's novella, harbingers of death during the cholera plague, are also retained in Visconti's adaptation, for they are not only portents of decay and death but also mirror images of what the composer is eventually to become during the sexual transformation he experiences before succumbing to the plague. Few film images of death are more haunting than that of Aschenbach on the beach, gazing upon Tadzio's resplendent, nubile body as he points out toward the golden sunset. At that moment, Aschenbach's garish makeup and face powder, put on by the hotel's barber in a futile attempt to disguise his age, drip down his tearful face as he dies. The intensely intellectual character of the film's plot, underscored by the philosophical discussions in many of the flashbacks,

together with Visconti's characteristically slow camera movements and
elegiac pans, ultimately produce a beautiful but chilling visual experience that never quite seems to engage our emotions.

The obsession in *Death in Venice* with solitude, sensuality, and mor-
tality becomes even more mannered in Visconti's portrait of King
Ludwig II of Bavaria, a romantic dreamer who constructed fantastic,
fairyland castles, spent a fortune on Richard Wagner's gradiose operatic schemes, and died a mysterious death after being deposed from
the throne for mental instability. After *Ludwig* opens with the King's
coronation in 1860, most of the film is developed through a series of
flashforwards that move between moments in Ludwig's reign and the
later legal inquiry that pronounced him insane. Once again, Visconti

Luchino Visconti's *Death in Venice* (1971). Aschenbach (Dirk Bogarde)
encounters Tadzio (Björn Andresen), the embodiment of his search for
spiritual and physical perfection.
(Photo courtesy of the Museum of Modern Art)

succumbs to the penchant he has always exhibited for the melodramatic and operatic spectacle of lavish sets and costumes. The Bavarian monarch (Helmut Berger) represents a personality type Visconti views as particularly characteristic of post-Romantic Germany and representative of both artists such as Aschenbach and perverted power seekers such as Martin von Essenbeck. For Visconti, such a man is caught between idealistic and poetic aspirations toward an abstract spiritual life, on the one hand, and baser expressions of vulgar sensuality or the will to power, on the other. The image of Adolf Hitler enraptured by Wagnerian melodrama while Berlin is being bombed suggests the historical counterpart of the kind of figure Visconti envisions in his trilogy. Ludwig pictures himself as the embodiment of the mythical Siegfried celebrated in Wagner's opera; the King innocently hopes to raise the spirits of his people through music. While Bavaria and its Austrian allies are defeated by Bismarck's Prussia on the battlefield, Ludwig amuses himself with fantastic musical projects and hours of enraptured planetarium gazing during which his nervous generals wait outside for his commands. As the monarch moves more and more into a closed and solitary existence, his physical deterioration parallels his descent into homosexuality; his drunken orgies with his troops and male lovers are shot in almost the same manner as was the Night of the Long Knives in *The Damned.* Seen by Visconti as a potentially positive but deeply flawed character, Ludwig is inevitably destroyed by the ugliness of a world that has no use for dreamers and poets, by the incomprehension of his friends, and by his own sexuality.

Many European critics have tried to interpret Visconti's "German" trilogy as a serious, historical vision of Germany's flirtation with Romantic idealism and its subsequent perversion in the Nazi era. But the three films fail to provide any coherent explanation of such a complicated process. It is far more accurate to conclude that in this trilogy Visconti has allowed his taste for visual spectacle, as well as his own personal preoccupation with old age, solitude, ugliness, and death, to overwhelm his philosophical or cultural intentions. Though he retained his matchless flair as a designer of period costumes and spectacularly operatic sets used within a traditional melodramatic framework—all of which is captured by a beautiful color photography—Visconti had, at the close of his career, abandoned more daring contributions to the art of cinematography for chilling but static visions of the passing of the culture that had produced him. A number of films by Antonioni and Fellini during this same decade were to surpass Visconti's work in originality, technical prowess, and intellectual profundity.

During the decade under discussion, Antonioni produced a number of immensely important works, beginning with the highly acclaimed trilogy—*L'Avventura* (1960), *La Notte* (1961), and *The Eclipse* (1962)—then shifting to color photography with *Red Desert* (1964), *Blow-Up* (1966), *Zabriskie Point* (1969), and *The Passenger* (*Professione: reporter,* 1975).[9] The last three works were made in English, an experiment which produced mixed results. In all of these films, Antonioni managed to make important contributions to film art, and with the gradual acceptance of his work, even among general audiences, he helped to shape our expectations of what cinematic narrative could be. Nowhere is this clearer than *L'Avventura.* Its plot is a simple one: Claudia (Monica Vitti), Anna, Claudia's wealthy girl friend, and Anna's lover Sandro (Gabriele Ferzetti) go on a cruise in the Mediterranean; when Anna mysteriously disappears, Claudia and Sandro go in search of her, along the way becoming lovers themselves. Outlined in this manner, the film seems to have a rather traditional storyline. Yet, Antonioni's originality lies precisely in his de-emphasis of the dramatic potential of film plot with its traditional problems, complication, and eventual resolution, all developed through some notion of psychological conflict between well-defined figures. Thus, in *L'Avventura,* Anna's disappearance, the subsequent inquest, the mystery of her location—in short, the crux of the story as another director would probably have conceived it—are ignored, or more accurately, become only as important as Claudia or Sandro feel they are (since both the storyline and the camera limits our knowledge to what the characters know). As Antonioni put it, he felt a need to "avoid certain established and proven techniques" and was "annoyed with all this sense of order, this systematic arrangement of the material" in cinema. Breaking away from conventional narrative techniques first involved a destruction of conventional plots so that the story's internal rhythms, rather than logical connections and sequential development, would move the action—the goal was to tie cinema "to the truth rather than to logic."[10]

Another aspect of Antonioni's originality is his exceptional sensitivity to the philosophical currents of the times, his ability to portray modern neurotic, alienated, and guilt-ridden characters whose emotional lives are sterile—or at least poorly developed—and who seem to be out of place in their environments. If the perfect existentialist film could be imagined, it would probably be one of the works in Antonioni's trilogy, or possibly *Red Desert*. As the director declared in a statement distributed in Cannes when *L'Avventura* was first shown, modern man lives in a world without the moral tools necessary to match his technological skills; he is incapable of authentic relationships with his environment, his fellows, or even the objects which surround him because he carries with him a fossilized value system out of step with the times.[11] As a result of this situation, man most frequently responds erotically, attempting to find in sex or love an answer to his moral dilemma; but this, too, proves to be a blind alley offering neither solutions nor possibilities for self-fulfillment. Self-knowledge and self-consciousness are an insufficient substitute for our outmoded values. Every emotional encounter must instead give rise to a new potential, a new adventure (the sense of Antonioni's title). Antonioni's characters thus suffer from the special kind of existential boredom or *noia* Alberto Moravia described so well in his novel *The Empty Canvas* (*La noia*, 1960):

> . . . boredom is not the opposite of amusement . . . boredom to me consists in a kind of insufficiency, or inadequacy, or lack of reality. . . . The feeling of boredom originates for me in a sense of the absurdity of a reality which is insufficient, or anyhow unable, to convince me of its own effective existence . . . from that very absurdity springs boredom, which when all is said and done is simply a kind of incommunicability and the incapacity to disengage oneself from it.[12]

Both Moravia and Antonioni see sexuality as a means of establishing a relationship with reality, and thus, the sexual act becomes something higher, more mysterious, and more complete than love, especially if

love is interpreted as the simple physico-sentimental relationship between man and woman, as Moravia has stated in *Man as an End* (*L'uomo
come fine,* 1964).[13] When sexuality fails as a means of communication
and provides only physical relief, then, in Antonioni's terms, Eros is
sick.

Antonioni's genius lies not in using this theme, a commonplace in
the literature of the postwar years, but in rendering it in starkly beautiful visual images. Ultimately, Antonioni's cinematographic *technique*
is his content. The visualization of subjective, often irrational states
of mind by representational means—what one film historian has aptly
termed "objective correlatives, visual embodiments of pervasive
mood and specific psychological states"—becomes, with Antonioni,
an original approach to cinematic expression.[14] A number of stylistic

Michelangelo Antonioni's *L'Avventura* (1960). Anna (Lea Massari) and Sandro (Gabriele Ferzetti) confront each other in a carefully composed frame
shortly before making love.
(Photo courtesy of the Museum of Modern Art)

devices, first appearing in *L'Avventura,* will characterize the work of Antonioni's maturity. First and foremost is Antonioni's absolute control over his composition. Every aspect of an individual shot is artistically organized for the fullest effect, just as if the director were a painter or a still photographer: a shot or sequence by Antonioni is marked as surely as though his signature were affixed to the celluloid. Characters frequently look away from one another, or remain speechless for lengthy periods; they are frequently framed by windows, doorways, long halls, and corridors, as if to emphasize their separation from others and their failure to communicate. Both black-and-white and color film are treated in a painterly fashion, and masses of shade or color are employed in much the same way as a fresco painter might use color to express weight and volume. An excellent example of this tight control may be found in the last few shots of *L'Avventura.* Sandro has just betrayed Claudia with Gloria Perkins, a cheap American actress whose favors he has purchased for the evening in his hotel in Taormina. Outside, Claudia and Sandro try to put their fragmented relationship back together again. First we see Claudia's hand on the back of Sandro's bench in close-up as it begins to rise and hesitates, turning into a fist; a close-up of her anguished face follows; then her hand moves to the back of Sandro's head and rests there—a white mass upon the darker mass of his hair. Antonioni then cuts to a long shot of the location—a carefully divided frame with a darker concrete wall on the right and snowy Mount Etna on the other side. As Antonioni has declared, the shot's composition employs the couple's environment (male figure/wall/pessimism versus female protagonist/volcano/optimism) to provide a beautiful but unconventionally inconclusive ending to this problematic work. As the film ends, we only know that Sandro and Claudia have managed to communicate through a mutual sense of pity, but we are uncertain as to whether this dynamic relationship, symbolized by the frame's careful composition, will long endure.[15]

With *La Notte,* Antonioni moves from the Mediterranean island of Sicily to the northern industrial city of Milan. His characters resemble those of *L'Avventura* in their emotional poverty and upper middle-class background, and the story is slim. Giovanni Pontano (Marcello

Mastroianni) and his wife Lidia (Jeanne Moreau) are no longer in love. Antonioni shows us a number of their activities during the course of a single day: they visit a dying friend in the hospital and attend a party for Giovanni's new novel; Lidia wanders by herself through Milan; later that evening, they attend a night club and visit the estate of a rich industrialist, who offers Giovanni a job; Giovanni meets the industrialist's daughter Valentina (Monica Vitti), while Lidia is offered a ride in the rain by a man named Roberto. Both are temporarily tempted into infidelity but neither actually commits adultery. Finally at dawn, they walk out on a golf course where Lidia reads Giovanni one of his old love letters, which he fails to recognize; in a desperate effort to communicate, they make love on the grass.

After *L'Avventura*, the story seems to be familiar territory. Perhaps more skillfully than in the earlier film, Antonioni now successfully exploits the artistic potential of duration, matching the characters' time with his film time. This is most often accomplished with long tracking or panning shots following the actors after they have delivered their lines, or, in the case of Lidia's walk through modern Milan, an entire sequence devoted to random behavior. Sound (or lack of it) is skillfully employed to advance his analysis of character. For instance, we do not hear the lengthy conversation between Lidia and her would-be seducer, Roberto, at the industrialist's party; the camera remains outside the car in the pouring rain and we only see the movement of their silent lips. Antonioni's tendency toward an abstract and poetic use of the frame is even more pronounced in *La Notte* than in *L'Avventura*. Characters are treated as if they were objects, captured as often by their reflection in a window or mirror as by a direct shot; they are observed in a number of different environments—modern homes, urban buildings, gardens. The absence of any traditional plot that might point to some conflict or development in the character creates an even more depressing assessment of contemporary love in *La Notte* than in *L'Avventura*. Even as Lidia and Giovanni make love at the end of the film, it is clear that this is a gesture of mutual pity (not unlike that extended by Claudia's hand to Sandro) within a marriage destroyed by the indifference of habit and an impenetrable loneliness.

Michelangelo Antonioni's *La Notte* (1961). Giovanni (Marcello Mastroianni) and Lidia (Jeanne Moreau) attempt to communicate their emotional feelings to each other at the film's conclusion.
(Photo courtesy of the Museum of Modern Art)

In *The Eclipse,* Antonioni pushes his increasingly abstract style almost to the limits. Once again, plot takes second place to technique: the opening sequence, a brilliant exercise in formalism, shows the end of an affair between Vittoria (Monica Vitti) and Riccardo; Vittoria then goes to meet her avaricious mother at the Roman Stock Exchange, where she encounters a stockbroker named Piero (Alain Delon) who strikes her fancy; after visiting a friend who has lived in Kenya and taking an airplane ride to Verona, Vittoria returns to the stock market, and a relationship with Piero blossoms; they arrange a rendezvous which they do not keep, and the final part of the film presents a montage of objects, people, and places at the appointed meeting place. Several remarkable sequences dominate *The Eclipse.* Its opening moments present Antonioni's own view of cinema quite effectively. As Vittoria and Riccardo break off their relationship, Vittoria is shown arranging a small abstract sculpture set on a table behind a propped-up picture frame; Antonioni then cuts to the other side of the frame, and from this new perspective the sculpture appears quite different. After this concentration upon painterly composition worthy of modern abstract painting, we are then introduced to Vittoria and Riccardo through a skillful series of reverse-angle shots, formally framed compositions juxtaposing characters to various geometrical shapes (or to each other) as they are separated by different angles and lines. To complement this expressly modernist atmosphere, in which objects and people seem interchangeable, Antonioni uses a sparse sound track: the insistent noise of a whirling fan effectively renders the notion that their affair has died from repetitive moments of boredom. Vittoria's search for meaning—or at least some pleasing organization—in the objects within her picture frame sets the leitmotif for the director's cinematic search for his own aesthetic organization of the starkly contemporary world his characters inhabit.

The problem of human communication remains, as always in Antonioni, at the center of his work: telephones ring but remain unanswered; characters are constantly photographed through barriers of all kinds (doors, hallways, windows, gates, fences). On one occasion, Piero and Vittoria even try to kiss through a windowpane; physical objects (most particularly various kinds of buildings, walls, or parts of architectural structures) separate characters and their gaze, (e.g., the Stock Exchange shot in which Vittoria and Piero are separated by a huge pillar is a classic example of Antonioni's careful compositions within the frame of each shot). Not an inch of film is used without artistic purpose.

In *L'Avventura*, Claudia and Sandro seemed to communicate at the close of the film through a mutual sense of pity, symbolized by a touch; the end of *La Notte* showed Lidia and Giovanni attempting to rekindle a moribund passion by making love; at the close of *The Eclipse,* Antonioni is more daring—his protagonists disappear completely and centerstage is devoted to the objects, people, or places associated with the spot in which they have previously met and at which their rendezvous was to take place. Some of these images recall the two characters (for example, the water barrel into which Vittoria tossed a twig while waiting for Piero); other shots suggest a foreboding atmosphere (the newspaper headline "The Atomic Age" and "Peace Is Weak"); still others may symbolize an aspect of their relationship or may be merely an intriguing composition (ants on a tree trunk, water trickling from the barrel, geometric architectural shapes); then, the director plays upon our expectations by showing us two characters who seem to resemble Vittoria or Piero but who turn out to be mere look-alikes. The final shot explains the title of the film. A sudden close-up of an illuminated streetlamp with a bright halo suggests the eclipse of natural, physical lighting from the heavenly bodies by the artificial light of the lamp—most likely a direct quotation from a modern work of art Antonioni would have known and admired, *The Street Light—Study of Light* (*Lampada—studio di luce,* 1909), by the Futurist painter Giacomo Balla (1871–1958).

The enigmatic and unconventional finale has puzzled the critics. Some see the last scene as proof that the final meeting of Vittoria and Piero will never take place, while others view the sequence as a chilling image of a completely dehumanized contemporary environment. But I am inclined to reject any overly symbolic viewing of this remarkable sequence. Piero and Vittoria were happy before their rendezvous, and there is really no reason to assume that their failure to keep an appointment means anything in particular. Antonioni surely meant the sequence to remain ambiguous—a step in the direction of the poetic cinema of abstraction he often advocates. Avoiding any facile resolution of the questions the film poses, he invites the viewer to speculate on what the outcome of Vittoria's love affair might be.

Red Desert may well be Antonioni's masterpiece. His first color film, its plot is deceptively similar to those of his trilogy. Giuliana (Monica Vitti)—married to Ugo (Carlo Chionetti), an electronics engineer, and the mother of a son, Valerio—has experienced a nervous breakdown and tried to commit suicide, although she is now out of the hospital. Ugo's friend, Corrado Zeller (Richard Harris), arrives, searching for workers from the factories in Ravenna to work in Patagonia. When

Ugo leaves town on business, Giuliana and Corrado have a brief affair. The film closes with a view of Giuliana and Valerio taking a stroll near Ugo's factory, the location at the beginning of the work.

In this film, Antonioni has moved beyond the material covered in his trilogy and now concentrates upon the characters' relationship to things around them rather than to their interaction. As he remarked in a conversation with Godard, "it is things, objects, and materials that have weight today."[16] In the three preceding films, Antonioni had thrust his unhappy protagonists into expressive Sicilian landscapes, or modernistic Milanese and Roman buildings. Now, they move within the environment of modern technology—oil refineries, radar stations, power plants—all of which possesses not only recognizably contemporary geometrical shapes but specifically artificial colors and sounds as well. But his point of view since the statement released at Cannes on L'Avventura remains unchanged: modern man's technological capabilities have far outstripped his moral values. And in contrast to many who offer the rather facile interpretations of Red Desert in which the film is seen as a condemnation of modern technological society in the name of ecological purity and a romantic return to the past, Antonioni believes that Giuliana's neurosis is caused by a failure to adapt to a new world. Her alienation is not the result of her supposedly dehumanized and hostile surroundings:

> . . . my intention, on the contrary . . . was to translate the beauty of this world, in which even the factories can be very beautiful. . . . The line, the curves of factories and their smoke-stacks, are perhaps more beautiful than a row of trees—which every eye has already seen to the point of monotony. It's a rich world—living, useful.[17]

Elsewhere, he has compared the intrinsic beauty of the computer parts in Kubrick's 2001 to the "revolting" insides of a human being: "In my films it is the men who don't function properly—not the machines."[18]

Antonioni's positive evaluation of modern industrial society finds its most complete expression in his original use of color in Red Desert, so much so that color emerges as a central element in the film, equal in importance to plot, characterization, or editing. As Antonioni him-

Michelangelo Antonioni's *Red Desert* (1964). The careful organization of the individual frame, juxtaposing Ugo (Carlo Chionetti), Giuliana (Monica Vitti), and Corrado (Richard Harris), within a composition emphasizing the abstract use of color reminiscent of contemporary paintings. (Photo courtesy of the Museum of Modern Art)

self remarked in a conversation with a French film critic, "people often say 'write a film.' Why can't we arrive at the point of saying 'paint a film'?"[19] An obvious impression of Antonioni's color in *Red Desert* is its modernity. Only a single scene of the film (Giuliana's fantasy of a desert island far from civilization) is shot in what we have come to consider as natural color; the rest of the film presents a particularly modern form of color, the kind we have come to associate with artificial fabrics or materials such as plastics. Few of the colors, in short, are from the world of nature. Secondly, and more importantly, color is integrally linked to character, as landscape was in *L'Avventura* or architecture in *The Eclipse,* and the director uses color in many cases in place of dialogue. In what Antonioni describes as "psycho-physiology of color," the director employs color to represent Giuliana's subjective states—a process he was to continue in the more recent *The Mystery of Oberwald* (*Il mistero di Oberwald,* 1981), employing the latest videotape and laser-transfer technology permitting him to alter colors during the very act of shooting the film itself.[20] Several famous examples of Antonioni's "painting" should be noted. When Giuliana leaves the boutique she is organizing, she sits beside a fruit vendor's cart, the fruit in which has been tinted a dull gray color (perhaps suggesting a monotonous sense of uncertainty on her part). Later, after making love to Corrado in his hotel room, the entire room and its objects are bathed in a pink uterine hue (perhaps emphasizing her sense of fulfillment). Antonioni not only artificially changes the normal colors of natural objects as a way of revealing the protagonist's state of mind, but he also frames colored objects in a pure, formalized fashion. Art—before possessing a thematic content—consists in its simplest form of lines and colors organized in a special manner. In like fashion, Antonioni invites his viewer to consider objects from this technologically advanced world primarily as art forms and only afterward as things with a purely functional human purpose. Closeups of various objects accomplish this in a clever fashion. Before Corrado arrives at Giuliana's boutique, for instance, we see a completely filled frame which seems to be a green canvas reminiscent of many works of contemporary abstract art; only after Corrado drives into the frame do we realize that what we have been viewing is only a concrete wall. In other instances, Antonioni continues his technique of the trilogy, shooting objects or characters framed within various objects (people are framed through wires or gratings, or against machinery that takes on an abstract, painterly quality). And even more importantly, Antonioni rejects great depth of focus in his color photography, employing, instead, a more frequent diffused and out-of-focus shot of colored objects, giving things which normally possess more mundane associations the formal characteristics of objects in abstract painting. The lack of depth of field in his backgrounds is usually juxtaposed to the clearly focused presence of Giuliana in the same frame. An excellent example of this technique is the closing shot of the film: at first, we see a hazy, diffused focus shot dominated by a beautiful yellow color, but as the film ends, the focus is sharpened to reveal a stack of yellow barrels. Even industrial debris and slag heaps have a peculiar beauty for Antonioni.

Red Desert's formalistic vision of Ravenna's industrial culture is an ironic perspective, in one sense, since Antonioni sets his abstract, color photography in a city which is the site of some of the world's most beautiful Byzantine mosaics. Yet, Antonioni discovers a new quality of beauty, one associated with our own culture, in a town normally linked to the art of a very distant and preindustrial past. No doubt Ravenna was chosen as the location of the film to emphasize Antonioni's view that man's outmoded codes of behavior and romantic view of nature must give way to a fresh morality. Thus, Antonioni's *Red Desert* represents an ecological film in reverse: Giuliana's neurosis is not caused by her environment (or, as Marxist critics would prefer, by the capitalist economic system which operates in Ravenna); her mental instability stems, rather, from her inability to evolve, to adapt to a world filled with chemicals, plastics, machines, and microwaves. She is clearly set in contrast to her husband, who is perfectly at home with his machines, or Valerio, who plays with robot toys that terrify his mother. Even her dream of a magic, desert island—with its clear, natural colors, wild animals, clean water, and pink sand—represents for Antonioni a pathetic romantic nightmare that is out of step with the modern world. She would do better to abandon her childish dreams and learn to adapt to a world of DDT, smog, radiation, and computers. This is also the meaning of the story Giuliana tells Valerio outside the factory at the close of the film.

After Valerio asks why the industrial smoke is yellow, Giuliana explains that it is poison, and when the child innocently remarks that if a bird flies through the smoke, it will die, Giuliana responds: "That's true, but by now the birds know this and don't fly through it any longer."[21] Antonioni's message is within Giuliana's grasp, and by the end of the film it appears that she has dimly comprehended its significance and has begun to attain "normality."

With *Blow-Up*, Antonioni achieved unprecedented commercial success all over the world. In retrospect, it appears to be far less complicated a work than *Red Desert,* just as hindsight reveals that Antonioni's much maligned *Zabriskie Point* was a much better film than it appeared to be when released. *Blow-Up* represents a new direction for Antonioni. There is a new language (English) and setting (mod London in the era of the Beatles). Abandoning his alienated and sensitive women, Antonioni concentrates upon a male protagonist, a somewhat shallow photographer named Thomas (David Hemmings). He employs a new rhythm or pace in his editing; rather than continue the obsessively long takes typical of his trilogy, he now shifts to the fast-paced editing more common to television commercials. And finally, the sound track assumes an importance it never possessed in his other works.

As the choice of his leading character and title implies, Antonioni creates in *Blow-Up* a film which makes an intriguing statement about the nature of the medium itself. Thomas orders the world through his camera, controlling those around him by arranging them within his lens; in one of the more celebrated sequences, he practically makes love to Verushka, a popular fashion model, with his camera. Besides the commercial world of fashion photography, Thomas aspires to realistic camerawork with purer artistic pretensions and is in the process of assembling a series of photographs which will expose, in typical neorealist fashion, pressing social problems and the seamy side of London life. To conclude his book of violent images, he believes he has accidentally stumbled upon a lyrical scene he describes as "very peaceful, very still'—a couple in a deserted city park. The irony is that he has accidentally photographed not an idyllic moment in a park but, instead, a brutal murder there, and his perception of what his picture contains will gradually change throughout the course of the film as the photograph is enlarged or blown up. Antonioni has addressed himself in *Blow-Up* to a question as old as metaphysics itself: how do we perceive the outside world, or more specifically, how does the camera capture what we see of reality? The director is highly skeptical of the omniscience of his medium:

> The camera hidden behind a keyhole is a tell-tale eye which captures what it can. But what about the rest? What about what happens

beyond the limits of its field of vision . . . make ten, a hundred, two hundred holes, install as many cameras and shoot miles and miles of film. What will you have obtained.? A mountain of material . . . Your task will then be to reduce, to select. However, the real event also contained these aspects, it had the same marginal details, the same excess of material. By making a selection you are falsifying it. Or as some would say, you are interpreting it. It's an old argument. Life is not simple, nor is it always intelligible, and even the science of history is unable to express it in its entirety . . . there is one fact which cannot be ignored, and that is that this camera, like any other, needs to be programmed.[22]

The blow-up sequence, in which Thomas's photograph of the park is progressively and dramatically enlarged, lies at the heart of Antonioni's exploration of the nature of photography. While enlargement of an image makes the identification of a part of it (a gun barrel or a body) easier, it also increases the distortion the image suffers. Thus, an enlargement simultaneously assists and impairs our perception of the object captured on film. As we move closer and closer to a particular detail in the picture, more and more of its connotative context is lost. This sequence is quite remarkable, for during the technical process of enlarging his photograph, Thomas also reconstructs the elements of a narrative from a moment frozen in time. We actually feel motion and energy as we follow Antonioni's camera from one enlargement to another. We sense Thomas's confusion as he gets things out of order. When he finally arranges events properly—that is, a sequence of photos of decreasing scope but of increasing importance—Antonioni's camera records each enlargement as if it were real, as if the images had substance, and the sound track repeats the same wind Thomas heard earlier in the park.

But the act of interpretation must always come between the reality "out there" and the "reality" on the celluloid. At first, Thomas misconstrues completely the meaning of what he has photographed. Seeing only the gun barrel but not the corpse in the bushes, he believes he has saved the victim from ambush. Only after an erotic interruption by two fashion "groupies" does Thomas begin to suspect the truth; he returns to the scene of the crime (significantly without his camera), and finds the corpse. Without conclusive photographic proof, since

Michelangelo Antonioni's *Blow-Up* (1966). Thomas (David Hemmings) searches for the "truth" in the blow-up sequence.
(Photo courtesy of the Centro Sperimentale Cinematografico, Rome)

the murderers have earlier ransacked his studio and stolen his prints and negatives, he is unable to convince his friends of what he has seen. Discouraged, he passes out at a pot party, and awakens the next morning to discover that the corpse has disappeared from the park. The film concludes with Thomas's encounter of a group of student mimes who pretend during Ragweek to play tennis with an imaginary ball; when they pretend the ball has been hit outside the court close to Thomas, the photographer sets his camera on the ground, picks up the imaginary ball, and tosses it back, joining in their spectacle. Suddenly, Antonioni's camera cuts to a high, overhead shot, Thomas is reduced to the size of a dot on the field, and then he disappears, as if erased by some master enlarger or editor.

Thomas believes he can control reality with his camera, either by manipulating it in his commercial fashion photography, or by capturing it in his realistic work. But Antonioni does not share his confidence in photography, and *Blow-Up* demonstrates the vulnerability of the photographic image to the infinity of interpretations to which it may be subjected. Thomas has failed to interpret the chain of events he photographed accurately, even though the camera presented all he needed to know for a correct explication of the image. Irony dominates our view of Thomas, since Antonioni clearly separates Thomas's vision from his or ours. The director and his audience need not misconstrue the enlargement's significance any more than they need be convinced of the reality of the game of tennis at the close of the film. We are certain that no tennis ball exists. But we should be equally convinced that a very real corpse was photographed in the park by Thomas. However, while Thomas loses control of his own perceptions, Antonioni is clearly in control of the film we view, dominating it so completely that he chooses, in godlike fashion, to erase his protagonist from the narrative in the final frame.

When *Blow-Up* appeared in 1966, the critics and reviewers reacted as if Antonioni had tackled—and largely resolved—most of the weighty problems of Western metaphysics.[23] Rarely has so much hot air been released over a single film, and only very seldom in the history of the Italian cinema has a film been received so clamorously abroad, surpassing even the reception of the best works by Fellini, Bertolucci, Sergio Leone, or Lina Wertmüller. A more dispassionate evaluation of the work today will fail to substantiate such wild claims. In reality, Antonioni had moved away from the remarkable achievements of the severely formal and highly original works he completed prior to *Blow-Up.* And whereas he formerly avoided reliance upon plot structure, in *Blow-Up,* he exploits to the hilt the suspense inherent in the classic detective thriller, replacing the detective with Thomas, the photographer. He even drops a hint of this to the attentive viewer in a conversation Thomas has with his friend Bill, whose abstract paintings resemble the grainy texture of Thomas's enlargements:

> Bill: They don't mean anything when I do them—just a mess. Afterwards I find something to hang onto—like that—like—like . . . (A closer view of the painting. Bill points at it.)

Bill: . . . that leg.
         (Bill glances across at Thomas.)
Bill: And then it sorts itself out. It adds up. It's like finding a clue
         in a detective story.[24]

Blow-Up is nevertheless an important film. Not only is it an intriguing statement on the ambiguous nature of the film medium itself,
scrutinized by a master photographer such as Antonioni, but it is also
a strong statement in favor of the director's absolute artistic control
over his material. And, with its surprising commercial success, it
helped to create a substantial market for Italian products abroad and
enabled Antonioni to obtain foreign financial backing for both *Zabriskie Point* and *The Passenger.*

If *Blow-Up* was praised too effusively, *Zabriskie Point* was attacked
unmercifully by reviewers and critics.[25] In addition, MGM, the American studio which furnished the capital for its production, took the
rushes out of Antonioni's hands for a time and eventually forced him
into editing a different film than he may have intended. The film's
plot concerns the younger generation during the height of the Vietnam
era, and Antonioni offended many viewers by taking what they considered to be an overly simpleminded view of American politics. Employing two nonprofessionals—both of whom play themselves in *Zabriskie Point*—an anthropology student from Berkeley named Daria
Halperin and a dropout named Mark Frechette—Antonioni set out
to explore America and its mythology. The focus of the film remains
primarily upon Daria, who works for Lee Allen (Rod Taylor), a Los
Angeles real-estate developer about to begin construction on Sunnydunes, a village in the desert. Daria eventually encounters Mark, a
student radical who is wanted by the authorities for the killing of a
policeman during a student riot (a crime he did not commit) and for
stealing the plane with which he has flown into the desert. They make
love at Zabriskie Point. After he returns the plane to the airport, and
is subsequently killed by police, Daria imagines a spectacular vision
of the destruction of Lee Allen's desert mansion and drives on toward
Phoenix.

Much of the film does seem designed to attack the American consumer society and the Establishment in the name of revolution and the younger generation to which Mark and Daria belong. As Mark drives around Los Angeles, Panavison shots reveal streets filled with giant-sized models of human beings employed for commercial advertising, billboards, and automobiles. The publicity film for Sunnydunes Enterprises employs dehumanized, plastic figures in an unnatural and artificially constructed desert, all of which is ironically juxtaposed to a sound track praising such outmoded Western myths as "rugged individualism." A billboard advertising the Bank of America with a setting sun is eventually repeated by nature in the closing shots of the film, as if nature imitated consumer society images. Everything seems out of synch, an impression forcefully underscored by Antonioni's careful photography, which confuses normal proportions: thus, Lee Allen is portrayed as larger than the Richfield Building, which is located behind his office window. Establishment figures (policemen, businessmen) are impersonal and interchangeable; the average middle-aged American—for example, tourists in ridiculous Bermuda shorts—seems ugly and offensive; even Daria's visit to an old Western town reveals only senile, old cowboys sipping their beer and a commune of mentally disturbed children. We might conceivably become interested in the odyssey that takes Mark and Daria to the desert, except for the fact that they are miserable actors and Antonioni's script never engages our interest in them as characters. Rarely has the casting of a film done more damage to its reception than in *Zabriskie Point*.

And yet at least two sequences in the film are quite remarkable. Both of them present a vision of sexuality and violence threatening to the established order of Lee Allen. In the desert at Zabriskie Point, the lowest point in Death Valley, Daria and Mark make love, and Daria's fantasy is visualized on the screen—a number of couples joyfully rolling in the dust in a hymn to the liberation of the senses. Later, when Daria hears of Mark's death back in Los Angeles, she stares at Allen's mansion, a magnificent Frank Lloyd Wright-type building in the middle of the desert, and Antonioni gives us a privileged view into her thoughts. Initially, she is angry over Mark's death, and we see a spectacular series of slow-motion explosions destroying the house (shot by the director with a total of 17 cameras in different positions). Eventually, this violent vision is replaced by a cooler one dominated by an icy sky-blue color: slow-motion explosions of various objects (bookshelves, television sets, refrigerators) yield to a marvelously entertaining series of free-floating objects in a sea of blue— a lobster, Wonder Bread, Special K cereal, flowers, and many other objects normally associated with American consumer society. Now, they have been released by Daria's imagination and become aesthetic objects that may be perceived and enjoyed without linkage to an economic system she despises. As we have come to expect from Antonioni, the sequence is of great technical interest—the cool explosion sequence employed special cameras capable of producing 3,000 images per second, an astonishing technical achievement that obviously intrigued the director. In its pure imagistic power, the film's conclusion is reminiscent of that in *The Eclipse*, in which objects also dominated the human characters' presence in the final sequences.

Zabriskie Point is a film with great unrealized potential. Had Antonioni been permitted to complete his film without studio interference, perhaps we would have a convincing Italian vision of a new American myth, the emergence of a new Adam and Eve from the desert wasteland through the liberation of sensuality and the birth of revolutionary politics. Unfortunately, *Zabriskie Point* as we have it today is a flawed work. It is also something one would never have suspected from Antonioni—a simpleminded work of art which nevertheless contains a number of interesting visual innovations (its use of Panavision and special effects photography). Even in *Zabriskie Point*, Antonioni seeks to increase and deepen our perception, our vision of the world around us, and our relationship to it.

Visconti's films during this decade were characterized by an obsession with historical or cultural problems, presented within a melodramatic and elegiac style. Antonioni, on the other hand, employed less spectacular means but greater originality to develop the potential of cinema for heightening our aesthetic perception of the modern world as well as photography itself. With Fellini's films during the same period, we are faced with an even more complicated style, often as flamboyant as its director. His major works include *La Dolce Vita*

(1959), *8 ½ (Otto e mezzo,* 1962); *Juliet of the Spirits (Giulietta degli spiriti,* 1965); *Fellini: A Director's Notebook (Block-notes di un regista,* 1968); *Fellini Satyricon (Fellini Satyricon,* 1969); *The Clowns (I Clowns,* 1970); *Roma (Roma,* 1971); and *Amarcord (Amarcord,* 1974). Rarely has a personality dominated Italian cinema so thoroughly as Fellini did during these years. Though his career in this period seems less unilinear than that of either Visconti or Antonioni—and therefore more difficult to analyze—there are nevertheless certain key themes that unite all of the above works and reveal a consistent purpose in the director's art.[26]

Fellini's view that Italian neorealism entailed a commitment primarily to artistic honesty rather than to a particular style or content has already been mentioned. Beginning with *La Dolce Vita,* Fellini creates a highly idiosyncratic and surrealist world of images and dream fantasies which leave behind forever any connection to traditional cinematic "realism." Yet, Fellini's obsession with his private, egocentric vision reflects his positive concern with combatting the outmoded, obsolescent ways of seeing or thinking, rejecting dead mythologies that no longer sustain modern civilization but, rather, serve as obstacles to human development. His interest in the creation of new belief systems and new mythologies explains why childhood, adolescence, growing up, and the move from the provinces to the city loom so large as themes in his films. Fellini has compared himself to a man in the sinking ship of our civilization but comfortably at ease, since a time of intellectual, moral, and artistic crisis is also a time of new possibilities and potential rebirth:

> I feel that decadence is indispensable to rebirth. I have already said that I love shipwrecks. So I am happy to be living at a time when everything is capsizing. It's a marvelous time, for the very reason that a whole series of ideologies, concepts and conventions is being wrecked. . . . This process of dissolution is quite natural, I think. I don't see it as a sign of the death of civilisation but, on the contrary, as a sign of its life.[27]

To be sure, Fellini is the fascinated chronicler of decadence and dissolution. But—more importantly—he agrees with Hegel's dictum that the flight of Minerva's owl takes place at dusk and that the artist's function in a period of crisis is to serve not only as observer but also as midwife to the birth of new values. As he remarks,

> unmasking the lie, identifying the inauthentic, and taking apart the indefinite or false absolutes continues to be, for now, the only corrective resource . . . against our bankrupt history while we are waiting to be prepared to pose and to live under a new hypothesis of the truth.[28]

Fellini's view of the director is, in some respects, terribly romantic and somewhat old-fashioned: he dreams and collects his recollections and fantasies in a dream book. His films ultimately derive from images culled from his subconscious, images that impinge upon his waking life almost like a physical illness until he frees himself of them by giving them artistic form in a film:

> A film takes form outside your will as a constructor: all genuine details come through inspiration. And what do we mean by inspiration? The capacity for making direct contact between your unconscious and your rational mind. When an artist is happy and spontaneous, he is successful because he reaches the unconscious and translates it with a minimum of interference. . . . The transformation from dream to film takes place in the awakened conscious state, and it's clear that consciousness involves intellectual presumption which detracts from creativity.[29]

And while this Freudian textbook explanation for artistic creativity implies that Fellini views all of his films as autobiographical extensions of his own personality, it would be a fatal error to judge his works as merely chapters in his own life history. On the occasion of his sixtieth birthday, he surveyed his career for a major Italian magazine and declared:

> It is not memory that dominates my films. To say my films are autobiographical is an overly facile liquidation, a hasty classification. It seems to me that I have invented almost everything: childhood, characters, nostalgias, dreams, memories, for the pleasure of being able to recount them. In the sense of the anecdotal, there is nothing autobiographical in my films. . . . I could easily make a film com-

> posed of memories and nostalgias on Turkey, a country that I do
> not know at all. . . . Certain locations I have constructed on the set,
> brick by brick, selecting color after color, I have inhabited in a much
> more participatory, vital, and true fashion than so many other places
> where I have personally lived.[30]

For Fellini, the cinema exists solely for the purpose of individual self-expression; fantasy, rather than reality, is its proper domain, because only fantasy falls under the director's complete and absolute artistic control. Cinema entails expression, not the communication of information, and therefore its essence is imagery and light. To guarantee control, Fellini prefers to work within the massive studio complex of Cinecittà where he manufactures his own version of the outside world (in *La Dolce Vita*, Via Veneto is a constructed set, not the actual street location in Rome; in *Roma*, Fellini prefers his own *autostrada* to that just outside the studio; he prefers an obviously plastic sea in *Amarcord* or *Casanova* as more "real"—since he has imagined it that way—than the actual ocean near Rimini or Venice). And since Fellini's particular vision of the world involves affirmation and acceptance rather than intellectual analysis or dialectic, this vision embraces life, warts and all, as a fascinating spectacle or stage production. As a result, the dominant metaphor or image in his films is the parade or spectacle: the circus march, music-hall performance, orchestra rehearsal, fashion show, military review, or beauty contest—in short, the endless procession of humanity in its infinite variety, captured by the fluidity of his mobile camera and his grotesque imagery, and accompanied by his peculiar atmosphere of festivity, good humor, and celebration.

As a corollary of his view that cinema must be a means of personal expression, Fellini is compelled to oppose any social convention, institution, or ideology which inhibits the complete freedom of the individual: "What I care about most is the freedom of man, the liberation of the individual man from the network of moral and social convention in which he believes, or rather in which he thinks he believes, and which encloses him and limits him and makes him narrower, smaller, sometimes even worse than he really is."[31] Thus, his cinema portrays not only the disintegration of outmoded mythologies (the image of ancient or modern Rome in *La Dolce Vita, Fellini Sa-*

tyricon, or *Roma*; Fascist Italy in *Amarcord*; the demise of the institution
of the circus and its clowns in *Clowns*) but also the birth of new values
(the open-ended conclusion of *Fellini Satyricon*; the triumph of the
director in 8 ½ or of the emancipated protagonist in *Juliet*; and Fellini's
own creativity in *A Director's Notebook, Clowns*, and *Roma*). In all of
his works, the city of Rome looms large as the creative matrix in which
imagination and tradition, decadence and rebirth meet. And, in like
manner, the conflict between outmoded mythologies and new, more
creative ways of living is connected to the liberation of the individual,
whether the individual be a journalist, a housewife, a group of provincials, or a film director.

In his trilogy on conversion—*La Strada, The Swindle, Nights of
Cabiria*—Fellini had employed an existing Christian mythology for
very different, personal concerns. With *La Dolce Vita* and *Fellini Satyricon*, Fellini uses the city of Rome as a metaphor for Western culture, viewed from a double perspective—before the advent of Christianity (the dominant mythology, now disintegrating) and in the
present. Reportedly, Fellini once intended *La Dolce Vita* to be called
2000 Years After Jesus Christ. The first film reveals Rome after the
final disintegration of Christian mythology and shows us life based
upon public relations stunts, meaningless intellectual debates, and
sterile love affairs. The central event in the film is the suicide of the
intellectual Steiner (Alain Cuny), who believes that "to succeed one
has to be detached" from life and who must play natural sounds (rain,
thunder, the wind, birdsongs) on a mechanical device in order to enjoy
them. Likewise, the many encounters Marcello (Marcello Mastroianni), the central character, experiences in the course of his aimless
journalistic wanderings almost all result in failures. For example, he
can gain nothing from jaded women such as Maddalena (Anouk
Aimée), whose only link to reality is through sexual games, nor from
the naive and innocent Paola at the beach, who can offer him nothing
but the illusion of lost innocence. Marcello's neurotic mistress, Emma
(Yvonne Furneaux), suffocates him with her unreasonable emotional
demands. Steiner's suicide graphically underlines the emptiness of
modern values and the loss of meaning in our life. The theme of *La
Dolce Vita*—life defined as all façade and masquerade—is summarized

in the remark of one of the female impersonators after a typically Fellinian all-night revel: "I was all made up but now I look ghastly." This cultural confusion finds its visual parallel in the most famous of the many remarkable images in the film—the shot of the helicopter carrying the statue of Christ with its ironic benediction over the ruins of an ancient Roman aqueduct. Instead of producing a richness and diversity of meanings, such a confusion of ancient, Renaissance, Baroque, and modern Roman imagery results only in spiritual poverty.

Robert Richardson has described *La Dolce Vita* as a film organized around an "aesthetic of disparity," where a number of images are juxtaposed to render visually a quite complex theme, the disparity between modern life, on the one hand, and the cultural achievements of the Roman past on the other.[32] The sex goddess and film actress

Federico Fellini's *La Dolce Vita* (1959). Ancient, Christian, and modern Rome are juxtaposed in a single image.
(Photo courtesy of the Museum of Modern Art)

Sylvia (Anita Ekberg), whose animal energy overwhelms Marcello's jaded sensibility, takes the journalist on a whirlwind tour of Rome through the relics of past civilizations—ancient Rome (the Baths of Caracalla), Christian Rome (St. Peter's), and the Rome of the Popes (Trevi Fountain). She becomes a water nymph, wading in the fountain, the very essence of spontaneous and innocent sensuality; however, when Marcello tries to join her in the water, it mysteriously ceases to flow, a clear sign of his spiritual impotence. Later Sylvia's boyfriend (Lex Barker, the Tarzan of the Hollywood movies) knocks Marcello down in the street. Ironically, as the journalist's picture is taken by the *paparazzi*, he, too, now an item in a tabloid gossip column, becomes a part of the world he normally exploits.

Not unlike St. John, Augustine, and Martin Luther, Fellini has pictured Rome as the whore Babylon, the center of moral corruption in a contemporary world devoid of moral values. Yet his point of view is not that of the indignant moral reformer or the prophet—as he neatly puts it, *La Dolce Vita* is "not a trial seen by a judge but rather by an accomplice."[33] As such, Fellini sets himself clearly apart from the venerable tradition of discourse on Roman vice and Roman virtue that extends back to Petrarch's revival of interest in the Eternal City in the early Renaissance.

Fellini Satyricon uses a classical text to comment upon the modern world, much as *La Dolce Vita* employed a modern story to underline how much we have lost from our past. The fragmentary, incomplete nature of Petronius's masterpiece appealed to Fellini, since its very incompleteness forced his work into the realm of fantasy. Since he felt that pre-Christian Rome was as unfamiliar as a distant planet or a dream world, everything had to be reconstructed in his imagination and in the studios of Cinecittà. Very few of the sequences were shot outside the studio. Moreover, he changes his characteristic cinematic style radically, seeking distance and alienation rather than identification from the characters, and as a result his characteristically mobile camera is often replaced by a series of extremely static shots—indeed, the extraordinary tracking shot following Gitone (Max Born) and Encolpius (Martin Potter) through the Roman brothel is almost out of place in this contemplative, dreamlike ambience. The controlling vision that links the film's many disparate episodes together is a vision of a dehumanized, chaotic, disintegrating, pagan world with important analogies to our own times. This symphony of corruption concentrates upon two major concerns—the status of the arts in ancient Rome, and the ancient myths or religions of pagan times.

Fellini's view of Roman culture is far from favorable. If we take Vernacchio's theater as typical, we find that acting has degenerated into breaking wind on stage and that the theater of Sophocles and Terence has fallen to the level of the bloodletting in the Coliseum. The artist and his creation are rarely appreciated. Eumolpus (Salvo Randone) complains that the relics of the past in museums put con-

Federico Fellini's *Satyricon* (1969). The decadence of ancient Roman culture, in analogy with that of modern times, is revealed in Vernacchio's theatre.
(Photo from the author's private collection)

temporary Roman art to shame, and in the superficial spectators of Eumolpus' age there is a suggestion of the tourists who race through the Sistine Chapel or the Villa Borghese in order to return to the comfort of their American Express buses. Eumolpus seems to be the only character who is genuinely moved by the recitation of the Greek tragedians at Trimalchio's banquet. Ancient myths and religions are seen as equally corrupted. Fellini continues the hints he discovered in Petronius of a mock epic in which Odysseus is reduced to the comic proportions of Encolpius: rather than begin a noble quest homeward, to wife and hearth, Encolpius embarks upon a sexual quest to cure his "blunt sword"; his odyssey contains a Cyclops, but it is the one-eyed Lichas (Alain Cuny), his homosexual bride, who replaces that great mythological figure so worthy of a true hero's cunning and valor. Fellini's Theseus in the labyrinth succeeds only in winning another male lover and fails miserably in the performance of his manly duties with Ariadne, who has been reduced to a mere prostitute.

The episode of the Villa of the Suicides, placed roughly in the middle of the film, illuminates the themes of decadence and corruption which precede and follow. The fate of this noble couple highlights the confusion, loss of values, and instability in the ancient world stripped of structure, stability, and tranquility. Like Steiner in *La Dolce Vita*, the couple is obviously out of step with the times, and their quiet belief in their household gods, the divinities of a distant past, is shared by no one else in the world. That pagan religion has come to be dominated less by any moral force than by magic, sorcery, and superstition is forcefully brought home in the sequences treating the hermaphrodite or the witch Oenothea. Yet, paradoxically, the overall structure of the film seems to be governed not by pagan but rather by Christian mythology; it follows the New Testament pattern of sin, punishment, and expiation. Encolpius commits a transgression and his impotence, the opposite of the flesh's resurrection, is the punishment for which he seeks atonement; the marriage of Lichas and Encolpius seems to be a parody of a pre-Christian sacrament, just as the visit to the hermaphrodite represents the pagan equivalent of a pilgrimage to a saint, adored by the faithful who hope to obtain a miracle from his powers and who remind us of the modern believers in *The Nights of*

Cabiria and *La Dolce Vita* vainly seeking a miracle that is never to occur. The closing sequence, the eating of the body of Eumolpus by his heirs, is clearly a parody of the Christian eucharist. And it is most signficant that the young men, whom Fellini presents as the ancient ancestors of the Piazza di Spagna hippies who are searching for a new morality in our own times, reject this horrible sacrament; they set sail for new lands, new adventures and, presumably, new, and incompletely formulated standards of conduct that have not yet been calcified into confining laws and traditions. In no other of Fellini's many works is the analogy between the degradation of the past and our own present so manifest. The viewer of the twentieth century recognizes himself easily in the surrealistic images, the stylized makeup, the rhetorical flourishes, and the discontinuous, fragmented narrative. Paradoxically, the frightening, nightmare universe conjured up by Fellini's fertile imagination is far closer to the present than to the Rome of the Silver Age. The chronological chasm is bridged by the fact that Fellini's picture of the world of Petronius embodies what the director calls "the eternal myth: man standing alone before the fascinating mystery of life, all its terror, its beauty and its passion."[34]

In *Roma*, Fellini combines the portrayal of Rome's mythic past and present with a Rome entirely of his own invention. The work is a completely discontinuous narrative—given coherence only by Fellini's private fantasies of his adopted city—viewed from three different perspectives: the image of Rome remembered from a young schoolboy's experiences in class and at the cinema; Rome as remembered by a young provincial (Fellini's alter ego?) arriving there in 1939; and the "objective" picture of Rome presented by the adult Fellini, now making a documentary on the Eternal City. Fellini's city is a city of illusions and myths—it is the center of Italian cinema, the headquarters of the Roman Catholic Church, as well as of the Italian government, and Fellini seems to view religion, politics, and cinema as human institutions all relying upon the manipulation of images and myths. Furthermore, there is no single Rome but a number of images, all of which interpenetrate and enrich the connotations of the others: the Rome of classical antiquity, symbolized by the many architectural wonders still surviving and made famous by the Livian tales of virtuous republicans as well as by less edifying stories of decadence, sexual license, and corrupting thirst for power from Tacitus or Suetonius; the Rome of the Renaissance and Reformation, the Baroque city that represents not only the Church Militant but also the darker underside of the Inquisition, the Jesuits, and the reactionary "black" nobility of the city; modern Rome, that of Mussolini and his dream to re-establish an imperial dominion modeled upon the Eternal City's former greatness; and finally, Fellini's Rome, that of the cinema, the music hall, the prewar brothels, and autostradas. Before presenting his own summation of Roman myth, Fellini moves to deflate various myths from the past. The Fascist rhetoric in the schools of his childhood is satirized mercilessly: a ridiculous schoolmaster crosses the Rubicon in imitation of Caesar (whose statue in the town is merely a pigeon target), discovering that this ancient stream has degenerated into a tiny trickle. Then Fellini evokes his childhood memory of Roman costume films popular during the Fascist period, and his subjective camera angles and points of view recapture the sense of wonder that must have typified his first experiences in the movie theaters, while it pokes fun at such films' rhetorical and bombastic style.

This satirical attack is followed by sequences that obviously evince Fellini's nostalgia. Perhaps most typical is the image of the Roman boarding house in 1939, inhabited by characters more likely to be found in an asylum than a hotel (a Chinese gentleman; the effeminate, sunburned son of the landlady, who is a monstrous woman with inflamed ovaries; a midget grandmother; an actor; a character who resembles Mussolini and declaims his speeches after leaving the toilet). Fellini's young provincial wanders outside to an open-air trattoria and is served an enormous Roman meal, as he is reminded: "What you eat you shit!" Later on that evening, in the deserted street, the light of an abandoned trolley car throws the shadows of stray dogs upon a wall, and they are magically transformed into images of the she-wolf, the ancient symbol of Rome. The theme of discovering the Roman past everywhere in the Roman present becomes one of Fellini's major preoccupations and will eventually culminate in the sequence portraying the excavation of a subway beneath the city's surface.

At this point in the film, Fellini shifts to the present as he and his camera crew enter Rome by the circular road around the city. Now we are greeted by an infernal vision, a journey into a modern mechanical hell—a cattle truck crashes, policeman clash with Maoists, prostitutes appear on the side of the road, a riderless horse (from *La Strada?*) mysteriously appears, the crew passes diabolic factories lit up at night near ancient ruins. The sequence culminates in front of the Coliseum in a tremendous traffic jam. Then Fellini cuts to a sequence in which he and his crew are making a "documentary" in a park, and a group of students attacks him for directing films not intended to resolve social problems. As if in response to this attack, Fellini then moves by flashback to a variety theater, the wartime Jovinelli, and he presents a number of acts which parody the Andrews Sisters, Fred Astaire, and various production numbers from Hollywood musicals (of the "Dames at Sea" variety).

Federico Fellini's *Roma* (1971). The flashback to the Roman brothels compares sexuality in the Fascist period to that of the hippies in the Piazza di Spagna.
(Photo courtesy of the Museum of Modern Art)

This fantastic sequence is rapidly followed by Fellini's visit to the subway excavation, where the discovery of a Roman home with ancient frescoes intact ends in tragedy: when the frescoes are touched by the modern air, they vanish mysteriously and are ruined. Subsequently, Fellini moves from a shot of sexually uninhibited hippies on the Spanish Steps to the memory of the furtive, guilt-ridden sex of his youth in the official Roman brothels. From the brothel, we move to another vignette, an ecclesiastical fashion show in which the modern church is held up to derisive ridicule: after a number of surrealistic images are conjured up (skating priests, disembodied priests' habits made from plastic and neon lights, bridal gowns worn by skeletons, and the like), the parade ends with an impressive "beatific" vision of a plastic Pope Pius XII before whom the audience falls to its knees in awe. Then Fellini moves to the bohemian district of Rome, Trastevere, to witness the Festa de Noiantri (the "Festival of We Ourselves"), in which the Romans celebrate themselves: Gore Vidal pretentiously declares he lives in Rome because it is the perfect spot to observe the end of the world; Anna Magnani is accosted by Fellini in the street, vestal virgin and tramp, the perfect embodiment of the Roman she-wolf or *lupa*. The final sequence seems to represent Fellini's modern version of the ancient barbarian hordes invading the Eternal City: a band of motorcyclists roar about the city at night, passing most of the major monuments of ancient Rome (the Capitoline, the Forum), Baroque Rome (Piazza Navona), and they converge upon the Coliseum—the site of Fellini's previous traffic jam and his unsuccessful attempt to penetrate to the center of the city—before roaring out into the night along the Via Cristoforo Colombo. It would seem, therefore, that *Roma* is a parody of the autobiographical documentary, a "notebook" of Fellini's obsessive preoccupation with the past.

And yet, *Roma* is a far more complicated view of the Eternal City's multifaceted significance. First and foremost, the film represents the quintessential Fellini in its treatment of the interplay of reality and illusion, autobiography and history. The importance of bizarre characters, eccentric faces, and grotesque makeup continues a tendency of *Fellini Satyricon*, as does the extravagant usage of elaborate sets constructed in Cinecittà or immediately outside the great studio complex. Almost everything in the film—the variety theater, outdoor scenes, even the Coliseum and the Roman autostrada—has been reconstructed by Fellini and in most cases, perfectly serviceable "real" locations have been consciously avoided. It is as if Fellini were declaring to his audience that reality consists solely in what the artist creates: the actual autostrada or Coliseum will not suffice, since they are not constructed as Fellini's imagination pictures them. Moreover, the archetypal Fellinian image of the parade or procession in *Roma* encompasses an enormous range of human experience—the theater, street traffic, the church, brothels, motocyclists, hippies. All of humanity passes before the director's camera as if the world were a bizarre, grotesque circus performance. Yet, at the center of this fragmented but exciting vision there is always the creative presence of Fellini, the character who plays in this particular film Fellini the director, continuing his role of *A Director's Notebook* and *The Clowns*. Only the imaginative fantasy of the maestro makes sense of all the confusion. And only the imagination ultimately leads to the creation of a new mythology for the future. Fellini does not replace one shopworn myth of Rome with another of his own invention. Instead, he renders the essence of his alternative myth, if it may be called that, with the final motorcycle ride through Rome; a close examination of the final sequence of the film reveals that it is ultimately Fellini's *camera*, not the cycles, that speeds down the center line of the road toward the Roman Coliseum. And this time, unlike Fellini's earlier attempt to penetrate the Eternal City with his crew, the way is unblocked and easy—no chaotic and infernal traffic jam impedes the camera's path because it now embodies the liberated and creative imagination. It is fitting that Fellini's vision of the city is one of continuous movement, a cinematic image that portrays for his audience the director's exhilaration with the creative moment and the ultimate artistic experience—synonymous for Fellini with human freedom.[35]

Fellini's preoccupation with human freedom is evident in his masterpiece, *8 ½*, which also constitutes an important statement of his views on the cinema itself. The harried protagonist of the work, Guido Anselmi (Marcello Mastroianni) is a director who embodies many of

Fellini's personal characteristics; he is trying to complete a science-fiction film treating the experience of people on earth after an atomic war, and most of *8 ½* concerns his personal problems with producers, mistress, wife, critics, and friends that arise during his efforts. Fellini's narrative moves rapidly back and forth between Guido's "reality," his fantasies, and flashbacks to the past or dreams; it is a discontinuous storyline with little logical or chronological unity. Instead, the film acquires coherence by remaining faithful to Guido's subjective and often irrational perspective. The influence of psychoanalysis (both Freud and Jung) upon Fellini's portrayal of his director is obvious, especially in Guido's relationships to his wife, Luisa (Anouk Aimée), his mistress Carla (Sandra Milo), and his parents. After Guido makes love to Carla, his mother visits him in a dream and together they visit a cemetery, where Guido (dressed in the black cape and hat he will later be wearing in flashback to his school days) assists his father into a grave. His mother kisses him first maternally, then sensuously (Guido obviously suffers from an Oedipal complex), and she suddenly turns into his wife Luisa in his waking life. Even the smallest incident in Guido's daily experience may touch off wild fantasies or involuntary memories from his past. After Guido's mind is read by a telepath named Maurice, we flash back to a happy and carefree infancy in which he was cared for in a large farmhouse by a number of family servants—the nonsense word ASA NISI MASA in Guido's mind is explained as a children's word game, not unlike our English "pig-Latin" and actually means *anima*, a Jungian concept as well as the Italian word for "soul." When Guido meets the Cardinal at the spa, he experiences a flashback to his days in Catholic school, and much of his sexual behavior is explained by the repressive morality of his teachers—Guido views women as either virgins or whores and is constantly haunted by the vision of La Saraghina, an enormous woman who would perform suggestive dances for the schoolboys on a nearby beach.

Often, Guido moves from the present to a daydream rather than to his past. At the mud baths, for example, he imagines a surrealistic descent into the spa and a Dantesque encounter with the Cardinal in which the church's only message for him (no salvation outside the church) lacks any meaning. Later, when Luisa and Carla both sit at the

Federico Fellini's 8 1/2 (1962). Guido (Marcello Mastroianni) forms the magic circle at the conclusion of the film, reconciling his artistic aspirations with his private life.
(Photo courtesy of the Museum of Modern Art)

same cafe, Guido imagines that they become good friends, and this daydream leads to another flashback to the childhood farmhouse which is now transformed by his imagination into a harem, where almost all the women in his life serve his every whim. Yet, one woman is significantly missing from Guido's harem—the character played by Claudia Cardinale who magically appears at the spa's mineral fountain to deliver to Guido the purifying and healing waters of the resort. Claudia Cardinale plays a number of roles in *8 ½*: she is first and foremost the image of Guido's Ideal Woman; secondly, she is the actress herself, Claudia Cardinale; and, of course, she is the character in Fellini's film who plays both the Ideal and herself. In some respects, Claudia parallels Guido as a Pirandellian figure. And the link between Fellini and Pirandello is significant. In Pirandello's trilogy of the theater, the separation between audience and stage, actor and person, art and illusion was obliterated; *Six Characters in Search of an Author* (1921), *Each in His Own Way* (1924), and *Tonight We Improvise* (1930) were concerned not with the traditional clash of personalities or plot but with the dramatization of the very act of artistic creation itself (as in the celebrated irrational appearance of Madame Pace in *Six Characters*). The influence of Pirandello upon Fellini is obvious. Both men emphasize two basic features that set their work off from that of other playwrights or film directors who have examined the nature of the theater or the cinema: both Pirandello and Fellini include in their works all of the possible criticisms that might be leveled at them, and, more importantly, both men produce a completed work of art whose subject concerns another work of art which remains incomplete. In *Six Characters*, Pirandello's play is not that of the six characters, whose romantic and sentimental drama is never realized, but the completed dramatization of the impossibility of *their* play. In *8 ½*, *Fellini's* film is completed, for it is the representation of Guido's failure to complete *his* science-fiction film. Just as it seems that *8 ½* has ended in an artistic impasse for Guido, the magic creative event occurs. In the grand finale that takes place in the magic circus circle (the traditional symbol for divine perfection), the director Guido announces: "Life is a festival. Let us live it!" He is then redeemed, saved by an act of artistic grace that is just as miraculous as its Christian counterpart. All the various characters in his life or fantasies assemble at the launching-pad set of the film he is unable to complete—all, that is, except the Ideal. Now most are dressed in white, purified by Guido's irrational willingness to accept them for what they are. Guido and Luisa join the parade, and we suddenly shift to night, where the characters in the circular procession are replaced by four clowns and little Guido, now dressed in white and shot alone in a spotlight. Thus, in a magnificent portrayal of the sources of artistic inspiration and a moving dramatization of the moment of creation itself (always irrational and mysterious, according to Fellini), Guido's failure to realize *his* film is magically transformed into the successful conclusion and realization of *Fellini's* film: creation from nothingness, or more precisely, creation from the deepest reaches of the artist's liberated imagination, is ultimately Fellini's only "message" to his audience. As Fellini has repeatedly remarked, "I am Guido."

Fellini's emphasis on the liberated imagination is also the theme of *The Clowns*—a work made for television—which combines elements of his personal biography (his childhood memories of circuses and clowns), a parody of film documentaries implicit in the suggestion that the imagination is more "real" than reality, and finally, a conclusion in which Fellini's imagination revives the moribund institution of clowning. During the course of Fellini's research on the history of clowns, we are led to conclude that clowns are dead. Just as Fellini turns to represent the funeral of a dead clown, he is asked what the message of his work has been, but before he can reply, a clown covers his head with a bucket. Messages, in the words of a great Hollywood producer, come from Western Union—not works of art. The magnificent funeral procession revives the institution of clowns for a brief moment, however, as Fellini's creativity triumphs even over death before a moving trumpet duet by two clowns in the center of the magic circus ring concludes the film. As one perceptive interpretation of *The Clowns* concluded, Fellini's comic vision here, as in *8 ½*, depends upon acceptance rather than rational analysis. Fellini accepts the absurdity of his obsession with a dead institution, and in the process of laughing at himself, he accomplishes the impossible, resurrecting the dead clowns in a "world beyond reality" which is the same artistic realm in which Guido's apotheosis takes place.[36]

While Fellini is normally obsessed with the problems of the artist, (usually a director such as he is), *Juliet of the Spirits* and *Amarcord* deal with more universal problems—those of women in repressive and male-dominated societies or of individuals living in an era of social or political conformity. *Juliet* was Fellini's first feature film in color, and he has described it as

> the story of the struggle taken up by a woman against certain monsters in herself, which are certain psychic components in her deformed by educational taboos, moral conventions, false idealisms. . . . The film takes all of its meaning, finds its true justification on the level of the imagination.[37]

Federico Fellini's *The Clowns* (1970). The two types of clown—the white clown and the Auguste—which represent different aspects of human nature are reconciled at the concluding trumpet solo.
(Photo courtesy of the Museum of Modern Art)

Juliet (Giulietta Masina) is a demure housewife with an unfaithful husband named Giorgio (Mario Pisu); the film recounts her discovery of Giorgio's infidelities, her confused attempts to deal with her own sexuality, and her eventual emancipation and maturity. The film is a remarkable argument for woman's liberation in a country where masculine values have traditionally dominated thinking on a woman's role in society.

In *Juliet*, Fellini continues the argument of *8 ½* that childhood memories and traumatic experiences shape adult life and must be confronted if their negative influence is to be avoided. But the past, for Fellini, is not merely a source of psychological neurosis; it is also a source of potential freedom and individual liberation. The healthy individual, such as Guido became at the end of *8 ½*, can be redeemed by an acceptance of his past. Juliet demonstrates just how much more difficult this acceptance is for an ordinary Italian woman than for an artist. The opening shot of a strange gingerbread home (reminiscent of René Magritte's surrealistic picture, *The Empire of Lights*) in which Juliet and her husband live sets the tone of the work: it resembles a doll's house, appropriate for Juliet's role as the faithful housewife who dutifully remembers her wedding anniversary while Giorgio completely forgets it. While Juliet dresses simply and in a costume reminding us of a coolie's outfit, the other characters—in particular her mother and sister—display outlandish and lavish clothes, setting her apart from their fashionable world.

Juliet's quiet life is assaulted by a number of outside forces, her "spirits." A seance scene produces a spirit who announces that she is "nobody." Later, in a dream on the beach, she experiences a surrealistic vision with obvious psychoanalytical implications: a man pulling a rope ashore hands it to Juliet (he is later revealed to be the detective she hires to investigate Giorgio), and as Juliet pulls a boat ashore, a boatload of strange savages armed with swords and horses lands on the beach just before a passing jet plane brings her back to reality. Subsequently, we discover in a flashback that these savages are circus characters and that her grandfather, whom she dearly loved, once ran off with a circus ballerina. In other flashbacks, we learn that Juliet has suffered a traumatic experience during the performance of a class play.

Its plot was a Christian saint's life: Romans roast a Christian woman
for refusing to renounce her faith (appropriately, Juliet played the
martyr), and as the grate is being raised to heaven, Juliet's irate grandfather interrupts the performance, denying Juliet the vision of God
which the nuns promised she would find on the other side of a ceiling
panel. Her Catholic education, symbolized by this traumatic event,
causes Juliet to suffer from sexual repression, and whenever she is
tempted to betray Giorgio (as she is at the fantastic party given by
her neighbor Susy [Sandra Milo]), the vision of this burning martyr
paralyzes her and chains her to an outmoded morality.

Juliet's neuroses—personified by a number of bizarre and surrealistic figures including the martyred girl, somber nuns, Nazi generals,
and her eccentric friends and relatives—all crowd about her, appearing
in her closets, behind doors, and the like. Only after she disobeys her
mother does a door open, and we watch the mature Juliet free the
little child Juliet from the martyr's grating; they embrace and the spirits
immediately disappear. The final shot of the film reveals a liberated
Juliet free to leave her prisonlike home, advancing in harmony with
the camera's forward motion toward the future. She no longer relies
upon her role as wife to provide her identity and is freed from the
feelings of guilt when she compares herself to her erotic neighbor
Susy; by her act of self-understanding, her "spirits" have been transformed into benevolent rather than evil presences. Disobedience to
her mother—originally the cause of an inferiority complex that stifles
Juliet's personality—leads to a renewal of her hope for the future. It
would be a simple matter to criticize the superficiality of Fellini's belief
that the mere acceptance of psychological problems (as in the case of
Guido or Juliet) necessarily yields therapeutic results. In both 8 ½
and *Juliet*, the intellectual level of Fellini's argument never rises to
match the tremendous emotive and persuasive power of the director's
imagery. But it would be difficult to imagine more aesthetically
satisfying conclusions to films organized around Fellini's particular
concern for human freedom.

While Fellini's works from *Amarcord* to the present are consistently
interpreted by the critics as segments of the director's autobiography,
Fellini himself has consistently declared that *Amarcord, Casanova* (*Ca-*

sanova, 1976), *Orchestra Rehearsal* (*Prova d'orchestra*, 1979), and *The City of Women* (*La città delle donne*, 1980) have important sociological and political dimensions as well. Thus, while *Amarcord* was enthusiastically received as a nostalgic return to the world of the *vitelloni* in Fellini's early works, the director's goals were very different:

> The province of *Amarcord* is one in which we are all recognizable, the director first of all, in the ignorance which confounded us. A great ignorance and a great confusion. Not that I wish to minimize the economic and social causes of fascism. I only wish to say that today what is still most interesting is the psychological, emotional manner of being a fascist. What is this manner? It is a sort of blockage, an arrested development during the phase of adolescence. . . . That is, this remaining children for eternity, this leaving responsibilities for others, this living with the comforting sensation that there is someone who thinks for you (and at one time it's mother, then it's father, then it's the mayor, another time Il Duce, another time the Madonna, another time the Bishop, in short other people): and in the meanwhile you have this limited, time-wasting freedom which permits you only to cultivate absurd dreams—the dream of the American cinema, or the Oriental dream concerning women; in conclusion, the same old, monstrous, out-of-date myths that even today seem to me to form the most important conditioning of the average Italian.[38]

All of the collective events in the provincial town during the Mussolinian era—the absurd classrooms taught by pedantic, incompetent, or neurotic professors; the visit of the Fascist *federale* on April 21 (the anniversary of the mythical foundation of Rome celebrated by the regime); the passage of the ocean liner *Rex* before an awed group of townspeople; the burning of the great bonfire to celebrate the pagan rites of springtime—are, for Fellini, "occasions of total stupidity," part of a gigantic leveling process which buries individuality in mass conformity before symbols of power. This is clearest in the imaginary Fascist wedding staged by Fellini before an enormous bust of Mussolini made of pink and white flowers: the entire population seems anxious to become a collective, unthinking entity under Il Duce's benevolent gaze.

Federico Fellini's *Amarcord* (1974). The imaginary Fascist marriage takes place before the fantastic image of Mussolini.
(Photo courtesy of the Museum of Modern Art)

Yet central to Fellini's view of Italy's collective past is his own complicity in this experience and his attempts to come to grips with it in his memory. His critical vision of provincial life also has its poignant side: the poetic arrival of the puff balls signaling the change of the seasons; the Hollywood characters, townspeople resembling American movie stars, that dominate the village's mentality; the sympathetic Gradisca (Magali Noël), who swoons before the *Rex*, the *federale*, or other symbols of the regime's power and eventually marries a patriotic policeman who shouts "Viva L'Italia!" at their wedding; the adventures of the young Titta (Bruno Zanin) as he discovers his nascent sexuality in the cinema or with the buxom tobacconist in town; the outbursts of Titta's neurotic mother against his honest and hardworking ex-Socialist father. These poetic sequences touch us in a manner that the political argument of *Amarcord* could never do, for they uncover the sense of loss and unrealized potential we all share, even if we have never experienced the same social structure that permeated Italian life during Mussolini's day. But it is a profoundly negative vision, one which underlines at every opportunity the disastrous effects such a society had upon the individual and his self-expression.

If we accept Fellini's assertion, as I believe we must, that he and his films are obsessed with the liberation of the individual, then it is legitimate to inquire of him whether he has anything but negative visions to offer us. What does Fellini propose to counter the cultural void repeatedly reflected in so many of his recent films? I believe Fellini's answer—the positive, life-affirming message of his works—lies precisely in the image of the liberated creative individual, in creativity itself. What his cinema can provide, not only by his example but also in specific films, is the image of the completely liberated creator. And nowhere is this concept better expressed than in the conclusions to many of his best works—Guido's procession, Juliet's escape from her evil "spirits," the apotheosis of the clowns, and the director's camera racing through Rome's historic monuments. *8 ½* was originally intended to be titled *La bella confusione*, a confusion that was "beautiful" because it comprised the necessary precondition for the godlike leap from artistic intention to the creative and individual fulfillment concluding the best of Fellini's films. In an essay entitled "The Unpopular Cinema," Pasolini attacked the prevalent notion in Italy that an avant-garde film must embody a political or ideological position; the truly liberated cinema, Pasolini claimed, represents not outmoded political views but, rather, the spectacle of the creativity of its maker; its medium is ultimately its message.[39] It is not any specific and limited political content, but the joy we as spectators experience from the sight of the artist's absolute freedom in his creation of images, stories, and fables that constitutes the unique humanistic vision of the cinema. Fellini declares as much in his recent *Orchestra Rehearsal* when the harassed German conductor tells his strife-torn orchestra that "the notes save us, the music saves us." We see this even more directly in *A Director's Notebook*. In Fellini's office at Cinecittà, the director is attempting to audition characters for *Fellini Satyricon*, and the scene is one of unbelievable confusion, not unlike that which is resolved in *8 ½*. A father brings his son, whose only talent consists of whistling like a bird, to see the maestro; a confidence man tries to sell Fellini a painting by an artist "greater than Raphael" but whom he refuses to identify; another grotesque character insists upon playing the accordion while the director talks. Each figure seems taken directly from the sketchbook of a master caricaturist and presents the spectator with the vision of what one critic has called "a fresco of human absurdity and loveliness."[40] As the camera records this chaos from Fellini's subjective perspective, the director remarks:

> Yes, I know it must seem sinful, cruel, but no, I am very fond of all these characters who are always chasing after me, following me from one film to another. They are all a little mad, I know that. They say they need me, but the truth is that I need them more. Their human qualities are rich, comic, and sometimes very moving.[41]

Never has Fellini, so fond of frivolous declarations to critics and scholars, been so honest and open in discussing the sources of his inspiration. All he has to offer his audience is his celebration and affirmation of life, and the passion with which he pursues his own personal vision. Yet, as Pasolini reminds us, this image of human creativity freed from all restrictive fetters which Fellini's cinema celebrates— even when concerned with the topic of decay, corruption, and cultural disintegration—is an exhilarating image that somehow, and quite mysteriously, manages to bridge the distance between the cinema screen and our deepest emotions in what Fellini would term the only act of grace that ultimately holds artistic significance.

A Fistful of Pasta: Sergio Leone and the Spaghetti Western

As one of the most popular and durable of all Hollywood film genres, the Western inevitably had an influence upon postwar Italian cinema. We have already seen how a number of works during the neorealist period by Germi and De Santis reflected their interest in the genre. But this is insignificant compared to the remarkable phenomenon we have come to label the "spaghetti Western," which flourished between 1963 and 1973 and included at least 400 films. Westerns dominated Italian film exports (in terms of box-office profits) between 1956 and 1971, a period that produced some of the most important Italian masterpieces. Although Sergio Leone (1929–89) is usually given the lion's share of credit for launching this Italian version of an American staple, some 25 Westerns had been produced at Cinecittà before he began *A Fistful of Dollars* (*Un pugno di dollari*, 1964). And since Leone completed only five Westerns, admittedly among the best, his genius is insufficient to explain the sudden increase in these many films in such a brief period of time.[1]

As Christopher Frayling has perceptively explained in a recent analysis of the Italian Western, economic factors played an important role in the genesis of the genre. Hollywood's annual production of Westerns had dropped from 54 in 1958 to a mere 11 in 1962–63 and would rise to 37 only in 1967 after the international success of Sergio

253

Leone's films. For a number of reasons, there was a stronger demand for such a product than Hollywood could meet, especially in years of financial crisis. In Rome, however, the huge infrastructure of the Italian film industry—second only to that of Hollywood—had just passed through a period of cooperation with Hollywood producers, directors, and actors working in Italy, and a number of Italians had worked closely with Americans on a wide variety of films, especially historical costume dramas. The Italian industry was looking for international financing for popular films, and with American money available, as well as relatively inexpensive Spanish locations and extras, the Western may well have been the logical choice, especially since it offered the possibility of exploiting the lucrative American market as well. The desire to pass Italian products off as authentic "American" Westerns certainly explains why most Italian directors and actors (including Leone, as "Bob Robertson"), disguised their national identities with English pseudonyms and characteristically employed at least one or two recognizably American actors to stand out in a sea of Italian and Spanish extras.

The economic explanation is insufficient to explain the phenomenon entirely, since by 1964 it seemed that the once promising market for Westerns "Made in Italy" had failed to materialize. All this changed with the appearance of Sergio Leone's *A Fistful of Dollars, For a Few Dollars More* (*Per qualche dollaro in più*, 1965), and *The Good, the Bad, and the Ugly*, (*Il buono, il brutto, il cattivo*, 1966). Leone also completed two less successful works—*Once Upon a Time in the West* (*C'era una volta il west*, 1968), and *Duck, You Sucker!*, also released under the title *A Fistful of Dynamite* (*Giù la testa*, 1971)—but more important were the imitations of his major films. The best include *Django* (*Django*, 1966) by Sergio Corbucci (1927–   ); *A Bullet for the General* (*Quien sabe?*, 1966) by Damiano Damiani (1922–   ); *They Call Me Trinity* (*Lo chiamavano Trinità*, 1970) by Enzo Barboni; and *My Name Is Nobody* (*Il mio nome è nessuno*, 1973) by Tonino Valerii, supervised by Leone and constituting a parody not only of the Western but of Leone's works as well. By the time the popularity of the genre had been worked to death, the Italian Western had moved from Leone's stylized works through comedy, parody, and political themes, culminating in the bizarre *Don't Touch the White Woman* (*Non toccare la donna bianca*, 1975) of Marco Ferreri (1928–   ).

Much of the impact of Leone's first Western was generated by its conscious departures from what had come to be known as the "classic" Western formula. John Cawelti outlines this formula in *The Six-Gun Mystique* as a combination of narrative possibilities generated by three central roles: the townspeople (agents of civilization); savages or outlaws who threaten the first group; and heroes, men who share certain characteristics of the second group but who act ultimately on behalf of the representatives of civilization.[2] Elsewhere, Cawelti has argued that the classic Westerns of the 1940s and 1950s "depended on and reaffirmed for us the traditional American view that violence was the fault of evil and corrupt men; good men might be forced to use it in purging society of corruption, but this would lead to a regenerated social order."[3] With *A Fistful of Dollars*, Sergio Leone willfully set out to modify the conventions of the traditional genre. The plot of the film is derived in part from Kurosawa's *Yojimbo* (1961) and in part from Carlo Goldoni's play, *The Servant of Two Masters*.[4] The Stranger, or the Man With No Name (Clint Eastwood) is released from a Southwestern prison by its warden in order to clean up a town across the Mexican border infested by two rival clans—the Baxters, a group of American gunrunners dominated by the mother, Consuelo; and the Mexican Rojos band, led by the sadistic Ramón (Gian Maria Volonté) and his two brothers, who deal in liquor. The Stranger plays one gang off against the other and eventually kills off the surviving Rojos in a climactic gunfight at the close of the film. Leone immediately plunges us into a violent and cynical world far removed from that of Howard Hawks or John Ford. The hero acts out of a single motivation (financial gain) which he shares with the villainous Baxters and Rojos. The town of San Miguel is far from the microcosm of a threatened outpost of civilization and is, instead, a surrealistic spot where nobody works except the coffin maker Piripero and the saloon owner Silvanito, since killing is the only means of gaining respect. Except for Marisol, a poor Mexican woman exploited sexually by Ramón Rojo, women (traditionally the symbol of civilization and stability in the western) are absent or, if present, are widows. Violence must be met by equal

violence: the authorities are reduced to using criminals to uphold the
law, and even the cavalry is corrupted, selling liquor and guns to the
Indians rather than protecting civilization. Leone also injects a note
of black humor into the West of his imagination: typical of his comic
wit is a scene preceding a gunfight as The Stranger tells the coffin-
maker to prepare three coffins and confronts three Baxter men who
have "insulted" his mule; in the inevitable shootout that follows, he
miscalculates and shoots an additional gunman ("My mistake—four
coffins!"). But it is not only Leone's changes in traditional Western
plots or his grotesque gags that constitute his originality. Perhaps no
more skillful composer has ever been employed by a Western director
than Ennio Morricone (1928–   ), whose unusual sound track composed from gunfire, richocheting bullets, cries, trumpet solos, traditional Sicilian folk instruments (especially the Jew's harp), and whistles
would become increasingly important in the Leone films, even central
to the narrative itself, and there is evidence that close collaboration
between Morricone and Leone actually shaped the final outcome of
both the shooting and editing process.[5] More important for the evolution of Leone's style is his insistence, even in his first Western,
upon lengthy and extreme close-ups of the faces of his actors, a stylistic
trait which will become more and more mannered in subsequent films.
Leone has explained this obsession with close-ups as part of his reaction against the formulaic codes imposed upon him by mediocre
directors who were more interested in following the so-called rules
of cinematic narrative than in pursuing their own individual style:

> I made 58 films as an assistant—I was at the side of directors who
> applied all the rules: make it, for example, a close-up to show that
> the character is about to say something important. I reacted against
> all that and so close-ups in my films are always the expression of an
> emotion. . . . so they call me a perfectionist and a formalist because
> I watch my framing. But I'm not doing it to make it pretty; I'm
> seeking, first and foremost, the relevant emotion.[6]

Leone's emphasis upon elemental and often brutal emotional impact
in his films conflicted with the implicit moral message audiences expected from the classic Western formula. Yet A Fistful of Dollars was

a revolutionary work, reinvigorating a dying genre and earning more money than *any* other Italian film made until that date. And, it cost only about $200,000 to make. Its success made Leone's task of locating financing for his next works quite simple.[7]

In *For a Few Dollars More*, Leone attempts to retain popular elements of *A Fistful of Dollars* in combination with several new narrative twists and variations. Clint Eastwood returns as The Stranger with his Tuscan cigars and his Mexican serape; now he has become a bounty hunter who kills purely for profit. To this familiar figure, Leone adds Colonel Mortimer (Lee Van Cleef), a retired soldier and bounty hunter motivated not only by profit but also the thirst for revenge: he is searching for the rapist of his sister, whose memory is evoked by a musical pocket watch. To complete the cast, there is Indio (Gian Maria Volonté), the dope-crazy Mexican killer Mortimer is seeking and whose perverse pleasure in violence is linked to the moment, years ago, when the death of Mortimer's sister traumatized him sexually—a moment recalled by the musical watch Indio took from the woman which was the mate of that carried by Mortimer. Like the effect of Proust's famous madeleine, the watch chimes evoke a flashback in Mortimer and Indio. Leone employs the flashback brilliantly in this film, linking the emotions of two of his three protagonists with it and preparing us for the inevitable showdown and settling of accounts between them that will conclude the film. Moreover, the initial hostility between Mortimer and The Stranger, both in competition for the same prey, makes the ultimate resolution of the plot—a face-off between The Stranger, Mortimer, and Indio—more exciting. Mortimer is a bizarre individual, a professional who stalks his target from a distance with an assortment of rifles rolled up in his saddle bags; his chilling obsession is in sharp contrast to his preacher's costume and his habitual reading of the Bible. Once again, Leone's grotesque humor permeates the film: when Mortimer and the Stranger first meet, they have an infantile encounter, each scuffing the other's boots in an attempt to establish a bounty hunter's pecking order. In another memorable sequence, Mortimer strikes a match for his ubiquitous pipe on the physically deformed back of one of Indio's men (Klaus Kinski); elsewhere, Indio, standing in a church pulpit preaches to his gang of murderers an irreverent

sermon (the parable of the carpenter) concerning a bank they are about
to rob, where the safe has been hidden within a cabinet—a piece of
information Indio obtained from its carpenter before he killed him!

The entire movie builds up to an inexorable confrontation between
Mortimer, Indio, and the Stranger. The motivation for the Colonel's
vendetta is somewhat unclear in American prints, since absurd cuts
have obscured the information Leone conveyed in his flashbacks—
not only did Indio kill Mortimer's brother-in-law on his wedding night
and rape his sister, but afterward the woman committed suicide with
Indio's gun. Thus, the perverse sexual makeup of the psychotic bandit
and his irrational activity can be explained by a sexual trauma he suffered; in addition, Mortimer's drive to settle accounts springs from
the same event. The confrontation is the first of many classic Leone
gunfights: as a number of sharp close-ups capture the faces, gun hands,
weapons, and minute expressions of the protagonists, the Morricone
score based upon the watch's chimes creates an emotional climax.
Indio's death is almost an afterthought, for the settling of accounts in
Leone's works takes on a symbolic function, a ritual act which concludes a narrative cycle and employs music in a manner similar to that
of grand opera, where death is often linked to spectacular aria accom-
paniments. With the death of Indio, the partnership between Mortimer and the Stranger is ended: the Stranger is left to pile up the
bodies to collect his bounty, while Mortimer, his vendetta concluded,
rides off into the distance.

A Fistful of Dollars and A Few Dollars More were brilliantly made
films with relatively low budgets. In Leone's subsequent two works—
The Good, the Bad, and the Ugly and Once Upon a Time in the West—
the production costs jump substantially, enabling the director to shift
perspective toward an epic tone and grander historical themes; moreover, the presence of established Hollywood stars, in addition to the
now famous Eastwood and Van Cleef, reflect the importance the
American film industry granted Leone's work. In the first two films,
there were few values, besides money or revenge, that motivated the
protagonists. However, in his treatments of the American Civil War
and the development of the West with the arrival of the railroad, Leone
began a more traditional concern in the Western with larger historical

issues, even if they are often ambiguously treated. The three characters of *The Good, The Bad, and The Ugly*—the bounty hunter Blondy
(Eastwood), the Mexican bandit Tuco (Eli Wallach), and the murderer-
for-hire Angel Eyes (Van Cleef)—all seem familiar figures motivated
by gold and bounty. Yet, as Leone presents them to us in separate
sequences, all ending in violent murder (with a title on the screen
denoting their respective moral connotations), such simplistic distinctions are immediately blurred. The film's plot centers on a complex
chase by the three men for $200,000 in gold stolen from an army
payroll and buried in an unmarked grave at Sad Hill Cemetery, in the
midst of a Civil War battlefield set in a rather unspecified location in
the Southwest territory. Once again, Leone's complex storyline culminates in a climactic gunfight between his heroes, who struggle over
the gold. But a number of highly interesting historical elements are
injected into the film. The moral ambiguity of the three protagonists,
ironically labeled "good," "bad," and "ugly," is overshadowed by the
even more shocking moral ambiguity of the Civil War itself. Right
and wrong, good and bad, change in Leone's universe as rapidly as do
uniforms: indeed, one of the most telling comments about the two
sides in the conflict comes from a comic sequence in which Tuco and
Blondy, disguised as Confederate soldiers, hail what they think is a
column of Southern horsemen and are taken prisoner by them after
the troops brush off the gray dust from their blue uniforms. The prison
camp to which they are taken is even more revealing: modeled more
on the Nazi *lagers* than upon the infamous Andersonville Prison, it
includes a sadistic guard (Angel Eyes, himself disguised as a Union
soldier) who beats his prisoners to the tune of a prison orchestra—
an obvious reference to Auschwitz. The battle for Langston Bridge is
an idiotic and murderous struggle for a "flyspeck on the map" at headquarters, and the bridge itself is useless to anyone except for the fact
that it is wanted by the opposing army. The visuals of the battle scene,
employing hundreds of extras, recall the senseless slaughter in the
trenches during World War I. Though the scene shows automatic
weapons never actually employed in the Civil War, it also features
sequences in which Leone's camera reveals images taken directly from
Matthew Brady battle photographs.

Sergio Leone's *The Good, the Bad, and the Ugly* (1966). The site of the climactic gunbattle between Blondy (Clint Eastwood), Angel Eyes (Lee Van Cleef) and Tuco (Eli Wallach).
(Photo courtesy of the Museum of Modern Art)

Leone seems to prefer the smaller but infinitely less immoral universe of his three gunfighters to general warfare: at least they live and die by a code with rules and a certain sense of dignity. And he continues his black humor in his third Western. In the final triangular confrontation over the gold, only Blondy knows the actual location of the grave in which it is buried. Therefore, he has written that name on a rock placed in the center of a ringed mud flat (the symbolic *corrida* circle of death and violence that Leone uses for his showdowns); the three men face off against each other, and Leone devotes a full three minutes or more to the crescendo of suspense leading to the actual gunfire. Here, Leone's manneristic gunbattle reaches an emotional peak never before achieved: as Morricone's music increases the tension, the director cuts rapidly back and forth between extreme close-ups of the eyes, pupils, hands, fingers, and weapons of the three men until the inevitable shot signals the wounding and then (with another bullet) the death of Angel Eyes. But we discover that Blondy has tricked Tuco, removing his bullets the night before to even the odds, and gallows humor returns with Blondy's callous remark: "In this world, there're two kinds of people, my friend—those with loaded guns and those who dig. You dig!" We seem to have been transported back to the amoral world of Leone's first two films, and yet a change has overtaken Leone's gunfighter. While *The Good, the Bad, and the Ugly* aims at the demystification of traditional moral values associated with gunfighters, a number of so-called edifying moments in the film tempers its tone: Tuco tells his brother, a priest, that he was driven into a life of crime to support his parents; Blondy compassionately offers a cigar and a warm coat to a dying Confederate soldier; Tuco is eventually spared by Blondy and even given half of the gold, when he could just as easily have been murdered. Male cameraderie, a bond central to the traditional Western formula, has crept back into Sergio Leone's interpretation of the American West, and such traditional themes will become even more important with the arrival of civilization and the railroad in his next film.

Once Upon a Time in the West was a film Leone had not intended to make. After the international success of his first three Westerns, he went to Hollywood seeking financial support for his still unmade work on American gangsters in the 1920s, *Once Upon a Time, America (C'era una volta America)*, but this proved impossible (however, his discussion about this project with Warren Beatty did precede Beatty's proposal to film *Bonnie and Clyde*). Armed with Paramount money and Henry Fonda as his star, Leone returned to location in Spain and Cinecittà and commissioned a script from Bernardo Bertolucci, who included in what he eventually showed to Leone numerous quotations from a lifetime of watching Hollywood Westerns in the Paris Cinémathèque. While Bertolucci's script was eventually discarded, *Once Upon a Time in the West* remains the most deeply indebted of all Leone's Westerns to the classic Western, with references to *High Noon, Shane, My Dar-*

ling Clementine, The Iron Horse, The Man Who Shot Liberty Valence,
and many films which influence the choice of Leone's shots, names,
costumes, and even his plot. Not only is the film a celebration of the
classic American Western, but it is also Leone's last and most elaborate
effort in the "spaghetti Western" genre he created almost single-
handedly, for his subsequent work would include a move in the direction of the so-called political Western with *Duck, You Sucker!* and
a production which parodied his own style in *My Name Is Nobody*.

Leone's casting alone establishes an interesting link to American
tradition. During the five-minute sequence that opens the film and
provides the credits, Leone presents two of the most familiar Western
character actors—Jack Elam and Woody Strode—who have been sent
to the train station to murder Harmonica (Charles Bronson) by Frank
(Henry Fonda), the hired killer working for a railroad magnate, Mr.

Sergio Leone's *Once Upon a Time in the West* (1968). Harmonica (Charles
Bronson) confronts the three gunmen sent to kill him at the train station.
(Photo courtesy of the Museum of Modern Art)

Morton (Gabriele Ferzetti). The sequence is an obvious quotation from *High Noon*, but Leone's style is totally different: for an enormous amount of time, compared to the importance of the sequence in the plot, Leone concentrates with obsessive and extreme close-ups upon the mannerisms of his two Hollywood actors: Elam's eye, Strode's bald head, the fly that buzzes about Elam until he traps it in his revolver, the water dripping upon Strode's hat. It is a brilliant segment wherein Leone's love for exploiting the emotive power of the extreme close-up is given free rein. Then, as the credits are completed, Harmonica suddenly kills off the two gunfighters, and they disappear from the story entirely. Leone has thus tantalized his audience with familiar Western faces, then removed them after they have served their purpose as iconographical representations of a familiar genre which he is in the act of transforming. An even more interesting and similar operation is carried out with the first appearance of Henry Fonda in the subsequent sequence, which shifts from the train station to a farmhouse where Frank McBain and his family await the arrival of his new bride, Jill (Claudia Cardinale), from New Orleans. (Later we learn that she comes from the finest brothel in that city to the town of Sweetwater to start a new life.) An Irish immigrant, McBain has bought land where the railroad will eventually need a refueling station, and Mr. Morton sends Frank to remove this obstacle from his path. As the family awaits the arrival of their new mother, they are suddenly massacred from ambush by Frank's men. We then cut to the appearance of Frank, a close-up of his famous blue eyes, then his gun, then the lone surviving child, then Frank's smile, and Frank brutally murders the last McBain child as the sound of his gun blends into the sound of a train whistle. Leone is counting on the audience's shocked response to his transformation of Henry Fonda, from John Ford's blue-eyed and heroic Marshall Wyatt Earp in *My Darling Clementine* (or a host of other lesser Westerns) into a cold-blooded and merciless killer of women and children. Moreover, this single sequence, with its juxtaposition of the murdered family and the arrival of the railroad, enables Leone to introduce the plot of the film—the clash of an older way of life on the lawless western frontier with the arrival of civilization, symbolized by the railroad.

Unlike many classic Westerns, *Once Upon a Time in the West* does not celebrate the coming of civilization. In fact, everything connected with the railroad and Mr. Morton results in violence and death, and is in sharp opposition to the more positive forces of civilization at work in the Western universe of John Ford (evoked by Leone with his shots of Monument Valley near the McBain ranch), or other classic American Western directors. While Jill McBain's attempts to claim her inheritance and to build the refueling station embody Leone's projection of the West's future, his sympathies clearly remain with the old outlaw Cheyenne (Jason Robards), who falls in love with Jill and whose sense of honor reflects the traditional gunfighter's code. Cheyenne and men like him, or like Leone's earlier Western protagonists, no longer have a role in the new society the railroad represents. Frank is a more complicated figure: a gunfighter like Cheyenne but with far fewer scruples, he seeks to transform himself into a rapacious capitalist like Mr. Morton, scheming to seize Morton's fortune after his inevitable death from the paralyzing disease that will eventually cut short his dream of reaching the Pacific with his rails. When Morton asks him how it feels sitting behind the plush desk in his private railroad car, Frank replies: "It's almost like holding a gun, only more powerful. . . . I'm beginning to think big too!" But Frank's desire to move from one era to another, from the code of the gunfighter to that of the industrial capitalist, is doomed to failure since the sinister figure of Harmonica stands in his way. And the entire film leads to the eventual showdown between them that will conclude Leone's story. At first, in two earlier flashbacks shot out of focus, we see Harmonica's memory of some past event which links the two men but which is, as yet, left unexplained by Leone. Each of the four main characters—Frank, Harmonica, Cheyenne, and Morton—have a musical theme from Morricone's score, and the music of Harmonica's mouth organ begins to assume an importance equal to that of the watch chimes in *For a Few Dollars More*. Each time Frank asks Harmonica who he is, Harmonica's only reply is a list of the dead men Frank has killed in the past.

While Cheyenne and Harmonica work to save Jill McBain's ranch (thereby blocking Frank's plans to take it over) and Morton's men are massacred in the process, the stage is set for the final settlement of accounts, which also corresponds to the process of revealing Harmonica's identity. As Frank and Harmonica face off, their conversation reveals Leone's continued juxtaposition of the old West he loves with the civilization that will eventually destroy it:

> Frank: Surprised to see me here?
> Harmonica: I knew you'd come. . . . So you found out you're not
>   a businessman?
> Frank: Just a man.
> Harmonica: An ancient race.

Frank realizes he will discover Harmonica's identity when he, Frank, is on the point of dying. As they face each other in the familiar circular *corrida* to a crescendo of Morricone's brilliant music and a variety of camera angles and close-ups, a tight close-up of Bronson's face shifts to a flashback explaining Harmonica's single-minded vendetta: a younger Frank strides slowly forward, stuffing a harmonica into the mouth of a young Mexican boy, on whose shoulders sits his brother, a noose around his neck; the camera cranes back to frame this scene through a semi-circular adobe structure, and through all this in the background we catch a glimpse of Monument Valley, "Ford country." But Ford's classic geographical setting never witnessed anything like Leone's vision in *Once Upon a Time in the West*. The older brother pushes his younger brother away, preferring to die a manly death by hanging rather than to beg Frank for his life, and we cut rapidly from the flashback to the gunfight as Harmonica shoots Frank in revenge for what we now discover was his brother's death many, many years ago. To complete the bizarre cycle of death, Harmonica thrusts his mouth organ into Frank's mouth, as Frank shares Harmonica's recollection at the point of death.

Cheyenne, who has concealed the fact that in killing Morton he himself received a gunshot wound that is slowly killing him, bids farewell to Jill and rides off to die by himself. Leone then shifts his attention to the arrival of the train, and the hustle and bustle of the new civilization which has symbolically replaced that of the gunfighter: the film's last image shows Jill carrying water to the thirsty railroad

Sergio Leone's *Once Upon a Time in the West* (1968). Frank (Henry Fonda)
learns the truth concerning the identity of Harmonica (Charles Bronson)
only at the point of death.
(Photo courtesy of the Museum of Modern Art)

men, an affirmation that the Old West of the solitary male gunfighter
with his special code of values has been transcended by the matriarchal culture of urban civilization.

With *Once Upon a Time in the West*, Sergio Leone bids farewell to
the Western genre as he has understood it in the classic American
formula and even as he has transformed it in his own successful "spaghetti Westerns." Once upon a time, as Christopher Frayling has concluded, "these characters lived and died in a world of simple icons,
where they enacted a series of rituals in which even life and death
became external, melodramatic gestures—and these gestures were
codified, as the story was retold, to become a full-fledged myth."[8]
The Italian director's works have explored many of the implications

of this myth, which they transfigured and finally abandoned. Yet, Leone's style was not without influence: his creative use of superb sound tracks by Ennio Morricone, his genius in employing close-ups to reveal emotions rather than information, and his brilliant editing rhythm changed the face of an entire genre. It would be impossible to imagine the films of such contemporary Western directors as Sam Peckinpah (*The Wild Bunch*, 1969), Don Siegel (*Coogan's Bluff*, 1968), or Ted Post (*Hang 'Em High*, 1968) if the work of Leone had not preceded them.

Besides having an influence upon the American Western, it was inevitable that the spectacular success of Leone's "dollars" trilogy would lead to immediate imitation within the Cinecittà studio system, as producers sought quick profits from fashionable subject matter. Hundreds of Italian Westerns of varying quality were the result, as was a series of new heroes modeled upon Leone's Stranger. Perhaps most interesting are the Django films, begun by Sergio Corbucci's *Django* (1966) with Franco Nero in the lead role. Borrowing from the "servant of two masters" plot-type, the film has Django caught between racist Ku Klux Klan members who shoot Mexican peasants for sport, on the one hand, and Mexican bandits on the other. The gun skill typical of Leone's protagonists is exaggerated in Corbucci's hero, who drags a machinegun concealed in a coffin around with him. The success of this bloody film (banned in England for its violence) spawned a number of Django imitations by various directors: Alberto de Martino's *Django Shoots First* (*Django spara per primo*, 1966); Giulio Questi's *Django, Kill* (*Se sei vivo, spara*, 1967); Leon Klimowsky's *Django, the Bounty Hunter* (*Django cacciatore di taglie*, 1968); Sergio Garrone's *Django the Bastard* (*Django il bastardo*, 1969); and numerous others. All in all there were more than twenty works exploiting the success of Corbucci's film. Other clusters of Westerns arose, employing different protagonists, repeating the pattern set by the earlier musclemen epics that preceded the Western as the staple product at Cinecittà. Besides Django, other characters emerged: Sartana, the best films on whom were made by Giuliano Carmineo; Ringo, a series associated with Duccio Tessari (1926–   ); Sabata, a hero created by Gianfranco Parolini; and the comic Western series on a character named Trinity, invented by Enzo Barboni. And just as Ursus, Maciste, Ulysses, and Hercules had eventually been crammed into the same film in order to squeeze the last lira of profit out of the *peplum* epic, in like manner, Westerns began to combine two or more of their heroes for the maximum appeal at the box office.[9]

It was perhaps inevitable that the spaghetti Western would also be made to carry the burden of ideological arguments, produced, as they were, in a country where political debate is so important an element in the popular culture of the audience. Of course, the classic American Western certainly reflected an ideology, or at least a political slant, but it was rarely an overtly Marxist one. However, the traditional Hollywood Western with a Mexican setting could easily be diverted for political purposes, since Mexico served so frequently as the location for revolution. Films such as these were usually based upon what Frayling (following Corbucci's suggestion) defines as the "Zapata-Spaghetti plot."[10] They often employed two protagonists—one a Mexican peasant or bandit who is or becomes a revolutionary, the other a European or American mercenary who opposes or assists the Mexican. The relationship between Blondy and Tuco in Leone's *The Good, The Bad, and The Ugly*, the obvious source of the plot, is thus transformed: the "Gringo" character remains an alien figure, often unconnected or even opposed to the revolution that the Mexican character eventually embraces. He may, however, also join forces with the Mexican. The first important political Western was Damiani's *A Bullet for the General*, which featured the familiar Gian Maria Volonté as the bandit El Chuncho, Klaus Kinski as his priest-turned-bandit brother Santo, and Lou Castel (an actor often used by such ideologically oriented directors as Marco Bellocchio) in the role of the American mercenary Bill Tate, sent to Mexico by American agents to assassinate the revolutionary leader, General Elias. When El Chuncho discovers the truth, he kills Tate and becoming a true revolutionary he tells a peasant not to buy bread but explosives. Made in an era of increasing criticism over America's involvement in Vietnam and the Third World, the film has a message that is painfully obvious—Yankee go home!

A number of such overtly political Westerns were produced, but perhaps none was so interesting as Sergio Leone's *Duck, You Sucker!* starring Rod Steiger as Juan, a Mexican bandit who eventually becomes a true revolutionary, and James Coburn as Sean, a jaded Irish revolutionary and explosives expert who eventually joins Juan and dies fighting for his cause. The Leone style is recognizable immediately: in an opening sequence (underlined by a quotation from Mao), Juan is insulted by a wagon-load of wealthy people, including not only Mexican landowners and a priest, but also an American who compares peasants to pigs; the close-ups of them eating and speaking owe an obvious debt to Eisenstein. The flashback, so well used in *For a Few Dollars More* and *Once Upon a Time in the West*, now reveals Leone's doubts about the morality of social upheavals: from them, we learn that under torture, Sean's best friend betrayed him, and that Sean had to kill this friend in a gunbattle that ended with his escape from the English authorities. History seems to repeat itself as Dr. Villega (Romolo Valli), a Mexican doctor and one of the revolution's leaders, is forced by a diabolical army officer to betray Juan under torture. When Sean discovers this betrayal, his past experience moves him to understand Villega (as he failed to do with his friend) and to give him a chance to die a hero by ramming a locomotive into a troop train. As Sean declares: "When I started using dynamite, I believed in many things. Finally, I believed only in dynamite. I don't judge you, Villega. I did that only once in my life." Mortally wounded later in the fight around the derailed troop train, Sean bids farewell to Juan, experiences one last flashback (in which he, his best friend, and his fiancée are all reunited in an Irish meadow, photographed in a romantic manner), and he eventually blows himself to bits. While Leone obviously sympathizes with the plight of Juan and Sean and seems to prefer the side of the exploited to that of the exploiters, his interest in *Duck, You Sucker!* seems focused upon Sean's transformation from an embittered killer of his best friend to a man who understands that life's complexities cannot be encompassed by revolutionary slogans.

The impact of the political spaghetti Western was not limited to the work of Leone or a number of lesser directors at Cinecittà. Jean-Luc Godard's *Wind from the East* (*Vent d'Est*, 1969), was originally intended to be a politically oriented statement with a script by the

German revolutionary Daniel Cohn-Bendit, and Gian Maria Volonté
was cast in the role of an Indian-torturing cavalry officer to explore
the parallel between the conquest of the American West in the nineteenth century and American "imperialism" in the Third World.[11]
Another interesting variant on the genre is Gillo Pontecorvo's *Burn!*
(*Quiemada*, 1969), with Marlon Brando as Sir William Walker, a British agent and soldier of fortune who first foments a native revolution
against the Portuguese and then helps to organize the middle-class
settlers of the island to exploit the peasants and keep the island open
to British trade. When the man Walker has trained to overthrow Portuguese rule leads another uprising against the landowners, Walker
returns to the island, burns out and destroys the rebels, and hangs his
friend (after he refuses Walker's offer of escape); just as Walker is
about to leave the island, he is assassinated by a dock worker. Pontecorvo implies that a popular revolution, like the one he recreated
in Algeria, is impossible to stop. While not technically a Western,
Burn! nevertheless employs the so-called Zapata-Spaghetti plot typical of the political western, locating it slightly outside its normal geographical location.[12]

An even more obviously political message was delivered by Marco
Ferreri's *Don't Touch the White Woman*, a film which combines political
as well as comic themes. Influenced by the bizarre sense of humor
associated with surrealist film, Ferreri parodies the famous Errol Flynn
role in Raoul Walsh's *They Died With Their Boots On* (1941), and sets
his ludicrous General Custer (Marcello Mastroianni) and the battle of
the Little Big Horn in the excavations made during construction on
the site of the old Les Halles market in Paris. Ugo Tognazzi is Custer's
faithful Indian scout, and Alain Cuny plays Sitting Bull. Ferreri's sense
of humor manages to save the film from its Godardian pretensions
and propagandistic content. The sight of Sitting Bull riding into contemporary Paris with his braves in the midst of rush-hour traffic to
meet Custer, who is seated with his men at a sidewalk cafe, in some
measure alleviates the heavy-handed parallel of the Indian Wars in
America in the last century and what Ferreri views as President Nix-
on's genocide in Vietnam. Nevertheless, *Don't Touch the White Woman*
reveals just how flexible the formula of the spaghetti Western was

and how easily it could accommodate a variety of themes, characters and plots.[13]

The political Western, in the highly intellectualized form practiced by Godard or Ferreri, had little impact upon the evolution of the genre in Italy, although works by lesser-known directors which never subordinated ideology to action were often quite successful. It was the comic western, however, which superseded even Sergio Leone's spectacular profitability at the box office. Most popular of all the comic Westerns were a series of films made by Enzo Barboni that began with *They Call Me Trinity*, starring Terence Hill (an anglicized stage name for the Italian actor Mario Girotti) as Trinity, a lazy, blue-eyed, adolescent who is described as "the right hand of the devil" and set off against Bud Spenser (whose Italian name is Carlo Pedersoli), his bearlike brother Bambino, "the left hand of the devil." Dressed in ragged and filthy clothes, Trinity travels through the West sleeping, as his horse drags him along on an Indian litter. His favorite activities are eating enormous quantities of beans, brawling, and bizarre shootouts that stretch the limits of credibility. *They Call Me Trinity* contains all the familiar elements from Leone's films and those of his imitators: bounty hunters, innocent Mormon settlers who refuse to defend themselves from a band of idiotic Mexican bandits; a group of Yahoos led by a jaded Southern aristocrat (Farley Granger). Both the complex psychological plotting of Leone's best works and his characteristic formalism yield to lengthy barroom brawls and elaborate stunts. Political themes are completely ignored. Leone's grotesque black humor is replaced by a series of comic gags that recall early film comedy (typical is a brawl scene in which Trinity hits a man's head on a cash register, which obligingly registers "Thank You"). The Trinity series should probably be studied as much for the information it reveals about the Italian audience and film industry as for the generic changes it creates in the traditional Western. While the series pokes fun at both the classic formula and Leone's hybrid, it aims at pure matinee entertainment and exploits the daydreams of a rather unsophisticated audience of young Italian males, who project themselves into Trinity's cool style, his aversion to serious work, and his macho prowess.

Tonino Valerii's *My Name Is Nobody* (1973). The parody of the Western
hero in both the classic American genre and in Leone's interpretation of
it: Nobody (Terence Hill) stuffs himself with beans.
(Photo courtesy of the Museum of Modern Art)

The most interesting comic Western, one which combined the same
goodhearted zest for slapstick and humor of the Trinity series with a
rather sophisticated view of the genre, is Valerii's *My Name Is Nobody*,
produced by Leone. This clever work may be defined as the comic
counterpart of *Once Upon a Time in the West*, since it treats the passing
of an era of gunfighters and cowboy heroes in a zany fashion. Henry
Fonda plays Jack Beauregard, an aging gunfighter whose only goal is
to leave the West and to retire in Europe; he is plagued by a young
man named Nobody, who aspires to become "Somebody" by replacing
Beauregard after assuring him a place in the history books by arranging
a successful shootout with "150 pure-bred sons-of-bitches on horse-

back," a grotesque enlargement of Peckinpah's Wild Bunch. The film parodies numerous scenes from Leone's own works: the opening sequence of *Once Upon a Time in the West*; the symbolic circular *corrida*; the omnipresent Leone graveyards (in which there is a tombstone marked Peckinpah); even the typical showdown music of Morricone. But *My Name Is Nobody* also parodies the Trinity series, recalled by casting Terence Hill as the "nobody" who has now replaced the "somebody" Henry Fonda, the representative of Leone's style. Comic gags abound: when a number of cowboys throw custard pies at some hapless blacks for entertainment, Nobody replaces the custard pie with one made from concrete and hits a white man with it; when he is confronted with a dwarf on stilts, he whittles the stilts down with shots from his revolver until the dwarf is his size; elsewhere Nobody displays his prowess and lightning-fast speed by engaging in a face-slapping contest with an arrogant gunfighter, who is so much slower than Nobody that he cannot ever reach his revolver before his face is smacked over and over. Of course, the basic gag of the film—which revolves around the protagonist's name, Nobody—can be traced all the way back to Homer's *Odyssey* (in which Ulysses cleverly announces his name as No Man to Polyphemus so that the other cyclops think Polyphemus has been drinking when he claims "No Man" has blinded him). As a man remarks at the beginning of the film after Beauregard kills three men so quickly it seems his gun has never left the holster, "Nobody is faster." And Nobody must therefore establish his preeminence over Jack in a public showdown, after Jack's fame has reached its apogee with his destruction of the 150 riders that guarantees his entrance into the history books as a myth.

Rather than present a typical Western plot, Valerii focuses in his film upon the confrontation of two characters embodying different myths. More than a film about the West, *My Name Is Nobody* is a work about films on the West and the myth of the West. The event which gains Jack mythical status—his gun battle with 150 men whose saddlebags have been stuffed with dynamite by Nobody to ensure an explosive finale—constitutes a parody of Sam Peckinpah's typical slow-motion photography of violence, here blown out of all rational proportion by the excessive numbers of dead men as well as a humorous comment on the music Morricone usually supplied for Leone films (Wagner's *Ride of the Valkyries* replaces the familiar Sicilian Jew's harp, gunfire, and whistles). Beauregard's fictitious death in a final gunbattle with Nobody is filmed in the presence of a photographer, as if to underline the film's self-reflexive character. As he is about to leave for Europe, Jack writes a letter to Nobody telling him that his era, in which men still believed a pistol shot could resolve everything, has now been transcended and that the kind of violence typical of Nobody's age is quantitively and qualitatively different from the code of behavior he and men like him lived by. Earlier, Nobody had told Jack a parable of a little bird, a cow, and a coyote: the bird became trapped in cow manure, and the only person willing to help him out of the mire turned out to be a hungry coyote. The parable is now explained:

> Folks that throw dirt on you, aren't always trying to hurt you. And folks that pull you out of a jam aren't always trying to help you. But the main point is: when you're up to your nose in shit—keep your mouth shut![14]

On that philosophical note, Sergio Leone bids farewell to a West created by his fertile imagination, returning to Europe along with Jack Beauregard. But the West on celluloid would never be the same after the impact of his work.

8

Myth and Marx: Pier Paolo Pasolini and Bernardo Bertolucci

Of the younger filmmakers who emerged in the postneorealist generation, Pasolini and Bertolucci received the greatest attention from critics and intellectuals and eventually gained the broadest, most international audience. While both directors reflect in their later films a heuristic encounter with two major intellectual trends, psychoanalysis and Marxism, neither director can be said to embody totally orthodox Freudian or Marxist positions in their work. Pasolini's career is perhaps the most enigmatic of the pair: after *Hawks and Sparrows*, Pasolini's cinema moved further and further away from his neorealist heritage toward a concern with myth and ideology. In *Oedipus Rex* (*Edipo re*, 1967), *Teorema* (1968), *Medea* (*Medea*, 1969), and *Pigpen* (*Il porcile*, 1969), Pasolini explored various aspects of mythical consciousness, employing not only traditional narratives from Sophocles and Euripides but also tales of his own invention. From these highly intellectual films, Pasolini then moved to seek out a more popular audience with his tremendously successful "trilogy of life" derived from three narrative masterpieces from the Middle Ages: *The Decameron* (*Il Decameron*, 1971); *The Canterbury Tales* (*I racconti di Canterbury*, 1972); and *The Arabian Nights* (*Il fiore delle mille e una notte*, 1973). After this celebration of sexuality and storytelling, Pasolini then rejected his "trilogy of life" with his last film, taken from the Marquis de Sade: *Salò, or the One Hundred and Twenty Days of Sodom* (*Salò o le*

120 giornate di Sodoma, 1975), a black vision that seemed ironically appropriate to the violent manner in which Pasolini met his death shortly after the film's release.[1]

Curiously, *Oedipus Rex* has never been distributed in the United States, although it was widely screened in Great Britain and Western Europe. Pasolini takes great liberties with the Sophoclean plays, recreating the protagonist to suit his own personal sensibilities: Oedipus becomes less a tragic figure destroyed by a mysterious fate than an individual whose ruin derives from a consciously willed refusal to examine himself rationally. Rather than a tortured intellectual, Pasolini's Oedipus is a man who responds to intellectual dilemmas by violence and rage. The Freudian interpretation of the classic tale is introduced by a brief autobiographical prologue, which takes place in prewar Italy around 1930. In it we see a middle-class family much like Pasolini's: a tiny baby provokes resentment in his soldier father, with whom he competes for attention from the wife/mother (played by Silvana Mangano, who wore a dress in the scene that once belonged to Pasolini's mother). When the father cruelly squeezes the young baby's foot, the film shifts to the traditional story of Oedipus ("swollen foot"), which Pasolini has located in Morocco rather than Greece, continuing his characteristic construction by analogy that was so successful in *The Gospel*.

The most striking changes in the classical texts occur precisely in the traditional section of the storyline: Oedipus (played by Franco Citti of *Accattone*) blunders into his tragic destiny, murdering his father and escort in an incident that has no apparent relationship to any mysterious or predetermined fate that might explain his actions; unlike Sophocles' Oedipus, who in a confrontation with the Sphinx solved a difficult riddle, thereby establishing himself as an intellectual, Pasolini's Oedipus attacks the Sphinx and kills it. The blind, brutal nature of Pasolini's Oedipus thus overshadows either the theme of parricide or that of incest in Sophocles, and his eventual blindness is emblematic of his basic refusal to understand his destiny. Pasolini's interpretation of the Greek myth then concludes wth a return to the modern era, as a blinded Oedipus absurdly wanders among factories and buildings in Northern Italy, returning finally to the place of his

.

birth. While the apparently Freudian prologue and epilogue might suggest that the Oedipal myth of parricide and incest serves as the mythical structure underlying all modern human relationships centering around the institution of the family, the film *Oedipus Rex* ultimately utilizes the metaphor of blindness to chronicle contemporary man's refusal to come to grips with his consciousness and to chart his own destiny.

Sophocles serves Pasolini as a springboard to comment on man's individual destiny, but the director found in Euripides' *Medea* a convenient vehicle for the personal mythology that had dominated *The Gospel* and most of his early films. The plot is outwardly traditional: Medea, a sorceress and daughter of Aeëtes, King of Aea in Colchis, aids Jason, who has come with his Argonauts to steal the Golden Fleece, which he requires in order to regain his kingdom; during the theft, Medea kills her own brother, Apsyrtus, and returns with Jason to Corinth, where she is subsequently abandoned by Jason, who decides to marry Glauce, daughter of King Creon. With her magic powers restored, Medea destroys Glauce and Creon; she also vengefully murders the two children she has borne Jason. Influenced not only by his own attachment to pre-industrial peasant cultures but also by readings in anthropologists Mircea Eliade and James George Frazer, Pasolini transforms Euripides' classical story into a drama concerning a clash between two cultures with diametrically opposed views of reality, a clash having more relevance to philosophical and religious problems than to traditional Marxist theories of class conflict. Medea, played brilliantly by Maria Callas in her first cinematic role, represents the archaic, clerical, and hierarchical universe of human prehistory, a stage of civilization typical of pre-industrial peasant cultures still found, according to Pasolini, in the Third World. Working by analogy, Pasolini sets the ancient mythical kingdom of Colchis in remote portions of Syria and Turkey. Jason (Giuseppe Gentile), on the other hand, embodies an entirely different perspective, the rational, antimythical and pragmatic universe of the technician. As Pasolini states, *Medea* could easily be the story of a Third World people and its disastrous encounter with materialist Western civilization, while Jason's inability to understand such a pre-industrial culture marks him as part of the modern world we all inhabit. Thus, Corinth is shown as the famous courtyard of Pisa's Cathedral, symbolic of the triumph of reason over myth brought about by the middle-class culture of the Italian Renaissance.[2]

The most impressive sequences in Pasolini's *Medea* present dramatic imagery reflecting this clash of two worlds, barbarism and civilization. Jason's blindness to myth is clear from the opening sequence with his tutor, the Centaur: the half-man half-beast explains to the young child that "all is holy, wherever you look, there is a god; when nature seems natural, that is the end; everything is holy." In successive film cuts, Jason grows to manhood, and the Centaur (Laurent Terzieff) is transformed into a mere man, symbolizing the drastic diminution of Jason's mythic consciousness. Later, after Jason steals the fleece, both Centaurs appear—the mythical Centaur remains silent (since its message is no longer comprehended by the rational Jason), as the completely human Centaur must explain its sentiments. Yet, mythical consciousness is not totally obliterated by its rational counterpart, Pasolini believes, and the heritage of modern man's origins in pre-industrial mythical culture is never totally destroyed in the human psyche, as the mute presence of the original Centaur implies. The lesson of the Centaur leads to Pasolini's brilliant evocation of mythical culture on Colchis: peasants gather for a human sacrifice that is part of a fertility cult of prehistorical origins, the victim's blood being employed to fertilize the wheat fields. This visual rendering of the kind of ritual found minutely described in any good anthropological textbook then shifts to the dramatic clash between the rational Greek invaders and the relatively defenseless peasants. Jason and his men overwhelm their opponents by their superior technology in much the same manner the Spanish Conquistadores destroyed Indian civilizations in South America. When Medea betrays her origins and flees with Jason and the fleece, she discovers that outside the mythical realm of Colchis, she has no roots, no identity ("Speak to me, Earth, I no longer remember your voice, speak to me, Sun!"). According to Pasolini, Medea thus finds herself in the same position as contemporary man: without a sense of identity provided by ancient myths, Medea exists without a soul and is alienated, separated from the beneficial power of illusion.

When Jason returns with the fleece, he is curiously uninterested in it; he tells King Pelias, who holds the kingdom that is rightfully his, that the goatskin no longer possesses any power, and the sequence underlines Pasolini's belief that the loss of myth entails a loss of human potential. Jason sets aside his claim to the kingdom of Pelias and proceeds to Corinth/Pisa.

Pasolini then returns to Euripides and the concluding revenge of Medea. Now, however, Medea's vendetta reflects her reacquisition of her mythical powers of sorcery, and they triumph over the facile rationalism of Jason and Corinth. Pasolini shows us this revenge in a novel manner, providing the viewer with two narratives of the burning, fiery deaths of Glauce (Magareth Clementi) and Creon (Massimo Girotti): the first embodies a subjective dream Medea experiences, while the second scene constitutes the actual event. The finale of the film thus juxtaposes Medea's mythical consciousness to Jason's world of reality. True to his particular reading of Gramscian Marxism, Pasolini believes that both capitalism and orthodox Marxism aim at the destruction of the pre-industrial cultures he admires both in Italy and in the Third World. Alienation derives not merely from working in a world where one's work product is controlled by an exploitive capitalist class, but it may also be caused by the loss of a sense of mythical identity, a sense of harmony with nature that is destroyed by a pragmatic, technological civilization. And the ultimate triumph of Medea provides Western viewers with a profoundly prophetic vision of the anger alien cultures feel when their values are attacked. Thus, the impact of Freud, Jung, cultural anthropology, and Marx produces in Pasolini's *Medea* not only an engagingly original synthesis of the director's personal views on the human condition, but also a highly successful cinematic spectacle.

With *Teorema* and *Pigpen*, Pasolini places us in totally unfamiliar territory, relying now upon a mythology entirely of his own invention rather than upon well-known, although radically transformed, literary texts. Yet, *Teorema* and *Pigpen* may reveal more about Pasolini's cinematic techniques and his personal ideology than any of his more accessible works. *Teorema* means "theorem" in Italian, and the entire film is constructed as a hypothesis, a demonstration of an abstract idea

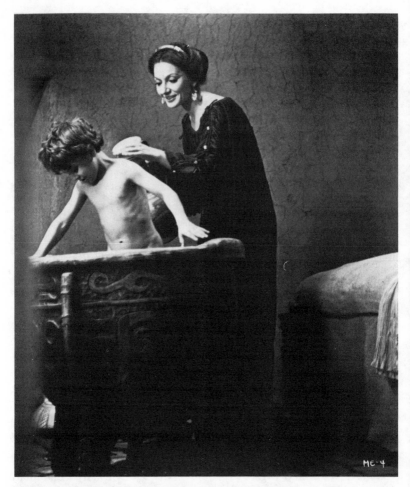

Pier Paolo Pasolini's *Medea* (1969). Medea (Maria Callas) prepares Jason's children for execution.
(Photo from the author's private collection)

that resembles a parable or an allegory. What if, Pasolini seems to ask his viewer, a god or some form of divine being appeared before a middle-class family, formed relationships with each of its members, and then departed? His unequivocal answer is that the bourgeois family members would achieve a sense of self-consciousness and would self-destruct; he adds the important corollary that any element of the subproletariate (specifically, the peasantry) would manage to achieve salvation. And, as we might expect in a film by Pasolini, the achievement of self-consciousness comes from specifically sexual encounters.

A prologue shot in color and utilizing documentary techniques reveals a factory owner turning over his plant to his workers, and is followed by an abrupt cut to the arid, smoking slopes of a volcano. Pasolini then shifts to a soundless, black-and-white introduction to the first part of the film in which the members of the family are presented: the father, Paolo (Massimo Girotti); his son, Pietro (Andrès Cruz); his daughter, Odetta (Anne Wiazemsky); his wife, Lucia (Silvana Mangano); and the maid, Emilia (Laura Betti). A sudden cut moves us to color again and a cocktail party during which a messenger, significantly named Angiolino (Ninetto Davoli), delivers a telegram announcing the arrival of a "visitor." The visitor suddenly appears, and he makes love successively with the servant, the son, the mother, the daughter, and the father (with several abrupt cuts to the same volcanic wasteland). A new message announces the visitor's departure and leads to the second part of the film, in which the visitor (Terence Stamp) speaks with each of the family: he has revealed the son's true nature, uncovered the mother's false values, caused the daughter to recognize her illness, and destroyed the father's smug complacency. Only the servant fails to speak with him, but she returns to her peasant origins, where she fasts, cures the sick, levitates, and becomes transformed into a saint before she goes to a construction site, buries herself, and cries "tears of renewal." Juxtaposed to her epiphany is the disintegration of the other members of the family: the daughter falls into a catatonic state; the son urinates upon his abstract paintings but continues his ill-chosen profession without sincerity or skill; the mother cruises around town, picking up strangers at street corners; and the father strips himself naked in the Milan train station as the camera follows his bare feet directly from the station onto the volcanic slopes to which the film has repeatedly referred.

Without reference to the archetypal story of Christ, *Teorema*'s storyline would have little meaning. And yet, the enigmatic visitor to this middle-class family is obviously an entirely different kind of divinity. Most intriguing are the visitor's relationships with the servant girl and with the father, who embodies not only an ideological significance, as the owner of the factory and of the means of production, but a psychoanalytical one, since he is the image of the primal authority figure. Their very different responses to the visitor are juxtaposed sharply at the close of the film: while the maid Emilia saves herself by a return to her peasant origins, the father is cast adrift in valueless

Pier Paolo Pasolini's *Teorema* (1968). The servant Emilia (Laura Betti) returns to her peasant origins and is buried, crying "tears of renewal." (Photo courtesy of the Museum of Modern Art)

industrial society, and his only response is a desperate howl set against a desolate volcanic wasteland, Pasolini's visual metaphor for the emptiness of the values his class embodies. Perhaps in no other film has Pasolini so graphically expressed his hatred of the middle class. As he has bluntly declared, "the point of the film is roughly this: a member of the bourgeoisie, whatever he does, is always wrong."[3] But this bitter hatred of a class that has destroyed his beloved subproletariat by assimilating its values into those of petit bourgeois consumer society extends to Pasolini himself, for he recognizes his own image in the family he despises:

> I too, like Moravia and Bertolucci, am a bourgeois, in fact, a petit-bourgeois, a turd, convinced that my stench is not only scented perfume, but is in fact the only perfume in the world. I too am thus endowed with the characteristics of aestheticism and humour, the typical characteristics of a petit-bourgeois intellectual. This is not a run-of-the-mill confession, but purely and simply a statement of fact.[4]

In *Teorema*, Pasolini makes extraordinary demands upon his audience. He insults their values and forces them to untangle an essentially experimental film narrative through allegory and parable; moreover, he constructs his parable by juxtaposing elements from traditional religion (the arrival of a divine being) and scandalous transgressions of sexual taboos (both hetereosexual and homosexual experiences). But as he remarks, the real scandal lies not in his controversial opinions, or even in his unfamiliar cinematic style with its elliptical explanations and abrupt cuts, but rather in the fact that his contemporaries lack a sense of the sacred and the mysterious, a sense that manages to save the peasant woman from the fate experienced by the middle-class family.[5]

Pigpen, an even more complicated personal allegory, employs the same abrupt editing techniques used in *Teorema* but juxtaposes not several responses to the same experience but, rather, two very different narrative storylines set in completely different eras. In one, we witness the origin and spread of a society of cannibals during the fifteenth century on the slopes of Mount Etna, the volcanic wasteland

Pasolini employed earlier in both *The Gospel* and *Teorema*. Here, a strange individual (Pierre Clementi) feeds first upon insects, then snakes, then finally upon human flesh, hurling the decapitated heads of his victims into the volcano's mouth, an action that eventually becomes part of a ritual repeated by the group of followers he soon attracts. When the local representatives of Church and State organize against the cannibals, all are captured and all but their leader repent; he merely declares that "I killed my father, I have eaten human flesh, and I tremble with joy" before he and the others are staked down to be devoured by wild dogs. The second storyline, linked to the first by a number of themes (including the transgression of society's taboos, cannibalism, and gargantuan consumption), deals with modern, neo-capitalist West Germany and a reconstructed Nazi industrialist named Klotz (played by Alberto Leonello, who bears an uncanny resemblance to Adolf Hitler and who plays the "Horst Wessel" song on the harp); his strange son, Julian (Jean-Pierre Léaud), a vaguely revolutionary student who is capable of responding sexually only to swine; and another ex-Nazi and rival industrialist named Herdhitze (Ugo Tognazzi). The relationship between these two separate but related tales remains ambiguous: most likely, they represent two separate stories occurring in different historical eras with important philosophical parallels; it is also possible that the Sicilian episode may be a fable capable of the same kind of psychoanalytical interpretation as the myth of Oedipus that currently underpins Western consciousness.

Herdhitze (formerly a Nazi named Hirt who once collected the skulls of Jewish Bolshevik Commissars during the war!) and Klotz first oppose each other's growing industrial power, then decide to forget the past and effect a merger which "is as natural as the return of spring." As Klotz exclaims in a burst of joy, "Germany—what a capacity to consume and to defecate!" Their accommodation takes place amidst the blackest of grotesque humor: Klotz trades his silence about Hirt's Nazi past for Hirt's silence about Julian's erotic affairs with the pigs. Thus, a story about pigs is exchanged for a tale about Jews! Pasolini employs pigs as the film's dominant metaphor to symbolize the gigantic German neocapitalistic machine of consumption and defecation that has risen from the ashes of the Holocaust. Central to the film is the juxtaposition of the cannibal and Julian. Both are "perverts" as their society defines the term, but the cannibal is a classic heretic, a threat to society by virtue of his unrepentant and proselytizing nature, and he suffers the same fate that other such characters suffered in premodern Europe under the full weight of repression by both Church and State. Julian is a "modern" deviant, seemingly less dangerous to the fabric of society but actually more of a threat to it, for his secret reveals the true essence of the ruling industrial class and its Nazi past. Julian is treated in the "modern" way—by secret understandings, agreements, and compromises—in order to cover the real scandal of the past, and the last shot of the film has Herdhitze speaking directly to the film's spectators, warning them to remain silent about what they have witnessed.

Pier Paolo Pasolini's *Pigpen* (1969). Klotz (Alberto Leonello) and Hirt/Herdhitze (Ugo Tognazzi), remnants from Germany's Nazi past, swap stories and effect their business merger.
(Photo courtesy of the Museum of Modern Art)

A single character links both episodes—the actor Ninetto Davoli, who usually represents Pasolini's subproletariat in his many works. In the cannibal storyline, he is a peasant who falls down upon his knees in a gesture of worship when he views the execution of the cannibals. Later, as an Italian immigrant and peasant worker on Klotz's estate, he comes to inform the father that Julian has been eaten by the pigs. Only he and his fellow peasants seem to be at all shocked by Julian's fate. But the two stories reveal entirely different responses to evil, even though the cannibalism in Sicily seems indirectly related to the industrial cannibalism of modern Germany. In the fifteenth century, transgression of social rules is first graphically shown and then immediately punished; in modern Europe, the even more horrible crimes of murder are never actually shown upon the screen. The viewer is horrified more by the relatively insignificant crime he witnesses in the past than those that are only mentioned in passing in the present. Surely, Pasolini could not have imagined a more severe condemnation of our contemporary sensibility than by juxtaposing our own emotional responses to the first crime and to the horrifying genocide which has been neatly swept under the luxurious carpets of the Klotz estate.

Pigpen was completed in 1968, the year of student upheavals in Europe that seemed to promise radical change throughout the continent. And yet, the vision of student radicals in the film—Julian and his girl friend Ida (Anne Wiazemsky)—is totally negative. Ida begins as a self-proclaimed revolutionary, then compromises herself, marries, and becomes part of the system she claims to detest; Julian, a complete intellectual, remains blissfully detached from his father's world and withdraws into his perversity until it destroys him. Although traditionally regarded as a Marxist, Pasolini nevertheless attacked radical students during the 1968 demonstrations as anticultural, antihistorical, and ignorant sons of the middle class, while he defended the embattled policemen, usually sons of peasants who had been drafted by the Italian government to defend a system that provided them with little benefit.[6] Thus, in the portrait of Julian we see in embryo the genesis of the shifts in Pasolini's personal ideology which form such an important part of *Salò*'s bleak vision of the world.

By the time Pasolini began making the first of his "trilogy of life,"

The Decameron, he had become Italy's most controversial filmmaker, who in almost everything he created or did was decidedly anticommercial. (It is no accident that works such as *Teorema* and *Pigpen* found a more receptive audience in the student population of Paris than in Italy.) With his three films based upon medieval narratives, Pasolini rejected his small, elite following and its intellectual preoccupations in order to broaden his appeal and to tell for the simple pleasure involved stories that nevertheless retained an ideological dimension that could not be ignored. Pasolini's choice of Boccaccio's collection of one hundred stories as his inspiration was quite deliberate.[7] In his own words, *The Decameron* is a work that reflects the historical optimism of an era that witnessed the triumph of the newly formed merchant class.[8] In fact, of the some 338 characters treated by Boccaccio, 140 come from the middle class and 68 are of lower-class, proletarian origins.[9] As Erich Auerbach has put it, in Boccaccio's masterpiece, "the literature of society acquired what it had not previously possessed: a world of reality and of the present."[10] In the magnificent fictional universe that emerges from the one hundred tales recounted by ten different narrators (three young men and seven young women), Boccaccio outlines a noble human goal, earthly glory attained through praiseworthy deeds, that implicitly denies the otherworldly goals of his great contemporary, Dante.

Pasolini's *Decameron* modifies the humanistic message embodied in his source, not because Pasolini rejects Boccaccio's anthropocentric view of society but, rather, because he sees Boccaccio's perspective as a partial, middle-class perspective. Therefore, Pasolini omits the celebrated frame describing the plague of 1348 and its ten storytellers, thereby eliminating the perspective of the merchant class to which these young men and women belong. In his film, we see only a single narrator—a popular Neapolitan storyteller whose obscene gesture and remark that one of Boccaccio's stories should be told "in the Neapolitan way" underscores Pasolini's geographical, ideological, and linguistic departure from his original. Boccaccio's Florentine location has been replaced by that of the Italian *mezzogiorno* (Naples); the middle class yields to the historical ancestors of Pasolini's beloved subproletariat; and Boccaccio's elegant literary language of an elite leisure class (Florentine) is replaced by the speech of the ordinary people of Southern Italy. Pasolini tantalizes the viewer familiar with Boccaccio's original by making references to the careful symmetry of *The Decameron*: he takes ten episodes from Boccaccio and adds to them ten of his own invention; the film is framed by two characters, the first from *The Decameron* (I, 1)—Ser Ciappelletto (Franco Citti)—and the second of Pasolini's invention—Giotto's best pupil (played by Pasolini himself), based upon Boccaccio's account of Giotto (VI, 5). While both sections of the film contain five of Boccaccio's original tales, the ten episodes added by Pasolini are scattered asymmetrically throughout each section (three in part one and seven in part two), a conscious reference to the number of male and female storytellers in the original. And, of course, the constant reference to the number ten in the film's structure plays upon a similar use in Boccaccio.

Pasolini's *Decameron* transforms its original into a film which is both self-reflexive (metacinema) and ideologically quite sophisticated. Take, for example, the manner in which Pasolini employs two of the most famous tales in Boccaccio—the tale of Riccardo and Caterina who "listen to the nightingale" (V, 4), on the one hand, and that of Lorenzo, Isabetta, and the famous pot of basil (IV, 5), on the other. Two pairs of lovers brave the objections of their families to enjoy each other's favors, but the outcome of each tale is radically different. Because Riccardo comes from a wealthy family, when he and Caterina are discovered naked on the balcony with the famous "nightingale" in Caterina's hand, her father resolves the moral problem with a merchant's cleverness, forcing the well-born Riccardo to take his daughter as his wife. To establish a contrast to this triumph of "business logic," Pasolini then relates the tragic end of Lorenzo, who has been transformed from Boccaccio's Pisan into a Sicilian servant and part of a despised, exploited lower class; Lorenzo is murdered by Isabetta's brothers because his origins provide no economic advantage to her family. With only a few subtle changes in the original, Pasolini is thus able to attack both a specific class (the bourgeoisie) and an institution (the family) that is its typical expression, thus completely reversing Boccaccio's habitual admiration for his practical merchants who guiltlessly reconciled economic interests and sexual drives. Elsewhere, the hilarious tale of Ser Ciappelletto's sanctification becomes a metaphor for the predatory practices of both the Church and the middle class; Father Gianni's magic transformation of an ignorant peasant woman into a mare (IX, 10) attacks the clergy's exploitation of popular ignorance; and the tale of Meuccio and Tingoccio (VII, 10) concludes with the ultimate message of Pasolini's film—that human sexuality is no longer a sin. In fact, Pasolini's expressed intention in his "trilogy of life" was to celebrate what he termed "the ontology of reality, whose naked symbol is sex,"[11] and it was his sexual explicitness in the film, generally misunderstood both by critics and voyeuristic audiences, that earned for the film one of the largest box-office grosses in the postwar era.

By casting himself as Giotto's best pupil, Pasolini asserts his own awareness of the reflexive nature of his film. In the Neapolitan marketplace, we see Pasolini/Giotto's pupil framing various characters with his fingers, much as a director might do with a lens. The view of the artist's creation of a fresco in Santa Chiara Church reminds us of the collective effort required for production of a film on a set. Finally, the director/artist dreams a vision, that of Giotto's *Last Judgment* (the original from the Arena Chapel of Padua, painted around 1306), but in Pasolini's dream, the figure of Christ the Judge is replaced by a benevolent Madonna portrayed by Silvana Mangano (Pasolini's mother in *Oedipus Rex*). At the film's conclusion, an enigmatic question is posed by the director/artist to the audience: "Why realize a work of art when it is so nice simply to dream it?" The answer to this vexing question arises from the structure of *The Decameron* itself. As Pasolini has noted, the making of his trilogy represented a "fascinating and marvelous experience," an examination of

> the most mysterious workings of artistic creation, this proceeding into the ontology of narration, in the making of cinema-cinema, cinema as we used to see it as children, without however falling victim to commercialism or lack of care. I find it the most beautiful idea I have ever had, this wish to tell, to recount, for the sheer joy of telling and recounting, for the creation of narrative myths, away

Pier Paolo Pasolini's *The Decameron* (1971). Pasolini's role as Giotto's best pupil underlines the parallel of making a film and composing *The Decameron.*
(Photo courtesy of the Museum of Modern Art)

from ideology, precisely because I have understood that to make an ideological film is finally easier than making a film outwardly lacking ideology.[12]

The sensational box-office success of Pasolini's *Decameron* guaranteed a negative reaction from Italy's intellectuals and critics. Writing on the six-hundredth anniversary of Boccaccio's death in 1975 in the prestigious *Corriere della Sera*, Vittore Branca, the dean of Boccaccio scholars, fulminated against works such as Pasolini's (without ever mentioning the director), describing such interpretations of Boccaccio's masterpiece as examples of a kitsch approach to Boccaccio's "higher" culture.[13] Branca was doubtless provoked less by Pasolini than by a group of blatantly pornographic films that were cheaply and rapidly produced by Italian studios to profit from Pasolini's success. We have already commented on this economic phenomenon in relation to the Italian costume epic and the "spaghetti Western." Once again, the Italian film industry turned to sequel mania, setting its contemporary preoccupation with sexuality in a patently artificial medieval background. Some of the titles are quite amusing: *Black Decameron* (a kind of National Geographic nudist tour through Africa with the camera leering at natives in various stages of undress); *Decameron Sinners*; a work with a comic Italian title, *Racconti proibiti di niente vestiti*, which might be rendered best in English as *Forbidden Tales of Bare Tails*; and the most ingenious of them all, *A Million and One Nights of Boccaccio and Canterbury*, which managed not only to assimilate all three works of Pasolini's trilogy but also to mistake Canterbury as an author![14]

The Canterbury Tales and *The Arabian Nights* continue Pasolini's experiments in cinematic narrative that is both self-reflexive and directed toward the celebration of human sexuality as a means of undermining middle-class values.[15] In the first film, Pasolini himself portrays Chaucer, who during the course of the film moves from the medieval marketplace and its many characters to the safety and solitude of his study. The tales Pasolini selected for his film include the Merchant's tale, the Friar's tale, the Cook's tale, the Miller's tale (never so graphically portrayed), the Wife of Bath's prologue, the Reeve's Tale, and the Summoner's Tale. Many of the themes of Pasolini's

Decameron are continued, although Pasolini is less at home with the English text. The hypocrisy of the Church is underscored by the evil summoner (played by Franco Citti, Ser Ciappelletto in *The Decameron*), who spies through keyholes upon homosexuals, bribing wealthy perverts and condemning poor ones to be burned alive while the public looks on, eating griddle cakes sold at the execution. Perkyn of the Cook's Tale (Ninetto Davoli) assumes the dress and manner of Charlie Chaplin, and the entire sequence represents Pasolini's homage to the gags and comic sketches of the American silent cinema. But unlike his evocation of medieval Italy, Pasolini's vision of Chaucerian England is colored by what in retrospect must be considered his gradual loss of confidence in the liberating powers of human sexuality. The director's preoccupation with bodily functions of all sorts, evoked throughout the film by images of anality, voyeurism, and grotesque exploitation, culminates in the bizarre vision of Satan's anus at the conclusion of the film (inspired from the Summoner's Tale as well as from the art of Bosch). This infernal vision of human sexuality run amok and ending in the very bowels of Hell itself is juxtaposed to the Edenic vision of a pure, Earthly paradise that opened the film in the Merchant's tale sequence. As one perceptive critic has noted in summarizing the film, "the powers of creation—taletelling—have thus reduced themselves punningly to powers of excretion and exhaustion—tail-telling."[16] Only the redemptive power of art, embodied in the Chaucer/Pasolini enigmatic smile that closes the film, seems to offer any hope.

With *The Arabian Nights*, Pasolini moves to a search for idyllic sexuality in the Third World, shooting on various exotic locations in Nepal, Yemen, Iran, and Ethiopia. Pasolini hoped to discover there a joyous sexuality freed from the exploitive manner of Western industrialized culture. And here, once again, he recounts his stories for the pure joy of narration. True to its literary inspiration, the film has a structure that is the most intricate of the trilogy. In the original text, the narrative evolved from a series of stories told each night by a woman to her husband in order to avoid execution; Pasolini's *Arabian Nights* plays once again with the device of narrative framing as found in Boccaccio and Chaucer. In this new film he frames his stories within the "Tale of Nur ed Din and Zumurrud," only a single episode in the original. By inserting a number of stories within this opening episode, Pasolini creates a narrative that embodies a Chinese box technique: stories set within stories set within stories.

The most remarkable features of *The Arabian Nights* are its breathtaking evocation of exotic and unfamiliar Oriental landscapes and locations, on the one hand, and its unique interpretation of Oriental sexuality on the other. Zumurrud (Inez Pellegrini), an extremely clever slave girl, is separated from Nur ed Din (Franco Merli), a rather dim-witted young boy, and the account of their reunion becomes Pasolini's account of the triumph of feminine sexuality and intelligence over male dominance and presumption. Disguised as a man, Zumurrud reaches the magic city of Sair where, as the first arrival after the previous ruler's death, she becomes heir to its throne; her disguise fools everyone, including Nur ed Din, who is brought to the King's bedroom; he expects a homosexual rape until his smiling mistress reveals her identity and rescues him from a fate he fears worse than death. The ironic conclusion to *The Arabian Nights*—the triumph of female heterosexuality—is a surprising and unexpected ending in a film directed by an avowed homosexual who had consistently viewed homosexuality as a weapon for undermining middle-class values. The joyous evocation of unfettered sexuality in the film, both heterosexual and homosexual, was to be Pasolini's final elegiac tribute to a force he then considered, along with the redeeming power of art, to be a vital civilizing presence in the modern world.

Pasolini's trilogy of life juxtaposed the carefree sexuality of the past in three different medieval cultures to his own era's manipulative, exploitive sexuality and deceptive sexual freedom. But his darkening mood and his increasing sense of alienation from the world around him caused him to reject not only the trilogy itself but most of the key ideas embodied in his major films. This view is given in his last important essay, "Disavowal of the 'Trilogy of Life'," which he published as a preface to the scripts of the three films.[17] The essay contains the explanation of the rejection, in *Salò*, of his earlier views on the mythical potential of sex. In an era of sexual liberation, *all* forms of sexuality have been assimilated into a cultural system Pasolini despises: consumer capitalism; even Pasolini's three films celebrating the liberating potential of human sexuality have been co-opted into the system of values he rejects. Now, Pasolini declares, it is clear that the lower-class characters he had always admired in other films and had seemed to discover in the Third World were always potentially petit-bourgeois figures, anticultural members of an ignorant lumpenproletariat whose only remaining function was that of consumer. This bleak admission of intellectual bankruptcy led the director to an inevitable conclusion: "I am adapting myself to the degradation and I am accepting the unacceptable. . . . The beloved faces of yesterday are beginning to turn yellow. Here before me—slowly materializing without alternative—is the present. I am readapting my own commitment to a greater legibility (*Salò?*)"[18]

Salò combines a storyline Pasolini took from the Marquis de Sade's *120 Days of Sodom*—the retreat of four powerful individuals into a château to satisfy all their penchants for lust, cruelty, and power—with a structure taken from Dante's *Inferno*—concentric narrative circles descending into the depths of Hell. He locates this pastiche of Sade and Dante in the town of Salò, the capital of Mussolini's Social Republic during the last days before the final downfall of the Fascist regime (1944–45). The four men who organize this horrifying retreat are Fascists, each of whom represents an arm of society's power: a magistrate, a banker, a duke, and a bishop. Following Sade's mania for symmetry, Pasolini includes, along with the four symbols of repressive power, four female narrators (ex-bawds), four of the men's daughters (who are married off among them), four soldiers, four collaborators, eight male and eight female victims, and five servants.

Pasolini's fascination with symmetry and order reflects the film's theme—the progressive unfolding of sadistic power wielded by contemporary consumer society. The film moves from the "Anti-Inferno" (in which a town is destroyed and the victims are assembled) through three Dantesque "circles": the "Circle of the Manias," in which lust for power is portrayed; the "Circle of Excrement," concerned with consumption and defecation; and finally the "Circle of Blood," which concludes with the sadistic destruction of all the victims. In contrast to the exuberance and vitality of his three adaptations of the trilogy,

Salò is a somber, static work, emphasizing highly stylized period sets (Art deco, Italian Bauhaus), intricately formal compositions, and relatively long takes and few camera movements. This static style underlines the increasingly closed and repressive nature of the activities taking place in the villa. Storytelling—a creative activity leading to individual liberation in the trilogy—is in *Salò* presented in a peculiar fashion: the female narrators appear in formal dress and relate scabrous events from their lives to the carefully posed torturers, guards, and victims; sexual arousal is achieved by the storytelling, desire thus being relegated to one stage in a sadistic ritual. Ritual overshadows the entire film: Pasolini uses sadistic parodies to attack a number of familiar institutions (the family, marriage, and religion), but most particularly human sexuality. The most shocking event in the film, and the one clearly designed to embody Pasolini's hatred for contemporary consumerism, is a meal during which human excrement is consumed. The logical result of a life based upon consumption and defecation is, it seems, self-consumption, a closed circuit of eating and evacuation. The film concludes with a ritualistic slaughter of the remaining victims, observed from a distance through binoculars so that without the sound of the victims' screams this horrifying spectacle may be enjoyed as an abstract object of aesthetic contemplation.

Salò is a film which Pasolini designed to be difficult to swallow, if I may be permitted to continue the dominant metaphor of the work. It is a desperate and highly personal attack against what Pasolini had come to view as a society dominated by manipulative and sadistic power and organized around mindless consumption and exploitation. Ironically, homosexuality becomes in *Salò* the very epitome of sexual repression rather than a counter-cultural phenomenon designed to undermine social taboos (as it was in Pasolini's earlier works). The single instance of normal, heterosexual love between a soldier and a young servant girl from the Third World is punished by immediate execution. No doubt Pasolini would have continued to evolve beyond this bleak vision of a totally unredeemed humanity in *Salò* had he lived past 1975. But his brilliant and problematic career ended on this note of despair, and film historians can only lament the passing of one of the Italian cinema's most original and controversial figures whose zest

Pier Paolo Pasolini's *Salò* (1975). The victims, soon to be executed, are first reduced to the status of animals.
(Photo from the author's private collection)

for life might have eventually uncovered an artistic escape from his intellectual impasse.

Bernardo Bertolucci began his cinematic career as Pasolini's assistant, although his films soon departed substantially from Pasolini's influence. Bertolucci's works also embody a more orthodox understanding of psychoanalysis and Marxist theory different from Pasolini's rather eccentric readings of Freud, Jung, Marx, and Gramsci. Nevertheless, the two men reflect not only similar intellectual influences but also a parallel development in their work. Like Pasolini, Bertolucci moved from films directed toward a small, elite intellectual audience, such as *Partner* (*Partner*, 1968), to films which were accessible to commercial audiences—first *The Spider's Stratagem* (*La strategia del ragno*, 1969) made for television; then the adaptation of Alberto Moravia's novel *The Conformist* (1970), followed by the internationally acclaimed

Last Tango in Paris (*Ultimo tango a Parigi*, 1972); then *1900* (*Novecento*, 1975–76), and *Luna* (*La luna*, 1979).[19] With the last three works, Bertolucci consciously aimed at breaking out of the art-film circuit and into large-scale commercial distribution, utilizing American money, English-language original versions, and carefully chosen American actors whose renown might guarantee box-office success. His move to increasingly commercial films did not, however, imply a lessening of his talent. On the contrary, Bertolucci's abilities seemed to be liberated by his move away from the hermetic world of the Parisian *cinéphile* reflected by his early films.

Partner was made at the height of the 1968 student upheavals when Bertolucci was still under thirty. Consequently, it bears the imprint of that emotionally charged era, as well as the sometimes oppressive influence of Jean-Luc Godard. Made during the initial stages of Bertolucci's lengthy psychoanalysis, *Partner* is a free adaptation of Dostoievsky's *The Double*: Jacob (Pierre Clementi), a young drama teacher in love with his professor's daughter Clara (Stefania Sandrelli), is rescued from suicide by his alter ego (Jacob II, also played by Clementi), who engages him in a number of philosophical conversations about the nature of theatrical spectacle. Jacob I, obviously reflecting the theatrical theories of Judith Malina and Julian Beck's Living Theatre (then popular in Italy), suggests that the stage should become the entire world, with revolution as its text. When the two doubles are deserted by the students, who betray their planned spectacle/revolution, Jacob II informs Jacob I that the spectacle/revolution will take place without them, then, before joining his double on a balcony to commit a double suicide, turns directly to the camera and announces somewhat abruptly that the major enemy in the world is American imperialism. While much of the film is humorlessly didactic, a number of "lighter" moments surface from the Godardian maze of political messages: a baby carriage is pushed down steps with a bomb in it (a clear reference to the Odessa steps sequence of Eisenstein's *Potemkin*); a detergent saleswoman visits Jacob II, who has taken Jacob I's place, and in a parody of advertising based upon sex, she offers herself to Jacob II and is eventually murdered in a washing machine overflooding with suds.

Much of *Partner* is intimately related to Bertolucci's obsessive personal concerns, problems he encountered under psychoanalysis. Yet, the seemingly Freudian theme—the confrontation of a man with his double or alter ego—is less indebted to Freud than to Marx, for it allows Bertolucci to construct a dialectical argument between Jacob I and his more politically committed split personality. The style of *Partner* is intentionally anticommercial: Bertolucci considered the traditional and frequent use of cuts the mark of a conservative director, and he consistently searches for the extremely long take, avoiding dramatic cuts at the places we might expect them from a studio-produced film. Yet, relatively sophisticated special effects (such as matte shots) are employed, and the work is shot in Cinemascope—as Jacob remarks, such a process is suitable to a film with broad ideas! Even in this work made for a very small audience, Bertolucci's eventual move toward commercial spectacle can be detected. When the upper-class students fail to present themselves for the spectacle/revolution, they betray the revolution just as surely as Fabrizio did with his marriage in *Before the Revolution*. The schizophrenia inherent in the split personality of the would-be revolutionary may properly be viewed as Bertolucci's personal admission that revolutions are carried out by the masses and are ultimately not undertaken by middle-class artists with movie cameras. Jacob, like Fabrizio before him or like Bertolucci himself, is condemned to live in an era *before* the revolution.

The Spider's Stratagem is a minor masterpiece. Produced for RAI, the Italian state television network, it is also one of the first of many excellent films RAI has sponsored during the last two decades. Based upon a short story by Argentina's Jorge Borges, "Theme of the Traitor and the Hero," the film marks a rejection of the Godardian style of *Partner* and a return to the lyrical evocation of Bertolucci's provincial origins that marks *Before the Revolution*. Bertolucci transposes Borges's setting from revolutionary Ireland to the Renaissance town of Sabbioneta, called Tara in the film: the film moves between the present and events that took place in 1936 during the Fascist period. Athos Magnani (Giulio Brogi) returns home thirty years after the assassination of his father, an anti-Fascist hero, meets his father's former mistress Draifa (Alida Valli), and tries to discover the truth obscuring the events leading up to his father's death by speaking with his father's anti-Fascist friends. Freud eclipses Marx in *The Spider's Stratagem*, as the film chronicles the oppressive hold of the father over his son. We see this control arising immediately as Athos Jr. encounters a statue erected to his father's memory in the town square upon his arrival (its blank, unchiseled eyes embody the persistent motif of blindness and its Oedipal connotations that will also mark the imagery of *The Conformist*). Gliding past the statue, Bertolucci moves the camera so that the statue obliterates our view of the son, prefiguring his eventual entrapment in the father's web at the film's conclusion.

Bernardo Bertolucci's *The Spider's Stratagem* (1969). Athos Magnani (Giulio Brogi) reaches Tara and is immediately drawn into the mysterious web his father spun years earlier.
(Photo courtesy of the Museum of Modern Art)

A series of repetitions dramatizes how the present repeats the past: numerous flashbacks to 1936 employ exactly the same actors and locations as in the present with no change of costume, and the flashbacks are so abrupt and continuous that they obscure chronological distinctions. When Athos Jr. accompanies his father's friends to the shack where they had met years ago to plan the assassination of Mussolini before his father betrayed them and was killed, past and present merge: Athos Jr. becomes terrified, runs away, and Bertolucci cuts back and forth between the present (Athos Jr.) and the past (Athos Sr.). Moreover, he employs a technique used in *Before the Revolution*: the running figure—his identity confused by constant flashbacks—is photographed by a swiftly moving camera in a brilliant visual evocation of the protagonist's inability to escape not only from his father's influence but from Bertolucci's obsessive camera as well.

The notion of political spectacle from *Partner* now finds its perfect aesthetic expression. Athos Jr. discovers that the traitor in the group of conspirators was actually his own father who then collaborated with his comrades to produce an operatic anti-Fascist myth, since the Fascists are blamed for his murder. Athos Sr. thus dies in a drama in which the town of Sabbioneta becomes a theater influenced by references to Verdian melodrama and Shakespearian tragedy. As Gaibazzi tells Athos Jr., it is not truth but the consequences of the truth which matter. Sabbioneta/Tara (a name taken from the cinema, the plantation from *Gone With the Wind*) becomes transformed into a mythical location of the mind, and the son learns the truth about his father as he was at the precise moment when he was murdered in the town's opera house—during the famous *Rigoletto* aria "Maledizione", a performance of which he, too, attends in the present. But the truth does not set the son free. On the contrary, it imprisons him in a mythical web his father, not unlike the spider, has created. When Athos Jr. tries to leave Tara by train (which never arrives), he sees that the tracks are completely overgrown with weeds. The father and the past have triumphed over the son and the present. Athos Sr. remains an enigma to his imprisoned son: whether he betrayed his comrades because of his cowardice, or whether he embraced his martyrdom consciously, engineering the melodramatic spectacle resulting in his death to create an enduring anti-Fascist myth, will never be completely clear. *The Spider's Stratagem* is a near-perfect example of the sublimation of an artist's individual neuroses into a brilliant work of art.

With his adaptation of Alberto Moravia's *The Conformist*, Bertolucci produced what is perhaps his most visually satisfying film, although many reviewers and critics question its ideological coherence. Working with a fairly conventional chronological narrative told by an omniscient narrator—Moravia's tale of a child's psychic development that begins with a view of his parents making love, leads to a traumatic homosexual encounter, and results in his compulsive search for normality or conformity by joining the Fascist Party—Bertolucci produced a completely subjective film—shaped by his own experiences under analysis—that rejects chronological narration and juxtaposes time sequences in a manner even more complicated than that found in *The Spider's Stratagem. The Conformist* also marks Bertolucci's decisive break with Godard's brand of anticommercial cinema: made with money from Paramount, the film caused a rupture between Bertolucci and his former mentor, a biographical fact that Bertolucci inserts into the plot of his film. Though *The Conformist* is greatly indebted to the cinema, it is not the cinema of Godard: its lighting reflects that of a 1930s studio film in its expressive and poetic qualities, and Bertolucci himself has mentioned the influence of Sternberg, Ophuls, and Welles on this work.[20] The plot of the film can be assembled only after a complete viewing of it, since the many flashbacks and flashbacks within flashbacks disrupt any linear sense of time. As one excellent study of Bertolucci's adaptation of Moravia remarks, "the film presents the viewer with a jumble of elements and chronologies which can be described only as oneiric. . . . These first scenes not only lack causal and chronological coherence, they operate by condensation, displacement, projection, and doubling—all techniques of what Freud has termed the latent dream work."[21] Marcello Clerici (Jean-Louis Trintignant) uses a honeymoon trip from Rome to Paris with his new wife Giulia (Stefania Sandrelli) to cover a political mission he undertakes for the Fascist Party: he must eliminate a bothersome anti-Fascist Italian refugee, Professor Quadri (Enzo Tarascio), his former philosophy

professor at the university. Along the way, he is escorted by Special
Agent Manganiello (Gastone Moschin) and encounters Anna Quadri
(Dominique Sanda), a lesbian who allows herself to be manipulated
by Marcello so that she may seduce his wife, Giulia. The entire story
is related through a complex series of flashbacks that begin at the
moment Marcello and Manganiello pursue Quadri into a dark forest
to kill him. The action shifts back from that moment in time (October
15, 1938) to follow Marcello's search for conformity within Fascism,
his marriage, his homosexual encounter with Lino (Pierre Clementi),
a chauffeur (March 25, 1917), and his meeting in Paris with the Quad-
ris. The film culminates in the murder of the professor and his wife
in October, and ends with a coda set in 1943, when the Fascist regime
falls.

Bernardo Bertolucci's *The Conformist* (1970). Giulia (Stefania Sandrelli)
and Anna Quadri (Dominique Sanda) perform a sensual tango together.
(Photo from the author's private collection)

With this ingenious confusion of levels of time, Bertolucci brilliantly manages to render the sense of entrapment in the past felt by Marcello. Central to Bertolucci's reconstruction of the novel is Marcello's constant search for surrogate fathers, authority figures he seeks both to appease and (in typically Oedipal fashion) to destroy. In flashback at the opening of the film, we encounter the first of these figures, his blind friend Italo Montanari (Jose Quaglio), a Fascist ideologue who broadcasts a radio program celebrating the "Prussian aspect" of Mussolini and the "Latin aspect" of Adolf Hitler! Later, when the regime falls, Marcello will denounce Italo to a crowd of angry anti-Fascists. A flashback within the flashback moves from the radio station to a government ministry, where Marcello visits another father surrogate, an even more obvious authority figure—a highly placed Fascist minister. At the ministry, the visuals underline Marcello's position behind barred windows and doors, a motif of entrapment continued throughout the film. Moreover, he encounters there the minister's mistress, a character whose face will reappear two more times—once as a prostitute in a brothel which is a front for Fascist secret police headquarters, and again in the person of Anna Quadri. Thus, when Marcello finally meets Anna Quadri, he has an uncanny sense of *déjà vu* that disconcerts him throughout the film. Marcello's strange relationship with Special Agent Manganiello embodies the father-son link, since the more experienced agent is charged with Marcello's "education." And Manganiello is eventually replaced by Professor Quadri himself, the father/teacher par excellence. To underline the repetition of this intimate relationship in Marcello's life, Bertolucci also confronts him with his real father—in a de Chirico-like asylum—who rejects him. Thus, Marcello's entire existence revolves around a desire to please successive surrogate fathers, and a feeling of inadequacy brought on by a chance homosexual encounter in the distant past which motivates his search for "normality" in the present.

Marcello's assignment to murder Professor Quadri reflects not only the protagonist's Oedipal conflicts but those of Bertolucci as well. Quadri's address and telephone number (17, rue St. Jacques; MED-15-37) belonged in 1971 to Jean-Luc Godard, Bertolucci's former best friend and cinematic mentor. As Bertolucci admitted,

> *The Conformist* is a story about me and Godard. When I gave the
> professor Godard's phone number and address, I did it for a joke,
> but afterwards I said to myself, 'Well, maybe all that has some sig-
> nificance . . . I'm Marcello and I make Fascist movies and I want to
> kill Godard who's a revolutionary, who makes revolutionary movies
> and who was my teacher.[22]

Thus, the director's private neuroses are transposed to those of his
protagonist on the screen, and once again, as in *The Spider's Stratagem*,
the framework of Freudian psychoanalysis provides the inspiration for
a brilliant work of art.

Even though some knowledge of Freudian theory is essential for
understanding *The Conformist*, most film critics acknowledge that this
stunningly beautiful work cannot be exhausted by a psychoanalytical
interpretation. In fact, as a coherent explanation of the birth of a
Fascist, *The Conformist* fails just as certainly as did the theories of
Wilhelm Reich in *The Mass Psychology of Fascism* (1933) or of Erich
Fromm in *Escape From Freedom* (1941), works which obviously influenced Bertolucci's adaptation of Moravia's novel. By placing the ultimate origin of Marcello's conformity and his desire for normality in
the realm of Marcello's unconscious (the lingering memory of a homosexual attack), Bertolucci undermines any Marxist explanation of
the rise of Italian Fascism through class struggle or middle-class repression of the working class. Paradoxically, although Bertolucci asserts
in a number of interviews that Marcello embodies the middle-class
origins of Italian Fascism, there is no evidence in the film to support
this position. On the contrary, the only milieu ever reflected in *The
Conformist*, that of the decadent bourgeoisie, includes not only Marcello and his family but also the anti-Fascist Quadri couple as well.
Anna Quadri's lesbianism, as well as her husband's obvious voyeuristic
pleasure in observing her sexual escapades with members of her sex,
mark the anti-Fascists of the picture as members of the same decadent
class to which Marcello belongs. Thus, far from an explanation of
Fascism, *The Conformist* is, in reality, only an indictment of it, and the
verdict has already been delivered before the film is made.

Though Bertolucci's understanding of a complex political phenomenon may be unsatisfying, the viewer of *The Conformist* cannot help

Bernardo Bertolucci's *The Conformist* (1970). Closed within his automobile, Marcello (Jean-Louis Trintignant) watches passively as Anna Quadri (Dominique Sanda) is murdered.
(Photo courtesy of the Museum of Modern Art)

but be overwhelmed by the film's strikingly brilliant visual texture, a feature indebted in large measure to the extraordinary talents of cameraman Vittorio Storaro (better known for his work on *Last Tango* and Coppola's *Apocalypse Now*). Careful composition of individual shots, as well as intricate attention to the effects of light and shadow, emphasize the film's dominant motifs of Marcello's entrapment and the metaphor of blindness. Light and shadow in *The Conformist* often say more than the dialogue implies. For example, in Bertolucci's version of Plato's Allegory of the Cave, transferred to Quadri's office, the interplay of shadow and silhouette underscores the ambivalent relationship between illusion and reality, sight and blindness. Marcello is offered ambiguous ideological guides: not only is his Fascist friend

Italo blind, but so is the little Parisian flower girl who sells violets from Parma (Bertolucci's home town) and who sings the Socialist "Internationale." The images of bars and prisons, suggested first by the horizontal and vertical windows at the Fascist ministry, are constantly repeated: light and shadows pick up this motif at Giulia's home, where Marcello's impending marriage represents another form of bourgeois entrapment and conformity, as her zebra-patterned dress implies; Marcello is constantly imprisoned in tight spaces, such as church confessionals, and especially in Manganiello's automobile enroute to Quadri's assassination. The eerie and surrealistic asylum inhabited by Marcello's father resembles a prison, and the father even locks himself in his straitjacket, muttering an enigmatic phrase over and over ("massacre and melancholy"). A recurrent pattern in the cinematography is a shot of Marcello through a pane of glass that picks up the reflections of others outside his imprisoned psyche: at the radio station, in the train heading for Paris, in the sequence in which Anna and Giulia perform a sensual tango, and within the car. Bertolucci's mature grasp of his craft is especially evident in the famous tango scene, with its quickly shifting camera angles, positions, graceful motions, and brilliant editing. Ultimately, Bertolucci's poetic talents and his consummate technical skills triumph over the sometimes over-insistent ideological structure contained within his storyline.

With *Last Tango in Paris*, Bertolucci achieved a commercial *and* critical success almost unprecedented in the history of the Italian cinema. Pauline Kael declared that it was "the most powerfully erotic movie ever made, and it may turn out to be the most liberating movie ever made," and Norman Mailer said of the famous scene in which Paul (Marlon Brando) the protagonist of the film, couples with the young French girl Jeanne (Maria Schneider) that "the cry of the fabric is the most thrilling sound to be heard in World Culture since the four opening notes of Beethoven's Fifth."[23] Deeply indebted to Freudian concepts of sexuality, Bertolucci's plot is less complicated and far more concentrated in its impact upon the emotions than that of *The Conformist*. Bertolucci himself has described the film as a tragic version of *An American in Paris*[24] or as "a form of dream" in which the entire story is an Oedipal projection on the part of the girl (who is 19) and Brando (who is 48).[25]

The dominant image of the film is a starkly empty room in which Paul and Jeanne accidentally meet while searching for vacant apartments. After their first passionate lovemaking, in which no words or names are exchanged, each is drawn back to this location for a number of different and equally unusual encounters—the most famous (infamous?) of which involves the use of butter as an aid to sodomy— during which most of society's taboos are broken. In each of these encounters, Paul sets the rules, forbidding the use of names or discussion of the world outside the room. As the director has remarked, the sex in the film is "simply a new kind of language that these two characters try to invent in order to communicate. They use the sexual language because the sexual language means liberation from the subconscious, means an opening up."[26] This is most apparent in their third act of love, when their words degenerate into animal grunts. But their attempt to maintain an absolutely pure sexual relationship is doomed to failure ("every sexual relationship is condemned" Bertolucci notes); the psychological and sentimental backgrounds of the two characters interfere with this sexual experiment and ultimately destroy their relationship.[27]

Paul has just lost his wife, Rosa, who is a suicide, and clearly seeks in Jeanne a love with no emotional commitments (Rosa and Jeanne are directly linked in the film when Jeanne arrives at the apartment dressed in a wedding dress similar to that worn by Rosa in her coffin). Jeanne had an obviously incestuous affection for her dead father, a colonel in the French army. Much of her attraction to the older Paul may be explained by this fact, yet when Paul follows her home at the end of the film and playfully dons her father's army hat, Jeanne kills him with her father's revolver. These psychoanalytical underpinnings to the film's plot are enriched by references in *Last Tango* to cinema itself. Paul is described by one character in the film in this manner:

> Nervous type, your boss. You know he was a boxer? . . . That didn't work . . . so he became an actor, then a racketeer on the waterfront

> in New York. . . . It didn't last long . . . played the bongo drums . . . revolutionary in South America . . . journalist in Japan . . . One day he lands in Tahiti, hangs around, learns French . . . comes to Paris and then meets a young woman with money.[28]

Such a description might be expected of a typical American expatriot, but Bertolucci employs Marlon Brando in *Last Tango* as a living icon (much as Sergio Leone did with Henry Fonda in *Once Upon a Time* and *My Name Is Nobody*). Thus, the description of Paul also corresponds to a resumé of Brando's own biography and work in the cinema, from his early role as a boxer in *On the Waterfront* to famous parts in *Viva Zapata, Mutiny on the Bounty*, and *Sayonara*. One perceptive critic has noted that Brando was the "last romantic cinematic idol" much of whose appeal is based upon his "rebel" image.[29] When Paul, Brando's alter ego, succumbs to his romantic attachment to Jeanne and wants to deepen a relationship begun on a purely sexual level, this romantic love leads to his death.

The cinematic myth of the romantic "leading man" embodied in Paul's character is juxtaposed by Bertolucci to the ludicrous figure of Tom (Jean-Pierre Léaud), Jeanne's *cinéphile* fiancé, whose attempt to produce a film about their engagement parodies aspects of both Truffaut (who casts Léaud frequently in his works) and Godard. While Paul attempts to banish sentiment from life in the hermetically sealed apartment building that is their trysting place, Tom reduces emotion to game-playing with a movie camera and silly discussions about naming their children after revolutionaries. Beneath Brando's stoic suffering there is a layer of genuine feeling, set in relief by the superficiality of Tom's sentiments. And the two characters reflect two historic cinematic styles, the older of which (Brando's Hollywood image) Bertolucci obviously prefers, even though he realizes that it embodies an attitude doomed to failure in a world composed of shallow people like Jeanne.

The dance-hall scene in which Jeanne and Paul stage a ridiculous tango together is prefaced by a number of imitations by Paul taken directly from the American cinema (Cagney, mannerisms of film tough guys). But when the facade is removed, Paul becomes transformed

Bernardo Bertolucci's *Last Tango In Paris* (1972). Paul (Marlon Brando) and Jeanne (Maria Schneider) perform a parody of the tango shortly before Paul is shot by her.
(Photo from the author's private collection)

from a mythic embodiment of Jeanne's father to an aging American with a romantic attachment and no future. Cinematic conventions fail to function in the pop-culture world Jeanne inhabits. The film closes upon a bleak picture of broken illusions (from both cinema and life): in the words of one critical review, "trapped in the conventions and fantasies of their culture, Tom is ridiculous, Paul is dead, and Jeanne is a killer."[30] Paul's failure to establish a new sexual language and his subsequent death ultimately argue not for more eroticism in the movies but, paradoxically, for the more old-fashioned love and affection contained in the classic American cinema Bertolucci knew and loved as a child, and to which he now nostalgically refers us.[31]

One remarkable feature of *Last Tango* is the role played by Marlon Brando in the film's production. No Italian director, regardless of his knowledge of American culture, could have created by himself dialogue with such authentic and complex cultural and cinematic references. Brando's advice and improvisation on the set were instrumental in creating the character of Paul; though the story analyzed many of the problems Bertolucci himself encountered in his private analysis, Brando clearly used his role to make a statement about his own life and work. Again, Storaro's participation in the film guaranteed a brilliant utilization of light and shadow. The empty apartment was lighted to underscore what Bertolucci terms a "uterine" or "prenatal" state, and the dominant imagery of the film was heavily influenced by the disturbing paintings of Francis Bacon, whose canvases are displayed under the film's opening credits. While *Last Tango* was being shot in Paris, a Bacon show was being held at the Grand Palais, and Bertolucci, Storaro, and Brando all went to study the English painter's works in order to assimilate their "devastated plasticity" into the film's visuals.[32]

With *1900*, Bertolucci's obsession with sublimating personal problems into art takes second place, and he is primarily concerned with offering a grandiose and ambitious Marxist vision of modern Italian society. In that film he aimed to rival the epic sweep of Tomasi di Lampedusa's *Leopard* and its cinematic adaptation by Luchino Visconti, to create an Italian equivalent to *Gone With the Wind*, combining the demands of commercial spectacle with the concerns of Marxist ideology. Fresh from the box-office triumph of *Last Tango*, Bertolucci used American capital to finance this Marxist extravaganza, and he employed major American actors in key roles to guarantee the film's reception at the box office. When *1900* was made, it was the most expensive film ever produced in Italy. The original Italian version was over five-and-one-half hours and was reduced by about a third for the version eventually exported abroad. Even with cuts, this version, like the Italian version, had to be shown in two separate parts, and the end result was, in effect, two different works: *1900 Act I* and *Act II*.[33]

Like *The Leopard*, Bertolucci's *1900* analyzes contemporary Italian history through family history by telescoping the events of this century into the juxtaposed chronicles of two different clans: on the first day

Bernardo Bertolucci's *1900* (1975–76). The fates of Alfredo (Robert De Niro) and Olmo (Gérard Depardieu) are intertwined even in their love affairs. (Photo from the author's private collection)

of 1900, two sons are born—one, Alfredo (Robert De Niro), the grandson of the wealthy landowner Alfredo Berlingheri (Burt Lancaster), the other Olmo (Gérard Depardieu), the grandson of the peasant Dalcò (Sterling Hayden). Bertolucci follows the two children whose twin destinies are closely intertwined from the day of their birth through their old age, touching upon a number of major historical events in contemporary Italian history: the rise of peasant cooperatives and agrarian strikes around 1908, World War I, the advent of Fascism, the Partisan experience, and the fall of Fascism. However, Bertolucci's plot opens with the Liberation of Italy on April 25, 1945, cuts back to the birth scene in 1900, and then ends *Act I* of *1900* with the apparent victory of the Fascists under the violent leadership of Attila (Donald Sutherland); *Act II* follows the demise of the regime, the destruction of the hated *padrone* (boss), and ends with a picture of Olmo and Alfredo as old men in 1975, still struggling with each other. Along the way, Alfredo marries a liberated young woman who takes cocaine and declaims Futurist poetry (Dominique Sanda), while Olmo weds a young Socialist teacher named Anita (Stefania Sandrelli); juxtaposed to these two couples is the Fascist Attila and his perverse wife Regina (Laura Betti), Alfredo's cousin.

Bertolucci's vision of Italian history has been attacked as either too ideological in its praise of his beloved peasants or as too softhearted in his portrait of Alfredo Berlinghieri, a weak-willed bourgeois whose friendship for Olmo does not prevent him from being used by Attila and his Fascist bullyboys, who eventually terrorize and murder a number of the peasants. Set against the decadence of the Berlinghieri (especially Alfredo's Uncle Ottavio, who dallies with Alfredo in casinos and Mediterranean resorts, snorting cocaine and taking photographs of nude and semi-nude peasant boys dressed in classical garb), the humanity of peasant culture and the generosity of the lower classes provide an element of sanity in a world which seems terribly out of joint. Alfredo's ambivalent character reflects that of Bertolucci himself, who was born only a few miles from the enormous nineteenth-century farm in Northern Italy where the film was shot. Indeed, there is much in the work that reflects more of the director's biography than authentic social history. Critics have attacked *1900* for its ahistorical character, but Bertolucci intended the film to represent a utopian dream—that of the end of the boss or *padrone* with the Liberation in 1945. Nevertheless, as an astute observer of the Italian scene, Bertolucci knows full well that the *padrone* was not completely destroyed in 1945; instead, he successfully regrouped his forces when the Liberation failed to generate a true social revolution in Italy. Thus, the opening sequences of *1900* show us a liberation *manqué*, just as Visconti's *Leopard* did: Alfredo is "arrested" by a young peasant boy (reminiscent of Olmo as a boy), and although Attila is eventually executed by the peasants for his crimes during the Fascist era, the real *padrone*, Alfredo, escapes true punishment. But his trial is postponed to the end of *Act II*, and after the opening sequences of the Liberation, Bertolucci cuts directly to 1900 and the birth of Olmo and Alfredo. The evocation of peasant life in Bertolucci's province shows the director at his best and most lyrical. Shot over a famous painting depicting a peasant demonstration, the opening credits remind us of the visual source of much of Bertolucci's views of peasant life—the canvases of the Italian *Macchiaiuoli*, a school of nineteenth-century Florentine painters who were influenced by Impressionism but concentrated their attention upon rural life in the period. Much of the impressive photography of *Act I* is indebted to this artistic source, and we are reminded of Bertolucci and Storaro's debt to Francis Bacon in *Last Tango*, or to the classic cinema of the 1930s in *The Conformist*. Perhaps the most beautiful moment in the entire film is a recreation of an afternoon peasant festival, shot with an extremely mobile and fluid camera to the tune of an ocarina concert. This pastoral interlude is juxtaposed to other episodes that expose the violence of the ruling classes: Attila sodomizes a young boy, then murders him after an orgy with Regina; Fascist *squadristi* burn down a *Casa del popolo* where Anita teaches illiterate peasants to read, killing four helpless old men; Attila smashes a kitten to bits with his head, declaring to his fellow Fascists that Communism plays on human sentiments much as the tiny animal does.

In making his transition from *Act I* to *Act II*, Bertolucci becomes more and more didactic, concluding with a celebration of the *idea* of the *padrone*'s demise (complete with Red banners and flags reminiscent of a Red Chinese ballet production), a celebration that only highlights the survival of the real *padrone*. (As Alfredo remarks after the symbolic trial that pronounces the *padrone* "dead," "The boss is still alive!"). The second part of the film embodies an increasingly oppressive ideological perspective. Bertolucci is never so naive as to assume that the struggle between boss and worker has been resolved in contemporary neocapitalist Italy, but he does believe that the ultimate victory will belong to the working class. The progressive forces of Italian history are symbolized by a train that, in *Act I*, carried Olmo and the other sons of striking workers to city schools in 1908 while their parents struggled on the land for a better life. When they were children, Olmo dared Alfredo to lie between the tracks while trains passed over his body. At the close of the film (set in the present of 1975 when Olmo and Alfredo are both old men), they scuffle and fight down a hill, headed toward the train tracks of their youth. Now, Alfredo lies not between the tracks but *on* them, and as Bertolucci cuts back to a picture of the younger Alfredo, the execution of the *padrone*—postponed on the day of Liberation in 1945—is now transformed into a self-willed suicide. For Bertolucci, the Italian ruling class has collapsed of its own dead weight, and the victory of the class to which Olmo belongs is inevitable.

Bertolucci thus repeats in *1900* the substance of the ideology of *Before the Revolution*. A middle-class intellectual, he believes that he, like Alfredo, can never actually become an integral part of the class he admires for its progressive role in Italian history. Thus, *1900* is a utopian view of a revolution that has yet to occur, made by a director who is doomed (so he believes) to make films in an era *before* the revolution. Bertolucci's ideological compromises stem from this perspective: to make a film in a capitalist system, he must follow the unwritten rules of cinematic spectacle and must bow to some of the dictates of his financial backers (few of whom were Marxists). The finished product reflects this ambivalent position and makes of it a far more honest work than many of its severest critics realized.

Despite its basically Marxist stance, *1900* maintains a Freudian perspective that is not completely submerged by politics: in a general sense, Bertolucci's view of the landed class in his film reflects his belief that the sins of the fathers are always visited upon their sons. With *Luna*, the director turns from his therapeutic preoccupation with his father to the image of his mother. After years of being obsessed in analysis with his father, he suddenly began to speak of his mother. His first memory of her recalls an evening when she is pedaling her bicycle down a country road with the infant Bernardo in a basket facing her; he remembers confusing the face of the moon with that of his mother, and the inspiration for *Luna* was taken from this early recollection.[34]

Luna was financed entirely by Americans, stars Americans, was shot in English, and is a conscious attempt on the director's part both to appeal to a wide audience and to provide an excuse for him finally to make a film in the land of Hollywood and Marilyn Monroe. The plot concerns an opera singer, Catherine Silvers (Jill Clayburgh) who takes her teen-age son, Joe (Matthew Brady), with her to Rome when she is asked to sing at the Baths of Caracalla. Along the way, she discovers that neglect and the absence of his father have turned Joe into a drug addict, and in an attempt to save him, she not only provides him with the drugs he needs but even offers herself to him sexually. Thus *Luna* analyzes an incestuous relationship between mother and son, breaking one of the few cinematic taboos left in the wake of *Last Tango*. With *Luna*, Bertolucci combines Freudian plot with Verdian melodrama, two elements that functioned perfectly in *The Spider's Stratagem*. Two prologues preface the New York sequence and the death of Joe's father before the film moves to Rome. An opening sequence shows a baby choking on the thick honey his mother has fed him with her finger (a reference to his later dependence on heroin, as well as his attraction to his mother); a shadowy figure, not yet identified, dances a twist with his mother, while the baby drags a ball of unwinding twine toward his grandmother playing the piano (an image meant to suggest the umbilical cord linking mother and son). Only at the conclusion of the film do we discover that this mysterious stranger is Joe's real father, an Italian named Giuseppe, who could not bear to leave his own mother to marry Catherine. A second, and stunningly beautiful sequence follows immediately, capturing Bertolucci's own memory of his mother on the bicycle: the confusion in the baby's mind between his mother's face and that of the moon suggests a mysterious link between them that is later developed in their incestuous lovemaking. Immediately we shift to New York, the sudden death of Joe's legal father, and Joe's trip to Rome with his mother. He takes a young Italian girl to see Marilyn Monroe in *Niagara*, and while he is trying to make love to her in the darkened theater the roof opens (not an uncommon phenomenon in Italy before air conditioning) to reveal a full moon. Joe abandons the girl and searches out his mother at the opera, where she is singing in *Il trovatore*. Later, at Joe's fifteenth-birthday party, his mother discovers him shooting up with a girl, and is horrified (initially, she thought they were making love and this only caused her to smile mischievously). She is mystified by the sight of Joe and others like him, who have nothing to live for: "When I look at you and your friends—it's scary. I feel like I'm on Mars . . . I come from a world where singing, dreaming, creating—they mean every-thing." Joe later explains why he takes dope ("Because I don't give a

shit!") and accuses his mother of making no attempt to understand
him. In an effort to communicate, she caresses his genitals, and he
suckles her breasts.

Her attempts to reach Joe fail miserably: when she takes him to
Villa Verdi to see the home of her idol, Joe is completely indifferent,
and she angrily exclaims: "Joe, how can you be like this? He [Verdi]
is like a father to me. You're a lost person, a junkie. That's all." While
Catherine has a father (Verdi), Joe has lost his and the man he lost
was not even his real parent. In a desperate attempt to make him care
about something, Catherine tells him where his true father works as
a school teacher. Joe goes to see him, then follows him to a beach
house which we recognize as the location of the film's opening sequence, but Giuseppe throws Joe out of the house. Rejected, Joe

Bernardo Bertolucci's *Luna* (1979). Ambivalent relationships between Catherine (Jill Clayburgh) and her son Joe (Matthew Brady) will eventually lead
the mother to break the incest taboo.
(Photo from the author's private collection)

races back to his mother, who is rehearsing *Un ballo in maschera* at the Baths of Caracalla. Art then begins to copy life in *Luna*, as the opera on stage begins to explain the scene in the audience: Joe watches his mother walk through her role, and Giuseppe joins him, slapping his son, then making up with him as Catherine sings "lasciatelo" ("leave him alone") on the stage. The stage immediately darkens, and as Bertolucci's camera moves into Catherine while she is singing, a full moon sets over the stage at the Baths. Joe has finally discovered his real father, and although his true parents will not be reunited (since Joe's father is more in love with his own mother than with Catherine), the last words sung by Catherine on the stage ("ei muore"—he is dying) inform us that Joe has become an adult and the child has died within him. What this implies for the relationship between Joe and his mother Bertolucci leaves unanswered.

Bertolucci's latest work, *The Tragedy of a Ridiculous Man* (*La tragedia di un uomo ridicolo*, 1981), first released at Cannes, continues his fascination with the relationship of fathers and sons: an industrialist (Ugo Tognazzi) learns that his son has been kidnapped, and when the boy is killed, his father exploits the situation in order to divert the ransom money to rebuild his shaky business. While set in Bertolucci's province of Parma and thus continuing both his favorite location and his interest in Freudian themes, *The Tragedy of a Ridiculous Man* nevertheless reflects Bertolucci's increasing attention to contemporary Italy's most pressing social problems—drug addiction and terrorism— two themes that have become an integral part of Italian cinematic plots during the last decade.

Pasolini and Bertolucci represented, before the former's tragic death, the best talents of the generation that emerged in the 1960s. Both utilized ideas they had assimilated from psychoanalysis and Marxism to create highly original and controversial films that gradually attracted a wide and enthusiastic following both among critics and popular audiences. Bertolucci's visual virtuosity and his ability to score at the box office offer considerable promise for the future. In retrospect, however, Pasolini's contributions to Italian cinema loom ever larger with the passage of time since his death, and the memory of him may ultimately be the last father-figure that Bertolucci must overcome in his art.

9

Politics and Ideology in the Contemporary Italian Cinema

As recent Italian history demonstrates, the years between 1968 and 1970 marked a turning point in Italian culture, even though the disruptive upheavals that began with student riots in Italy left the political fabric of the nation less damaged than was once imagined.[1] Violence and terrorism became a way of life for Italians, beginning with the bombing at Piazza Fontana in Milan (December 12, 1969), continuing with terrorist bombings in Brescia (May 28, 1974), on the Florence-Bologna express (August 4, 1974), and culminating with the shocking kidnapping and eventual assassination of Aldo Moro, former Prime Minister and head of the Christian Democratic Party, by the Red Brigades (March 16, 1978). Italy's "economic miracle" of the 1960s ended abruptly, as inflation, reduced productivity, foreign competition, and the disastrous Arab oil embargo closed an era of relative prosperity. Social changes of far-reaching proportions included the advent in 1970 of divorce despite stiff opposition from the Vatican, and the weakening of public confidence in the government, the bureaucracy, the military, political parties, and trade unions following the discovery of successive scandals that touched the highest levels of Italy's governing class. It is no exaggeration to say that in the last decade on several occasions the very existence of Italy seemed to be in question, and that if the nation passed through such a period intact it was thanks to the good sense of the Italian people rather than as a result of the political leadership its ruling class provided.

Such rapid historical and cultural change inevitably had a serious impact upon the Italian cinema. With shifting patterns of popular entertainment (especially the increasing competition of television, both state-operated and private channels), the infrastructure of the Italian theater circuit, once the largest in Europe and second only to that of the United States, suffered staggering losses. Many of the local neighborhood theaters of the popular *seconda visione* circuit were forced to close: from 5,902 movie theaters in the peninsula in 1955, the number decreases rapidly to 4,619 in 1971 and 4,000 in 1975, and the decline has continued until the present.[2] All available statistics reveal a sharp drop in total ticket sales in Italy, one source reporting 513,700,000 ticket sales in 1975, dropping drastically to 276,300,000 in 1979. Box-office receipts remained relatively stable (362.5 billion lire in 1975 compared to 363.6 billion lire in 1979), but this stability was deceptive, as it reflected a doubling of the average ticket price (from 706 lire in 1975 to 1,322 lire in 1979) as well as extremely high inflation.[3] In real lire, therefore, the industry suffered a disastrous drop in income, which was reflected in the drop in the number of films produced: after reaching a high of 294 in 1968, production dropped gradually until it reached a low of 98 films in 1978, while American films distributed within Italy between 1968 and 1978 remained at a relatively high level, averaging almost 140 each year.[4] While production in 1981 would stabilize at around 100 Italian films, fewer and fewer of these films could compete for the mass commercial market abroad, although the handful of films produced by major directors continued to garner awards and the praise of critics at international festivals. By the beginning of the 1980s, the crisis in the Italian film industry had become prime-time television news, and such embarrassing bits of information as the enormous indebtedness of Cinecittà and that institution's difficulty in meeting employee payrolls became common knowledge.[5] The enduring paradox of the Italian film industry—individuals of genius working within a weak and increasingly vulnerable economic system—thus reemerged, and the gigantic Italian industry continued to stumble along in cadence with the equally faltering government with no assistance in sight from the state, except for a number of productions sponsored for Italian state television.

   The political and economic crises successively striking Italy found
ready responses in the best works of all major directors in the 1970s,
not only those artists who had established their reputations on work
of an essentially nonideological character (Fellini, Antonioni, De Sica,
Dino Risi, Mario Monicelli, and Luigi Comencini), but also in the best
films of a group of aggressively ideological directors, not unlike Pasolini and Bertolucci, who embodied the contradictions inherent in
Italian society in their work (Elio Petri, Francesco Rosi, Marco Bellocchio, Liliana Cavani, Lina Wertmüller, Giuliano Montaldo, Marco
Ferreri, and Franco Brusati). An examination of how the Italian cinema's "old guard" confronted contemporary politics and ideology will
set in perspective the very different responses of their often younger
and usually less famous colleagues.
   Federico Fellini signaled a shift in his work with the political message of *Amarcord*, attacking the infantile mentality of his countrymen,
which he had termed the "Fascism within us." With *Casanova, Orchestra Rehearsal* and *The City of Women*, Fellini continued, often with
mixed results, in the same direction, blending his uniquely personal
vision of the cinema with contemporary social issues.[6] In *Casanova*,
Fellini returns to the past and to a literary source just as he had done
with *Satyricon*; like that earlier film, *Casanova* deals with decadence
and is an extravagant and visually impressive work, the sets and costumes of which alone reward study. Fellini completely rejects the
obvious in his film: rather than a portrait of the archetypal Latin lover,
he offers Casanova (Donald Sutherland) to us as a mechanical man,
whose sexuality is reduced to the automatic movements of a machine
and whose final and most satisfying partner is a mechanical doll. His
character thus continues the argument of *Amarcord*, for Fellini inter-
prets Casanova as the "anticipation" of the Fascist personality type of
Amarcord—an eternal adolescent with no individuality whatsoever.
While the film is set in the eighteenth century, its target is the present-
day glorification of sex. Casanova's tireless quest for ever newer sexual
adventures produces no change in his character, no improvement in
his condition, and no increase in his self-understanding. His ultimate
failure to attain the unattainable is prefigured by the opening Carnival
sequence—a classical example of Fellinian bravura—with its frenetic

crowds, lavish historical costumes, and extravagant set constructions: a huge head of Venus rises momentarily above the waters, then suddenly breaks free of its cables and sinks into the murky waters of the lagoon. Like this enigmatic symbol, love and women are forever inscrutable to Casanova, and the Venus figure appears again at the beautiful close of the film, where in a dream Casanova imagines himself skating upon a frozen lagoon with his mechanical doll, a chilling image of misdirected sexuality and impotence in old age. As his assistant director remarked on the set, "only a middle-aged man growing cynical could make such a statement. How sad. How honest."[7]

Fellini's refusal to acknowledge contemporary sexuality as a liberating force is a direct response to radically shifting sexual mores during this decade. *Orchestra Rehearsal* responds dramatically to the social and political upheavals of the period. This 70-minute film made for television is dominated by a single extended metaphor: an orchestra in revolt against not only its German conductor but also against itself reflects the situation of contemporary Italy, torn by class conflict, corruption, lack of shared purpose, and a continual mean-spirited pursuit of selfish interests. The most humorous part of the film, and that which recalls such earlier films as *Clowns* or *Roma*, views the members of the orchestra from the perspective of a cartoonist—individual instruments embody various personality types and, therefore, the musicians that play them. But this examination of the psychological links between instrument and musician is submerged beneath Fellini's pessimistic vision of Italy as an orchestra out of synch: the unionized musicians bring in a giant metronome to replace their director, shout slogans ("Viva record players," "Down with Beethoven" and the like), and eventually even attack the metronome, advocating complete freedom. This, of course, results in the destruction of the music. Suddenly the building is shaken by a huge explosion, part of a wall crumbles and a huge demolition ball is revealed; the imminent destruction of the entire group forces the musicians back to their rehearsal. The close of the film fades to black, as the sound track carries the Hitlerian commands of the authoritarian German conductor—Fellini's ominous warning that total anarchy eventually leads not to freedom but to tyranny.

In *The City of Women*, Fellini deals with the advent of radical feminism in Italy: Snàporaz (Marcello Mastroianni), a character whose sexual fantasies make him reminiscent of so many Fellinian males, falls asleep on a train trip with his wife, and in a dream he finds himself in a feminist convention. There he is captured, tried for his "crimes," and freed; ever in search of the ideal woman—symbolized by a hot-air balloon shaped like a beautiful woman—Snàporaz soars above the assembled feminists before one of their more radical number brings him abruptly to earth with a burst from an automatic weapon. Snàporaz awakens in the train compartment to find himself with his wife. His puzzled and confused response to new feminine sexual mores reflects that of his creator, who obviously feels himself increasingly uncomfortable in a world that seems to be outside the range of his habitual illusions, fantasies, and images. Cast adrift in his city of women, Fellini's protagonist, like Casanova, fails to comprehend not only the sexual enigma that is woman but also her newly awakened political awareness and radicalized ideas.

While it was perhaps inevitable that a director whose preoccupation with his private fantasy world was as great as Fellini's would react to, rather than assimilate, the social upheavals taking place all around him, Visconti's penultimate film, *Conversation Piece* (*Gruppo di famiglia in un interno*, 1974), seems more open to the changing Italian scene, as political terrorism and social instability intrude into the hermetically sealed world of an old professor (Burt Lancaster) who collects "conversation piece" family paintings. Yet in Visconti's final film, *The Innocent* (1976), he returns to more familiar territory, a portrait of *fin-de-siècle* society in a beautiful adaptation of Gabriele d'Annunzio's novel. However, Visconti's protagonist, Tullio Hermil (Giancarlo Giannini), is very different from the main character of the novel: his suicide at the end of the film embodies Visconti's belief that the grandiloquent posturings of d'Annunzio's Nietzschean superman figures have no relevance for our times; however, the director leaves us with a beautiful vision of a world that has disappeared.[8]

Two other directors of Italy's neorealist generation—Antonioni and De Sica—seemed less bound to their familiar cinematic experiences in a number of excellent works. Antonioni's open attitude to new developments led him to accept the Chinese government's invitation to make a documentary on the "new man" in Red China—*China* (*China Kuo Cina*, 1972), aired for television in Italy, France and the United States.[9] The film was bitterly denounced by the Chinese authorities for what they believed was a grotesquely distorted view of their country. In retrospect, the Chinese reaction can be explained more by the internal politics of that country than by an honest examination of the content of Antonioni's work. However, of more importance as a film was the English-language *The Passenger*. It signaled a return to *Blow-Up* with its objectivity, its outwardly conventional suspense-story plot, and its focus upon the themes of self-knowledge and human identity. A television journalist named David Locke (Jack Nicholson) goes on assignment in North Africa to make a film about a guerrilla movement; Locke meets David Robertson, a gunrunner dealing with the rebels, and when Robertson dies of a heart attack, Locke changes passports and identities with him. His wife, Rachel, and his producer, eventually believing Locke to be dead, produce a television homage to his work, utilizing scraps of film Locke shot in Africa. Meanwhile, Locke meets a girl (Maria Schneider) and uses her to dodge the investigations of his producer and his wife. However, he does not realize that while he has been following Robertson's itinerary he has been trailed by secret government agents sent to assassinate him in order to stop the flow of arms to the rebellion. The film concludes with a second hotel death—this time Locke dies as Robertson—when the secret police reach him before his wife does.

Antonioni thus combines an inquiry into the nature of documentary with a suspense thriller. Locke's confused identity parallels the confused attempts of the journalist to reach "objective truth" in his footage. Three very different types of documentary film are examined by his wife and producer: the first is an interview with an African leader, full of government propaganda and lies; the second and most disturbing bit of film is that of an actual execution in Africa (shown to us first as it actually happens and then on the studio monitor, juxtaposing what we first perceived as "real" with what has become "objective" reporting); finally, a third sequence concerns a well-spoken witch doctor, who, during Locke's interview, turns the camera around upon the journalist, underlining how Locke's quest for information reveals more about himself than about Africa. Antonioni's films generally end with a cinematic *tour de force*, and *The Passenger* is no exception. Locke's eventual assassination as Robertson is shown obliquely as captured by Antonioni in a virtuoso seven-minute sequence without cuts: beginning inside Locke's hotel room, the camera travels out the barred windows, attached first to the room's ceiling, then guided by a connection to a huge crane more than a hundred feet high; the camera continues to circle about the square outside, finally peering back into the room where Locke's dead body now lies. The sequence was made with a new Canadian camera controlled by gyroscopes to neutralize the transition from the track inside the room to the crane outside, and the result is a stunningly beautiful evocation of the mystery of the relationship between human reality and the more problematic "reality" the camera is capable of capturing.

While in this period of political upheavals abroad Antonioni's sensitivity expressed itself by a conscious attempt to assimilate the "reality" of politics in China or Africa within his own continuing investigation of the "reality" of cinematography, Vittorio De Sica, rounding out his long career, turned away from the commercial comedies he made after his neorealist period to several excellent works—*The Garden of the Finzi-Continis* (*Il giardino dei Finzi-Contini*, 1970) and *A Brief Vacation* (*Una breve vacanza*, 1973). The first was an evocation of the destructive results of anti-Semitism during the Fascist period and the second a brilliant portrait of industrial life in Milan.[10] De Sica's adaptation of Giorgio Bassani's novel fails to do justice to the complexity of its highly critical portrait of an aristocratic Jewish family from Ferrara, whose aloofness from the more commonly born Jews of the city does not save them from the destruction of the Holocaust. However, the film captures quite beautifully the elegaic nostalgia of Bassani's portrait of the Edenic garden of this family, an idyllic pastoral oasis where the film's narrator comes of age emotionally and sexually in his ill-fated infatuation for the enigmatically beautiful Micòl Finzi-Contini (Dominique Sanda). Photographed with a deeply romantic diffused focus, the work was awarded an Oscar for the Best Foreign Film in 1972.

It is *A Brief Vacation*, however, which shows De Sica's most sensitive poetic touch, worthy of comparison to his neorealist masterpieces, in a memorable treatment of the Italian working class: a Calabrian housewife now a Milan factory worker, Clara Mataro (Florinda Balkan), contracts tuberculosis and is sent to recuperate in a convalescent hospital in the Italian Alps (the ironically named "brief vacation"). There, she encounters an entirely new range of experiences and different ideas, as well as members of the upper class, and she falls in love with a man named Luigi. Here, the misty, romantic soft-focus shots of *The Garden of the Finzi-Continis* are replaced by the gritty, industrial colors of Northern Italy, reminiscent of Antonioni's *Red Desert*. The portrait of the patients at the hospital in Sondalo provides a cross-section of women from Italian society. Class and regional distinctions are marked but eventually blur, as Clara's simple good nature wins over even the rich wives and mistresses of Northern industrialists who, unlike the workers who come to the hospital under health insurance plans, are paying patients. Nevertheless, the gulf between Italy's working class and the wealthy in this microcosm of modern Italy is shocking: Clara's economic condition is so wretched that a trip to a sanatorium seems like a resort vacation; her rich friends ask insipid questions ("Did Karl Marx write a novel?") and side with the hospital administrators when hospital workers go on strike for higher benefits; when Franco (Renato Salvatori), Clara's unemployed husband, visits her accompanied by their entire Calabrian clan, he tries to force himself upon her sexually, reveals his unchanged sexist attitudes toward women, and moves Clara to realize that an entirely different kind of life could be possible outside her family and its archaic Southern mores.

Ironically, her love affair, her discovery of her personal potential—until then submerged under her husband's macho demands—and the promise of a better life all come to nought when she is cured and forced to return to her former life. As Clara returns home on the train, the last image we see is that of two political slogans scribbled on a wall by the tracks—"Viva Mao!" and "Down with Mao!" Clara's problems are ultimately left untouched by the political solutions proposed by those around her; like the protagonists of De Sica's earlier masterpieces, Clara must face her destiny alone, without the comforting illusions of help from her family, her coworkers, or even the lover she must now abandon.

The impact of rapid social and political changes during the past decade has had an effect upon the Italian cinema's most commercial product, the *commedia all'italiana*. Mario Monicelli, Dino Risi, and Luigi Comencini have produced a number of films within this tradition, and while most of them are aimed at the middle-brow audiences who have always taken to the genre, several are remarkable barometers of Italian problems. Some films, such as Risi's *How Funny Can Sex Be?* (*Sesso matto*, 1973), continue the episodic tradition established in the early 1960s, and perhaps the best of them is *Viva Italia* (*I nuovi mostri*, 1977), a work by Risi, Monicelli, and Ettore Scola which consciously refers us back to the early comic portrait of Italian society in transition in Risi's *The Monsters* (1963). As its Italian title—"the new monsters"—implies, the three directors assemble even more grotesque episodes, fourteen vignettes of even more comic decadence than appeared in 1963. Now the laughter is bittersweet, as Italian society has become more and more violent. A man sees a stabbing in the street but is more concerned with the quality of the cheese on his pasta than in calling the police; a couple are incensed that their young actress daughter must work in the nude in a pornographic film but eventually agree to allow her to make love with a monkey for four million lire; a rich industrialist broadcasts special radio appeals to the kidnappers of his wife, pleading with them to provide her with the special medicine she needs to survive, but the final shot of the episode reveals he has cut the telephone wire to avoid their return calls; a businessman dumps his aging mother at a nursing home; a Latin-lover type seduces a beautiful airline stewardess but only to plant a bomb in her plane; the final scene, in the face of this corrosive indictment of Italian life, recalls Fellini's *Clowns*, for it is the funeral of an Italian comic during which the lighthearted celebration and dancing around the open grave offer us the hope that comedy may triumph over the tragedy filling an Italian's daily life.

The best comic films of the period underscore a black, grotesque vision of contemporary society. Monicelli's *We Want the Colonels!* (*Vogliamo i colonelli*, 1973) is a thinly disguised reference to both the contemporary Greek Army dictatorship and the unsuccessful coup attempt organized earlier by Prince Valerio Borghese among elements of Italy's armed forces. An even more important work, in which Alberto Sordi gives an unforgettable performance as a minor government functionary whose son is accidentally murdered by terrorists, is Monicelli's *A Very Petit Bourgeois* (*Un borghese piccolo piccolo*, 1977). It is a macabre vision of an entire society gone berserk: when the grieving father tries to find a grave for his son, he discovers hundreds of people lined up at the state burial office, waiting for endless unburied caskets; on two different occasions, a police lineup fails to identify the killer (who is nevertheless present), and eventually the father takes the law into his own hands, captures the terrorist, and eventually kills him accidentally. Our last view of this pathetic figure shows his impotent rage still bubbling over as, intent upon killing anyone who seems to present a threat to his conventional values and political views, he trails a young man. A similar story may be found in Risi's *Dear Dad* (*Caro papà*, 1979), a bittersweet portrait of an ex-Partisan industrialist (Vittorio Gassman) whose son studies semiotics at the university but is also a member of a terrorist group which has plotted his father's assassination. The plot is complicated by the father's discovery of his son's diary in which he discusses an unnamed but impending terrorist act. Not realizing that he is the target, the father protectively fails to alert the police to his son's activity, and he is shot and paralyzed by a professional killer in Canada. Back home and reduced to helplessness, the father is practically deserted both by mistress and wife; eventually, he tearfully discovers that his son Marco has not abandoned him and had apparently argued against his execution, leaving the terrorist group when his opinion was rejected. Although shifts in contemporary Italian politics and ideology present obvious threats to the family in such works as *A Very Petit Bourgeois* or *Dear Dad*, traditional values connected to that hallowed and rudely buffeted Italian institution may still be offered by the cinema.

Luigi Comencini produced both frothy comic vehicles for the scantily clad Laura Antonelli, such as *Till Marriage Do Us Part* (*Mio dio, come sono caduta in basso*, 1974)—a film capitalizing upon the widespread popularity of this charming actress during the last decade—as well as several films of greater value, particularly *Traffic Jam* (*L'in-gorgo*, 1978), and *Turn Around, Eugene!* (*Voltati, Eugenio*, 1980). The first film is composed of a number of episodes and a large collection of major stars (Alberto Sordi, Marcello Mastroianni, Ugo Tognazzi, and others). Fellini's allegory of Italy as an orchestra out of tune is matched by Comencini's use of an extraordinary traffic jam to project an image of Italy's disorganization, lack of discipline, and chaotic social conditions. (As the industrialist Sordi portrays ironically remarks, things are better in Moscow where there are always free traffic lanes.) Every character in the film is shown in the worst possible light—a typical feature of recent Italian comedies—and the last image of the film offers no possible solution, only a long line of motionless cars honking and going nowhere. *Turn Around, Eugene!* is a far more com-plex film, for it focuses upon the family life of a couple who came of age during the 1968 upheavals and student riots: thoughtlessly con-ceived by his parents during student protest marches, young Eugene is neglected by his mother and father who see him only as a nuisance who interferes with their liberated life style. Only the child's grand-parents—representatives of an earlier era in which Italian life still centered around the affection generated by a united family—emerge as positive figures; the ex-revolutionaries reveal themselves to be spoiled adolescents, unworthy of the responsibility implied by the momentous social changes they advocated when they were younger.

The most unusual of Italy's comic directors, Marco Ferreri, has produced a number of outrageous and interesting works, each of which embodies surrealist themes and grotesquely unconventional plots. *Don't Touch the White Woman*, Ferreri's parody of the Western genre and an attack upon American military adventures in the Third World, has already been discussed. With *La Grande Bouffe* (*La grande abbuf-fata*, 1973) and *The Last Woman* (*L'ultima donna*, 1976), Ferreri turns his jaundiced eye toward contemporary consumer society and man's relation to women. Both works are set in France (not Italy) and were co-productions with the French film industry. The first film, an un-settlingly graphic description of how four men (a chef, a television writer, a pilot, and a judge) go on a weekend retreat and eat themselves to death, employs the metaphor of overconsumption in a manner which may have influenced Pasolini's more ideologically coherent, if no less revolting, *Salò*. In the process of describing these culinary suicides, Ferreri creates a lengthy and somewhat overblown metaphor for the decadence of the society his characters are carefully chosen to represent. *The Last Woman* more successfully attacks the male myth of virility and reveals the instability of contemporary family life: Giovanni (Gérard Depardieu) lives alone with his infant son after his wife has left him, and he begins an erotic relationship with Valeria (Ornella Muti), the girl who looks after the boy. An unreconstructed male chauvinist, Giovanni consistently fails to understand female needs and emotions, even though he desperately needs the security and comfort of a family life. The recurrent visual motif in the film is that of kitchen accidents with knives, leading to the frightening conclusion of the film when Giovanni cuts off his sexual member with an electric knife in order to offer Valeria the ultimate symbol of his manhood and, therefore, his affection. While Valeria seeks a substitute for what she considers to be the now outmoded nuclear family and hopes to "invent" a new form of male-female relationship, Giovanni can only focus upon his penis as the center of his male-dominated set of values.

As is evident from even this brief survey of the best examples of the *commedia all'italiana* of this decade, many such films avoided complex plotting and developed, instead, a series of images around a dominant metaphor. They reflect the insecurity and the instability their directors sense in the contemporary Italian scene, even though few works manage to transcend this unilinear vision with the creation of a truly complex form of comedy, typical of the preceding decade's production. It is this superficiality of approach that ultimately limits their appeal, causing such works as *Orchestra Rehearsal, The Last Woman*, or *Traffic Jam* to fall short of the more richly wrought comic masterpieces of Lina Wertmüller or Ettore Scola (to be discussed in the last chapter). Thus, while many works in the tradition of the *commedia all'italiana* are worthy of mention in the context of the cinema of politics and ideology, they often fail to come to grips with the ideological complexities that a number of dramatic works from the same period present in a far more engaging manner.

Perhaps the most brilliant comedy of the period is *Bread and Choc-*

olate (*Pane e cioccolata*, 1973) by the relatively unknown Franco Brusati
(1923–   ). Largely ignored in Italy until it received rave reviews at
film festivals around the world, it is an indictment of the conditions
of Italian guest-workers living in Switzerland. In it Nino Manfredi
gives a memorable performance as Giovanni Garofoli, a Southern
Italian worker who is pathetically out of place in Switzerland, yet
forced by economic exigencies to remain there in order to survive.
The clean, tidy nature of Swiss culture is juxtaposed to the more
exuberant and humane (if somewhat tacky) Latin culture beginning
with the first sequence of the work: as Brusati's camera pans slowly
over a Swiss family and a quartet playing Haydn in the beautifully
manicured park, Garofoli appears, wearing a garish tie and sport shirt
and eating a bread and chocolate sandwich. He procedes to break all
of the rules of polite Swiss society—he litters the park, smokes where
it is forbidden, and is generally out of step with those around him.
Yet death lurks in this blissful Arcadian setting: a sexually demented
cleric has just murdered a young girl in the forest nearby, a crime for
which the foreigner is initially blamed. Throughout the film, the surface cleanliness of Switzerland is contrasted to the darker reality underneath its civilized surface.

Garofoli must compete with another foreigner, a Turk, for the only
permanent position in a restaurant, and the misadventures he experiences there recall similar episodes in Chaplin films. The most moving
moments of the film chronicle Garofoli's visit to a workers' barracks,
in which Italians are squeezed into living quarters more like a prison
or a concentration camp than a home: there, in a poignant evocation
of the scene in Renoir's *The Grand Illusion* in which Allied prisoners
stage a variety show, Brusati shows us his homesick Southerners doing
the same. When "Rosina" (a young worker in drag named Renzo),
unable to stand the separation from home any longer, breaks into
tears, Garofoli comes to understand that singing away problems, an
attitude so typical of Italian culture, has never solved them and, in
fact, has kept Italians from changing their condition. Even more disturbing is Brusati's surrealistic vision of a group of clandestine immigrants who live and work in a chicken coop: surviving by piece
work (the more chickens they pluck, the more they earn), these pa-

Franco Brusati's *Bread and Chocolate* (1973). Giovanni (Nino Manfredi), an Italian working in Switzerland, is unaware that the neatly kept Swiss parks may conceal great evil (in this case, the brutal murder of a young girl by a demented cleric).
(Photo courtesy of the Museum of Modern Art)

thetic individuals, trapped in a building which forces them to stoop when they walk, have themselves turned into a grotesque parody of the animal they kill. They even speak in henlike clucks. From within the coop they see an outdoor vision of Germanic purity—blond young men and women bathe nude in a limpid stream to the accompaniment of Teutonic music. We cut immediately to Garofoli, who has tinted his hair blond in one last desperate attempt to assimilate himself into Swiss society. But even this masquerade fails when, in a bar crowded with German-speaking Swiss, while watching the televised soccer

match between Italy and Switzerland, Garofoli is provoked by the
racist insults to his native land and screams "Viva l'Italia!" when his
countrymen score a goal. He is immediately tossed out of the bar.

Brusati's comic vision of Italy's feeble economic status in Europe
never allows us to laugh away the dilemma we see presented upon
the screen. Garofoli realizes the attraction of his own culture, yet each
time he starts home toward Southern Italy, the sight of singing immigrant workers on the trains turns him back to Switzerland. It is a
desperate situation, one experienced not only by hundreds of thousands of Italians abroad but by millions of others in Europe as well:
forced to leave their homelands and their cultural roots, these workers
fail to discover anything abroad to replace their old values and at-
tachments. Like Garofoli, they are trapped between a world which is
incapable of supporting them and another in which they feel they have
no identity.

The political cinema of the past decade has been dominated by a
number of directors who first came to prominence in the postneorealist generation. Francesco Rosi continued the richly documented
legal briefs against the political system in Italy with a number of original works.[11] *Men Opposed* (*Uomini contro*, 1970), an Italian *Farewell
to Arms*, uncovers the stupidity of the commanders of the Italian army
during the disastrous battles leading up to Caporetto in World
War I. *The Mattei Case* (*Il caso Mattei*, 1972) forces the viewer to
speculate on the reasons behind the mysterious death of Enrico Mattei, the director of the state-owned petroleum complex ENI, and in
the process investigates the complex links between private enterprise
and the public corporations sponsored by the Italian government. Perhaps the most interesting of these "documented" films denouncing
the Italian establishment is *Lucky Luciano* (1973), a probing look into
the strange history of this Italo-American gangster who mysteriously
returned to Italy with Allied troops in the invasion of Sicily. Working
in the style he employed in *Salvatore Giuliano*, Rosi builds up a ver-
itable legal brief against both American politicians and Italian authorities, showing that there is little difference between those within
and those "outside" the law in an era when power and profit dominate
Italian life.

After several adaptations of literary works—*Excellent Cadavers* (*Ca-*

daveri eccellenti, 1975), a chilling parable of the intricate link between political power and corruption from Leonardo Sciascia's novel *Equal Danger*, in which the Sicilian Mafia is transformed into a universally comprehensible metaphor for corrupt, absolute power anywhere in the world, and *Christ Stopped at Eboli* (*Cristo si è fermato a Eboli*, 1979), a television version of Carlo Levi's neorealist classic about poverty in the South of Fascist Italy—Rosi made *Three Brothers* (*Tre fratelli*, 1981), a didactic film which presents a view of contemporary Italy through the juxtaposition of three brothers, who return from the North where they have made their fortunes to attend their mother's funeral. Their individual histories reflect typical Italian experiences: Raffaele (Philippe Noiret) has become a Roman magistrate leading an antiterrorist group and his life is in constant danger; Rocco (Vittorio Mezzogiorno) attempts to retrain delinquent minors in an over-crowded correctional institution; Nicola (Michele Placido) works in a factory in Turin, rejects traditional unions, and is a member of an autonomous workers' group that supports urban terrorism. A nostalgia for the peasant culture of another, less complicated era causes each of the brothers to reflect upon their lives. In a flashback to the American invasion, Rosi provides a neat reversal of the confrontation immortalized in Rossellini's *Paisan*: the soldiers Rocco encounters as a boy are Italo-Americans, who jump from their tanks and kiss the soil from which their parents came. These soldiers, in search of their cultural roots in Italy, are contrasted to contemporary Italians like the three brothers, who in abandoning their peasant roots have lost their identities.

A fresh look at Italy's encounter with America, so important a theme in the neorealist period, thus characterizes not only a number of Rosi's works but also dominates an excellent film by Giuliano Montaldo (1924–   ), *Sacco and Vanzetti* (*Sacco e Vanzetti*, 1971), which combines Rosi's pseudo-documentary style with an attempt to recreate the authentic atmosphere of Boston's Italian community during the famous trial of the two Italian immigrant anarchists in 1927. Gian Maria Volonté's brilliant performance as Bartolomeo Vanzetti, especially his moving speech during the trial, provides Montaldo with a means of effectively examining not only American injustice in the past but also Italian injustice at the time the film was made.[12] Disturbing parallels between the situation during the Red scare of the 1920s in America and contemporary Italy may not be noticed by the non-Italian viewer of the film, but Montaldo employs them skillfully in a discourse about the corrupt nature of political power that recognizes no national frontiers.

The best examples of the political film genre may be found in the important works of Elio Petri (1929–82), such as *Investigation of a Citizen Above Suspicion* (*Indagine su un cittadino al di sopra di ogni sospetto*, 1969); *The Working Class Goes to Heaven* (*La classe operaia va in paradiso*, 1971); *Property Is No Longer Theft* (*La proprietà non è più un furto*, 1973); and *One Way or Another* (*Todo modo*, 1976). Rosi's films, with their fundamental connection to Italian life, often seem incomprehensible abroad, but Petri's films have gained a number of festival prizes, even an Oscar (for *Investigation*), and have achieved wide international distribution. His success is in part explained by his ability to blend politics and ideology with good entertainment—a lesson well learned by Bertolucci and Pasolini. *Investigation* succeeds because it presents a specific political situation, that of contemporary Italy, in an abstract, almost philosophical manner: the film is like one of Kafka's parables, applicable not only to power in Italy but everywhere. Its plot centers around a police inspector (Gian Maria Volonté), transfered from homicide to the political section, who murders his mistress Augusta (Florinda Balkan) in the film's first sequence and then defies the police to arrest him even when he has provided ample evidence of his guilt. The conceit behind the plot is the puzzle: who will guard the guardians? Petri's view of power is that it reduces us all to an infantile state. Thus, Augusta and the Inspector play, in a flashback, ritualistic games that center around the policeman's role as father surrogate: he interrogates her as if she were in jail, since he reminds her of her father; when he informs her that the police play upon the guilty feelings all citizens share and that confronted by the state, everyone becomes a child, she angers him with her remark "you're like a child," which leads to her eventual murder while they make love. The Inspector wishes to have the cathartic experience of confession available to the average citizen, and commits his crime hoping to be caught.

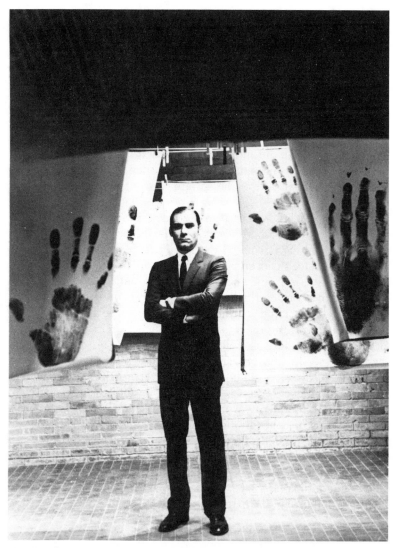
Elio Petri's *Investigation of a Citizen Above Suspicion* (1969). Irrefutable proof of the guilt of the police inspector (Gian Maria Volonté) goes un-heeded.
(Photo courtesy of the Museum of Modern Art).

Ultimately, the Inspector is confronted by the highest authorities of the government, but instead of arresting him, they greet him with a smile and a scolding tug on the ear (repeating a gesture symbolizing the link between father and child, which the Inspector had earlier used with one of his political prisoners). The Inspector is finally forgiven when he declares, "I confess my innocence." His superiors leave, and we realize that this sequence was a dream. Yet, as the Inspector reties his tie, we see the authorities appear outside, and it is clear that the dream will be repeated in reality. The film closes with a citation from Kafka: the servants of the law are above the law, and therefore, above suspicion.

Investigation of a Citizen Above Suspicion is engaging cinema: the strange, jerky music of Morricone, the skillful and abrasive editing techniques, and the fast-paced rhythm of the film force the audience along the director's chosen path with little time to pause for analysis. Petri produces an exciting suspense thriller built around our expectation that the murderer will eventually be caught, then surprises us with the Kafkan ending and the ideological message about the nature of political power. But the impact of the film is purchased at a price— a lessening of the work's ideological coherence and historical veracity. Far less successful but perhaps more honest a film is *The Working Class Goes to Heaven*, again boasting an excellent performance by Volonté as Lulu Massa, a factory employee whose life centers about his skill as a superproductive worker on the plant assembly line until a moment's loss of concentration causes him the loss of a finger and moves him to consider his alienated condition. The world of the factory in Petri's film resembles a machine itself: dehumanizing in its demands upon the worker and its barrage of constant noise, the assembly line ultimately shapes the worker in its own image. As Massa ironically defines human nature:

> You put in a little raw material called food; various machines in the body go to work on it; and the final product that comes out the other end is . . . shit! Man is a perfect little shit-factory. Pity there's no market for the stuff, we could all be capitalists.[13]

Everything is reduced by the factory to the mechanical, even sex: Massa is able to produce more than anyone else because he endows the metal products his lathe produces with his frustrated sex drive ("a piece, an ass, a piece, an ass" he mutters, keeping his rhythm steady with the machine). Yet, his prowess on the assembly line alienates him from his fellows, who resent his productivity, since his record production is used as an excuse to speed up the pace of the work. And when a strike breaks out, Massa feels lost without the factory. Petri's ideological position is far more convincing here than in the somewhat confusing mixture of politics and sexuality of *Investigation*; as James MacBean notes, there is no need to examine the psychoanalytical background of a factory worker to explain his neuroses—just examine the brutalizing conditions on the job.[14] In fact, when Massa is examined by the plant psychologist, it is clear from Petri's satirical presentation of the doctor's desire to reduce Massa's neuroses to a sexual dysfunction that the company provides him with medical treatment only to defend its production and is not really interested in discovering the illness's true roots in the factory system itself.

When the union finally obtains a "victory," it is paradoxically one that sends Massa back to work, back to the place responsible for his alienation. And the film closes on a chilling note: staccato images of the assembly line are presented in rapid, disconcerting succession, while the sound track bombards us with the noises and screams of the workers, as Massa relates to his friends a dream he had about breaking down a wall separating them all from Paradise. Petri obviously believes that the working class will never reach Paradise until it destroys the wall (industrial capitalism) separating it from its dream of unalienated labor.

In *One Way or Another*, Petri employs a novel by Leonardo Sciascia to deliver a frontal attack upon the system of Christian Democratic rule that has controlled Italy since the war. The plot concerns a surrealistic monastery in which the major leaders of a political party (obviously the Christian Democrats) assemble for "spiritual exercises" established by Loyola (the title itself refers to Loyola's dictum that all means must be employed to seek the will of God). During the retreat, a number of the men are killed by an unknown avenger, and at the film's conclusion, everyone, including the "President" of the party, is murdered. While Sciascia's novel was a philosophical parable uncovering the guilt associated with the exercise of power, Petri's adaptation

Elio Petri's *The Working Class Goes to Heaven* (1971). The dehumanizing conditions of the factory produce neuroses in a radicalized Lulu Massa (Gian Maria Volonté).
(Photo courtesy of the Museum of Modern Art)

(in spite of the closing titles that claim any link of the film to real events is a result of pure coincidence) aims directly at a specific institution, the Christian Democratic Party. The President (Gian Maria Volonté) looks exactly like Aldo Moro, and other Christian Democratic politicians are clearly recognizable (Andreotti, Fanfani). The President, like Moro, speaks of a "historical compromise" (a reference to his *compromesso storico* with the Italian Communist Party) and even remarks, "I never distinguish between right and left" at one point in the investigation of the murders. Petri's film is thus both a caustic denunciation of the corruption and the *trasformismo* that marks Italian politics and an impassionated call for a violent mopping-up operation to throw all the rascals out. But the ending is somewhat puzzling: Petri argues for the extermination of Italy's ruling class but their violent destruction is left unexplained, nor is it clear who has actually committed the murders.

One Way or Another remains too imbedded in the confusing morass of Italian political squabbles for it to be appreciated outside the peninsula, although it is a curiously prophetic work about the end of an Italian politician (Aldo Moro) who, only two years later, was actually to be murdered for his role in the *compromesso storico*. The film demonstrates how difficult it is to produce a genuinely political or ideological film: if the laws of cinematic spectacle are followed to guarantee an audience as in *Investigation*, the thrust of the specific historical context may be obscured; if ideology takes over the picture completely, as it does in *One Way or Another*, only the initiated may follow the storyline.

The rage that bubbles over from Petri's *One Way or Another* also characterizes the political films made by Marco Bellocchio (1939–) during this period.[15] Though the genius clearly evident in *China Is Near* or *Fists in the Pocket* has yet to be fully realized in the works of this interesting director, several of his films from the past decade still deserve mention. *Slap the Monster on the Front Page* (*Sbatti il mostro sulla prima pagina*, 1972) examines in a rather superficial manner the way in which political factions manipulate Italian newspapers; *Triumphant March* (*Marcia trionfale*, 1976) analyzes the relationships between those with power and authority in the army and the draftees under their control. Bellocchio's best work to date, however, and one which continues many of the themes of his promising early films in the 1960s is *In the Name of the Father* (*Nel nome del padre*, 1971), which not only situates the action of the drama in an identifiable historical era related to the present (the 1958–59 academic year, the year in which Pope Pius XII died) but also embodies a fascinating discourse on the repressive nature of educational institutions themselves. The setting, a college for the sons of the well born, is clearly a metaphor for the entire social system as well as an explanation for the causes of the social upheavals that were to sweep over Italy a decade later. The college is organized like Italian society: the priests are feeble academics, but they try to instill in their pupils a sense of their "duties" as future rulers; the wealthy students are a motley lot, dominated by one individual named Angelo (Yves Beneyton), who despises his fellow students for their sheeplike behavior and his teachers for their incompetence and "half-way measures." The working class is represented by the men who do the cleaning for the priests and students. In Angelo, Bellocchio portrays his view of the true neo-Fascist: for centuries priests have ruled by fear, Angelo explains, but now secular leaders (such as he obviously aspires to be) can employ even more efficient methods. The class play Angelo directs ruthlessly attacks traditional values and cultural artifacts: in it, a veterinarian named Faustolo (a parody of Faust) confronts God dressed in a Santa Claus costume and is unafraid to lose his soul, since he claims he has none.

Marco Bellocchio's *In the Name of the Father* (1971). During the class play, the students attack their clerical teachers by having God appear as Santa Claus.
(Photo from the author's private collection)

While Bellocchio's audience will probably sympathize, as all ex-students must, with Angelo's attack upon academic authority, it is the director's contention that such puerile rebellions—like that of his middle-class protagonists in *Fists in the Pocket* or *China Is Near*—arise more from a need to replace outmoded authority figures (here represented by the priests) with new ones rather than from any truly revolutionary desire for real political change. Thus, Angelo's student revolt rejects an alliance with the revolt of the college's menial employees for better conditions, as the spoiled students refuse to have anything to do with the despised lower classes. By situating his story during the last year of the reign of Pius XII (the symbol for most Italian leftists of religious reaction and complicity with a government dominated by the Christian Democrats), Bellocchio means to show us how such a system produced not only docile cogs in the government's repressive machinery but, from time to time as in Angelo's case, a potentially dangerous individual whose thirst for power could not be quenched by the "half-way" measures advocated by the priests. And as the film was released during the height of the student uprisings in Italy, Bellocchio's message about the ideologically limited goals of the student population was not lost on those who advocated a truly revolutionary change in Italy's social structure.

Vittorio (1929–   ) and Paolo (1931–   ) Taviani made two of the most original political films of the period: *Allonsanfan* (a mispronounced Italian version of the first lines of the French national anthem, "Allons enfants," 1974); and *Padre Padrone* (*Padre padrone*—literally "father boss," 1977).[16] The second film was originally produced for Italian television and received both the Golden Palm Prize at Cannes as well as the New York Film Festival award for the same year. The first work recalls Bertolucci's attitude toward revolution in his early works, although it is set in post-Napoleonic Italy during the reactionary restoration that followed the destruction of the democratic changes in the peninsula. Fulvio Imbriani (Marcello Mastroianni), an aristocratic Jacobin accused of revolutionary acts, is released from prison, only to be accused by his fellow Jacobins (members of a group very much like the Masons) of betraying their "Grand Master"; but when Fulvio is taken by them to confront the leader, they discover that the latter has committed suicide. Fulvio returns home to the family estate and seems to have put political activism behind him, until his former mistress, Charlotte, appears. Once again, and quite against his wishes, Fulvio is embroiled in subversive schemes, despite the fact that he really wants to abandon the struggle and take his son to America.

The Tavianis' picture of Fulvio, the reluctant revolutionary, reflects their view that middle-class participation in political upheavals must, of necessity, always be limited and constrained by a class-oriented utopianism. Fulvio only accidentally becomes part of a Jacobin scheme to support peasant revolt in Sicily, and the Jacobins are so far from understanding the complex social and political relationships in still feudal Sicily that when they arrive, they are attacked and brutally murdered by the very peasants they had come to assist. When one of the Jacobins mistakenly informs Fulvio that the peasants have joined the rebellion, he finally commits himself, dons a red Jacobin shirt, and meets his death. Just before he is shot, the Tavianis show us a mass of red-shirted Jacobins and white-shirted peasants, dancing a traditional Sicilian folk dance together. Although this image is a projection of the aspirations of the Jacobins and is actually a dream experienced by one of Fulvio's friends, it expresses quite beautifully the Tavianis' conception of revolution as utopia, a view already suggested in their earlier works.

Padre Padrone, a film based upon Gavino Ledda's autobiographical account about how he, an illiterate Sardinian shepherd, became a professor of linguistics, represents the best work of the Tavianis to date. Though it employs a number of the major themes typical of the political film, it transcends this genre's usual lack of historical and ideological depth. The Tavianis are fond of playing with the conventions of the genres within which they work, and *Padre Padrone* is full of shifts from documentary to fiction. The real Gavino Ledda is introduced at the opening sequence and gives the actor playing himself a stick, explaining that his father once came to take him from school with one; from this sequence, we cut abruptly to an account of the traumatic moment when the father entered young Gavino's classroom and terrified everyone, including the teacher, threatening all of the children with the same fate: "Hands on the desk: today it's Gavino's turn, tomorrow it's yours!" In Sardinian families completely dependent upon their herds, children must be kept at home to help support the family. The stern, archaic rules of this primitive society therefore provide the Tavianis with a perfect image of the primal father of psychoanalysis; at the same time, this father represents an historically accurate portrait of a real, not imagined, society. Thus, *Padre Padrone* employs a theme used by most of the political directors of the period—the authoritarian link between father and son—in a context that has philosophical implications but which retains an air of complete veracity. This is not unlike earlier films on Sardinia, such as De Seta's *Bandits of Orgosolo*.

But the Tavianis play with the conventions of realism, they do not

Vittorio and Paolo Taviani's *Padre Padrone* (1977). The young Gavino (Fabrizio Forte) is traumatically removed from school by his authoritarian father (Omero Antonutti).
(Photo courtesy of the Museum of Modern Art)

follow them. Much of the film follows Gavino's slow education from an illiterate peasant boy to a young man who learns a number of different languages or codes: he assimilates the language of sex by observing the animals about him coupling (or his fellow shepherds coupling with them!); he tries to learn to play an accordion, which he purchases from a passerby when he hears him playing a Strauss waltz in the fields; later when Gavino is drafted, he begins to acquire a mania for language, words, and their origins, discovering for the first time that his own language is a dialect, prohibited in the barracks. Returning home from the army, he announces his intention to go to the university, rejecting his father and the archaic, patriarchal system of repressive authority he represents. This act of rebellion finally breaks his father's will, and Gavino leaves home for the "continent" and a new world of experiences.

At the close of the film, the real Gavino Ledda appears once more, speaking directly to the camera and explaining that to employ his newly acquired education in a position of privilege would only represent his father's final victory. We cut back to the scene where the father came to take him to the fields from school, but now his terrifying words have an entirely new and revolutionary significance, one of hope rather than of despair, for if Gavino was able to evolve from an illiterate peasant into a professor of linguistics and even a bestselling author, then all of the school children have that same potential. Now the tune of the Strauss waltz, first heard on Gavino's accordion and later picked up by the radio he was taught to build in the army, is heard again, a reminder that true revolutions begin in the human mind and with the seemingly insignificant actions of brave individuals. And yet, the price of this personal evolution is not overlooked by the Tavianis, for the last image of the real Gavino (not the actor) that closes the film shows him holding his knees and rocking back and forth silently, recalling the same gesture he habitually made while left alone in the hills, tending his father's flocks.

It is not surprising that the poignant story of *Padre Padrone* moves us in a way few avowedly ideological films can, because the ideological import of Gavino's life emerges naturally from this portrait of the provinces with no need for tiresome metaphysical arguments or full-blown political messages. While theirs is decidedly not a work in the neorealist tradition—given its playful and self-conscious mixture of fact and fiction—the directors continue the honesty and simplicity of the best neorealist films dealing with provincial problems. An entirely different kind of film, Olmi's *The Tree of the Wooden Clogs* (*L'albero degli zoccoli*, 1978), also the winner of prizes at Cannes and New York and originally made for Italian television, focuses upon peasant life on a farm near Bergamo around the end of the nineteenth century.[17] Recalling the conventions of neorealism, Olmi's work employs amateurs (the peasants still living in the region) who speak their local dialect, still difficult for speakers of Italian to comprehend. Most of the film's three hours is devoted to an elegiac recreation of the slow rhythms of life in a culture that has almost disappeared but is still very much a part of the collective memory of contemporary Italians.

How distant Olmi's spectators are from this world is evident from the scene picturing the slaughter of the peasants' hogs: we are shocked by the blood and gore of the scene, but for the peasants, this seemingly cruel execution of a docile animal represents a necessary part of their daily lives. And even when they are forced to kill their animals, the peasants obviously feel more affection for their livestock than the landlord feels for the peasants. The central event in the film occurs when a farmer's son breaks his wooden clogs on the way home from school: intent upon safeguarding his son's education, his only means of achieving a better life, his father (having no other wood) cuts down one of the *padrone*'s trees to replace the clogs. When this act is eventually discovered, the entire family is driven from the land. Here, in a simple and apparently insignificant event, Olmi tells us more about a cruel and exploitive economic system than all the richly choreographed scenes of Bertolucci's *1900*. The revolutionary upheavals sweeping over Italy during this troubled period are only glimpsed briefly during a visit to the city, where street demonstrations and class warfare are shown. But the world of the peasants and that of the city do not yet intersect. Yet, Olmi's patient, relentless evocation of the daily lives of his Bergamo peasants makes a far more convincing ideological statement than many of the highly charged political films so characteristic of the past decade. It is a message at once revolutionary and traditional, for it contrasts the simple Christian steadfastness of his peasants to the insensitive cruelty of their superiors, reminding his viewers of the many virtues that have been lost in the rapid transition from an agrarian, peasant culture to one based upon rapid industrial development and urbanization.

The vast range of ideological positions contained within the genre of the so-called political film of the past decade represents a rich commentary upon both Italy's past and present. The frequent thematic concern with relations of fathers and sons serves a double purpose: not only does it provide a concrete image of the more general problem of authority and rebellion in a society characterized by rapidly changing values, but it frequently reaffirms the need for a return to the security of the nuclear family, traditionally a dominant value in Italian culture. The highly critical attitude taken by the majority of these "political" directors toward the state and its institutions is an amazingly accurate barometer of social problems in the peninsula. Regardless of their ideological position or their individual style, Italian directors in the past decade have remained true to the essential vision of Italian neorealism—they have cast a critical eye on the society that produced them and have attempted, insofar as it is possible through artistic means, to change their world for the better. With their works, they have broadened the idea of the cinema as "entertainment" and have created for the movies an essentially positive, civic function as a public forum in which hotly debated social issues and great art have joined together in an often uncomfortable but ultimately healthy marriage of convenience.

10

The Contemporary Scene
and New Italian Comedy

The Italian cinema's preoccupation with politics and ideology remains a factor to this day, and it seems highly unlikely that the best directors will ever turn primarily to escapist entertainment, even if the bulk of the industry's annual production aims at a relatively lowbrow audience. Several important developments in the last decade, not unconnected to the general trend toward political themes already noted, should be signaled for special treatment here. (1) For the first time in the history of the Italian cinema, women—Liliana Cavani and Lina Wertmüller—have gained prominence as directors. (2) In the last few years, Ettore Scola has developed from one of Italy's greatest scriptwriters in the comic tradition into one of the country's most talented directors, and his work often provides a complex commentary upon the Italian cinema itself. (3) A number of new faces have arisen, young directors who have produced only two or three films to date, but who have already displaced their more famous colleagues at the box office by producing a variety of comic film that must be considered a hybrid form of traditional Italian film comedy. (4) Finally, the economic crisis of the film industry continues, but a possible solution for the industry's recovery has been seen in television productions, preferably productions with a foreign market. However, it should be noted that in the last few years, many of Italy's greatest and best known directors have made few new films, and a number of major figures have died.

347

Liliana Cavani (1937–) moved from a literary background to earn a place at the Centro Sperimentale, and upon her graduation, she won a competition (out of some ten thousand candidates) to work for the RAI, Italy's state-owned television network. Her first work was therefore in documentary film, and between 1962 and 1965, she produced a number of brief programs on Nazi Germany, Stalin, Pétain, the role of women in the Resistance, and other topical themes. Her first feature-length television film was *Francis of Assisi* (*Francesco d'Assisi*, 1966). The film provoked the first of the many polemical reactions to her work, for Cavani's St. Francis (portrayed by Lou Castel, the star of Bellocchio's *Fists in the Pocket*) avoids the traditionally pious interpretation sanctified by years of hagiography or traditional sermons to the birds and concentrates upon a simple man who revolutionized European culture by his potentially subversive concern for the poor and his rejection of the hierarchy of the Church. Her next film, *Galileo* (1968), coproduced by Italian television, provoked an equally hostile reaction and was therefore not even shown on Italian television. Though some of the criticism was directed at its depiction of the Church's role in the persecution of Italy's greatest scientist, it was its simple realism, and not its Brechtian ideological message, that made the film controversial. Cavani's Galileo is the historic Galileo— not a man in revolt against his Church but a Christian scientist who felt himself, a true believer, to have been betrayed by a Church which, he wrongly believed, was as opposed to ignorance as he was. More didactic than Rossellini's study of Louis XIV, *Galileo* is a moving testimony to the memory of a brave man, and it deserves more attention than it has so far been given.[1]

Cavani's rise to fame began with her turn from television documentaries. Infected, as all the younger directors were, with the rebellious spirit sweeping across Italy and Europe in the wake of the 1968 student riots, she produced a political allegory, *The Cannibals* (*I cannibali*, 1969) based loosely upon Sophocles' *Antigone*: after a military government has quelled a revolution in an unnamed nation in our own day, the authorities decree that the bodies of the fallen rebels are, upon pain of death, to be left where they fell; only a mysterious foreigner (Pierre Clementi) shows any compassion for the dead by breaking the law and burying them; his act of defiance causes a young girl, Antigone (Britt Ekland), to join him in a gesture which ends in their death. *The Cannibals* never succeeds in moving beyond Cavani's desire to make an important ideological statement; it not only fails to engage the viewer's emotions but even manages to include an absolutely terrible musical score by Ennio Morricone—a feat which few films scored by this musical genius have ever achieved. Its failure at the box office forced Cavani to return to television for several years.

When *The Night Porter* (*Il portiere di notte*, 1974) first appeared, there was little in Cavani's former career to foreshadow the tremendous polemical but favorable reaction to the film in Europe or its utter condemnation by the New York critics. One delirious writer described the work as "a thinly-disguised Fascist propaganda film" or a "high point in social, cultural and political barbarism,"[2] proving once again that the term "Fascist" as employed by leftist reviewers in this country has been completely emptied of any meaningful historical or intellectual content. The single serious critical analysis of the work in this country quite rightly called the film's critical reception in America "a disgrace," revealing "a total lack of historical, social, and artistic awareness in the critics."[3]

A brief plot summary of *The Night Porter* will immediately reveal the source of such undisguised venom: a chance encounter in Vienna in 1957 between Max (Dirk Bogarde), a former SS officer in a concentration camp and Lucia (Charlotte Rampling) a female inmate with whom he carried on a sado-masochistic affair during the war, leads both characters to revert to their relationship of twelve years earlier. Max's former comrades, all of whom are undergoing therapy to remove their guilt complexes, disapprove of Max's return to their murky past. After refusing to continue his therapy, he and Lucia lock themselves inside his apartment; eventually, they are murdered. Cavani's plot moves in a series of flashbacks from the present in Vienna to the past, probing deeper and deeper into the strange relationship which quite rightly horrifies her viewers.

The portrayal of evil, nevertheless, does not imply praise of it, and the superficial attacks on the film's supposed "Fascist" character entirely miss the point. Cavani reports that in her earlier documentaries on the Third Reich and in conversations with veterans of the death camps and readings of their memoires, she was struck by a constant theme: one woman who had survived the concentration camps told her that she hated the Nazis the most for revealing to her the depths of evil every human being is capable of, and she advised Cavani not to consider all victims as innocents, for like their captors they were human.[4] In other words, evil was not only practiced in the *lagers* but it was also taught there as well, and the lessons learned were to haunt the survivors and saddle them with guilt for the rest of their days. The kind of group therapy Max undergoes with his ex-comrades consists of a mock trial at which all surviving witnesses are brought to testify (and are then eliminated), and its purpose is to absolve the criminals of the guilt that still troubles their victims.

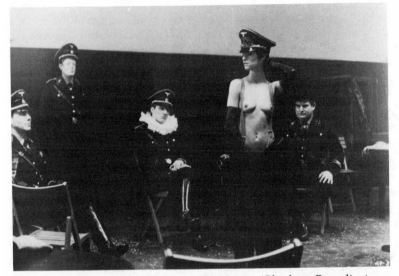

Liliana Cavani's *The Night Porter* (1974). Lucia (Charlotte Rampling) performs the dance of Salomé in the flashback to the "Biblical" sequence in the concentration camp.
(Photo courtesy of the Museum of Modern Art)

The key to the film's theme lies in a scene in which Max tells a decadent Countess that "his little child" has returned to him; when she is moved by his feelings to remark that his affair with Lucia is "a romantic story," he corrects her, calling it a "Biblical story." This remark leads to the most shocking flashback of the film. Lucia is dancing in a military barracks for Max and other SS officers; wearing suspenders over her naked breasts and sporting an SS cap, she sings a German nightclub song in Marlene Dietrich's style; after the number is completed, Max rewards her with a present, and when she opens it, she discovers the severed head of one of her fellow prisoners. Her cry of mingled horror and pleasure implies that from that moment on, she was forever linked to her lover-torturer. Max's explanation that the man was a troublemaker who had constantly bothered Lucia—she had requested only his transfer to another camp—fails, of course, to wipe away the guilt this traumatic event inspires in her. Rightly or wrongly, from that moment on she views herself as guilty of murder and no different from the SS troops Max led.

Cavani's story is, as Max asserts, a Biblical tale, underlined by the obvious reference to the story of Salomé and John the Baptist in the depiction of Lucia's dance and the death of her fellow inmate. Lucia returns to Max to relive their past affair in order to purify and liberate herself from its grip, while Max rejects the pseudo-psychoanalytical schemes of his ex-comrades, thereby embracing the responsibility for his past actions. In the clinical sense, Max was and is mad, but if he is therefore found innocent by reason of insanity, then how can any of the Nazis be considered guilty? When Max rejects his therapy, he ultimately asserts his sanity and accepts his own guilt. And in so doing, he removes Lucia's burden of guilt from her conscience. This explains why he dresses her in the little girl's outfit and why he finally dons his own SS uniform at the end of the film. He has freed her from her past, and in a certain sense, his is an act of selfless love.

Far from being a "Fascist" film, *The Night Porter* celebrates the ability of the human spirit to survive and ultimately to overcome the worse excesses of physical and psychic degradation. What disturbs most critics, of course, is Cavani's use of eroticism (and a particularly perverted eroticism at that) as the vehicle for a reaffirmation of what constitutes a traditional goal of Christian morality—consciousness of sin and guilt, expiation, and purification through punishment. The film rejects the Old Testament notion of revenge or *lex talionis*—an eye for an eye, a tooth for a tooth—that often and quite naturally colors our attitudes toward the Holocaust and the trials of war criminals; instead, it suggests an essentially Christian notion of individual redemption. It is no wonder that Max's former comrades murder the couple as they stroll across the city bridge: by their very presence, Max and Lucia undermine the pathetic attempts made by others to sweep their individual responsibility for the Holocaust under the carpet by indulging in farcical sessions with their analyst. Whether or not *Night Porter* is a specifically "woman's film," as one critic has claimed,[5] it certainly is a powerful and disturbing statement about the dialectical relationship between good and evil. With Lina Wertmüller's masterpiece *Seven Beauties* (*Pasqualino Settebellezze*, 1975), it stands as a most controversial and thought-provoking view of the existential dilemma life in the concentration camps posed for inmates.

Cavani's next film, *Beyond Good and Evil* (*Al di là del bene e del male*, 1977), moves from the Viscontian atmosphere of *Night Porter* to examine the life of Friedrich Nietzsche (Erland Josephson) and his love affair with Lou Salomé (Dominique Sanda) and with his friend Paul Ree (Robert Powell). It is a highly personal view of the practical effects of the famous German philosopher's theories of morality, and it is surprisingly enough the liberated woman, Lou Salomé, who emerges from the film as the most uninhibited character: she encourages the philosopher and his friend to share a *menage à trois*, and Cavani explores the thinly disguised homosexual tendencies that emerge between the two male friends. Paul is eventually killed by a gang of male toughs after being gang-raped, and when he returns from the dead in a séance, he reports with a smile to Lou that he has achieved happiness since he admitted his homosexual tendencies and that she should tell Nietzsche to do the same. By this time, however, Nietzsche has gone insane from the venereal disease he picked up years earlier in Sicily. When Lou greets him at his home, she cheerfully announces that "our century is about to arrive, Fritz!" Cavani cuts to a playful country scene in which Nietzsche and Lou had once made passionate love in the mud, and we then return to the final shot of this remarkable woman leaving Nietzsche forever, as she smokes a cigar beside a young blond man (perhaps a symbol of the future Germany which would constitute "their century"). While *Beyond Good and Evil* proposes a highly personal interpretation of Nietzsche's private life, the most interesting feature of the film is its portrait of a totally liberated and libertine woman who in her private life was far ahead of any theory Nietzsche might have proposed.

First screened at the Cannes Festival in 1981, Cavani's *The Skin* (*La pelle*, 1981), an adaptation of Curzio Malaparte's description of Naples under American occupation, is her most ambitious film. With a cast aimed at an international market—Burt Lancaster as General Mark Cork (Mark Clark), Marcello Mastroianni as the novelist Malaparte, and Claudio Cardinale as Malaparte's aristocratic ex-mistress—Cavani investigates a moment of Italian history already familiar from many well-known neorealist films; however, she captures it from an entirely different perspective. In place of the nobler values of sacrifice and courage neorealist films celebrate, Cavani forces us to reconsider the dramatic story of occupied Naples as the relationship between victor and vanquished. The director implicitly protests the cultural hegemony of America over Italy that began during the last year of the war. Malaparte's grotesque realism survives from the novel: Italy's "liberators" purchase women and children for packages of cigarettes; gangster chiefs sell captured German soldiers to the Americans; parked American vehicles are stripped and stolen, leaving only a tiny puddle of oil. The romanticism associated with the war by those who fought on the winning side, or who participated in the Resistance, is removed from Cavani's story, and what remains is a tale of survival, of saving one's skin in the midst of hardship, starvation, depravity, and uncertainty. When General Cork finally liberates Rome, his military parade is interrupted by a symbolic accident, as one of the Italians trying to grasp a chocolate bar from a passing vehicle is squashed under its treads. Once again, Cavani reminds us, human history is made at the expense of human sacrifice, literally from our hides. *The Skin* thus reflects a contemporary tendency to re-examine recent Italian history, in which World War II and the arrival of the Americans in Italy played such an important role. Cavani, like most of the directors of late, views this cultural interchange in a more ambivalent light than that in which it was seen by her neorealist predecessors.

Unlike Liliana Cavani's films, those of Lina Wertmüller were enthusiastically greeted by American critics and scholars alike; five of her screenplays were even published in English translation though they are still unavailable in Italian, and the first monograph on her works was in English rather than Italian.[6] Her films were championed by the most improbable of all American critics, the usually caustic John Simon. And yet, in Italy Wertmüller is rarely taken seriously. Perhaps the explanation for this strange turn of events is contained in Liliana Cavani's assessment of the difference between film criticism in Italy and in the United States. In Italy, critics tend to punish a director for commercial success, admitting only American films to the category of popular entertainment that may also embody great art; paradoxically, Italians are the least provincial of all peoples in their openness to foreign cultures and their cinemas, but this cultural openness has its price—everything from abroad is considered better than the domestic product![7] But American critical taste is also mercurial: with the arrival of her first five films in this country, Wertmüller's critical fortune seemed assured; then, after her collaboration with American production companies in a sixth film, she was relegated to critical obscurity almost overnight.

Perhaps only the work of Fellini and Bertolucci enjoyed the acclaim that greeted her first group of excellent films: *The Seduction of Mimi* (*Mimi metallurgico ferito nell'onore*, 1971); *Love and Anarchy* (*Film d'amore e d'anarchia*, 1972); *All Screwed Up* (*Tutto a posto e niente in ordine*, 1973); *Swept Away* (*Travolti da un insolito destino nell'azzurro mare d'agosto*, 1974); and her acknowledged masterpiece *Seven Beauties*. Greatly indebted to the exuberant imagery of Fellini, Wertmüller's work combined a concern with topical political issues and the conventions of traditional Italian grotesque comedy, with its vulgarity, its stock characters, and its frontal attack upon accepted values and mores;[8] therefore, much of the critical confusion over the intentions of her films stems from an ignorance of her work's cultural background. But within the genre of the Italian comic film, Wertmüller's works emerge as the most complex and visually rich of the last decade. *The Seduction of Mimi* is typical of her very personal combination of politics and comedy.[9] The seduction of the title is a political seduction, not one of the heart. After losing his job in Sicily for voting the Communist ticket against a Mafia-sponsored candidate, Mimi (Giancarlo Giannini) must look for work in Turin, where he becomes a metal worker, joins the Communist Party, and falls in love with Fiore (Mariangela Melato); transferred back home where in the interval his wife, Rosalia, has also become "modernized" by leaving the security of the home, finding an industrial job, and broadening her horizons, Mimi discovers that the archaic Southern values he thought he had abandoned still dominate his thinking. While he desires sexual freedom (keeping Fiore and his new child as well as Rosalia), he cannot permit the same liberty to his wife, who has betrayed him and is now pregnant. Seeking revenge by means of the traditional Sicilian vendetta, he forces himself to sleep with Amalia (Elena Fiore), the wife of the man who has cuckolded him; she too becomes pregnant. When Mimi confronts Amalia's husband in the square, his rival is shot by a Mafia gangster, but Mimi goes to prison for the crime, and when he comes out, he is forced to support both Rosalia and Amalia, as well as all their children, by working for the very Mafia he once fled Sicily to escape.

Wertmüller's view of power and authority in Italy is comically rendered by a series of characters—a Catholic bishop, a Mafia boss, a police inspector, a Communist Party member, a building contractor—all of whom sport on their faces three prominent moles that are captured by Wertmüller's zoom lens in close-up. Each time one of these figures appears, the Italian national anthem is heard on the sound track, implying a common bond between these seemingly very different organizations both inside and outside the law. They are all "brothers of Italy" as the opening line of the anthem implies. To show how rapid industrial development cannot hope to erase age-old sexual prejudices the film uses the conventions of traditional comedy. Music and mime are also effectively employed, as in the silent courtship of Mimi and Fiore to the music of Verdi's *La traviata*, a courtship accomplished solely by expressive Sicilian gestures and movements of

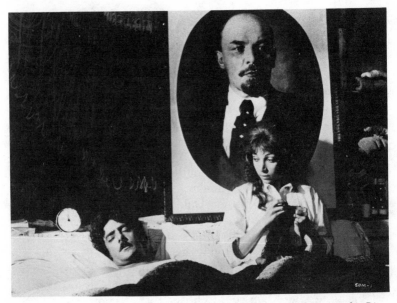

Lina Wertmüller's *The Seduction of Mimi* (1971). Mimi (Giancarlo Giannini) and Fiore (Mariangela Melato) beneath the benevolent gaze of Lenin,
a visual metaphor for the film's uneasy connection between sexuality and
politics.
(Photo from the author's private collection).

the eye. Giannini's performance is superb and provides much of the
film's comic force. Especially memorable (and attacked by many feminist critics) is the comic scene photographed with a fish-eye lens that
grostesquely portrays Mimi's seduction of the enormously obese
Amalia—a Saraghina-like figure reminiscent of Fellini's 8 ½—a seduction forced upon Mimi by the ridiculously outmoded code that
shapes his view of masculine honor.

Love and Anarchy offers an entirely different and more positive male
protagonist, again played by Giannini: Tunin, a peasant radicalized
against Mussolini's Fascist regime by the brutal death of a friend,
comes to Rome to assassinate Il Duce, and he meets his contact, a
prostitute named Salomé (Mariangela Melato) in a luxurious Roman

Lina Wertmüller's *The Seduction of Mimi* (1971). Mimi (Giancarlo Gian-nini) seduces Amalia (Elena Fiore) to gain revenge.
(Photo from the author's private collection)

brothel; soon, Tunin is torn between his desire to follow his anarchist principles (meaning certain death) and his love for Tripolina (Lina Polito), a prostitute with whom he falls in love. Salomé and Tripolina let Tunin sleep too late to attempt the assassination, and when Tunin goes berserk over their negligence, he is captured and eventually murdered in prison by the henchmen of Spatoletti (Eros Pagni), the macho head of the Fascist police. Once again, Wertmüller plays with the paradoxes that arise when love and politics combine. Spatoletti continuously associates political power and sexuality: Italy is metaphorically seen as a ravished woman, dominated by sexual and political adventurers like Mussolini and Spatoletti. The brothel, photographed in a way that explicitly recalls the brothel scene in Fellini's *Roma*, serves as a metaphor for all of Italy: both the Fascist government and the bordello are organized around authoritarian principles, while the private, intimate relationships of Tunin and the two women seem to embody old-fashioned, romantic views of love. Tunin's death shows him to be a saintly figure but ultimately a man whose energies are misdirected into meaningless political gestures with no possible hope of success. And Wertmüller's figure of Spatoletti is far truer to the reigning macho ideology of the Fascist regime than are the many repressed homosexuals employed by Visconti or Bertolucci to represent Italian Fascism. Indeed, Spatoletti's exuberance and misdirected sexual drive may be compared to Tunin's, for neither character offers a completely positive solution to the complex problems the microcosm of the brothel poses. Ultimately, neither love nor anarchy but, rather, only a more deeply felt ideological commitment on Tunin's part (and others like him) can lead to the end of the regime's tyranny.

All Screwed Up offers the image of a workers' commune in Milan as a possible alternative life style to the dehumanizing industrial development of the North. It is a film with some brilliant sequences: the satirical use of classical music to accompany a view of a slaughterhouse in which beef carcasses are skinned, cut, and quartered; a seduction scene in which a virginal Sicilian girl uses her hands not to fend off her ravisher but, rather, to keep her cherished consumer object (a new television) from falling on the floor; the hilarious view of a police official's car which has been completely painted with excrement. The most disturbing moment in this comic farce occurs when right-wing terrorists throw a bomb into the restaurant where some of the commune's members work. Suddenly all is silent, as if something truly revolutionary might come of this moment. But then the maddening dash for the customers' plates begins all over again as Wertmüller provides us with an engaging metaphor for contemporary Italy's chaotic problems which never quite works as a coherently organized work of art.

With *Swept Away* and *Seven Beauties*, the glaring inconsistencies and obvious flaws of plot structure typical of her other films are removed, and Wertmüller's art combines its exuberance and photographic virtuosity with a storyline well under control. *Swept Away* employs the traditional pastoral myth of the state of nature embodied in classics

Lina Wertmüller's *Swept Away* (1974). In a pastoral oasis far away from the more rigid constraints of civilization, the barriers of class and politics separating Raffaella (Mariangela Melato) and Gennarino (Giancarlo Giannini) are temporarily swept aside.
(Photo courtesy of the Museum of Modern Art)

of political theory, as well as in tales about modern men trapped on a desert island far from civilization. Writers have long been fascinated by the portrayal of life outside the bonds of society: what will occur when man, formed by his environment, class, or culture, is suddenly cut away from these determining influences and is free to lead a life in a pastoral setting far from civilization? Wertmüller's film provides a contemporary response to this perennial question. A rich, spoiled Northern Italian woman named Raffaella (Mariangela Melato) is marooned on a deserted island with Gennarino (Giancarlo Giannini), a Sicilian sailor who is both a Communist and a sexist holding the typically Southern Italian view of women as merely sexual objects. Raffaella, on the other hand, reflects a prevalent racist prejudice against Southern Italians (she calls Gennarino an Ethiopian and an African on numerous occasions) that is not uncommon in Northern Italy.

The storyline of *Swept Away* has been reduced to one of classic simplicity: a prologue on a yacht presents a microcosm of Italian society, representing not only a variety of social classes but political ideologies as well; this is followed by the adventure proper, with the two main characters cast adrift in what will become a parable of class and sexual relationships; finally, in the conclusion, the two protagonists are returned to the society they left, and the personal, sexual, and political relationships they established on the deserted islands are tested.

In the film's opening scenes on the yacht, Gennarino and Raffaella immediately clash. While constantly needling the Southern sailor about his dirty T-shirts, his overboiled coffee, and his soggy pasta, Raffaella harangues the other wealthy guests on the boat about political problems. Wertmüller's hilarious portrait of these wealthy industrialists as would-be socialists or leftists is a perfect display of the ludicrous kind of Italian "radical chic": pretending to a revolutionary ideology, the wealthy contentedly sail their yachts around the Mediterranean, loudly insisting that people of importance, even Karl Marx, have always retained a bevy of servants! Raffaella's attitude is neatly summed up by her biting remark to Gennarino: "Anyhow, as we await the end, the revolution, let's try and make the spaghetti *al dente* . . . at least once."[10]

Once Raffaella and Gennarino are abandoned to their own devices on the island, however, the master/slave relationship reflected in Gennarino's subordinate position to Raffaella on the yacht is radically transformed: in the original state of nature, power and command pass naturally to the man. His physical prowess and technical expertise make short work of the former *padrona*, whose lack of talent for survival makes her good only for menial tasks and exploitation. Thus, roles are neatly reversed: and once Raffaella is placed in the position Gennarino once occupied, she naturally rebels. Eventually, what emerges from this transformation is a strange, somewhat masochistic love affair—the woman who loved to dominate Gennarino on the yacht now submits willingly to Gennarino's slaps and curses, eventually even begging to be sodomized to show her total subjection to his domination. And now, Gennarino truly falls in love with her, and it is he (and not Raffaella) who wants to return to society in order to determine once and for all if the woman really loves him. Only Raffaella recognizes that this wish is a foolish one, for the strength of society's class barriers will necessarily destroy the affair that could blossom only beyond social limits. When they are found and returned home, the inevitable occurs: class always tells and determines the ultimate outcome of personal relationships.

Swept Away angered many feminists by what they felt was a degrading image of women in the film—particularly the sequence in which Gennarino slaps and kicks Raffaella over the sand dunes, calling her every conceivable ideologically charged name ("dumb Social Democratic whore," "industrial whore"), and blaming her for everything from high prices to a shortage of hospital beds. Such feminist criticism is unfounded, however, for it is clear that the director is more concerned with the social roles these characters play and the classes they reflect than their sexual identities. Wertmüller's allegory places a man in the role of the exploited class and a woman in the role of the exploiting class, while feminist critics would prefer to see all men of whatever class as exploiters of all women. As she has declared on numerous occasions, the sexes could easily be switched without undermining the allegory. Nevertheless, it is the sexual relationship between these two representatives of very different classes which ensured the film its commercial success, and Wertmüller was well aware that such an unusual and sometimes risqué storyline would guarantee the film large audiences.

With *Seven Beauties*, Wertmüller's art reaches its culmination in what must be termed a masterpiece.[11] Once again, she combines the familiar themes of Southern comedy with political issues, but now they involve much more than class relationships and include a treatment of the Holocaust, the concentration camps of World War II, and the moral questions involved in man's survival through this nightmare. In flashbacks, the film's plot moves from wartime Nazi Germany to prewar Fascist Italy—specifically Naples. The main character, Pasqualino Frafuso, nicknamed "Pasqualino Seven Beauties" (Giancarlo Giannini) is a Neapolitan *guapo*, a dandy who lives by his wits primarily off the wages of his seven adoring but rather plump sisters; when one of them,

Concettina (Elena Fiore) disgraces the family honor by dancing in a music hall and later becoming a prostitute in a brothel, Pasqualino feels compelled to kill Totonno, the man who seduced her into a life of this sort; he disposes of the body by mailing pieces of it all over Italy. Caught, he is first sent to prison and then to an asylum (when he feigns madness), but when he rapes a fellow patient, he is forced to join the army and eventually finds himself on the Eastern Front; after deserting, he is caught by the Nazis and interned in a concentration camp. Though Naples is known for the cunning of its citizens, who survive from day to day in a miraculous economic balancing act, Pasqualino may well be the ultimate Neapolitan. His cleverness always saves him from a situation he fears, but in each instance he is placed in an increasingly more desperate predicament; when he winds up in a death camp his ingenuity and his drive for survival meet their most difficult challenge. Nevertheless, he manages to seduce the buxom female commandant (Shirley Stoler), who then forces him to murder his friend Francesco in order to save his own life. At the film's end, we see him back in Naples—a virtuoso survivor who has sacrificed everything in order to remain alive.

Recounted in this fashion, Wertmüller's plot seems straightforward enough, but as in Bertolucci's *The Conformist* the chronology is completely juggled by flashbacks that explain Pasqualino's story only in bits and pieces. By avoiding a linear narrative, the director draws paradoxical parallels between the Neapolitan segment (involving a single murder for an affair of honor) and the German segment (involving the wholesale slaughter of many, many people in the death camps). The prevalent tone of the work thus becomes not completely grotesque or tragic but, rather, tragi-comic, as hilarious Neapolitan sequences are juxtaposed to chilling, horrifying German ones. Naples never becomes Germanic, but in Pasqualino's single-minded drive for survival, the potential is always there. The overriding instinct for survival that Wertmüller shows so humorously in a single individual can, when allowed to develop unchecked by any higher moral values, degenerate into a dehumanized obsession to live at any price, no matter how high. Ultimately, life is not worth the price Pasqualino pays, and the characters who receive the director's approval are those camp inmates who rebel and are killed rather than submit to the Nazi system: Pedro (Fernando Rey), the anarchist who believes in "man in disorder," a humane disorder meant to oppose the insane order of the German Reich; or Pasqualino's friend Francesco (Piero di Orio), who sees the guilt implicit in Italy's alliance with Nazi Germany.

Rarely has any film on the Holocaust treated the material with such a combination of comic and tragic moods, and it is this only apparent levity that offended some critics, who believed it implied Wertmüller's equation of petty crime and mass murder. But Wertmüller realized that only with this juxtaposition of moods could she move her viewer to react most fully to the horror of the state to which Pasqualino would eventually be reduced. Many of the Neapolitan sequences could be anthologized as classic moments in Italian film comedy. They reflect Fellini's influence on Wertmüller's broad, sometimes vulgar satire, and they also show her skill in handling large numbers of actors and brilliant imagery. For example, there is the masterful music-hall scene in which Concettina's obscene performance scandalizes her puritanical brother; the graphic but comic murder of Totonno, who is cut into tiny pieces like a slaughtered steer; the slapstick comedy scene when Pasqualino steals food from a German farmhouse, where a buxom blond woman plays Wagner's "Dreams" on the piano, a romantic prelude to the more terrifying entrance into the death camp (where Wagner's "Ride of the Valkyries" introduces the enormous camp commandant); or Pasqualino's murder trial in Naples, done completely in pantomime and exploiting the expressive talents of Giannini's face and eyes. Yet, the most memorable sequences of the film are in the death camp, pictured as a nightmare version of the bath sequence from *8 ½*, and indebted in its imagery not only to Fellini but also to Dante's vision of Hell. Here, Pasqualino touches rock bottom in his obsession with survival, and he is forced to earn his survival with a feat of sexual prowess, the seduction of the commandant.

Since our hero has been reduced by life in the camp to a physical wreck, the woman first makes Pasqualino eat a bowl of food, then forces him to quiver at her feet, a shot taken from an angle that underlines his worm-like state: "Now you eat, then you fuck . . . if you don't fuck, you die!"[12] The braggart Neapolitan dandy has been re-

Lina Wertmüller's *Seven Beauties* (1976). The Nazi commandant (Shirley Stoler) who must be seduced by Pasqualino in order to ensure his survival. (Photo courtesy of the Museum of Modern Art)

duced to nothing: once a macho rapist, to save his hide he has now been forced to perform a sexual act that disgusts him. It is the supreme irony in Pasqualino's existence, and it leads inevitably to his total capitulation, his collaboration with the guards, and the eventual execution by his own hand of his best friend. And when he returns home to postwar Naples, he discovers that everything he has done to guard the honor of his family—the entire train of events that led him from a relatively insignificant murder to collaboration with the greatest crime of the century—was done in vain. Now all of his sisters, and even his young virginal fiancée, have become prostitutes, selling themselves to American soldiers in order to survive. Their decision echoes his own. The final close-up of Pasqualino's haggard face convincingly suggests that some values are more vital to human existence than survival.

From the pinnacle of critical success with *Seven Beauties* (and a nomination for an Oscar as Best Foreign Film), Lina Wertmüller's fortunes collapsed disastrously with the first of what was intended to be three films made with Warner Brothers: *The End of the World in Our Usual Bed in a Night Full of Rain* (*La fine del mondo nel nostro solito letto in una notte piena di pioggia*, 1977). Starring Giancarlo Giannini as Paolo, an Italian journalist and Candice Bergen as a liberated American photographer, the film attempts to study the confrontation of two entirely different world views—that of the liberated feminist and that of an Old World male chauvinist. While not so bad a film as the critics made it out to be (it was quickly withdrawn from general distribution), *A Night Full of Rain* is, frankly, a shallow film saved only by a few brilliant sequences (particularly the love scene in the church in a small Calabrian town of Padula). Though Wertmüller's penchant for visual spectacle and careful set design (usually a reflection of the obvious talents of her husband, Enrico Job) is visible in the film, the confused plot and the necessity of bringing into her work a cultural tradition with which the director is obviously ill at ease, almost completely undermine the film.

Wertmüller's last film, *Blood Feud* (*Fatto di sangue fra due uomini per causa di una vedova* [*si sospettano moventi politici*], 1978), employs an outstanding cast—Giancarlo Giannini as Nick, an Italo-American

gangster; Sophia Loren as Concetta, a widow whose husband was murdered by a man who is now the head of the local Fascists; and Marcello
Mastroianni as Rosario Spallone, a Socialist intellectual—and a plot
that combines a familiar Sicilian love triangle with a political theme
of resistance to Fascism. As in *The Seduction of Mimi* or *Love and
Anarchy*, passion interferes with politics. Both Nick and Rosario fall
in love with Concetta, and each thinks she is carrying his child. After
a furious shootout with Fascists, as they attempt to leave Italy with a
false passport the gangster has purchased for Rosario, the three characters are trapped and the two men are killed at the dock. The last
shot reveals the two rivals joined in friendship at the point of death,
with Concetta whispering to them both that her unborn child is his.

Lina Wertmüller's last two works were disappointing after the mature talent revealed in *Seven Beauties* and *Swept Away*. Her failures,
however, are those of an excellent director who seeks an ever broader
audience and is not content with the narrower following of a few critics
and intellectuals. And yet these failures promise more in the future
than do Cavani's more limited successes. There is no doubt, however,
that the future of the Italian cinema in years to come will depend in
some measure on how successfully these two "female" directors function within the industry and how able they are to combine their personal artistic perspectives with films that reach a wider, commercial
audience.

Perhaps a recent development that holds equal promise for the
future is the steady maturation of Ettore Scola (1931–   ), a director
whose early career included collaboration with the humor magazine
Marco Aurelio in Rome, the same periodical on which Fellini worked
before moving to scriptwriting. After collaboration on some twenty
scripts, most without signature and the majority vehicles for the comic
genius of Totò, Scola became one of Italy's most fecund screenwriters,
completing a total of over fifty scripts before he began to direct his
own work in 1964.[13] Moving from the traditional *commedia all'italiana*,
Scola first showed his originality in *Will Our Heroes Succeed in Locating
Their Friend Mysteriously Disappeared in Africa? (Riusciranno i nostri
eroi a trovare il loro amico misteriosamente scomparso in Africa?*, 1968).
In a philosophical tale indebted to the travel satires and philosophical

contes of the eighteenth century, Scola follows the attempts of a Roman editor (Alberto Sordi) to track a brother-in-law who has disappeared in Portuguese Angola on the eve of the end of colonialism. Of course, like Voltaire or Montesquieu, who used exotic tales of travel as a means of commenting on their own society in the Age of Reason, Scola is more concerned with an analysis of the modern upper-middle class Italian than with a true and accurate portrait of life in Africa. He underscores this effectively by his hilarious depiction of Sordi's arrival in Luanda: emerging from a bus dressed in outlandish jungle garb worthy of the explorers in Hollywood Tarzan films, Sordi busily takes pictures of "exotic" Africa (actually a modern metropolis) while an amazed African takes pictures of him in his even more exotic and anachronistic costume.

Scola's recent works have reflected two different currents. In two excellent films—*A Special Day* (*Una giornata particolare*, 1977), and *Passion of Love* (*Passione d'amore*, 1981)—Scola relies upon brilliant acting performances in a dramatic vein and minutely analyzes the emotions of his characters in a manner that recalls the art of his cinematic model, Vittorio De Sica. In three other perhaps even more intriguing works—*We All Loved Each Other Very Much* (*C'eravamo tanto amati*, 1974); *Dirty, Mean, and Nasty* (*Brutti, sporchi e cattivi*, 1976), winner of the prize for direction at Cannes; and *The Terrace* (*La terrazza*, 1980)—Scola employs a metacinematic discourse to treat the very history of the Italian cinema itself, examining not only the heritage of neorealism (especially De Sica) but the entire course of postwar film in Italy. In addition, *Trevico–Turin: Voyage in Fiatnam* (*Trevico–Torino: Viaggio nel Fiatnam*, 1972), perhaps the most politically motivated film Scola has made to date, may be compared to Petri's *The Working Class Goes to Heaven* in its compelling reconstruction of the alienated existence of southern immigrants in Turin who work on the assembly lines of Italy's most important industrial complex.

A Special Day casts two of Italy's most popular actors, Sophia Loren and Marcello Mastroianni. Both are quite out of character, she as Antonietta, a dutiful and aging mother of six children who tries to fulfill the Fascist regime's propaganda praising motherhood and the family, and he, as Gabriele, a radio announcer who is about to be sent into confinement in Sardinia because of his anti-Fascist leanings and his homosexuality. With both Loren and Mastroianni playing roles that consciously negate their commercial reputations as glamour girl and Latin lover, Scola obtains perhaps their most successful dramatic performances to date. He focuses upon one special afternoon, that of May 6, 1938, the occasion of Adolf Hitler's visit to Mussolini's Rome. While the inhabitants of the crowded Fascist housing project in the San Giovanni district have left for the celebration, dressed in their various uniforms and encouraged by the government's propaganda to consider this visit a momentous event, Antonietta and Gabriele are left alone in the building; by chance, they are drawn together for a few brief hours during which time they seek to assuage their extreme solitude. Scola's fluid camera movements, panning up and down the apartment building and entering the two apartments, are in juxtaposition to the jarring and omnipresent sound track of the blaring microphones announcing the triumphs of the Fascist regime. Indeed, the sound track becomes a third protagonist of the film, so crucial is it to the drama of the work. In showing us the exhaustion and lethargy Antonietta feels while alone in her kitchen, Scola borrows brilliantly from the classic *Umberto D.* scene in which the young maid prepares her breakfast, matching screen time with real time in a poignant moment of extreme psychological realism. In a refreshing change, in *A Special Day* it is the anti-Fascist who is a homosexual, and a sensitive, intelligent one at that rather than the perverted, sado-masochistic brute shown in many of the less profound films on Italian Fascism. Thrown together, the two characters discover that their marginal place in Italian society is not dissimilar; they even make love in a desperate attempt to reach each other, but Gabriele is not transformed, even by the charms of a superb Sophia Loren, into a heterosexual: "It was beautiful," he remarks, "but it changes nothing." Both figures are tragically destroyed by the Fascist myth of virility: Gabriele has lost his job and his party membership (crucial for employment in the government), since such work is "only for real men"; Antonietta's obvious intelligence and sensitivity have been destroyed by a life of frantic childbearing necessary to gain government subsidies. Her Fascist husband, a frequent customer at the local brothel, announces on his return from the military parade welcoming the German dictator that he intends to initiate a seventh child that very night and to name him Adolfo. That same evening, Fascist police come to take Gabriele away.

A Special Day is a brilliant example of how fine acting, beautiful camera work, and an original use of a symbolic sound track can produce a classically simple indictment of the Fascist regime more devasting than most of the overblown ideological films made during the last decade.

The reversal of expectations brilliantly exploited by Scola in his casting of Loren and Mastroianni figures in Scola's most recent *Passion of Love*, an adaptation of *Fosca* by Igino Ugo Tarchetti (1830—69). The original novel is a fine example of the nineteenth-century *scapigliatura*, an Italian literary movement that opposed bourgeois in-

Ettore Scola's *A Special Day* (1977). The weary Antonietta (Sophia Loren) pauses for a moment from her household chores in a scene recalling De Sica's *Umberto D*. (Photo courtesy of the Museum of Modern Art)

sistence upon "normality" and focused on eccentric and often macabre themes stressing corruption, decay, and the links between beauty and death. In a beautiful reconstruction, characterized by sumptuous sets and romantic photography, of a vanished society, Scola analyzes the tragedy of Fosca (Valeria D'Obici), an intelligent and interesting woman who has the misfortune to be cursed by a disconcertingly ugly body. However, the power of her personality is such that it completely captivates a handsome young officer who abandons his love affairs and his brilliant career for one evening with her; the sensual pleasure Fosca derives from this brief moment destroys her delicate constitution, and she dies three days later. The bohemian mood of the *scapigliatura* dominates this dark tale "against nature" and is told to an ugly dwarf in a tavern by the officer; the dwarf, a male counterpart to Fosca's feminine ugliness, laughs bitterly at the officer's tale, for only he can understand that Fosca's fate was far more tragic than the officer's embellished and romanticized version of it.

Scola's films that deal explicitly with the nature and history of the Italian cinema owe a great debt to the example of Vittorio De Sica, to whose memory *We All Loved Each Other Very Much* is dedicated and in which the neorealist director himself appears in documentary footage. An extremely ambitious film, it combines a consideration of the many social and political changes Italy has undergone since the Resistance and the end of the Fascist regime with an equally comprehensive survey of the major developments in the history of Italian cinema, which so often reflected these changes. Opening in color, Scola presents three male friends who once fought in the Resistance: Gianni (Vittorio Gassman), now a wealthy lawyer but once the bravest of the Partisans; Nicola (Satta Flores), a provincial school teacher and minor intellectual who once lost his job because of his passionate defense of the social criticism in De Sica's *The Bicycle Thief* and who later lost a jackpot on a television program for providing the *correct* answer about a detail of De Sica's direction of that film; and Antonio (Nino Manfredi), a worker whose good sense and hard work serve as a corrective to the compromises and pretentions of his two comrades. Their personal history over the past thirty years provides Scola with a microcosm of Italian history. And these experiences are presented in a manner that recalls a number of different cinematic styles and periods. For example, the first flashback to Partisan days is shot in black and white in a documentary style typical of many neorealist works. Next, the tense atmosphere of the immediate postwar period is recreated as Nicola defends De Sica's masterpiece against the bigots of his hometown, who accuse *The Bicycle Thief* of "fomenting class warfare." Aldo Fabrizi, the actor who immortalized the Partisan priest in *Rome, Open City*, now plays a disgustingly obese gangster whose daughter eventually marries Gianni and whose wealth caused Gianni to be the first of the three old friends to bargain away their hopes for a new Italy in exchange for wealth and position. Perhaps no more devastating image of the end of Italian postwar aspirations may be seen in the film than the actual physical degradation of Fabrizi, whose gargantuan body bears witness to Italy's postwar excesses of self-indulgence.

References to cinema abound in the film. Film buff Nicola playfully recreates Eisenstein's Odessa Steps sequence on the Spanish Steps at the Piazza di Spagna, and in scenes of the 1950s, Scola shows us the characters in the squares and streets of Rome in a manner reminiscent of early Fellini films. With the 1960s, we switch to color, the prosperity of the Italian "economic miracle," and the atmosphere of Fellini's *La Dolce Vita*: Scola re-creates the shooting of the famous Trevi Fountain sequence from that film with the assistance of Federico Fellini, who plays himself and is mistaken for Rossellini by one of the crowd. Then Scola moves to paraphrase the mature style of Antonioni's *Eclipse*, employing it to dramatize the failure of communication between Gianni and his wife. Perhaps the most complex linkage between cinema and society, fiction and fact, in *We All Loved Each Other Very Much* involves the figure of De Sica. In the 1960s, Nicola had appeared on Mike Bongiorno's quiz show *Lascia o radoppia* (literally "quit or go for double," a program patterned on "The Sixty-Four Thousand Dollar Question" in America). The jackpot question involved an explanation of why the boy cries in *The Bicycle Thief* at the end of the film. Nicola explained that he cries because De Sica put cigarette butts in the boy's pocket and then accused him of stealing them, mistaking the "factual" answer for the "fictional" one, but Bon-

Ettore Scola's *We All Loved Each Other Very Much* (1974). Nicola (Satta Flores), Gianni (Vittorio Gassman), and Antonio (Nino Manfredi) meet for a nostalgic reunion over pasta.
(Photo courtesy of the Museum of Modern Art)

giorno disqualifies Nicola's answer with the "correct" reply—the boy has seen his father arrested for stealing a bicycle. Years later, Nicola sees a documentary featuring De Sica, and during the course of the program, De Sica recounts the story of how he forced the boy to cry just as Nicola had explained it years before!

Though each of the three friends falls in love with the same woman, Luciana (Stefania Sandrelli), at some point in his life, only Antonio, the honest worker, manages to win her affection. Despite Scola's intriguing mixture of historical styles and settings that constitutes an important statement about the interrelationship of film and society in Italy, his political message may therefore be grasped by even the most uneducated Italian spectator: the three men represent three separate social groups (middle class, intelligentsia, and proletariat) with the woman symbolizing Italy herself, and their evolving relationships reflect in microcosm the broader social and political interchange between Italy's major social classes.[14]

Dirty, Mean and Nasty also reflects Scola's admiration for De Sica, and the story of the film is a clear parody of De Sica's portrait of a utopian shantytown in *Miracle in Milan*. However, Scola completely changes the happy-go-lucky image of the urban poor that De Sica's fantasy celebrated, and his film also shows these shantytowns as devoid of even the elementary aspects of proletarian culture that Pasolini had found so fascinating in *Accattone*. In fact, before Pasolini's untimely death, Scola had meant to introduce *Dirty, Mean and Nasty* with some filmed remarks by him. While Scola sees Giacinto (Nino Manfredi), the greedy pensioner who lost one eye in an industrial accident and now cunningly hides his insurance benefits from his huge family, as a tragic product of a dehumanized capitalist society that reduces the inhabitants of the shantytown to mindless consumers, thieves, prostitutes, and assassins, Pasolini—then dominated by the bleak mood that culminated in his rejection of the subproletariat in *Salò*—argued that the corruption found there was as much attributable to the victims themselves as it was to the society around them.[15]

In its caustic indictment of Italian society, Scola's film completely overturns every favorable aspect of shantytown society in De Sica's earlier masterpiece: instead of patient, long-suffering—if downtrodden—poor people, Scola shows us vicious, brutish, mean and nasty individuals whose moral values have been completely destroyed by their economic depravity. It is a cycle of hopelessness and despair broken briefly by desperate couplings that lead only to unwanted pregnancies. In the ironic conclusion, shot from a hillside against the same dome of St. Peter's that was used to symbolize hope for a new and brighter Italian future in Rossellini's *Rome, Open City*, Scola offers us a quite different vision: a family of eighteen trapped in an inferno of ignorance and poverty. Rossellini's Christian humanism or De Sica's somewhat patronizing empathy no longer offer any possibility for a different future, and the children—so crucial a symbol for the neorealist masters—are now reduced to a concrete embodiment of the economic barriers that keep the poor forever doomed to repeat their tragic fate.

With *The Terrace*, Scola turns to examine the genre which had for some time provided him with a livelihood before he turned to direction: the *commedia all'italiana*. *We All Loved Each Other Very Much* buried the myth of Italian neorealism, and in *The Terrace*, Scola points up both the impossibility of making traditional film comedy and the impasse his generation had reached in its private and social life. The structure of the film also plays with that so typical of Italian comic works—the episodic vignettes starring different performers. Scola opens with a camera craning over a garden wall and onto a terrace where one of Rome's fashionable upper-class receptions is about to be held; in successive episodes, the reception begins anew each time,

Ettore Scola's *Dirty, Mean and Nasty* (1976). Giacinto (Nino Manfredi) tries to conceal his money from his relatives in his shantytown hovel. (Photo courtesy of the Museum of Modern Art)

and in each sequence Scola follows a different character. There is Mario (Vittorio Gassman), a Communist intellectual; Enrico (Jean-Louis Trintignant), a scriptwriter; Luigi (Marcello Mastroianni), a journalist who recalls Mastroianni's role as a gossip reporter in Fellini's *La Dolce Vita*; and Amadeo (Ugo Tognazzi), a film producer waiting impatiently for the script that Enrico will never write. The repetition of the different sequences, all ending nowhere, reveals the emptiness and lack of creativity that characterize these men, all of whom are directly or indirectly linked to the film industry. The presence of Italy's great comic actors—Gassman, Mastroianni, Tognazzi—makes this lack of creativity even more serious, for they are comic characters who are (for Scola) no longer funny, no longer in touch with the pulse of the nation. They are described by the women at the reception as has-beens, washed-out shadows of their former greatness—"it's not true that men grow old more gracefully than women," one remarks, while another makes the even more damning comment, continuing the theme of *We All Loved Each Other Very Much*: "if only you could have seen them during the Resistance . . ."

In *The Terrace*, Scola continues but deepens his investigation of the complex interrelationship between the cinema and Italian society employed so brilliantly in *We All Loved Each Other Very Much*. The characters portrayed by these comic actors point up the failure of Italy's intellectuals—especially the filmmakers—to actualize the potential of the Resistance period. And, of course, by employing the cream of Italy's comic actors, Scola also implies that the traditional *commedia all'italiana* has reached an artistic impasse and is no longer a vital force in changing the course of Italian behavior. It is a comic film about the impossibility of making a comic film, a bittersweet vision of a society in which laughter can no longer serve as a corrective. Indeed, the men at the reception even fight over the very meaning of the nature of comedy, and the fact that comic inspiration has dried up even drives Enrico, in a symbolic gesture full of desperation, to place the finger of his writing hand into an electric pencil sharpener when he is unable to produce his script. Yet, Scola presents a glimmer of hope, for his negative vision still reveals men in the film industry who retain a notion of their obligations not only to their craft but to the society their art reflects. Perhaps, like the beautiful creation Fellini's Guido managed to pull out of the abyss in *8 ½*, there are still some surprises in store for the spectator—provided that individuals such as these manage to put their houses in order. In the meanwhile, as Scola demonstrates, Italians can still make a good film about their inability to make better ones.

The emergence of Liliana Cavani, Lina Wertmüller, and Ettore Scola to positions of artistic preeminence is not the only development of note as the Italian film industry moves into a very uncertain decade. With the march of time, several major talents have inevitably disappeared: Visconti, Pasolini, Rossellini, De Sica, the scriptwriter Sergio Amidei, the musician Nino Rota, and scores of the actors and technicians who came of age in the neorealist generation and who were so integral a part of the industry's pool of experienced talent. Other major directors are approaching the end of their careers. It may well be too early to report that a third wave of great talent has appeared to equal the first wave that arose immediately after the war with Rossellini, or the second that followed in the early 1960s with figures like Pasolini and Bertolucci. However, there are encouraging signs which indicate that in the future as in the past Italian cinema will continue to arise like the phoenix from the ashes of each succeeding economic and artistic crisis.

One encouraging note is the revival of the Biennale, the Venice Film Festival, under the leadership of Carlo Lizzani. This important international film festival offers the industry an opportunity to test its wares in the international market, and it serves as a launching pad for new talents as well as for the reaffirmation of older artists' work. In the past few years, several of Italy's most promising directors have gained international attention with successful presentations of their first or second films at Venice, and that initial critical attention has enabled them to obtain crucial financial support for other works, which have been remarkably successful at the box office. Maurizio Nichetti's (1948–   ) *Ratataplan* (1979; the title is the Italian onomatopoeic equivalent for a drum roll), a brilliant comedy done almost completely in pantomime, literally stole the show at the 1979 Venice Festival from older directors such as Bertolucci, Pontecorvo, the Taviani brothers, and a host of Frenchmen and Americans. Made in 16 millimeter at a cost of around $100,000, its success at Venice helped the film to win immediate distribution and to earn over four million dollars. Nichetti's second feature, *Splash!* (*Ho fatto splash!*, 1980), another film based largely on pantomime that presents a satirical view of modern advertising, did almost as well.

Another young comic director whose success has been even more remarkable than Nichetti's is Nanni Moretti (1953–   ), who began working in Super-8 with four brief films made for less than a thousand dollars and initially shown to small film clubs in Rome. After gaining a small but enthusiastic following, Moretti made his first full-length film, *Ecce Bombo* (1978—the title is an irreverent reference to the Biblical "Ecce Homo"), which dares to poke fun at the tradition of

Maurizio Nichetti's *Ratataplan* (1979). Maurizio Nichetti stars in his pantomime comedy about a waiter's misadventures in Milan.
(Photo from the author's private collection)

Italian film comedy (particularly at Alberto Sordi, one of its foremost figures). It also casts a jaundiced eye on Moretti's own post-1968 generation, viewing his contemporaries as silly role-players who are far more similar to their parents, whom they pretend to hate, than they realize. Moretti resembles Nichetti in his debt to the classics of American film comedy (the Marx Brothers, Laurel and Hardy, Buster Keaton, Chaplin), as well as Woody Allen and Mel Brooks. Like many of the newer directors, Moretti not only directs his films and writes their scripts but plays a leading role in them as well. Most recently, his second major work, *Golden Dreams* (*Sogni d'oro*, 1981), earned a Golden Lion at the 1981 Venice Festival; like *Ecce Bombo*, it is filled with references to the cinema (Moretti plays a young director who is making a film entitled *Freud's Mama*), and *Golden Dreams* may well turn out to be the *8 ½* of the 1980s.

Two other new faces, also masterful comedians, are worthy of note. Carlo Verdone (1946–   ), son of the film historian Mario Verdone, has produced two good first works based upon his portrayal of a number of different roles in the same film: *Life Is Beautiful* (*Un sacco bello*, 1980); and *White, Red and Verdone* (1981, a play on the tricolored Italian flag with the director's name replacing green, or *verde*). Verdone's model may be Peter Sellers, but the comedy is completely Italian in its preoccupation with the social and personal problems of members of his generation. The most successful of all the younger directors has been Massimo Troisi (1954–   ), a young Neapolitan whose first feature, *Ricomincio da tre* (*I'm Starting From Three*, 1981), cost only $450,000 to make but is well on its way to breaking box-office records in Italy. While Troisi's work reflects some of the venerable *commedia dell'arte* and Neapolitan comic traditions, it has broader appeal than most such regional works and reveals, as do the films of Nichetti, Moretti, and Verdone, a sure comprehension of the preoccupations and the new values of the rising generation that constitutes much of Italy's cinematic audience.[16] Their success does not necessarily imply a complete turn away from political or ideological themes, since postwar Italian cinema has never strayed far from pressing social problems, but it seems clear that this new generation of comic directors has sought inspiration more from the American cinema than from its own national heritage and has begun to fill the demand for commercially successful and highly profitable products, the lack of which has long weakened the Italian industry.

Other recent and encouraging signs of continuing vitality and growth have appeared in a more dramatic vein. A brilliant tragedy is Salvatore Piscicelli's *Immacolata and Concetta: The Other Jealousy (Immacolata e Concetta, l'altra gelosia,* 1980). This sensitive and compelling portrayal of an affair between two women of different social classes ends in the murder of the wealthier lover who has betrayed her female companion for a man. Although made by a man, this film proves that gender poses no artistic barriers to a sympathetic treatment of lesbian passion. Valentino Orsini's (1926–) adaptation of Elio Vittorini's novel about the Italian Resistance, *Men and Non-Men (Uomini e no,* 1980), is also worthy of mention, as is Franco Brogi Taviani's *Masoch* (1980). The latter, based upon the letters written by Leopold Sacher Masoch to his mistress and eventual wife, presents a contemporary interpretation of sexual masochism within a surprisingly feminist view of this sexual persuasion. Both films were presented at the 1980 Venice Festival with some success. Another young dramatic director with great promise is Marco Tullio Giordana, whose *Damned, I Shall Love You! (Maledetti, vi amerò!,* 1980), and *The Fall of the Rebel Angels (La caduta degli angeli ribelli,* 1981) have attracted wide-spread critical notice.

Musicals have traditionally been regarded as the domain of Hollywood, but one of the most original Italian films to have appeared in some years is a musical, *Help Me To Dream (Aiutami a sognare,* 1981), by Pupi Avati (1938–). A bittersweet interpretation of Italy's love affair with America and American culture, its title is inspired by a Fats Waller song. The encounter with America played a major role in the genesis of Italian neorealism and has continued to represent a major theme in Italian films until the present. *Help Me To Dream* opens with the train on which Fats Waller died, then cuts to a farm in Emilia where a group of upper-class Italians are waiting for the arrival of American troops in 1943. Francesca (Mariangela Melato) is a star-struck movie fan, whose cinematic education was based upon her memories of American musicals and the popular entertainment fare permitted for importation by the Fascist regime. Her affection for American culture, even the somewhat romantic vision of it from Hollywood, is emblematic of the hope an entire Italian generation felt. The group sits around the fireplace, playing old American records and breaking into full-blown production numbers worthy of the American musical (doubly humorous, since they sing such songs as "Jeepers Creepers" "Pennies From Heaven," and "Some Of These Days" with marked Italian accents), and from time to time they rush outside to watch an American observation plane spotting German targets for the American Air Force. One day, however, the plane develops engine trouble and is forced to land on the farm; out steps an Italo-American named Ray (Anthony Franciosa), who has relatives in Castellamare, and who, like Francesca, is a passionate jazz pianist. (He claims to be a personal friend of Bing Crosby, Glenn Miller, and other famous musicians.) Ray's plane is named "Help Me To Dream," after the Waller song, and it embodies all of Francesca's dreams, her fixation with America, and her hope for a different future that many other Italians shared.

Ray is forced to spend the winter on the farm, hiding from the Germans while he repairs his craft, and the inevitable happens: Francesca falls in love with him and everything American he represents. Eventually, he leaves, and abandoning Francesca and her singing children, he returns to New York, apparently oblivious to the importance he and the culture he represents have played in the lives of the Italians he had met. A voice-over ending the film announces that for years, Francesca and her children waited for Ray's return but nothing arrived from the sky except the magic moon.

Help Me To Dream is much more than a musical. It represents a final good-bye to the myth of America that has dominated postwar Italian culture. Like Ray, the dream of America as the fortress of democracy and the land of exotic popular music appeared on the Italian scene, promised much, but delivered little. His seduction of Francesca is emblematic of Italy's predicament in the postwar period. Attracted by the enigmatic innocence and enthusiasm embodied in American music—and by free spirits such as Ray, who seemed to offer a new cultural model upon which many Italians have based their lives—

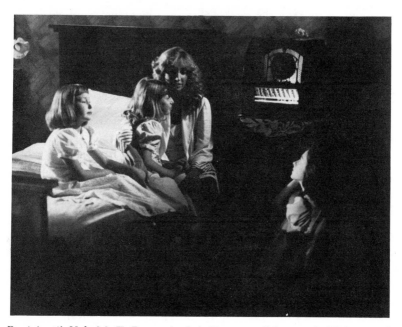

Pupi Avati's *Help Me To Dream* (1981). Francesca (Mariangela Melato) and her children listen to the magic radio with its American music during the last days of the war.
(Photo courtesy of the Museum of Modern Art).

Francesca and her friends are ultimately betrayed not by America herself (which promised little) but by their own naive perception of her culture which was ultimately a projection of their own aspirations and illusions. Rossellini's *Paisan* opened this cross-cultural dialogue, so crucial to the history of the Italian cinema, but films such as Avati's *Help Me To Dream* seem to have assessed it in a far more critical light. This is ironic in view of the fact that much of the inspiration for artistic revival in the contemporary Italian cinema comes from the classic American cinema.

Our brief examination of new, talented young directors makes it clear that the Italian film industry can look to the future with some confidence. As ever, the weakness of the film industry in Italy derives not from a dearth of individual talent but, rather, from the relative instability of its economic structure, and its production, distribution, and financial system. In the last two years, a positive trend has been seen in the increasingly successful box-office performance of young directors who have far outdistanced the earnings of their more illustrious older colleagues. Nevertheless, a fundamental defect in the industry still remains unresolved—its failure to exploit the exploding market for television films. The state-owned television networks have moved rather tentatively into this area, but their productions have focused upon large-budget projects aimed at a relatively high-brow audience. Some of the best Italian films in the past fifteen years have been RAI coproductions: these include Rossellini's historical documentaries; Fellini's *Clowns* and *Orchestra Rehearsal*; Bertolucci's *The Spider's Stratagem*; Castellani's *The Life of Leonardo da Vinci* (*La vita di Leonardo da Vinci*, 1971), a series shown with much success in the United States; Cavani's *Galileo*; Olmi's *The Tree of the Wooden Clogs*; and *Padre Padrone* by the Taviani brothers. These are films of great importance, winners of majœr awards and obvious works of great value. To this list should be added Luca Ronconi's relatively unknown adaptation of Ariosto's Renaissance epic poem, *Orlando Furioso* (1974), breathtakingly photographed by Vittorio Storaro, whose sets and costumes represent a testimony to the technical virtuosity of Cinecittà that even Fellini's best efforts could not surpass. But too often in the past, coproductions with government television have created artistic problems without offering economic solutions. There is the ever present threat of political censorship involved in granting or denying funding, and in addition these limited efforts cannot hope to offer effective competition to the deluge of television programming imported from American networks in the past few years. Every evening, the dozens of private channels and the three public channels in Italy present discontinued American series such as *Kojak, Laverne and Shirley, Ironsides*, and the like—all purchased at rates no national industry can match, since the huge costs of production have long been amortized by revenues from the gigantic American network runs. Only with a massive shift of resources toward programs produced in

Italy for domestic television with an eye to an additional export market can Italy ever hope to continue to control its own popular culture and avoid being submerged by American imports of far less artistic value than even the average Hollywood films that traditionally played such an important role within the Italian market. There is some indication that this problem has been understood, and several recent productions intended for world television distribution have already been success-fully completed or are about to be. Franco Zeffirelli's (1923–) *Jesus of Nazareth* (*Gesú di Nazareth*, 1977) represents one such success story. A film shot with a predominantly English and American cast, it was paid for by subscribers from a variety of world television net-works even before completion.[17] Another project recently released in Italy and abroad is Giuliano Montaldo's (1924–) *Marco Polo* (1982), which boasts one of the largest budgets in television history (almost thirteen billion lire); its costs, like those of Zeffirelli's film, have already been covered by foreign purchases.[18] Whether Italian directors, staunch individualists in the pursuit of their personal artistic visions, will fit within the constraints of such a market system remains to be seen.

Perhaps no other national cinema since the war has so consistently provided such an honest, entertaining, and important vision of a na-tional culture as has Italy's postwar cinema. It is one of the country's great national treasures, as aesthetically varied as the masterpieces guarded by the many major museums of the peninsula, but as threat-ened a species as that sinking Adriatic jewel—Venice. For the for-eigner, who is probably more aware of Italy's contributions to con-temporary culture because of Italian cinema than because of any understanding of modern Italian literature or art, the unstable con-dition, the continual crisis, and the precariousness of the very exis-tence of the Italian film industry always comes as something of a shock. But survival has always been an Italian talent. And it is probably most likely that the sense of continous crisis characteristic of the Italian cinema from neorealism to the present also explains much of its con-stant artistic development, its sense of cultural commitment, and its perennial originality.

Italian Cinema in the 1980s

The Italian cinema of the 1980s lacks a unified series of pressing social concerns, one of the central elements that explains the explosive impact of directors such as Rossellini, De Sica, and Visconti upon the development of international cinema during the immediate postwar period. In addition, although a number of emerging directors or actors and actresses have earned well-deserved critical praise within Italy during the last decade, no vigorous renewal of the industry, such as that which produced the exciting developments of the early 1960s beyond neorealism, has occurred. Once the art form most sensitive to Italy's pressing social problems and most expressive of its own particular political and aesthetic concerns, the Italian cinema has yet to produce a newly inspired third generation of filmmakers in the contemporary period. As a result, the critical profile of Italian cinema during the past decade is characterized more by continuity than by radical change. It is, however, a continuity that may conceal stagnation and decline.[1]

The most powerful Italian films of the last decade have mainly been the work of older directors who came of age during the neorealist period, such as Fellini, and the second, postneorealist generation of the 1960s, now mature artists in midcareer, such as Bertolucci, Scola, Leone, and the Taviani brothers. For years, these familiar faces have garnered the lion's share of international critical acclaim. The films of these directors generally express the personal vision of an *auteur*, a perspective that reflects a continuity of tradition rather than any radically new departures in cinematic style or content. Only two figures—Nanni Moretti and Pupi Avati, both undeservedly little known outside of Italy—may be said to have earned the right to be considered as first-rank directors with a body of work that stands in comparison to that of their older and better-established colleagues. Although a number of the newer directors have demonstrated great talent and promise in first films, they have too often found financing impossible to obtain and distributors unwilling to give their products proper promotion. Italian reviewers, who continue to be the Italian cinema's most pessimistic and negative critics, constantly assert that the Italian cinema is moribund (if not already dead). Perhaps a more accurate appraisal is to say that after three decades of unparalleled innovation and vigor from 1945 until the mid 1970s, a creative period unequalled in the sheer number of artistically notable films by any other national cinema, the creative development of Italian film may for the moment have reached a plateau while its economic substructure continues to stagnate or even to decline.

Unquestionably Federico Fellini remains the standard-bearer of Italian cinema abroad. Perhaps the most famous of all living directors, his unique brand of personal cinema has made his name synonymous with the most fanciful, poetic aspects of the so-called art film. And while none of his recent films has enjoyed the commercial success of *La Strada, La Dolce Vita,* 8½, or *Amarcord,* the body of his work is so substantial and unique that his major contributions to the Italian cinema are recognized by even his most adamant detractors. In 1985, Fellini received two unique honors: he was the first foreign director granted a retrospective at New York's Lincoln Center Film Festival; and he received the Golden Lion award for a lifetime of achievement from the Venice Film Festival. The three films he has completed in the last decade—*And the Ship Sails On* (*E la nave va,* 1983); *Ginger and Fred* (*Ginger e Fred,* 1985); and *Interview* (*Intervista,* 1987)—reflect the themes Fellini has developed since the mid-1960s: a metacinematic investigation into the nature of his art form along with a highly fantastic and idiosyncratic style relying upon the technical resources of the studios at Cinecittà.

Nowhere is Fellini's love for the cinema as evident as in *And the Ship Sails On,* yet its plot moves Fellini closer to contemporary history than is usually typical of his work.[2] The film describes the cruise of a ship, the

Gloria N., from its dock in Naples to the island of Erino, where the ashes of a famous opera singer, Edmea Tetua (Janet Suzman) will be scattered to the winds. Among the ship's passengers are a number of Tetua's friends, enemies, and colleagues from the world of grand opera; Orlando (Freddie Jones), a befuddled journalist who functions as Fellini's unreliable narrative voice and who constantly fails in his search for the "objective" facts of the voyage; and a contingent of royalty from the Austro-Hungarian Empire—the grand duke of Herzog (Fiorenzo Serra), his blind sister Lerinia (Pina Bausch), and the prime minister (Philip Locke). These wealthy first-class voyagers are joined in midjourney by a group of scruffy Serbian refugees who are fleeing the reprisals inevitably resulting from the assassination of Archduke Ferdinand at Sarajevo. An Austrian battle cruiser appears, demands that the refugees be handed over, and after Tetua's ashes are dispersed, in a puzzling sequence of events—perhaps initiated by a hand grenade tossed into the cruiser's magazine by the refugees—the *Gloria N.* is sunk by the cruiser.

Summarized in this fashion, *And the Ship Sails On* seems to be Fellini's version of the traditional "ship of fools" theme, which depicts a microcosm of European society immediately before the conflagration that destroyed *la belle époque*. Yet, the film is far more preoccupied with the nature of the cinema than with an explanation (however spurious) of the social causes of the outbreak of the First World War. The opening sequence of the film, the boarding of the ship, is an homage to the silent cinema: the port of Naples (the only outside location employed in the film, shot against the wall of a pasta factory) appears as if it is part of an early silent documentary. Fellini shot the entire film in technicolor, then decolored or toned various sequences to either sepia or black-and-white. Sound is evident only after several minutes of the first sequence have passed. Working without Nino Rota, whose death during the initial stages of *The City of Women* deprived the director of his greatest collaborator, Fellini not unexpectedly turned to the melodramatic music of Giuseppe Verdi, Gioacchino Rossini, and Vincenzo Bellini for this film filled with opera personalities, but he had the poet Andrea Zanzotto write new lyrics for their familiar music, thus creating the illusion that these three Italian masters had written a sound track expressly for Fellini.

Everything about the film, which was created in the gigantic Teatro 5 of

Cinecittà, is overtly fictitious. Six platforms with hydraulic equipment inside the studio simulated the motion of a ship on water and supported the weight of 170 tons of material and some 250 people during the production. The ocean upon which the *Gloria N.* sails is clearly made of plastic (a fact to which one of the passengers attracts our attention with the naive remark that the artificial sunset appears to be "false"). Even the apparently historical setting of the film provided by the Serbian refugees and the Austrian cruiser is called into question by the puzzling manner in which the sinking of the *Gloria N.* is depicted in the ending. A number of different versions of this dramatic event are shown, all possible and none definitively "true," thus confounding Orlando's desire to establish a documentary record for posterity. What remains for the spectator, however, represents the triumph of the director's creative powers. As the camera moves away from the sinking ship near the end of the film, it reveals the deck of the *Gloria N.* to be a complicated set construction in Cinecittà's Teatro 5, while the person whose eye operates the camera is mysteriously obscured (Fellini? Orlando?). The narrative then returns to the discolored tones of the opening sequence: Orlando has managed to save himself in a lifeboat, along with the mysterious rhinoceros in the ship's hold whose stench had overwhelmed the ship's passengers. While the historical "truth" of the incident remains unclear, we are invited, with Fellini's concluding revelation of the techniques of his medium, to consider the only "truth" that matters for him—the dream factory of Cinecittà. Finally, Orlando delivers the "moral" of the film—a puzzling remark about the excellent quality of the rhinoceros's milk! The style of this last sequence is clearly reminiscent of a television spot, with the small screen replaced by a porthole. [3]

Within the pseudohistorical story of *And the Ship Sails On,* Fellini presents his own abbreviated version of the history of the cinema. The initial evocation of the silent documentary recalling the Lumière brothers is followed by the coming of sound; subsequently, the cinema's fully developed expressive capabilities are demonstrated on the set of Fellini's completely artificial ship sailing upon an imaginary ocean. The result is a work of great poetic power, often expressing in images and music what cannot be expressed with dialogue. Furthermore, the final sequence, shot in the contemporary style of a television commercial, clearly implies that

Federico Fellini's *And the Ship Sails On* (1983). The count of Bassano (Pasquale Zito) watches silent footage of Edmea Tetua (Janet Suzman) as the *Gloria N.* sinks into the ocean.
(Photo courtesy of Studio Longardi, Rome)

this fragile, poetic medium has today been overshadowed by a more homogeneous and depersonalized electronic image.

The endangered hegemony of cinema in an age of electronic mass media concerns Fellini in both *Ginger and Fred* and *Interview*.[4] The first film recounts the nostalgic reunion of a pair of tap dancers named Amelia (Giulietta Masina) and Pippo (Marcello Mastroianni) who in the 1940s used the stage names Ginger and Fred in an act that recalled the more famous American dance numbers of Fred Astaire and Ginger Rogers. Their act, and the world of Hollywood it recalled, now form part of a dimly remembered past that seems totally out of place in the shallow, superficial world of electronic mass media where the wildest and most disparate personalities and subjects are introduced to a crass and insensitive public. Transvestites, look-alikes of famous characters, retired admirals, dancing dwarfs, mystics, and tap dancers become grist for the inexorable mill of a contemporary brand of entertainment that seems to involve voyeurism and instant gratification rather than sentiment, emotion, or genuine feeling. The only authentic emotion in the film derives from the poignant moment when Pippo falls as he attempts to execute the intricate dance number of his youth. For Fellini, the traditional cinema represents more than mere entertainment; it is also a kind of rite de passage, where the giant silver screen is a reflection of the dreams and aspirations of the audience's collective unconsciousness. Television, at its best, communicates information, but it is incapable of expressing emotions in a poetic fashion with its limited technical capabilities and its pandering to the homogenized desires of an audience whose expectations have been reduced to the lowest common denominator of bad taste.[5]

With *Interview,* awarded the Grand Prize at the 1987 Moscow Film Festival, Fellini goes beyond even his classic film 8½ in analyzing the

Federico Fellini's *Ginger and Fred* (1985). The vulgar master of ceremonies (Franco Fabrizi) for the tasteless television show "We Proudly Present" introduces Amelia (Giulietta Masina) and Pippo (Marcello Mastroianni) to the audience.
(Photo courtesy of Studio Longardi, Rome)

nature of the cinema. 8½ had been constructed around a solid script, written and rewritten countless times to offer the *illusion* to its audience that it emerged from extemporaneous improvisation. *Interview*, on the other hand, represents what Fellini has termed a "live" film: "This affable chat among friends represents the extreme limit of my kind of filmmaking: a point where there is no longer a story, no longer a script, nor even a feeling, unless it is precisely that of being inside a kind of creativity which rejects every kind of preconceived organization."6 Recalling not only 8½ but also other films in which Fellini himself plays a role *(Fellini: A Director's Notebook, The Clowns, Roma)*, *Interview* combines four films in one.7 On the simplest level, it is the reportage of a Japanese television crew that has come to shoot an interview with the director. The recording of "facts" leads to the more interesting personal memoirs of Fellini's first arrival at Cinecittà (both real and invented), where a younger Fellini (Sergio Rubini) is confronted by his first vision of the film director. The impressionable young man views the director (probably Alessandro Blasetti), who is the undisputed ruler over an imaginary celluloid universe, as an awe-inspiring figure. On a third level, we witness scenes from an abandoned Fellini project, a version of Kafka's *Amerika*. And finally, as the film winds to its conclusion, we realize that we have also enjoyed a fourth film, a film within a film—the film *Interview* composed of the three other films, which Fellini has created "live" before our very eyes with Cinecittà, his private dreamworld, as its main protagonist, and his own artistic creativity as its driving force. In Fellini's mind, Cinecittà's gigantic stage, Teatro 5, presents the greatest challenge when it is empty, for only then does it inspire him as a fecund womb to be filled with light and images by the figure of the director, the creative god of this artificial universe of moving pictures.8 The idea of artist as divine creator is further articulated by the novel conclusion of the work. As the four different levels of *Interview's* metacinematic discourse appear to reach a conclusion, we cut to a view of the inside of Teatro 5, illuminated by artificial lighting. Fellini's voice on the sound track tells us that the film should end here, where he can almost imagine one of his former producers complaining about his endings: "What, it ends this way? . . . without a ray of hope, a ray of sun? At least give me a ray of sun." To this imaginary criticism, Fellini can only respond: "A ray of sun? Well, I don't know, let's try."9 Saying that, he then

Federico Fellini's *Interview* (1987). Federico Fellini shows the actor playing the director at Cinecittà how directors should manipulate actors. (Photo courtesy of Studio Longardi, Rome)

follows with a concluding shot of the artificial studio light, which is for Fellini the quintessential quality of cinematic art.

Fellini's scriptwriter, Gianfranco Angelucci, reports that shortly before beginning work on *Interview*, Fellini visited the Museo del Cinema in Turin and remarked:

> People have constructed a castle of useless intellectual structures around the cinema the like of which has not occurred in any other art. Perhaps it is because we see those faces larger than dressers upon the screen that they have so conditioned the public to believe in the cinema as a sacred phenomenon, something to be beatified and to be discussed as if it were an extraordinary and miraculous event. Instead, the cinema has always remained the same: a rickety contraption with someone inside taking a picture of a clown moving around in front of him. [10]

Only a director completely at ease with his artistic medium and totally in control of his creative powers could have uttered such an elementary definition of the cinema, or could have produced such a deceptively simple and expressive poetic homage to his trade. Fellini's *Interview* is perhaps the director's most eloquent statement in defense of cinema as fiction, illusion, personal self-expression, and craftsmanship. And while he implies that the director's ability to conjure up a dreamworld with light, the primordial material of the universe, places him in a unique relationship to other mortals, Fellini has not forgotten that by placing himself in front of his camera in *Interview*, he has implicitly admitted that he is as much a circus clown as a godlike creator.

The role of the imagination, a theme so central to Fellini's art, has also come to dominate the cinema of Paolo and Vittorio Taviani during their production of the last decade: *The Night of the Shooting Stars* (*La notte di San Lorenzo*, 1982); *Kaos* (*Kaos*, 1984); and *Good Morning, Babylon* (*Good Morning Babilonia*, 1987). *Kaos*, produced in cooperation with the RAI, presents a number of Luigi Pirandello's short stories, the rural settings of which avoid even the pretense of a realistic re-creation of ambience so typical of traditional neorealist depictions of Sicily in the Italian cinema. This propensity to avoid realism and to search for a fanciful, fablelike style constitutes the originality of the Taviani brothers' other two more important films of this period.

With *The Night of the Shooting Stars*, the Tavianis continue their exploration of the heritage of neorealism, a central theme of *Padre Padrone*, by reconsidering the influence of Roberto Rossellini's *Paisan* upon their cinema. Their film should be interpreted as "a polemic against that landmark neorealist film which inspired the Tavianis' cinematic vocation and which shares with *Night of the Shooting Stars* its historic subject."[11] The origin of this highly acclaimed work (awarded various prizes by the Cannes Film Festival, the National Society of Film Critics, and the Premio David di Donatello) is to be found in an early documentary film (*San Miniato, July '44* [*San Miniato luglio '44*]), which the two brothers produced in 1954 with the assistance of Cesare Zavattini. This film chronicles the massacre of townspeople inside the cathedral of their native Tuscan village in retaliation for the death of a German soldier. After thirty years of reflecting on this topic, originally treated in the realistic, documentary style typical of the 1950s, the Tavianis altered their cinematic style in a radical re-creation of the same story. The plot of *The Night of the Shooting Stars* shares the wartime setting of *Paisan*. After mining the town of San Miniato, the Nazis and their Fascist allies instruct the townspeople to gather for safety inside the cathedral. Mistrusting the Germans, Galvano Galvani (Omero Antonutti) leads part of the populace toward the American liberation forces. While those who remain are betrayed and many killed inside the cathedral, Galvano's refugees fight a deadly battle in a wheat field before reaching safety.

Everything about the Tavianis' reconstruction of these events undermines the artistic and thematic heritage of neorealism. Whereas Rossellini's depiction of the encounter of Italy and America, following the geographical progression of the war from Sicily to the Po River Valley, focused primarily upon the journey of the Americans and their gradually developing empathetic awareness of another national culture, the Taviani brothers depict the confusing journey of Tuscan peasants who lack any clear destination or purpose. This lack brings to light the ideological confusion of the times in contrast to Rossellini's clear message of a Christian humanism that transcends national boundaries. Galvani's group experiences three "pseudoencounters" with the Americans.[12] First, when the music of "The Battle Hymn of the Republic" is played on a record player by one of their neighbors to poke fun at their childish desire to meet the Allies, they mistake it as an announcement of the Americans' arrival that equates the Liberation with the Second Coming. Then, a Sicilian woman named Mara (Enrica Maria Modugno), rushes forward to greet the liberators after hearing that an entire contingent of American soldiers is composed of Sicilian-Americans. She is shot by the Germans, and as she dies, she confuses the Nazis with her countrymen. In her delirium, she imagines receiving a miniature Statue of Liberty encased in a glass filled with artificial snow and being told she will be taken to visit her Brooklyn relatives. In the third and most amusing encounter, two young girls named Cecilia and Renata meet several GIs at a crossroad: they receive the obligatory Hershey bars, exchange gestures and funny faces, and are offered blown-up condoms in place of balloons. When the rest of the refugees come to investigate, only a half-empty package of Camel cigarettes testifies to the presence of the mysterious liberators. The encounter of Italy and America in the Tavianis' version owes an obvious debt to the Sicilian episode in *Paisan*. Besides the shooting star motif each film shares, the courageous actions of Rossellini's Carmela to avenge the death of Joe from Jersey contrast with the useless, illusion-filled death of Mara. The Christian brotherhood established between Italians and Americans in Rossellini is, in the Tavianis' film, replaced by an internecine civil war between residents of the same town, a struggle from which the Americans are physically absent.

This reversal of Rossellini's major themes is intensified by a completely different cinematic style. In juxtaposition to the documentary realism of *Paisan*, the Tavianis entrust the narrative of their story to the subjective memory of the six-year-old Cecilia filtered through the eyes of the adult Cecilia as she recounts the events from her childhood to her own daughter. The film's most typical editing technique is the wipe, which highlights the film's editing and emphasizes its cinematic qualities. The directors' ironic distance from their material is nowhere more evident than in the memorable battle between the black-shirted Fascists and the partisan peasants in a ripe and golden field of wheat. Interrupting this murderous struggle, members of both sides pause, pass water back and forth between them to tend their wounded, then return to the killing. The fictitious and antirealistic qualities of the narrative are equally obvious in the scene in which Cecilia saves herself during the battle from a bloodthirsty Fascist by closing her eyes and repeating a *filastrocca* or magical incantation learned from her mother. Cecilia's fantasy conjures up an epic scene recalling Homeric legend: the partisans are transformed into Greek hoplites, and the Fascist dies before he can harm Cecilia, pierced by an incredible number of ancient spears.

Few films of the last decade have so successfully combined poetic fantasy with original narrative. In an era when so many directors and critics have turned to taking stock of Italy's rich cinematographic heritage, the Taviani brothers have created both a unique tribute to their neorealist origins and an original expression of their departure from its realistic pretensions. Four generations after the historical events recounted in their early documentary took place, they have transformed the history of the Italian Resistance from a mere collection of facts and bitter memories into a popular legend placed in a mythological realm of poetic fantasy. If *The*

Paolo and Vittorio Taviani's *The Night of the Shooting Stars* (1982). Partisans and Fascists momentarily suspend their bloody quarrel. (Photo courtesy of Paolo and Vittorio Taviani and Umberto Montiroli)

Night of the Shooting Stars represents the Taviani brothers' settling of accounts with their neorealist heritage, *Good Morning, Babylon* contains a thoughtful consideration of the cinema and its historical origins. The plot involves two brothers—Nicola (Vincent Spano) and Andrea (Joaquim De Almeida) Bonanno—who have followed their father (Omero Antonutti) in his ancient trade as a cathedral builder in Tuscany. When the family business fails and the two young men emigrate to America, they eventually find work in the studio of D. W. Griffith (Charles Dance) as carpenters. During Griffith's production of *Intolerance*, the Bonanno brothers produce exactly the kind of elephant Griffith desires for his lavish sets (copying an animal they had observed while repairing the facade of Pisa's cathedral), and their cleverness launches them as set designers. The two brothers marry two sisters, Edna (Greta Scacchi) and Mabel (Desirée Becker), but with success, their close relationship begins to disintegrate. When Edna dies in childbirth, Nicola decides to return to Italy. The two men are united again on the Italian front during the First World War while a film of the action there is being shot for the Italian army. Just before dying from wounds suffered in combat, they shoot each other's picture in order to preserve their filmed images for their children.

Numerous details of *Good Morning, Babylon* underline the Taviani brothers' views on cinematic art. The fact that the protagonists are two brothers clearly calls our attention to their own close collaboration. As a historical reconstruction of the early years of the cinema, the narrative calls to mind the indebtedness of the first great American director to Pastrone's *Cabiria*. After attending the premiere of the Italian silent epic in America and then being inspired by a magic vision of the Italian pavilion at the San Francisco Fair, Griffith hires Italian workmen for the construction of the set of *Intolerance*. This much has a basis in historical fact. But the Tavianis go a step further in the film, drawing a direct parallel between Master Bonanno, the old cathedral builder who has passed down his craft to his two sons, and Griffith, the creator of the twentieth century's new "cathedral" of celluloid. After the two brothers use the model of the statues on the Pisan cathedral to fashion an elephant that not only satisfies Griffith but makes their fortune, Griffith himself offers a wedding banquet for the two brothers and their new brides Edna and Mabel on the set of *Intolerance* with Master Bonanno as Griffith's honored guest. Griffith's speech to the old man may be said to reflect the Taviani brothers' assessment of their craft:

> I do not know whether our work, that of your sons and mine, is as fine as that of those who built the Romanesque cathedrals. I do know that those works were born as these are born today—of the same collective dream. I believe that your sons, Bonanno, are like those obscure stonecutters who carved their masterpieces on the cathedrals you honour, who contributed to making them famous with their art, and who helped their neighbour to believe and live better. . . . This is why I love movie-making, and I respect it, Bonanno.[13]

Later, when the brothers lie dying on an Italian battlefield, the film cuts to a vision of ancient craftsmen upon the facade of a nearby Romanesque cathedral. A close-up reveals Master Bonanno directing his two sons as

Paolo and Vittorio Taviani's *Good Morning, Babylon* (1987). Jealous American workmen destroy the model of the elephant constructed by the Bonanno brothers for D. W. Griffith's *Intolerance*.
(Photo courtesy of Paolo and Vittorio Taviani and Umberto Montiroli)

they carve the bas-relief of the elephant that centuries later will inspire Griffith's set. The simple love for one's craft, whether building cathedrals or shooting films, finally triumphs over the negative vision of death and destruction that, with the war, darkens the last sequences of the film.

A decade ago, it would have seemed foolhardy to compare the philosophical assumptions of the Taviani brothers, the heirs to a tradition of politically engaged filmmaking that originated within a certain current of Italian neorealism, to those of Federico Fellini, identified historically with the transcendence of neorealism's social concerns and with a more purely poetic cinema of artifice and illusion. But both Fellini's *Interview* and the Taviani brothers' *Good Morning, Babylon* celebrate a certain kind of filmmaking that the three men believe to be most typical of Italy's cinematic heritage. It is an artisan's cinema, a poet's cinema, a kind of

filmmaking closer in conception to the honest labor and personal expression of a simple craftsman, and it is far removed from either the
ideologically engaged cinema aimed at a minuscule audience or the
commercial brand of industrialized filmmaking we usually associate with
the Hollywood system.

If Federico Fellini and Paolo and Vittorio Taviani have produced films
during the last decade that stress the personal expression of the *auteur* as
artisan, Sergio Leone and Bernardo Bertolucci have moved in an entirely
different direction. Always obsessed with cinema as a repository of cultural
myths, Leone's *Once upon a Time in America (C'era una volta in America*,
1984) and Bertolucci's *The Last Emperor (L'ultimo imperatore*, 1987),
explore two foreign cultures, uniting a highly personalized interpretation
of the subject matter and a style characteristic of the so-called art film of
the European *auteur* with the enormous budgets, expensive on-location
shooting abroad, international casts, and epic scope audiences have come
to identify with Hollywood productions.[14] Sergio Leone's portrayal of
Jewish (not Italian) gangsters in a work teeming with references to the
history of the cinema earned critical acclaim in Europe and America as
well as a special premiere at the Cannes Film Festival, but its length (218
minutes) caused its American distributor to mutilate the film in a shame-
fully abbreviated version that weakened its aesthetic impact and distorted
its meaning. Bertolucci's biography of the last Chinese emperor began with
even more difficulties than Leone's project eventually encountered, and
was initially rejected by both Italian producers and the major Hollywood
studios. Nevertheless, with an independent producer and the all-important
permission to shoot on location in Beijing's Forbidden City, Bertolucci
astonished the international film industry with an epic masterpiece that
garnered a total of nine Oscars—a record for any foreign director and third
place in the history of the Academy Awards.[15]

In Sergio Leone's ambitious re-creation of America during the era of the
gangster, based upon a novel entitled *The Hoods* by Harry Gray, the
familiar Italo-American criminal is replaced by a group of Jewish gangsters
in the Lower East Side of New York City. Leone traces the careers of two
close friends, Noodles (Robert De Niro) and Max (James Woods) from
their childhood in 1922 through 1933 (the Prohibition Era) and concludes

with their final encounter decades later in 1968. Although Leone spent thirteen years preparing the film and almost a year actually working on location, his perfectionism and meticulous attention to historical detail in his sets, costumes, and dialogues owe nothing to realism. The key to this film, like others Leone made earlier within the western genre, is to be found in the title itself ("Once upon a time. . . ."), the traditional opening line in fairy tales both in Italy and America. As Leone has noted: "My America is a land magically suspended between cinema and epic, between politics and literature."[16] And in this magic America of the imagination, the passage of time itself constitutes Leone's dominant theme.

The narrative of *Once upon a Time in America* hinges upon a complicated series of flashforwards and flashbacks between the three crucial years of 1922, 1933, and 1968. The film opens and closes in the 1930s: in one of the initial sequences and at the close of the film, we see Noodles in a Chinese opium den containing a shadow puppet theater, a subtle reminder that what is to unfold before the spectator's eyes is a cinematic work of the imagination and not a historical reconstruction of an era from the American past. Barely escaping from gangsters who are trying to kill him, Noodles flees the opium den and leaves New York from a bus station dominated by a wall painting in the period style advertising the amusements at Coney Island. When we then jump forward in time to 1968 to observe Noodles's return, the station's original advertisement has been replaced by an enormous Big Apple (the modern symbol for New York) as "Yesterday," a popular Beatles song from the 1960s, plays on the sound track. The intricate narrative of the film gradually reveals the explanation for Noodle's flight. For years, he and Max had argued over the direction their criminal enterprises should take. Although Noodles wanted to remain small, Max aimed to align himself with a larger criminal syndicate; in particular, he supported the efforts of a labor organizer, Jimmy O'Donnell (Treat Williams), who recalls the historical figure of Jimmy Hoffa. When Max seems to lose control of his senses and plans an impossible attack upon a Federal Reserve Bank, Noodles informs the police to save Max and his other friends from certain death, but something goes wrong when the police arrest the gang and all of Noodles's friends are killed. Noodles flees the syndicate's revenge in 1933 and remains in hiding until

Sergio Leone's *Once upon a Time in America* (1984). Noodles (Robert De Niro) begins his journey through time from Coney Island to the "Big Apple."
(Photo courtesy of Sergio Leone)

1968 when a mysterious summons calls him back to New York from Buffalo. For thirty-five years of his life, he has lived with the remorse he felt over his earlier betrayal.

What Noodles discovers upon his return is that his own betrayal pales before that of his friend Max. The elimination of the old Jewish gang was actually planned by the syndicate; Max survived and has now assumed the identity of a new character, the powerful Senator Bailey under congressional investigation for his connections to the underworld. Not only did Max betray his best friend and ruin his entire life, but he also stole his childhood sweetheart Deborah (Elizabeth McGovern) in the process. In partial atonement, Max offers Noodles a fortune if Noodles will accept a contract to execute him, since Max knows the mob will kill him sooner or later to cover up his years of collaboration with them as the influential

Senator Bailey. When Noodles refuses this offer and walks out of the senator's mansion on Long Island, Max is murdered in a surrealistic garbage truck that mysteriously appears without a driver and apparently mangles his body beyond recognition. The film ends with a close-up of Noodles's smiling face in the opium den of the initial sequences, as the credit titles run across this final enigmatic image.

In the process of unfolding this mythical view of America, Sergio Leone destroys our comfortable notions of narrative time and character development. In fact, there is no true present. While the episodes of 1922 and 1933 represent flashbacks from 1968, the episodes in 1968 are flashforwards from the past: "There is only the past seen from the future and the future seen from the past, memory is confused with fantasy, without reference points."[17] With the opening and closing sequences in the opium den and the drugged state of the protagonist Noodles, the entire intervening narrative of the film, with its complicated jumps back and forth between past and future, suggests that the film actually projects Noodles's guilt-ridden fantasy, dreamed in a narcotic stupor, in an attempt to relieve himself for the responsibility of his friends' death. The unusual length of the film, far from detracting from the dramatic impact of the work as its American distributors believed, is essential for the unfolding of Leone's theme of time. The spectator observes all the protagonists of the film passing from adolescence through maturity into old age, and since these figures also embody an archetypal cinematic myth of American culture, the gangster, their gradual deterioration before our eyes demythologizes this cinematic tradition in much the same manner that Leone's laconic gunfighters and bounty hunters altered the conventions of the American Western film in the 1960s.

Sergio Leone's gangsters are trapped in their immutable past. They grow old but never appear to develop or mature. In contrast, as Bertolucci has remarked, the theme of *The Last Emperor* is change: "Can a man change? The story of Pu Yi is a story of metamorphosis. From emperor to citizen . . . from caterpillar to butterfly."[18] The life of Pu Yi (1906–67), as described in the memoirs of Sir Reginald Johnston, the emperor's tutor between 1919 and 1922, or Pu Yi's own autobiography, written with the approval of the Maoist government after his "reeducation," spans all the tumultuous events of modern Chinese history. Named emperor at the age

Sergio Leone's *Once upon a Time in America* (1984). Noodles (Robert De
Niro) prepares to forget his remorse in a Chinese opium den.
(Photo courtesy of Sergio Leone)

of three by the empress dowager on her deathbed in 1908, Pu Yi was
shortly thereafter deposed by republican nationalists in 1911 and remained
confined inside the Forbidden City in the center of Beijing until 1924,
when he was finally evicted by a Chinese warlord and took refuge in the
Japanese legation at Tianjin. After passing a few years as a Western-style
playboy, Pu Yi eventually agreed to serve the Japanese puppet state of
Manchuria (the birthplace of his ancestors) as a collaborationist emperor.
Arrested by Soviet troops in 1945, Pu Yi was turned over to the victorious
Communist regime established by Mao in 1949. After ten years of relatively gentle "reeducation," he was released as a simple citizen, finding
employment as a gardener in the botanical gardens of the imperial city he
had once ruled. After publishing his autobiography in 1964, Pu Yi died
during the upheavals of the Chinese Cultural Revolution.

Bertolucci's interpretation of Pu Yi's life employs a narrative structure similar not only to two of his best previous films (*The Spider's Stratagem* and *The Conformist*) but also to Leone's *Once upon a Time in America*. A series of twelve major symmetrically balanced flashbacks and flashforwards, beginning with the reeducation of Pu Yi (John Lone) in Fushun Prison, weave an intricate web of details from which the spectator must reconstruct the protagonist's life. However, unlike Leone's quite different flashbacks and flashforwards, which tend to negate the difference between past and present and to prevent any sense of development in his characters, Bertolucci's narrative relentlessly returns over and over again to the prison scene where Pu Yi's motives are constantly called into question by the prison governor, Jin Yuan (played by Ying Ruo Chen, China's vice minister of culture). Accordingly, the jumps in narrative continuity in *The Last Emperor* serve to analyze and to explain the protagonist's motives and actions. This constant transition from the prison to the past and back again ceases abruptly during the film's last three sequences, which are the only sections of the work organized in chronological order. Significantly enough, these three sequences represent the final stages of Pu Yi's metamorphosis: his release from prison in 1959; his witnessing of the Cultural Revolution and the public humiliation of his former prison interrogator in 1967; and his final visit as a simple tourist to the throne room of his former palace in the Forbidden City. This shift to a smoother narrative continuity emphasizes the results of Pu Yi's reeducation and his final transformation into an entirely different kind of individual by the close of his life.

Other aspects of *The Last Emperor* confirm Bertolucci's heuristic encounter with Freudian psychoanalysis and his perhaps utopian search for a Marxist humanism. Pu Yi's sheltered existence within the Forbidden city is most often shot with "'forbidden' colors, the warmest colors," in the words of cameraman Vittorio Storaro, "because it was both a protective womb for him and a kind of prison . . . the more we go into his story, the more we discover new colors, new chromatics."[19] The collaboration of Bertolucci and Storaro in utilizing the lighting of the film to advance its narrative content, an achievement already brilliantly realized in *The Spider's Stratagem*, *The Conformist*, and *Last Tango in Paris*, constitutes one of *The Last Emperor's* most original features. Light and shade are juxtaposed to suggest a psychological struggle between Pu Yi's conscious and unconscious. For Bertolucci, the young emperor trapped inside the Forbidden

City represents the flight from painful self-awareness common to all human beings. Thus, he depicts Pu Yi's eventual exile from his womblike residence as the departure of a blind man, the dark glasses testifying not only to a lack of self-knowledge but also to the effects of an Oedipal complex growing out of the emperor's unusual family history, particularly the lack of a strong, paternal presence. As Pu Yi matures and reaches greater understanding of his life, the lights and shadows of the film's photography move into greater balance.

Nowhere is Bertolucci's belief that the child is father to the man clearer than in the brilliant and complicated sequence that narrates the young emperor's coronation: the three-year-old child scampers through the ranks of his courtiers on the Upper Terrace outside the Hall of Supreme Harmony, lured not by a thirst for adulation from his assembled retainers (a group of some two thousand extras provided by the Chinese People's Liberation Army to supply Bertolucci with the proverbial Hollywood "cast of thousands") but rather by the chirp of a cricket. Bertolucci's highly mobile and fluid camera movements follow the young boy (Richard Vuu) with a difficult Steadicam shot as he races along through the throng; the young Pu Yi eventually reaches the cricket's owner, who shows the child the insect inside a cage that the mature Pu Yi will eventually rediscover in 1967 when he returns to his throne room toward the end of his life. Bertolucci's use of this simple incident to provide narrative closure for his story underlines the fulfillment of Pu Yi's intellectual and psychological growth and recalls Sergio Leone's similar narrative closure with the image of the opium den. Bernardo Bertolucci has always been fascinated by the interplay of history and ideology. As early as *The Spider's Stratagem*, he portrayed the ideological underpinnings of the Italian Resistance movement as a consciously orchestrated fiction employed by the Left to dramatize its anti-Fascist interpretation of Italian history to the masses. *The Last Emperor* was authorized by the Chinese government (who habitually described its director as "a member of the Italian Communist Party"), and the portrait of Pu Yi in the film does, indeed, follow the Chinese Communist Party's official, post-Maoist view of his rehabilitation. The "official" status of the film moved one Italian critic to attack Bertolucci for his "ingenuity" and to denigrate the film as mere propaganda.[20] But there is little evidence in the completed film to support such a harsh verdict. In

Bernardo Bertolucci's *The Last Emperor* (1987). Pu Yi (John Lone) is exiled from Beijing's Forbidden City.
(Photo courtesy of Bernardo Bertolucci and Studio Lucherini, Rome)

Bernardo Bertolucci's *The Last Emperor* (1987). The three-year-old emperor (Richard Vuu) scampers about the court in a flashback to Pu Yi's happier and protected childhood.
(Photo courtesy of Bernardo Bertolucci and Studio Lucherini, Rome)

fact, Bertolucci shows Pu Yi to have suffered personally from ideological manipulation. At first, he incarnates the formal trappings of traditional political authority. Subsequently, Pu Yi is exploited by both the Japanese and later the Chinese Communists as a symbolic figure head. Even his rehabilitation becomes a crucial test for the legitimacy of the new Marxist state. His final conversion from emperor to citizen may well, by Western lights, represent only a transition from one form of authoritarian faith to another. But in the concluding scene, the now-wiser ex-emperor dimly perceives that like the cricket, he, too, had been trapped throughout his life by ideological myths. Pu Yi's release of the insect testifies not only to the emperor's final acceptance of his new personality but also to Bertolucci's deep faith in the possibility of changing human nature.

Once upon a Time in America and *The Last Emperor* represent the most ambitious achievements of the Italian cinema during the last decade. Within genres traditionally associated with Hollywood, the gangster film and the historical epic, Leone and Bertolucci attempt to move beyond a purely commercial spectacle, combining a style reflecting the experience of the European "art-film narration" with narratives of wide, commercial appeal.[21] Bertolucci has remarked: "I believe in movie theatres as big spaces where we dream the same dream together. Theaters are cathedrals for collective hypnosis."[22] While recognizing the differences in their personal cinematic styles and philosophical perspectives, Bertolucci, Fellini, the Taviani brothers, and Sergio Leone are all in basic agreement with this desire to return to a cinema of pleasurable, if not necessarily comfortable, narrative illusions informed by the poetic imagination.

During the last decade, Ettore Scola's critical reputation has risen steadily, and few Italian directors of the last few years have been as successful as Scola in joining together high artistic achievement with box-office appeal.[23] His latest films—*La Nuit de Varennes* (*Il mondo nuovo*, 1982); *Le Bal* (*Ballando, ballando*, 1983); *Macaroni* (*Maccheroni*, 1984); and *The Family* (*La famiglia*, 1987)—continue to alternate between investigations into the nature of metacinematic discourse and traditional dramatic structures relying upon strong acting performances. *La Nuit de Varennes* analyzes French society on the eve of the French Revolution: a carriage ride causes Tom Paine (Harvey Keitel), an aging Casanova (Marcello Mastroianni), Restif de la Bretonne (Jean-Louis Barrault), and

Countess de la Borde (Hanna Schygulla) to witness the French king's unsuccessful attempt to escape from Paris and his capture at Varennes on 22 June 1791. Scola captures this exciting moment of French history from a perspective similar to that of another of his works, *A Special Day*. He depicts the momentous events in *La Nuit de Varennes* from much the same private point of view, emphasizing how the most earthshaking historical revolutions ultimately depend upon small, seemingly banal personal decisions. The events leading up to Varennes are actually shown as a flashback from an opening prologue: a group of Venetian actors operate a magic-lantern peep show (the ancestor of the contemporary cinema) called "Il Mondo Nuovo" through which the audience is invited to observe the spectacle that follows.

This metacinematic approach to the history of the distant past becomes even more crucial in *Le Bal*. Set entirely inside a Parisian dance hall and filmed without dialogue, *Le Bal* examines change in French morals and attitudes over half a century. After a prologue in 1984, flashbacks move through crucial moments in contemporary French history: the Popular Front of 1936; the war in the early 1940s and collaboration with the Nazis during the Vichy regime; the Liberation in 1945 and the arrival of Americans, the black market, and jazz; the year 1956 and the war in Algeria with its racism; the student revolts of 1968; and a return to 1984. During the course of the film, twenty-four actors portray some hundred and forty characters; in each epoch, they represent caricatures of basic human emotions buffeted by the changing tides of historical events. Scola's deft skill at capturing the essential traits of an individual of a particular period in time with a single gesture, glance, or expression—all accomplished without any supporting dialogue except for the dance-hall music—testifies to his many years' apprenticeship on the Roman humor magazine, *Marc'Aurelio*, whose staff also boasted, at one time, such illustrious filmmakers as Federico Fellini and Cesare Zavattini as writers or cartoonists. A fascinating tribute to the possibilities of mime and the traditional acting techniques of the *commedia dell'arte*, choreography in *Le Bal* describes the history of contemporary France in much the same way that the evolution of the postwar Italian cinema in *We All Loved Each Other Very Much* chronicles the development of contemporary Italy.

Less daring, although no less well achieved projects, *Macaroni* and *The*

Family explore the sentiments of basic human relationships. The first film, treated rather superficially by American critics as nothing more than a vehicle for the acting talents of Jack Lemmon and Marcello Mastroianni, examines the relationship between an American businessman named Jack Traven (Lemmon) and a less-successful archivist named Antonio Jasiello (Mastroianni) that began during the war in Naples. Years later, while visiting Naples for three days, Traven realizes that his frenetic existence lacks meaning without friendship. He learns how to savor life's fleeting moments of happiness from his Neapolitan companion: at one point Jasiello announces: "How beautiful wasting time is!" At the premiere of this film, Scola declared that his title alludes to the confrontation of two different cultures. The American fast-food sandwich—often devoured standing up, hurriedly, and alone—is juxtaposed to Neapolitan macaroni, an even simpler fare that nevertheless requires more attention to detail and should be eaten with a group of friends and relatives to be best enjoyed.[24]

The Family is perhaps the most successful of all of Scola's recent films. It combines the superb acting talents of major stars, the technique Scola exploited in *Macaroni*, with the goal of telescoping a considerable range of historical change into the microcosmic lives of a few individuals, an approach that characterizes both *La Nuit de Varennes* and *Le Bal*. *The Family* recounts the bittersweet adventures of a middle-class Italian family from 1906 until 1986, recounted in the first person by Carlo (Vittorio Gassman), who is transformed by the passage of time in the film from a child into a grandfather. Shifts from one decade to the next are marked by dissolves that only heighten the concentration of dramatic tension achieved by employing the family apartment in the Prati district of Rome as the film's sole setting. The patriarchal family has traditionally represented the focal point of Italian life, but much of its strength has been eroded by the evolution in Italian society and morality that Scola's film narrates. Most of the dramatic moments in the lives of his protagonists take place around the dinner table, and Scola is particularly skillful in handling the subtle innuendos and undercurrents of domestic life during these tense moments. The enormous critical and commercial success of *The Family* has once again confirmed Scola's ingenuity in combining the daily dramas of everyday life with larger, panoramic views of an entire society or national culture in the throes of social, moral, and political change.

Ettore Scola's *The Family* (1987). The dining table becomes a battlefield: Carlo (Vittorio Gassman) seated beside his wife Beatrice (Stefania Sandrelli), entertains his former sweetheart Adriana (Fanny Ardant) and her French fiancé Jean-Luc (Philippe Noiret), toward whom his barely concealed jealousy is transformed into open hostility.
(Photo courtesy of Ettore Scola and Mass Films, Rome)

The production of Fellini, the Taviani brothers, Bertolucci, Leone, and Scola is the most consistently innovative and interesting of the past decade, but a number of notable films by other established directors argue against the constant critical cry in Italy that Italian cinema is dead. In the last decade, the operatic film, a genre popular during the 1940s and early 1950s, has renewed interest at the box office. Franco Zeffirelli, true to his early apprenticeship with Luchino Visconti, continues to work both in the cinema and in the musical world, and has made three interesting films with a musical theme: *La Traviata* (*La Traviata*, 1983); *Othello* (*Otello*, 1986); and *Toscanini, the Young Master* (*Il giovane Toscanini*, 1988). Adapted from Giuseppe Verdi's masterpieces, the first two are characterized by sumptuous settings and the rich detail that recall Visconti's own films and opera productions. *Toscanini, the Young Master* treats a critical moment in Toscanini's life when at the age of eighteen, he made his debut in Rio de Janeiro with Verdi's *Aida*. The narrative focuses upon Toscanini's relationships with his first love and with an imposing opera diva named Nadina Buliscioff (Elizabeth Taylor). In contrast, Francesco Rosi in *Carmen* (*Carmen*, 1984) and Luigi Comencini in *La Bohème* (*La Bohème*, 1988) create more realistic settings for the operas of Georges Bizet and Giacomo Puccini. The relative success of these works, building upon an audience of fanatic opera lovers all over the world, suggests that Italian filmmakers should continue to exploit the wealth of their lyric tradition in much the same manner that British television has prospered with the excellent and widely viewed adaptations of Shakespearean drama.

A number of first-rate films within the comic genre, the *commedia all'italiana*, prove that this rich vein of Italian humor has yet to be mined to exhaustion. Although Lina Wertmüller's critical reputation has suffered of late, the four comedies she has most recently produced deserve serious consideration: *Joke of Destiny (Scherzo del destino in agguato dietro l'angolo come un brigante da strada*, 1983); *Sotto . . . Sotto (Sotto . . . sotto . . . strapazzato da anomala passione*, 1984); *Camorra (Un complicato intrigo di donne, vicoli e delitti*, 1985); and *Summer Night (with Greek Profile, Almond Eyes, and Scent of Basil) (Notte d'estate con profilo greco, occhi a mandorla e odore di basilico*, 1987). In all four of these films, Wertmüller displays the wide range of her thematic interests and her characteristically exuberant camera style, dealing respectively with political satire, a husband's dismay over discovering his wife is in love with another woman, the deadly battle fought against the underworld of the Neapolitan drug scene by the mothers of its victims, and the contemporary ecological crisis.

With *Where's Picone? (Mi manda Picone*, 1983), veteran director Nanni Loy (1925–   ) produces a chilling comic portrait of crime-ridden Naples with the assistance of a memorable performance by Giancarlo Giannini as a small-time con artist named Salvatore who assumes the identity of Pasquale Picone, after this apparently unemployed steel worker has set himself on fire during a government hearing about unemployment in the South. With the assistance of Picone's wife Luciella (Lina Sastri), Salvatore soon discovers that Picone was never employed (and therefore never unemployed), that he has disappeared, that his true occupation was that of a collector and runner for the local mob, and that his death was faked by the use of an asbestos suit to shield Picone from the flames. Why Picone may have simulated such a dramatic death is never clarified, increasing the mystery for both Salvatore and the spectator. Salvatore follows Picone's traces through the underworld of Naples in a picaresque journey that owes more to the narrative world of Kafka than to the sunlit beaches of the tourist brochures. As he prepares to attend Picone's funeral, Salvatore is taken ill and carried off by the same kind of mysteriously appearing ambulance that has taken Picone away. The spectator is left to wonder about the possibility of ever comprehending the morass of corruption and criminality that characterizes the city.

The most important film comedy of this period is unquestionably Mario Monicelli's *Let's Hope It's a Girl* (*Speriamo che sia femmina*, 1986), which proved to be a box-office success. Based upon an original idea by Tullio Pinelli and masterfully scripted by Pinelli and Suso Cecchi d'Amico, *Let's Hope It's a Girl* boasts an outstanding female case and also provides an interesting perspective upon the current feminist debate in Italy.[25] Elena (Liv Ullmann) lives on a Tuscan farm, separated from her ineffectual husband Leonardo (Philippe Noiret), who is more concerned with his mistress Lolli (Stefania Sandrelli) then his wife or two daughters, Franca (Giuliana De Sio) and Malvina (Lucrezia Lante Della Rovere). This collection of sharply drawn female figures inhabiting a world virtually without men is completed by Elena's sister Claudia (Catherine Deneuve) and Elena's housekeeper Fosca (Athina Cenci). Fosca lives in the farm-house with her daughter and is separated from her husband, an emigrant in Australia. The only male in the house is a senile old uncle (Bernard Blier) who spends most of his time knitting. This unusual stable female environment is shaken by several crises. Suddenly, Leonardo appears with a scheme to turn the property into a tourist spa, but his willingness to follow the directions of his senile uncle results in his accidental death, as he backs his Mustang off a cliff. Then Franca discovers that she is pregnant, and leaves the house to live with her boyfriend (another male figure Monicelli presents as completely incapable of understanding women), followed by Malvina's departure to live in Rome with her aunt

Claudia. Just as the community seems to have fallen apart and Elena prepares to sell the farm to her lover, all of the women, including even Leonardo's mistress, return. At the close of the film, with the removal of all the ineffectual male figures, the united group of women await the arrival of Franca's child, hoping it will be another girl. Monicelli has shown that in their lives, men are completely superfluous.

Within the genre of the *commedia all'italiana*, usually noted for what contemporary feminists often simplistically term "sexist" humor, Monicelli has produced a devastating critique of the role of the modern male in a society that seems to be on the verge of wide-sweeping generic changes. Men are incapable of dealing with women as individuals or of understanding their psychological needs; they are even inept businessmen and frustrated or solitary figures. The history of the cinema is filled with films devoted to the traditional forms of male bonding, but *Let's Hope It's a Girl* demonstrates the possibility of a similar kind of close relationship between women who live, by choice, in a world without men.

If Monicelli's bittersweet comedy portrays an unusual vision of a feminist world, Ermanno Olmi's *Long Live the Lady!* (*Lunga vita alla signora!*, 1987) presents an amusing allegory of authority in a charming treatment of the adventures of six adolescents, the best students of a school for hotel workers, who are summoned to serve an important banquet given for a mysterious but powerful woman. With little dialogue and a fine attention to detail and facial expression, Olmi draws masterful performances from his amateur actors that recall *The Sound of Trumpets*. The high point of the film is, of course, the banquet, where the mysterious woman's physical appearance is echoed in the snout of her fierce dog and in that of the monster fish baked specifically for the banquet. The pretentiousness of power comes clearly into focus when juxtaposed to Olmi's innocent and sympathetic children, but as usual in Olmi's work, there is little political ideology in his denunciation of society's power elite. In fact, the film closes with an allegorical message that implies how love could change the woman's loneliness and transform her sterile power into a force for good.

Although comic films are almost always more popular among Italian audiences than dramatic works, a number of serious and provocative films have been produced in the last ten years. After twenty years of working abroad, Michelangelo Antonioni returned to an Italian environment with

Identification of a Woman (*Identificazione di una donna*, 1982), and his subject continues to remain the same crisis of values in a rapidly changing world that was an integral feature of his masterpieces in the late 1950s and early 1960s.[26] The film traces the attempts of a film director named Niccolò (Thomas Milian) to understand his relationships with two successive mistresses: Mavi (Daniela Silverio), a rich, spoiled aristocrat, and Ida (Christine Boisson), a stage actress. Antonioni's masterful photography of environments and objects remains his characteristic signature, but the director's viewpoint has shifted dramatically from earlier works such as *L'Avventura*: now, rather than analyzing male behavior through the eyes of a female protagonist, Antonioni's film depicts the point of view of a male director who attempts, without success, to "identify" and to understand the women in his life. Both Monicelli and Antonioni, in quite different styles, present women as a perplexing and unfathomable mystery for the male psyche.

More mundane and less philosophical problems between the sexes are presented in *Love Story* (*Storia d'amore*, 1986), by Francesco Maselli, a remarkable film that earned major awards at the 1986 Venice Film Festival, including that of best actress for Valeria Golino, an important new talent, who plays Bruna, the film's protagonist. Far removed from the intellectual, elite atmosphere of Antonioni's troubled characters, *Love Story* examines the daily problems of the working class in Italy and how these critical issues (the lack of housing, the dearth of good jobs) affect the emotional lives of couples trying to make a life together. Maselli's film succeeds in depicting the life of the proletariat without being patronizing or condescending, but when Bruna suddenly commits suicide at the close of the film, it appears that we are faced once again with the image of a perplexing female response to a life shared with a man.

Far more perverse a portrait of human eros is Liliana Cavani's *The Berlin Affair* (*Interno berlinese*, 1985). Set within the scrupulously re-created environment of prewar Nazi Germany (Berlin in 1938), Cavani's depiction of a ménage à trois between an official from the German Foreign Office named Heinz (Kevin McNally), his wife Luisa (Gudrun Landgrebe), and Mitsuko (Mio Takaki), the daughter of the Japanese ambassador, cannot fail to recall the somber images and atmospheres of Luchino Visconti's German trilogy. However, Cavani's perspective upon an erotic relationship traditionally considered as decadent shows an original twist, since her focus is upon the complete sexual and moral domination over the German couple by the young Japanese girl. *The Berlin Affair* is unusual among recent films because the female protagonist in a torrid love affair not only controls the relationship but acts with apparent disregard for differences in sexual gender.

The Basileus Quartet (*Quartetto Basileus*, 1983), a minor masterpiece about how the cloistered lives of the members of an internationally renowned string quartet are shaken by contact with human feelings, has finally earned Fabio Carpi (1925–   ) well-deserved critical attention.[27] With the death of the first violinist, his three companions decide to break up the quartet but soon discover that their three decades of self-imposed seclusion from the world of workaday affairs have rendered them incapable of coping with the world outside the microcosm of a concert hall. With the arrival of a young, brash violinist as a replacement, the quartet is reconstituted but no longer represents a secure refuge that protects its members from the buffeting effects of human emotions in the real world. Also worthy of note is Carpi's recent *Bluebeard* (*Barbablú Barbablú*, 1987), a fascinating story about a capricious, authoritarian old psychoanalyst (John Gielgud), who has outlived four wives. On what appears to be his deathbed, a television interview is being shot with the psychoanalyst, while downstairs the doctor's various children and his fifth wife await what promises to be his demise. Nonetheless, the tables are turned on them all; the television film is completed, and the resilient old doctor manages to survive and to continue to exercise psychological tyranny over his family.

Few new talents have emerged and matured into internationally recognized directors during the last decade in Italy, but two individuals deserve special mention: Pupi Avati and Nanni Moretti.[28] Relatively unknown outside Italy, Avati has actually made almost twenty films since 1968, most set in Emilia-Romagna, and is one of Italy's most productive directors, often working in connection with Italian television. His comic irony and his light touch have moved many critics to compare his recent work with both Truffaut or the sentimental comedies of Ernst Lubitsch. Unlike many of his colleagues, Avati is unafraid to work in a number of film genres— sentimental comedies, thrillers, fables, musicals (such as his superb *Help Me to Dream*), sports films, and historical narratives in period costumes.

With *We Three* (*Noi tre*, 1984), Avati anticipates Milos Forman's *Amadeus* and provides a lighthearted study of the young Mozart who in 1770 at the age of fourteen comes to Bologna to prepare for an examination on musical composition. The drama of this little jewel of a film lies in the conflict between Mozart's genius and the greatness that lies in his future and the temptation to abandon this destiny for a more emotionally rewarding life that allows room for simple pleasures and human passion.

This nostalgic look at Mozart's youth shares affinities with the mood of two other of Avati's best works—*School Trip* (*Una gita scolastica*, 1983) and *Graduation Party* (*Festa di laurea*, 1985)—whereas *Christmas Present* (*Regalo di natale*, 1986) contains a more biting, dramatic tone. All three of the films profit from the acting talents of Carlo Delle Piane, whose characters project an ingenuousness and basic goodness that more than compensate for their extremely homely features. In *School Trip*, the bittersweet events of a high-school excursion in 1914 from Bologna to Florence are recounted from the viewpoint of the last surviving member of the class, an aging spinster named Laura (Lidia Broccolino). The trip offers the bashful literature professor Carlo Balla (Carlo Delle Piane) his first taste of passion in a relationship with Serena Stanziani (Tiziana Pini), the drawing instructor who later betrays her husband with a student and loses her job. Meanwhile, Laura is traumatized by the callous rejection of a young man, which explains her refusal ever to marry. While love seems to triumph when Professor Balla defies his superiors and leaves his job with Serena to the cheers of their students, Avati's last scene shows each of the children on the school trip crossing over a river and into a thick fog bank, a metaphor for their deaths. Love cannot conquer death, and only the director's narrative has saved their personal dramas from oblivion.

Avati's skillful handling of his most typical theme, the clash of innocence with the agony of experience, reappears in *Graduation Party*. Once again, the director exploits the talents of Carlo Delle Piane in the role of Vanni, a pastry-maker and former factotum of the rich Germani family whose life was forever changed when the beautiful daughter of the house, Gaia (Aurore Clement), kissed him in her excitement over Mussolini's declaration of war on 10 June 1940. Exactly ten years later, Gaia asks Vanni to remodel her country villa and to handle all the details for the graduation party of her daughter Sandra (Lidia Broccolino), consciously exploiting the crush Vanni has had on her for ten years in order to receive these services without paying Vanni a penny. The entire affair destroys Vanni's beautiful memories of the single kiss that changed his life: Gaia refuses to understand his eventual declaration of love; she and her family and friends turn out to be merely a superficial collection of egotists; and even Sandra has lied about her successful completion of her schoolwork. Vanni loses his innocence and comes to realize that the woman of his dreams was a figment of his imagination but demonstrates his superiority over the wealthy but morally and emotionally bankrupt upper-class family he has faithfully served by refusing to be reimbursed by Gaia for his ruinous expenses.

With *Christmas Present*, Avati reverses the ingenue role usually played by his favorite actor, Carlo Delle Piane, and transforms Delle Piane into a calculating card shark named Santelia in a performance that earned him the Golden Lion at the 1986 Venice Film Festival. Santelia is introduced into a friendly card game among four friends by one of the group, who has agreed to split his earnings with Santelia. During an all-night game on Christmas eve, the friendships and close relationships of the four friends are shown to be based upon less than solid grounds. In the lives of Avati's protagonists, cheating at cards has become emblematic of a wider range of inauthentic emotional relationships.

While Pupi Avati's cinema is characterized by a bittersweet mood that emphasizes the theme of lost innocence, Nanni Moretti's recent works—*Bianca* (*Bianca*, 1983) and *The Mass Is Ended* (*La messa è finita*, 1985)—present an entirely different kind of cinematic comedy. Moretti, like Woody Allen, writes his own scripts, directs them, and plays the leading roles, and since Moretti's particular brand of caustic humor departs from the familiar slapstick routines of the more traditional *commedia all'italiana*, its self-conscious and ironic tone is quite unique in the spectrum of Italian filmmaking. In *Bianca*, Moretti plays a young professor of mathematics in a high school named Michele whose mania for perfection and neatness turns him into a murderer. Moretti's sarcastic opinion of the disastrous leveling effects of the cultural upheavals in Italy after 1968 finds perfect expression in the humorous depiction of Michele's high school. Named after Marilyn Monroe, it boasts a headmaster who tells Michele that his task is to "inform" his students and not to "form" them; a

Pupi Avati's *Christmas Present* (1986). Santelia (Carlo Delle Piane) prepares himself for the card game in which a close friendship is betrayed. (Photo courtesy of Pupi Avati)

psychoanalyst for the faculty (not the students); and various forms of games (toy trains, pinball machines) that seem to attract the students more than their education.

With *The Mass Is Ended*, Moretti achieved both critical and commercial success and earned the Berlin Film Festival's Silver Bear award. Moretti plays the role of Don Giulio, a young priest whose personality has affinities with the neurotic murderer Michele of *Bianca*, especially his impatience with empty rhetoric and his desire for perfection. However, Don Giulio not only has a genuine vocation for his work (thus sparing the audience the usual, banal scenes treating a priest's sexual temptation), but he also firmly believes he has a mission to help those in need. Yet, he is thwarted in every attempt to attend to his neighbor: his father abandons his mother for a younger girl; his sister becomes pregnant and insists on an abortion; his former friends from earlier, more revolutionary days are

Nanni Moretti's *The Mass Is Ended* (1985). Don Giulio (Nanni Moretti)
impatiently fulfills his duties as a priest in a world which no longer seems
to need his services.
(Photo courtesy of Nanni Moretti and SACIS)

either ex-terrorists, slightly mad intellectuals, or selfish egotists. But the
common denominator of all those who surround him is their complete
and absolute indifference to his desire to exercise his vocation as a priest.
Finally, Don Giulio decides to abandon his Roman parish and to work in a
tiny church in South America where the parishioners truly need someone's
assistance.

Despite some brilliant and original works, as well as the emergence of at
least a few new faces who have considerable talent, the Italian cinema
enters the last decade of this century suffering from a series of problems
that affect cinema all over the world. Production of films per year has
never returned to the high figures of several decades ago: the total films
(both Italian and coproductions) completed in Italy during the past few
years number 125 (1982), 113 (1983), 99 (1984), 86 (1985), 111 (1986),

and 129 (1987).[29] The RAI continues to provide funding for a number of Italian films and has even increased its activities during the last decade, but this important assistance by the state television cannot make up for the continually decreasing level of investment from the private sector. Both the Centro Sperimentale di Cinematografia and Cinecittà have just celebrated their fiftieth anniversaries respectively in 1985 and 1987. Although the Centro's functions seem to be paralyzed by a number of internal political problems, Cinecittà has finally begun to show a profit, thanks to a growing number of foreign productions (such as *The Name of the Rose*), the increased filming of commercials there, and new investments in high-technology special-effects studio equipment that will enable Cinecittà to compete with even the Pinewood Studios of Great Britain. However, the condition of the theater circuits in Italy suffers from the same kind of undercapitalization that characterizes the entire industry. Of the some 370 *prima visione* theaters in Italy operating on a continuing basis today, there are no more than 60 structured in the multitheater format now common in the United States that maximizes profits and increases audience interest in the products. Too few are equipped with Dolby sound systems, and too many employ old and outmoded lighting systems. The dilemma facing the industry can be summed up by the paradoxical situation that occurred after Bertolucci's *The Last Emperor* garnered its nine Oscar awards in the United States. When Bertolucci and his director of photography Vittorio Storaro began to organize the Italian premiere of the film, they were embarrassed to discover that only a single movie theater in all of Italy—one in a suburb of Milan—was equipped for the screening of a 70-mm print. With theaters in poor condition, it is no wonder that ticket sales have been steadily decreasing from a total of some 241,891,000 (1980) to 123,113,000 (1985), 124,867,000 (1986), and an estimated 116,000,000 in 1987.[30]

Not all of the developments within the industry during the last decade are negative. The videocassette revolution, already an established force within the American film industry and a source of much of its profits, has reached Italy. Even though American films outnumber Italian films in the video format (just as American prints dominate the theater circuit), the growing availability of both classic Italian masterpieces and recent releases may well provide the industry with additional capital that can be wisely reinvested in new films. And Italy, through the efforts of the RAI, has been in the forefront of investment and development of new techniques of electronic filmmaking in High Definition. In fact, the first feature-length film designed for High Definition transmission, *Julia and Julia* (*Giulia e Giulia*, 1987) by Peter Del Monte (1943–), was presented at the 1987 Venice Film Festival. At present, High Definition television has yet to be introduced around the world, so that films shot with this electronic process must be subsequently transferred from videotape to celluloid. The fundamental difference between shooting films with the traditional cameras and the new video technology is that rushes are no longer necessary; the director may immediately see the results of his takes and may even, if desired, modify the colors, lighting, and toning by electronic means. Eventually, the image broadcast upon a High Definition television set will be infinitely superior to anything available today, because it will contain some 1125 lines as opposed to the 625 lines on European video receivers or the even less satisfactory 525 lines on the American color format. At the moment, it is difficult to determine what the widespread use of such technology will mean for the artistic expression of the Italian cinema, but it is encouraging that the Italian industry seems to be in the forefront of its development. The recent announcement that the American director, Francis Ford Coppola, has decided to work for the RAI on a long-term project in Rome involving High Definition technology in the cinema suggests that such innovative ideas will guide Italian cinema in the future.

Perhaps no other national cinema since the war has so consistently provided audiences in Italy and abroad with such a brilliant tradition of great cinematic works. The Italian cinema may arguably be Italy's greatest contribution to twentieth-century culture; it is certainly the art form that has most successfully stimulated an interest in contemporary Italy throughout the globe. The continuous crises, artistic and economic, which have plagued its history from the neorealism of the immediate postwar period down to the filmmaking of the present day, have never succeeded in silencing its voice. It has long been fashionable in Italy to warn of the impending "death" of the Italian cinema. Critics appear to believe unique events in the life of a popular art form, such as the unrepeatable historical moment that witnessed the birth of neorealism, can be willed into existence. Yet, even in the last decade, supposedly the lowest point ever reached in the artistic development of the Italian cinema in the view of such negative voices, a large number of respectable films have continued to appear and a few genuine masterpieces have been created. Survival, after all, has long been an Italian talent.

Revised Notes for the Second Edition

The notes for this second edition have been substantially revised to reflect the rapid growth of scholarship on Italian cinema during the last decade. Notes have also been abbreviated wherever possible by employing only shortened titles of sources listed in the bibliography, or by referring the reader to the particular section of the bibliography pertinent to the argument. Whenever possible, the notes also attempt to guide the reader toward the most reliable and stimulating secondary material currently in print.

CHAPTER I

1. For specific studies of the Italian silent cinema, see the works listed in section III.B of the bibliography (particularly the three-volume history by Aldo Bernardini), as well as a number of more general histories in section III.A (especially Gian Piero Brunetta's *Storia del cinema italiano 1895–1945*). Perhaps the single most useful source on the Italian silent cinema is a documentary film produced from the archives of the Centro Sperimentale di Cinematografia in Rome—*Antologia del cinema italiano: il film muto (1896–1926)*, ed. Antonio Petrucci—which is available for viewing at the Centro.

2. For an account of Pastrone's relationship to D'Annunzio on *Cabiria*, see *Authors on Film*, ed. Harry Geduld, pp. 163–80; specific studies of Pastrone's works, including a detailed photographic record of the film itself, may be found in section IX.AA of the bibliography.

3. The links between the early silent films, such as *Cabiria* or *Messalina*, and modern film genres (the "neomythical" or *peplum* film, and the so-called spaghetti western) can be traced in a number of studies listed in section IV.D of the bibliography. In particular, see: Bondanella, *The Eternal City: Roman Images in the Modern World*; Elley, *The Epic Film: Myth and History*; Frayling, *Spaghetti Westerns: Cowboys and Europeans from Karl May to Sergio Leone*; and Solomon, *The Ancient World in the Cinema*.

4. Pierre Leprohon, *The Italian Cinema*, p. 60.
5. Carlo Lizzani, *Il cinema italiano*, 1895–1979, 1:23.
6. Michael Kirby, *Futurist Performances*, p. 213; in addition to a number of English translations of Futurist manifestos, Kirby's excellent study contains a summary of Italian scholarship on Futurism and the cinema (the fundamental works on which are those by Mario Verdone listed in section III.B of the bibliography).
7. Studies on the economic structure of the Italian film industry are found in section VI of the bibliography: in particular, see Libero Bizzarri and Libero Solaroli, *L'industria cinematografica italiana*; Lorenzo Quaglietti, *Storia economico-politica del cinema italiano* 1945–80 (which summarizes developments before 1945); and Enrico Magrelli, ed., *Sull'industria cinematografica italiana*.
8. Cited in Pierre Leprohon, *The Italian Cinema*, pp. 51, 58.
9. As was the case with the silent period, the most useful source for the cinema during the Fascist period is another documentary film on the subject produced from the archives of the Centro Sperimentale di Cinematografia: *Antologia del cinema italiano: il film sonoro* (1929–1943), ed. Fausto Montesanti. In the last two decades, scholarship on Italian cinema during the Fascist period has completely overturned the more traditional negative view of its contributions, a critical perspective usually based upon political opposition to the regime and its ideology. Rather than a sharp break between films in the Fascist period and those in the immediate postwar period identified with Italian neorealism, most film historians now see greater continuity in Italian production and closer links to genres and cinematic styles in France or America. For an example of the traditional approach, see Carlo Lizzani's *Il cinema italiano*, 1895–1979. The memoirs of Luigi Freddi, *Il cinema*, present a retrospective look at the period from the perspective of one of the regime's most important figures in the industry. Section III.C of the bibliography contains a comprehensive listing of major works on the topic. In particular, see: Francesco Savio, *Ma l'amore no* and *Cinecittà anni trenta*; Riccardo Redi, ed., *Cinema italiano sotto il fascismo*; Adriano Aprà and Patrizia Pistagnesi, eds., *The Fabulous Thirties*; James Hay, *Popular Film Culture in Fascist Italy*; Marcia Landy, *Fascism in Film*; and Elaine Mancini, *Struggles of the Italian Film Industry*. The three recent American contributions by Hay, Landy, and Mancini are particularly recommended. For specific studies of Blasetti and Camerini, the two major directors of the era, see sections IX.F and IX.H in the bibliography (which includes two detailed works on Blasetti's *Sun* and *The Iron Crown*), as well as Gian Piero Brunetta, *Storia del cinema italiano* 1895–1945.
10. José Luis Guarner, *Roberto Rossellini*, pp. 10–11.
11. Non-Italian historians of film theory have unfortunately ignored the important contributions of Umberto Barbaro and Luigi Chiarini due to their all-

too-frequent inability to read Italian. Yet, the first history of film theory in *any* language was Guido Aristarco's *Storia delle teoriche del film*, which contains (pp. 143–66) excellent discussions of the two men. For additional bibliography on the early contributions of Italians to film theory, see the works by Aristarco, Barbaro, Casetti, and Chiarini in section VII.A of the bibliography.

12. Monica Stirling, A *Screen of Time: A Study of Luchino Visconti*, p. 50.
13. Roy Armes, *Patterns of Realism: A Study of Italian Neo-Realism*, p. 50. Barbaro's essay, "Neo-Realismo" (*Neorealismo e realismo*, 2:500–504) departs from a discussion of Carné's *Port of Shadows* (*Quai des Brumes*, 1938) and Renoir's *The Bitch* (*La chienne*, 1931) and calls for a return to the realism found in Italian art and the early silent film, *Lost in the Dark*: "If we really wish to abandon the historical pot-boiler, the Nineteenth-century rehashes, and the minor comedy of errors, we must attempt the realistic film" (author's translation). For an attempt to reconstruct *Lost in the Dark* from its script and recently discovered still photographs, see Alfredo Barbina, ed., *Sperduti nel buio*.
14. For studies of the interchange between Italy and America during these years, consult sections II and III of the bibliography. In particular, see: Donald Heiney, *America in Modern Italian Literature*; Angela Jeannet and Louise Barnett, eds. and trans., *New World Journeys: Contemporary Italian Writers and the Experience of America*; and Cesare Pavese, *American Literature: Essays and Opinions*.
15. Pavese, *American Literature: Essays and Opinions*, p. 196.
16. Section IX.JJ contains a detailed bibliography on Visconti, including the script for *Obsession*; Overbey, ed., *Springtime in Italy*, contains the English version of "Anthropomorphic Cinema" cited here (pp. 83–85); the original Italian version is found in Adelio Ferrero, ed., *Visconti: il cinema*, which also includes Visconti's other theoretical statements on the cinema.
17. See Overbey, ed., *Springtime in Italy*, pp. 79–82 and 125–29 for English translations of Antonioni's "Concerning a Film about the River Po" and De Santis's "Towards an Italian Landscape." For a consideration of the influence of James M. Cain upon both Visconti's *Obsession* and Antonioni's *Story of a Love Affair* (to be analyzed in detail in chapter 4), see Allison Graham, "The Phantom Self: James M. Cain's Haunted American in the Early Neorealism of Visconti and Antonioni," *Film Criticism* 9 (1984), 47–62.

CHAPTER 2

1. This definition is provided by Geoffrey Nowell-Smith in *Visconti*, p. 32. For major critical discussions of Italian neorealism, see: Aristarco, *Antologia di "Cinema nuovo:" 1952–58*; Armes, *Patterns of Realism*; Bazin, *What Is*

Cinema? Part Two (or the original French edition); Brunetta, *Storia del cinema italiano dal 1945 agli anni ottanta*; Hiller, ed., *Cahiers du Cinéma—The 1950s*; Liehm, *Passion and Defiance: Film in Italy from 1942 to the Present*; Marcus, *Italian Film in the Light of Neorealism*; Miccichè, ed., *Il neorealismo cinematografico italiano*; and Overbey, ed., *Springtime in Italy* (English translations of critical articles and theoretical positions from the period). Faldini and Fofi, eds., *L'avventurosa storia del cinema italiano raccontata dai suoi protagonisti 1935–1959*, provides a rich collection of recollections of this period by actors, directors, producers, and other personalities.

2. See Bazin, *What Is Cinema? Part Two*.
3. See Zavattini's "A Thesis on Neo-Realism," in Overbey, ed., *Springtime in Italy*, pp. 67–78; a similar version of the same statement is also found translated as "Some Ideas on the Cinema," in Richard MacCann, ed., *Film: A Montage of Theories*, pp. 216–28.
4. Fellini, *Fellini on Fellini*, p. 152.
5. "A Discussion of Neo-Realism: Rossellini Interviewed by Mario Verdone," *Screen* 14 (1973–74), 70.
6. De Sica, *Miracle in Milan*, p. 4.
7. Cited by Gianni Rondolino, *Roberto Rossellini*, p. 5 (author's translation).
8. For example, Bazin's discussion of De Sica's *The Bicycle Thief* first defines the film as one of the best examples of "pure cinema," wherein there are "no more actors, no more story, no more sets" but continues, somewhat paradoxically, to state that the work represents "the perfect aesthetic *illusion* of reality" wherein "there is no more cinema" (*What Is Cinema? Part Two*, p. 60, my italics). Armes is even more aware of artifice's role in neorealist films, warning the naive viewer that "the neo-realist film remains a conscious artifact, never a simple transcription of reality" (*Patterns of Realism*, p. 187). Marcus, *Italian Film in the Light of Neorealism*, pp. 3–23, surveys the entire question of realism in postwar Italian culture. George Huaco's *The Sociology of Film Art* provides an interesting, if not completely convincing, attempt to explain neorealism by analyzing the directors' social backgrounds, their ideologies, and the political content of their works.
9. Calvino, *The Path to the Nest of Spiders*, p. vii; Calvino continues to make the suggestion that so far removed were neorealist novels from the canons of literary realism that "perhaps the right name for that Italian season, instead of 'neorealism,' should be 'neo-expressionism'" (p. xi).
10. Pavese, *American Literature: Essays and Opinions*, p. 197.
11. *Catalogo Bolaffi del cinema italiano 1945/1955* and *Catalogo Bolaffi del cinema italiano 1956/1965*, both edited by Gianni Rondolino, provide the most useful listing of films produced in the neorealist period; the second volume includes an invaluable listing of box-office receipts for the period by year of release. For discussions of the poor box-office showing of most

neorealist works within Italy itself, see: Lino Miccichè, "Per una verifica del neorealismo," in Miccichè, ed., *Il neorealismo cinematografico italiano*, pp. 7–30; or Spinazzola's *Cinema e pubblico: lo spettacolo filmico in Italia 1945–1965*.

12. These revealing statistics, as well as the texts of the agreements between ANICA and MPEA, may be found in Bizzarri and Solaroli, *L'industria cinematografica italiana*.

13. An English translation of the scripts of Rossellini's trilogy, from which all citations are taken, may be found in Stefano Roncoroni, ed., *Roberto Rossellini: The War Trilogy*. The most complete monographic study of Rossellini that exists is Peter Brunette, *Roberto Rossellini*; for complete bibliography on Rossellini, consult Adriano Aprà, ed., *Rosselliniana*; section IX.FF of the bibliography lists the major critical works on this director. Special attention should be called to several recent interpretations of *Rome, Open City*: Robert Burgoyne's "The Imaginary and the Neo-Real," *Enclitic* 3 (1979), 16–34; and Marcus, *Italian Film in the Light of Neorealism*, pp. 33–53.

14. Rossellini believed that montage was absolutely essential for the silent cinema but is no longer as crucial to filmmaking after the advent of the completely mobile camera: "Montage is no longer essential. Things are there, why manipulate them? . . . People who make films always believe that the cinema is a little like a miracle. . . . Technical procedures always astound people; not me, but many people. Well, the same thing is true for montage. It's a bit like the magician's magic wand. All those techniques are put inside and then a pigeon, a bouquet of flowers, or a water glass are made to appear. . . . Montage, taken at least in this sense, is something which disturbs me and which in my opinion is no longer necessary" (cited by Rondolino, *Roberto Rossellini*, p. 12, author's translation).

15. For a consideration of the interplay of illusion and reality in Italian neorealist films, see: Peter Bondanella, "Neorealist Aesthetics and the Fantastic: *The Machine to Kill Bad People* and *Miracle in Milan*," *Film Criticism* 3 (1979), 24–29; Ben Lawton, "Italian Neorealism: A Mirror Construction of Reality," *Film Criticism* 3 (1979), 8–23; and Leo Braudy, "Rossellini: From *Open City* to *General della Rovere*," in Baudy and Dickstein, eds., *Great Film Directors: A Critical Anthology*, pp. 655–73.

16. Bazin, *What Is Cinema? Part Two*, p. 37.

17. *Ibid.*, p. 62.

18. For Zavattini's various critical statements and scripts, see the bibliography in section X; in addition, see a special Zavattini issue of *Cinema & Cinema* 6, #20 (1979).

19. De Sica, "How I Direct My Films," in *Miracle in Milan*, p. 5. See section IX.O of the bibliography for the few scripts of De Sica's films available (both in English); John Darretta, *Vittorio De Sica: A Guide to References and*

Resources, provides an invaluable analysis of De Sica criticism; of special interest is Franco La Polla's "La città e lo spazio," *Bianco e nero* 36 (1975), 66–83, a brilliant analysis of De Sica's use of space and his original camera style in the neorealist period; see also Marcus, *Italian Film in the Light of Neorealism*, pp. 54–75, for a lengthy analysis of *The Bicycle Thief*.

20. Bazin, *What Is Cinema? Part Two*, pp. 51, 60.
21. While De Sica himself has rejected this comparison (Pierre Leprohon, *Vittorio De Sica*, p. 44), arguing that human solitude in his works has social rather than metaphysical causes, the distancing, alienating effects of his cinematic style clearly place his work close to Kafka's narrative technique in its impact upon the viewer.
22. Bazin, *What Is Cinema? Part Two*, p. 77.
23. *Ibid.*, p. 78.
24. Cited by Overbey, ed., in *Springtime in Italy*, p. 135.
25. An outline of the plots of these episodes may be found in *"La terra trema— appunti per un film documentario sulla Sicilia* (1948)," in Adelio Ferrero, ed., *Visconti: il cinema*, pp. 35–42.
26. Cited by Armes, *Patterns of Realism*, p. 126.
27. For both English and Italian versions of the script for *The Earth Trembles*, see section IX.JJ of the bibliography.
28. For a guide through the voluminous literature on Visconti, see Mancini, *Luchino Visconti: A Guide to References and Resources*. The most recent and complete account of Visconti's works is Di Giusti, *I film di Luchino Visconti*. Only very recently has American criticism been generally sympathetic to Visconti's particular brand of cinema, while his works have always been highly esteemed in Europe.

CHAPTER 3

1. For a general treatment of this period, see especially Brunetta, *Storia del cinema italiano dal 1945 agli anni ottanta*, and Faldini and Fofi, eds., *L'avventurosa storia del cinema italiano raccontata dai suoi protagonisti 1935–1959*; see also Liehm, *Passion and Defiance*; Marcus, *Italian Film in the Light of Neorealism*; Miccichè, ed., *Il neorealismo cinematografico italiano*, or its companion volume, *Il cinema italiano degli anni '50*, ed. Giorgio Tinazzi.
2. The best guide through the literature on Antonioni is Perry and Prieto, *Michelangelo Antonioni: A Guide to References and Resources*, which lists far more material than would be possible to include in section IX.A of the bibliography. The most useful recent critical works that analyze the director's entire career are Biarese and Tassone, *I film di Michelangelo Antonioni* and Chatman, *Antonioni or, The Surface of the World*; for a spectacular presenta-

tion of Antonioni's imagery and photographic style, see Mancini and Perrella, eds., *Architetture della visione/Architecture in Vision*.

3. See section IX.S for bibliography on Lattuada, the most recent and complete work being Cosulich's *I film di Alberto Lattuada*. No published script for *Without Pity* exists, although thanks to Tullio Pinelli, I was able to consult the unpublished original manuscript of the screenplay, which is now part of a newly acquired Fellini collection at the Lilly Library of Indiana University. A very useful interview with Lattuada may be found in Tassone, ed., *Parla il cinema italiano*, 1:141–74.

4. See section IX.M for bibliography on De Santis. For the complete script of *Bitter Rice*, including frame enlargements, see Carlo Lizzani, ed., *"Riso amaro": un film diretto da Giuseppe De Santis*; see also Marcus, *Italian Film in the Light of Neorealism*, pp. 76–95. For a consideration of the role played by the image of America and its cinema in the films of this period, see Peter Bondanella, "America and the Post-War Italian Cinema," *Rivista di studi italiani* 2 (1984), 106–25. A very important survey of the links between Hollywood and Italy (including much recently recovered footage from the silent era) is contained in an eight-part television program aired during 1988 by RAI's first channel: *Storie di cinema e di emigranti*, ed. Gianfranco Mingozzi.

5. Farassino, *Giuseppe De Santis*, pp. 26–27.

6. Armes, *Patterns of Realism*, p. 139.

7. For additional details on Italian censorship of the cinema, see a number of works in section IV.B of the bibliography on sex and censorship, in particular Argentieri's *La censura nel cinema italiano*.

8. Spinazzola's *Cinema e pubblico* contains an excellent treatment of the rise of "popular," as opposed to "art," cinema in Italy. This problem is perceptively analyzed by Aprà and Carabba, *Neorealismo d'appendice—per un dibattito sul cinema popolare: il caso Matarazzo*. For a discussion of so-called rosy neorealism in English with a detailed analysis of Luigi Comencini's *Bread, Love, and Fantasy (Pane, amore e fantasia*, 1953), see Marcus, *Italian Film in the Light of Neorealism*, pp. 121–43.

9. For Aristarco's works, see sections III.D (particular reference to films made during this period) and VII.A (more theoretical writings); the collected essays by Bazin on Italian cinema may be found in section VIII.A; Zavattini's collected works are listed in section X. The most convenient compilation in English of primary sources from this polemical debate that became known in the historiography of the Italian cinema as the "crisis of neorealism" may be found in two books devoted to Fellini: *Federico Fellini: Essays in Criticism*, ed. Bondanella, pp. 60–69; and *"La Strada": Federico Fellini, Director*, eds. Bondanella and Gieri, pp. 197–220. Artistarco's critique of the direction Italian cinema was taking is most persuasively argued, however, in his *Antologia di "Cinema nuovo": 1952–58*, pp. 1–151.

10. For this view (with particular reference to *Miracle in Milan*), see Canziani and Bragaglia, *La stagione neorealista*, pp. 95–99.
11. De Sica, *Miracle in Milan*, p. 13.
12. "A Discussion of Neo-Realism: Rossellini Interviewed by Mario Verdone," *Screen* 14 (1973–74), 70.
13. See Zavattini's "Some Ideas on the Cinema," in MacCann, ed., *Film: A Montage of Theories*.
14. The text of Boito's *novella* is included in Cavallaro, ed., *"Senso" di Luchino Visconti*; Aristarco, *Antologia di "Cinema nuovo": 1952–58*, pp. 90–98, 869–903, contains his important interpretation of *Senso* and discusses a number of differing views by major critics and writers; the best discussion of the film in English is in Marcus, *Italian Film in the Light of Neorealism*, pp. 164–87.
15. Baldelli, *Luchino Visconti*, p. 129.
16. Cited in Aristarco, *Antologia di "Cinema nuovo": 1952–58*, p. 880.
17. *Ibid.*, pp. 881–82 (author's translation).

CHAPTER 4

1. Maurice Scherer and François Truffaut, "Interview with Roberto Rossellini," *Film Culture* 1 (1955), 12; originally published in *Cahiers du Cinéma* 37 (1954). For detailed discussions of Rossellini's films from *The Ways of Love* to *Fear*, see: Brunette, *Roberto Rossellini*, pp. 85–176; and Masi and Lancia, *I film di Roberto Rossellini*, pp. 37–72. The influence of James Joyce upon *Voyage in Italy* is treated by Luciana Bohne, "Rossellini's *Viaggio in Italia*: A Variation on a Theme by Joyce," *Film Criticism* 3 (1979), 43–52.
2. Scherer and Truffaut, "Interview with Roberto Rossellini," p. 13.
3. Cited by Leprohon in *Michelangelo Antonioni: An Introduction*, pp. 89–90.
4. Cited by Geduld, ed., in *Film Makers on Film Making*, pp. 200–201.
5. *Ibid.*, p. 202.
6. Cameron and Wood, *Antonioni*, p. 66; for other detailed analyses of Antonioni's career in the 1950s, see: Biarese and Tassone, *I film di Michelangelo Antonioni*, pp. 69–95; Chatman, *Antonioni or, The Surface of the World*, pp. 12–50; and the Italian scripts contained in Di Carlo, ed., *Il primo Antonioni*, and Antonioni, *Sei film*. A more detailed analysis of the Antonioni bibliography can be found in Perry and Prieto, *Michelangelo Antonioni: A Guide to References and Resources*.
7. Richard Roud, *"The Passenger," Sight and Sound* 44 (1975), 134.
8. Fellini, *Fellini on Fellini*, p. 152. Critical comment on Fellini's works during this period is voluminous; for a guide through it, see Stubbs, *Federico Fellini: A Guide to References and Resources*; for Fellini's biography during the period, see Alpert, *Fellini: A Life*; Betti, *Fellini: An Intimate Portrait*; or

Kezich, *Fellini*. Fellini's own statements on filmmaking and his career during this decade may be found in *Fellini on Fellini* and in two Italian works: Fellini, *Fare un film*; and Fellini, *Intervista sul cinema*, ed. Grazzini. For a selection of some of the best criticism on Fellini's works, see Bondanella, ed., *Federico Fellini: Essays in Criticism*. Particularly useful for Fellini's development away from neorealism are the following: Bondanella and Gieri, eds. and trans., *"La Strada": Federico Fellini, Director*; Burke, *Federico Fellini: "Variety Lights" to "La Dolce Vita"*; Costello, *Fellini's Road*; Fava and Viganò, *The Films of Federico Fellini*; Marcus, *Italian Film in the Light of Neorealism*, pp. 144–63; and Rondi, *Il cinema di Fellini*.

9. Cited by Budgen in *Fellini*, pp. 91–92.
10. *Ibid.*, p. 92.
11. Nevertheless, Lattuada insists that while Fellini had the original idea for *Variety Lights*, the film was almost entirely his creation (see Tassone, ed., *Parla il cinema italiano*, 1:158); for a discussion of the creation of the film, see Cosulich, *Il film di Alberto Lattuada*, pp. 47–50. Lattuada's statement does not, however, explain why the film reflects Fellini's typical vision of the world rather than Lattuada's.
12. The *fotoromanzo* derives its name and peculiar character from the fact that its narrative is carried forward by photographs of actual people rather than cartoons, as in comic strips (*fumetti* in Italian). The *fotoromanzo* does, however, retain the balloon encircling the characters' words, typical of the *fumetti*. For the link between Fellini's cinema and the cartoon, see Mollica, ed., *Scenari: il fumetto e il cinema di Fellini*, or Kezich, *Fellini*, passim.
13. Fellini, *Early Screenplays*, p. 102 (from which all subsequent citations from the script of *The White Sheik* will be taken). Indiana University's Lilly Library Fellini collection now includes a number of the original treatments and screenplays of Fellini's early films written in collaboration with Tullio Pinelli: *Variety Lights*, *The White Sheik*, *I Vitelloni*, *La Strada*, and *The Nights of Cabiria*.
14. This interpretation of early Fellini was first advanced in my earlier essay, "Early Fellini: *Variety Lights*, *The White Sheik*, *The Vitelloni*," in Bondanella, ed., *Federico Fellini: Essays in Criticism*, pp. 220–39; the original Italian scripts of Fellini's first works are reprinted in Renzi, ed., *Il primo Fellini*; English versions of *I Vitelloni* and *The Swindle* are published in Fellini, *Three Screenplays*.
15. Taylor, *Cinema Eye, Cinema Ear*, pp. 27–29; for a detailed discussion of *La Strada*, including early reviews, the testimony of the director and his associates during the shooting of the film, and selected critical commentary, see Bondanella and Gieri, eds., *"La Strada": Federico Fellini, Director*.
16. "The Secret Life of Federico Fellini," in Bondanella, ed., *Federico Fellini: Essays in Criticism*, pp. 241, 247; reprinted in Bondanella and Gieri, eds., *"La Strada": Federico Fellini, Director*, pp. 240, 246.

17. "*La Strada*," in Bondanella, ed., *Federico Fellini: Essays in Criticism*, p. 58; reprinted in Bondanella and Gieri, eds., "*La Strada*": *Federico Fellini, Director*, p. 203.
18. "Italian Cinema," in Bondanella, ed., *Federico Fellini: Essays in Criticism*, p. 60; reprinted in Bondanella and Gieri, eds., "*La Strada*": *Federico Fellini, Director*, p. 204.
19. Agel, *Les chemins de Fellini*, pp. 128–29 (author's translation).
20. Fellini, *Three Screenplays*, p. 240.
21. Murray, *Fellini the Artist*, p. 97.
22. Cited from *Dante's Purgatory*, trans. Mark Musa (Bloomington: Indiana University Press, 1981), p. 52.
23. "Cabiria: The Voyage to the End of Neorealism," in Bondanella, ed., *Federico Fellini: Essays in Criticism*, p. 102.

CHAPTER 5

1. For more detailed information on the economic profile of the Italian film industry during this period, see the bibliography in section VI and especially Quaglietti, *Storia economico-politica del cinema italiano 1945–1980*, pp. 245–49. Of particular interest for the economic history of the Italian cinema are three extensive studies of two major Italian production companies: Barlozzetti, et al., eds., *Modi di produzione nel cinema italiano: La Titanus*; Bernardini and Martinelli, eds., *Titanus: la storia e tutti i film di una grande casa di produzione*; and Farassino and Sanguineti, *Lux Film: Esthétique et systéme d'un studio italien*. General discussions of the important films from this period may be found in: Brunetta, *Storia del cinema italiano dal 1945 agli anni ottanta*; Faldini and Fofi, eds., *L'avventurosa storia del cinema italiano raccontata dai suoi protagonisti 1960–1969*; Liehm, *Passion and Defiance*; Miccichè, ed., *Il cinema italiano degli anni '60*; and Michalczyk, *The Italian Political Filmmakers*.
2. For detailed discussions of Italian film comedy, see the bibliography in sections IV.D and V and especially: Aprà and Pistagnesi, eds., *Comedy, Italian Style 1950–1980* (the catalogue for the retrospective presented at the Museum of Modern Art in New York); d'Amico, *La commedia all' italiana: il cinema comico in Italia dal 1945 al 1975*; and a special 1987 issue of the French journal *CinémAction* edited by Michel Serceau. Interviews with major actors or directors of comic films may be found in Gili, *Arrivano i mostri: i volti della commedia italiana*, or in the two volumes of Tassone's *Parla il cinéma italiano*.
3. Cited by Gili, *Le cinéma italien*, p. 189.
4. Section IV.B contains a detailed bibliography on censorship problems in the Italian cinema; in particular, see Argentieri, *La censura nel cinema italiano* and Baragli, *Cinema cattolico*.

5. I owe this and subsequent definitions of comic form in film to Gerald Mast, *The Comic Mind: Comedy and the Movies*, pp. 5–6 and passim. The most lengthy analysis of Germi's work in English is in Marcus, *Italian Film in the Light of Neorealism*, pp. 228–44, but is limited to *Seduced and Abandoned*.

6. No script for this film exists, but see the excellent English translation of the film's source: *Bell'Antonio*, trans. Stanley Hochmann. For Bolognini, see di Montezemola, ed., *Bolognini*.

7. Cited in Ferlita and May, *The Parables of Lina Wertmüller*, p. 10.

8. Cited by Tassone, *Parla il cinema italiano*, 1:193–94; for Monicelli's collected remarks on film comedy, see his *L'arte della commedia*, ed. Codelli.

9. Sorlin, *Sociologia del cinema*, p. 101; for detailed studies of major Italian actors, see section V of the bibliography.

10. *Ibid.*, pp. 118–35, presents an excellent discussion of the Italian distribution network during this period.

11. The most important examples of episodic films directed by major figures in the Italian cinema are: Pasolini's *Ricotta* (*La ricotta*) from *Rogopag* (*Rogopag*, 1962); Visconti's *The Job* (*Il lavoro*) and Fellini's *The Temptations of Doctor Antonio* (*Le tentazioni del dottor Antonio*), both from *Boccaccio '70* (1962); and Fellini's *Toby Dammit* (*Toby Dammit*), from *Tales of Mystery* (*Histoires Extraordinaires*, 1968). The previously mentioned Fellini collection at Indiana University's Lilly Library includes the original screenplay with autograph corrections and sketches of *Toby Dammit*.

12. The word *peplum* derives from the Latin, referring to the robe of state worn by gods or men in classical times. For extensive bibliography on this important subject, see section IV.D and IX.L of the bibliography. Perhaps the most interesting director in this genre was Vittorio Cottafavi (1914–   ), who produced such representative films as *The Revenge of Hercules* (*La vendetta di Ercole*, 1960), and *Hercules Conquers Atlantis* (*Ercole alla conquista di Atlantide*, 1961). Sergio Leone's debut in the cinema as a director occurred in this genre: he was the director of the second crew on Mario Bonnard's *The Last Days of Pompeii* (*Gli ultimi giorni di Pompeii*, 1959), while *The Colossus of Rhodes* (*Il colosso di Rodi*, 1960), was his first film; in 1961–62, he assisted Robert Aldrich on *Sodom and Gomorrah*. The links between Hollywood and Cinecittà productions of such films set in classical times may be traced in Campari, *Hollywood-Cinecittà: il racconto che cambia*; Del Buono and Tornabuoni, eds., *Era Cinecittà: vita, morte e miracoli di una fabbrica di film*; and Kaufman and Lerner, *Hollywood sul Tevere*.

13. For the most detailed discussion of Rossellini's work for television during the period, see: Brunette, *Roberto Rossellini*, pp. 231–322; and Trasatti, *Rossellini e la televisione*, which also contains a number of the director's theoretical pronouncements on the relationship of cinema and television (esp. "Perché faccio film storici," pp. 185–88); for a detailed analysis of *The Rise to Power of Louis XIV*, see MacBean, *Film and Revolution*, pp. 209–29.

14. Cited from "'The Audience Should Not Be Just Passive Spectators': An Interview with Francesco Rosi," *Cinéaste* 7 (1975), 8; for additional analysis of Rosi's career, see section IX.EE of the bibliography, as well as Michalczyk, *The Italian Political Filmmakers*, pp. 19–63.
15. *Ibid.*, p. 8.
16. In addition to the Pontecorvo bibliography in section IX.CC of the bibliography, see Michalczyk, *The Italian Political Filmmakers*, pp. 182–209.
17. Ghirelli, *Pontecorvo*, p. 3.
18. David Wilson, "Politics and Pontecorvo," *Sight and Sound* 40 (1971), 161.
19. For criticism on Olmi, see section IX.Y of the bibliography; in addition, see the interviews with Olmi in Tassone, *Parla il cinema italiano*, 2:177–220; and in Samuels, *Encountering Directors*, pp. 99–115. For a detailed analysis of *The Sound of Trumpets*, see Marcus, *Italian Film in the Light of Neorealism*, pp. 211–27.
20. For criticism on the Taviani brothers, which has become quite substantial in the last few years, see section IX.HH of the bibliography; of particular interest are De Santi, *I film di Paolo e Vittorio Taviani*; and Ferrucci, ed., *La bottega Taviani: un viaggio nel cinema da San Miniato a Hollywood*.
21. Accialini and Coluccelli, *Paolo e Vittorio Taviani*, pp. 38, 10.
22. *Ibid.*, p. 12.
23. Pasolini's works have always elicited a copious amount of critical comment, and the major works and screenplays are listed in section IX.Z of the bibliography. The most recent critical survey of Pasolini's films is De Giusti, *I film di Pier Paolo Pasolini*, while in English, the best treatment remains Snyder's *Pier Paolo Pasolini*. Stack, ed., *Pasolini on Pasolini: Interviews with Oswald Stack*, contains an excellent introduction to the director's early works. Siciliano's biography, *Pasolini: A Biography*, presents the director's life story from the intimate point of view of a close friend. Pasolini's important theoretical statements on cinema from *Empirismo eretico* have been elegantly edited and translated by Barnett and Lawton in *Heretical Empiricism*.
24. Stack, *Pasolini on Pasolini*, pp. 42, 40.
25. "Pier Paolo Pasolini: An Epical-Religious View of the World," *Film Quarterly* 8 (1965), 32.
26. For critical analysis or screenplays of Bertolucci's works, see section IX.E of the bibliography.
27. For critical books and screenplays, see section IX.D of the bibliography.
28. Cited by Nichols, *Movies and Methods: An Anthology*, 1:552–55.

CHAPTER 6

1. A guide through the bewildering amount of material devoted to Visconti's mature cinema can be found in Mancini, *Luchino Visconti: A Guide to*

References and Resources; see section IX.JJ of the bibliography for major works and screenplays in print.

2. Nowell-Smith, *Visconti*, p. 177.

3. For analysis of Visconti's debt to melodrama, see Guido Fink, " 'Conosca il sacrifizio . . .': Visconti fra cinema e melodramma," in Ferrero, ed., *Visconti: il cinema*, pp. 84–97.

4. For this view of the trilogy, see Pietro Bianchi, "Trilogia germanica," in Visconti, *"Ludwig" di Luchino Visconti*, pp. 11–27.

5. Visconti, *"Morte a Venezia*: è un'opera della maturità," in Ferrero, ed., *Visconti: il cinema*, pp. 78–79 (author's translation).

6. Visconti, "Racconto storie come se raccontassi un Requiem," in Ferrero, ed., *Visconti: il cinema*, pp. 80–81 (author's translation).

7. The most strident of such attacks, a review of *The Damned* by John Simon, described Visconti's later output as "pretentious, posturing, bloated, and empty under all the window-dressing," and declared that "there is no more overblown, self-inflated and preposterous reputation in film than that of Luchino Visconti" (*Movies into Film*, p. 190).

8. David Wilson, *Sight and Sound* 39 (1969–70), 48.

9. See the major books and published screenplays listed in section IX.A of the bibliography; Perry and Prieto, *Michelangelo Antonioni: A Guide to References and Resources*, provides an excellent analysis of major critical statements on Antonioni during this period. The reader may also wish to read a collection of short stories by Antonioni with cinematic backgrounds, *That Bowling Alley on the Tiber: Tales of a Director*, that often provide clues to his film style.

10. Antonioni, *"L'Avventura": A Film by Michelangelo Antonioni*, ed. Amberg, pp. 213, 215.

11. For the complete translation of the Cannes statement Antonioni read at the film festival, see Antonioni, *"L'Avventura": A Film by Michelangelo Antonioni*, pp. 221–23.

12. Alberto Moravia, *The Empty Canvas*, trans. Angus Davidson (New York: Farrar, Giroux and Cudahy, 1961), pp. 3–4.

13. Alberto Moravia, *Man as an End: A Defense of Humanism*, trans. Bernard Wall (1966; reprint Westport, CT: Greenwood Press, 1976), p. 230.

14. Alan Casty, *Development of Film: An Interpretative History* (New York: Harcourt Brace Jovanovich, 1973), p. 277.

15. Antonioni, *"L'Avventura": A Film by Michelangelo Antonioni*, ed. Amberg, p. 223.

16. Cited in Andrew Sarris, ed., *Interviews with Film Directors*, pp. 28–29.

17. Cited in Sarris, ed., *Interviews with Film Directors*, p. 23.

18. Samuels, ed., *Encountering Directors*, p. 21.

19. Leprohon, *Michelangelo Antonioni* (French ed., author's translation), p. 100.

21. Sarris, ed., *Interviews with Film Directors*, p. 29.
22. Antonioni, *Sei film*, p. 497 (author's translation).
23. For a sampling of such articles, see Huss, ed., *Focus on "Blow-Up."*
24. Antonioni, *Blow-Up*, p. 45.
25. For more sympathetic views of *Zabriskie Point*, see: Angela M. Jeannet, "From Florence, Italy: on *Zabriskie Point*," *Italian Quarterly* 14 (1970), 93–104; Biarese and Tassone, *I film di Michelangelo Antonioni*, pp. 139–45; or Chatman, *Antonioni or, the Surface of the World*, pp. 159–68.
26. For major critical works and published screenplays, many in English, see section IX.P of the bibliography. Of particular interest are the detailed analyses of *8½* now available, as well as descriptions of the production of *La Dolce Vita*, *8½*, and *Fellini Satyricon*. See Fellini, *"8½": Federico Fellini, Director*, ed. Charles Affron; Benderson, *Critical Approaches to Federico Fellini's "8½"*; Boyer, *The Two Hundred Days of "8½"*; Hughes, *On the Set of "Fellini Satyricon": A Behind-the-Scenes Diary*; and Kezich, *Il dolce cinema*, which describes the making of *La Dolce Vita*. Indiana University's Lilly Library now owns the original manuscripts of several of these screenplays (including *La Dolce Vita*, *Juliet of the Spirits*, and *Fellini's Rome*).
27. Fellini, *Fellini on Fellini*, p. 157.
28. "*Casanova*: An Interview with Aldo Tassone," in Bondanella, ed., *Federico Fellini: Essays in Criticism*, p. 35 (Fellini's italics).
29. Samuels, ed., *Encountering Directors*, p. 121.
30. Fellini, "Ho inventato tutto, anche me," *Panorama* 18, #717 (14 January 1980), 92, 95 (author's translation).
31. Fellini, *Fellini on Fellini*, pp. 157–58.
32. Cited in Bondanella, ed., *Federico Fellini: Essays in Criticism*, p. 111.
33. Cited by Budgen, *Fellini*, p. 99.
34. Cited in Bondanella, ed., *Federico Fellini: Essays in Criticism*, p. 19. A detailed analysis of *Fellini Satyricon*, including a consideration of its literary source and the development of the film from the original story idea through various stages of the screenplay, may be found in Peter Bondanella, "Literature as Therapy: Fellini and Petronius," *Annali d'Italianistica* 6 (1988), 179–98 (an essay that was based upon an examination of the original screenplay now in the possession of Norma Giacchero).
35. For a more detailed description, to which my own viewing of *Roma* is indebted, see Walter C. Foreman, "Fellini's Cinematic City: *Roma* and Myths of Foundation," *Forum Italicum* 14 (1980), 78–98; for a discussion of Fellini's use of Roman imagery in *La Dolce Vita*, *Fellini Satyricon*, and *Roma*, see Bondanella, *The Eternal City: Roman Images in the Modern World*, pp. 237–55.
36. William J. Free, "Fellini's *I Clowns* and the Grotesque," in Bondanella, ed., *Federico Fellini: Essays in Criticism*, pp. 200–201; for Fellini's views on producing film for television, see pp. 11–16 of same volume.

37. Sarris, ed., *Interviews with Film Directors*, p. 182.
38. Fellini, "*Amarcord:* The Fascism within Us," in Bondanella, ed., *Federico Fellini: Essays in Criticism*, pp. 20, 21.
39. See Pasolini, "Il cinema impopolare," in *Empirismo eretico*, pp. 273–80.
40. Cited in Bondanella, ed., *Federico Fellini: Essays in Criticism*, p. 160.
41. *Ibid.*

CHAPTER 7

1. For critical studies of the Italian western or Sergio Leone, see sections IV.E and IX.T of the bibliography. The most important publications on this topic are Frayling, *Spaghetti Westerns: Cowboys and Europeans from Karl May to Sergio Leone;* and De Fornari, *Tutti i film di Sergio Leone.* The vogue of the so-called spaghetti western was initially attacked by a number of Italian critics (especially leftists), who identified the genre with American cultural or military imperialism. While many critics were unable to appreciate Leone's genius precisely because his films were popular with an enormous audience, young directors (Bernardo Bertolucci, Dario Argento) were immediately struck by his talent. Something of this leftist distaste for Leone's work may be discerned in Liehm's *Passion and Defiance* (pp. 184–87), which liquidates the phenomenon of Leone and the Italian western in several sparse paragraphs. In my opinion, such a negative view of Leone's contribution to the history of the Italian cinema, reminiscent of the equally puzzling critical neglect of the actor Totò by Italian leftist critics for many years, proves once again that popular audiences may sometimes recognize originality in the cinema before it is perceived by intellectuals or scholars with an ideological ax to grind.
2. Cited from *Focus on the Western*, ed. Jack Nachbar, p. 62.
3. John G. Cawelti, "Reflections on the New Western Films," in Nachbar, ed., *Focus on the Western*, p. 113.
4. According to Frayling (*Spaghetti Westerns: Cowboys and Europeans from Karl May to Sergio Leone*, p. 147), Kurosawa and his associates sued Leone and were awarded exclusive distribution rights for *A Fistful of Dollars* in Japan, Nationalist China, and South Korea, plus 15% of the worldwide box receipts; Leone's legal defense rested upon the claim that both directors should have paid Goldoni's estate for the use of his original plot.
5. For an excellent assessment of the impact of Morricone's music upon Leone's films, see Staig and Williams, *Italian Western: The Opera of Violence*, pp. 116–77.
6. Noel Simsolo, "Sergio Leone Talks," *Take One* 3 (1973), 30.
7. For box-office statistics on Leone's westerns, see Frayling, *Spaghetti Westerns: Cowboys and Europeans from Karl May to Sergio Leone*, p. 287; or De Fornari, *Tutti i film di Sergio Leone*, pp. 39, 51, 63, 75, 91, and 177.

8. Frayling, *Spaghetti Westerns: Cowboys and Europeans from Karl May to Sergio Leone*, p. 214.
9. For a guide through the maze of directors, films, characters, and pseudonyms, see Frayling, *Spaghetti Westerns: Cowboys and Europeans from Karl May to Sergio Leone*; or Moscati, *Western all'italiana*.
10. Frayling, *Spaghetti Westerns: Cowboys and Europeans from Karl May to Sergio Leone*, p. 52.
11. For a more sympathetic treatment of Godard's "western," see MacBean, *Film and Revolution*, pp. 116–38.
12. For critical analysis of *Burn!*, see: Ghirelli, *Pontecorvo*, pp. 72–89; Joan Mellen, "A Reassessment of Gillo Pontecorvo's *Burn!*," *Cinema* (1972–73), 38–46; and Michalczyk, *The Italian Political Filmmakers*, pp. 199–204.
13. For Ferreri's discussion of his intentions in this film, see the published screenplay (Ferreri, *Non toccare la donna bianca*) listed in section IX.Q of the bibliography.
14. Cited by Frayling, *Spaghetti Westerns: Cowboys and Europeans from Karl May to Sergio Leone*, p. 254.

CHAPTER 8

1. For criticism on Pasolini's films during this period, see the bibliography listed in section IX.Z; note that published scripts for all of the films except *Salò* are available in Italian or English. Since the first edition of this book was published, *Oedipus Rex* has indeed become available in America; in addition, a number of Pasolini's works are easily found in videocassette. For an account of Pasolini's death, see the biography *Pasolini* by Siciliano (first and last chapters). De Giusti, *I film di Pier Paolo Pasolini*, pp. 154–57, contains a very useful list of screenplays, essays, and interviews, only some of which have appeared in English translation.
2. For Pasolini's intentions in *Medea*, see the director's own remarks in Duflot, ed., *Entretiens avec Pier Paolo Pasolini*, pp. 112–13.
3. Stack, ed., *Pasolini on Pasolini*, p. 157.
4. Pasolini, "Why That of Oedipus Is a Story: Pier Paolo Pasolini," in Pasolini, *Oedipus Rex*, p. 7.
5. Duflot, ed., *Entretiens avec Pier Paolo Pasolini*, p. 85; for the most thorough analysis of *Teorema* in English, see Marcus, *Italian Film in the Light of Neorealism*, pp. 245–62; for a consideration of the links between Pasolini's cinema and his theoretical essays, see Naomi Greene, "Art and Ideology in Pasolini's Films," *Yale Italian Studies* 1 (1977), 311–26; or Teresa De Lauretis, "Language, Representation, Practice: Rereading Pasolini's Essays on Cinema," *Italian Quarterly* 21–22 (1980–81), 159–66.
6. Duflot, ed., *Entretiens avec Pier Paolo Pasolini*, pp. 59–71.

7. The most convincing interpretation of Pasolini's *Decameron* is Ben Lawton, "Boccaccio and Pasolini: A Contemporary Reinterpretation of *The Decameron*," in Musa and Bondanella, eds. and trans., Boccaccio, *The Decameron: A Norton Critical Edition*, pp. 306–22; it is republished as "The Storyteller's Art: Pasolini's *Decameron*," in Horton and Magretta, eds., *Modern European Filmmakers and the Art of Adaptation*, pp. 203–21.
8. Cited by Petraglia, *Pier Paolo Pasolini*, p. 16.
9. This statistical survey of Boccaccio's characters is found in Thomas G. Bergin, "An Introduction to Boccaccio," in Musa and Bondanella, eds. and trans., *The Decameron: A Norton Critical Edition*, p. 162.
10. Cited in Musa and Bondanella, eds. and trans., *The Decameron: A Norton Critical Edition*, p. 284.
11. Petraglia, *Pier Paolo Pasolini*, p. 15.
12. Cited by Gideon Bachmann in "Pasolini Today," *Take One* 4 (1973), 21.
13. Vittore Branca, "Boccaccio moderno," *Corriere della sera*, 20 March 1975, p. 3.
14. For an account of these sequels, itself contained in a girlie magazine masquerading as a serious critical review, see "The Merry Middle Ages" (no author listed) in the *Continental Film Review's* special number, *Italian Cinema in the Seventies*, pp. 42–51.
15. For *The Canterbury Tales* and *The Arabian Nights*, see Snyder, *Pier Paolo Pasolini*, pp. 142–63. An unintentionally humorous (not to mention misleading) discussion of Pasolini's views on homosexuality in *The Arabian Nights* may be found in Richard Dryer's "Pasolini and Homosexuality," in Willemen, ed., *Pier Paolo Pasolini*, pp. 57–63; for a sensible corrective, see Ben Lawton, "The Evolving Rejection of Homosexuality, the Sub-Proletariat, and the Third World in the Films of Pier Paolo Pasolini," *Italian Quarterly* 21 (1980), 167–73.
16. The phrase is from Snyder, *Pier Paolo Pasolini*, pp. 149–50.
17. Pasolini's rejection of his trilogy ("Abiura dalla *Trilogia della vita*") forms the introduction to the Italian script: Pasolini, *Trilogia della vita*, ed. Gattei, pp. 7–11. Pasolini's ideas on the Marquis de Sade are indebted to Roland Barthes's *Sade, Fourier, Loyola* (New York: Hill & Wang, 1976). For discussions on the making of *Salò*, see: Quintavalle, *Giornate di Sodoma*; and Gideon Bachmann, "Pasolini and the Marquis de Sade," *Sight and Sound* 45 (1974–75), 50–54, or his "Pasolini on de Sade," *Film Quarterly* 29 (1975–76), 39–45.
18. Pasolini, "Abiura dalla *Trilogia della vita*," in Pasolini, *Trilogia della vita*, p. 11 (author's translation).
19. For bibliography on Bertolucci, see section IX.E (in particular, the two books in English by Kline and Kolker, as well as the richly illustrated *Scene madri di Bernardo Bertolucci* by Ungari and Ranvaud). A number of important articles or interviews in English are devoted to Bertolucci's cinema. For *The Spider's*

Stratagem, see Peter Bondanella, "Borges, Bertolucci, and the Mythology of Revolution," *Teaching Language Through Literature* 27 (1988), 3–15; for *The Conformist*, see T. Jefferson Klein, "The Unconformist: Bertolucci's *The Conformist (1971),*" in Horton and Magretta, eds., *Modern European Filmmakers and the Art of Adaptation*, pp. 222–37; Marilyn Goldin, "Bertolucci on *The Conformist,*" *Sight and Sound* 40 (1971), 64–66; and Joan Mellen, "A Conversation with Bernardo Bertolucci," *Cinéaste* 5 (1973), 21–24. For *Last Tango in Paris*, see Gideon Bachmann, "'Every Sexual Relationship Is Condemned': An Interview with Bernardo Bertolucci apropos *Last Tango in Paris,*" *Film Quarterly* 26 (1973), 2–9.

20. Cited by Goldin in "Bertolucci on *The Conformist*," p. 66.
21. Klein, "The Unconformist," in Horton and Magretta, eds., *Modern European Filmmakers and the Art of Adaptation*, p. 231.
22. Cited by Goldin in "Bertolucci on *The Conformist*," p. 66.
23. Bertolucci, *Bernardo Bertolucci's "Last Tango in Paris,"* pp. 10, 202.
24. Cited by Mellen in "A Conversation with Bernardo Bertolucci," p. 24.
25. Cited by Bachmann in "'Every Sexual Relationship Is Condemned,'" p. 5.
26. *Ibid.*, pp. 4–5.
27. *Ibid.*, p. 7.
28. Bertolucci, *Bernardo Bertolucci's "Last Tango in Paris,"* pp. 46–47.
29. Julian C. Rice, "Bertolucci's *Last Tango in Paris,*" *Journal of Popular Film* 3 (1974), 161; for a more detailed consideration of Bertolucci's debt to other films and directors, see Ungari and Ranvaud, *Scene madri di Bernardo Bertolucci*.
30. Marsha Kinder and Beverle Houston, "Bertolucci and the Dance of Danger," *Sight and Sound* 42 (1973), 191.
31. Norman Mailer could not be further from the truth when he argued that Bertolucci's film would have been improved by including not less explicit sex but more of it: "Brando's real cock up Schneider's real vagina would have brought the history of film one huge march closer to the ultimate experience it has promised since its inception (which is to reembody life)" (cited in Bertolucci, *Bernardo Bertolucci's "Last Tango in Paris,"* p. 203). It is precisely the failure of pure, physical sex to satisfy human emotional needs that constitutes Bertolucci's story, and there is even less reason to suppose that a director with the extremely personal cinematic style that Bertolucci's works exhibit would be primarily interested in cinematic "realism" of the most elementary kind.
32. Cited by Tassone, *Parla il cinema italiano*, 1:80.
33. For a discussion of the making of 1900, see Gideon Bachmann, "Utopia Visited: Excerpts from a Diary on the Set of 1900," *Sight and Sound* 44 (1974–75), 28–33; or the documentary film made by Giuseppe Bertolucci (Bernardo's brother and the coauthor of the screenplay for 1900) entitled *The Making of 1900*.

34. Cited by Tassone, *Parla il cinema italiano*, 1:82; the most extensive discussion of Bertolucci and dreams is in Klein, *Bertolucci's Dream Loom: A Psychoanalytic Study of Cinema*.

CHAPTER 9

1. Kogan, *A Political History of Postwar Italy*, p. 47; for additional historical or cultural information on contemporary Italy, see the works cited in section II of the bibliography.
2. Contaldo and Fanelli, *L'affare cinema: multinazionali, produttori e politici nella crisi del cinema italiano*, p. 143. Figures reported by Quaglietti, *Storia economico-politica del cinema italiano*, p. 253, reflect a less-dramatic drop and a much higher total number of theaters in operation. Both sets of statistics show a definite decline. For other studies of the economic structure of the industry, see section VI of the bibliography.
3. For these figures, see the special cinema insert to *Panorama*, 20 October 1980, p. 135.
4. Quaglietti, *Storia economico-politica del cinema italiano*, pp. 245–46.
5. Cited from *Quo vadis cinema?* a television documentary aired on RAI's second channel 2 July 1981.
6. For available screenplays and criticism of these three films, see section IX.P of the bibliography. For *Casanova*, the fundamental statement by Fellini on the work is to be found in Betti and Angelucci, eds., *Casanova rendez-vous con Federico Fellini*, pp. 138–45; translated as "*Casanova*: An Interview with Aldo Tassone," in Bondanella, ed., *Federico Fellini: Essays in Criticism*, pp. 27–35. For the production of the film itself, see: Antonio Chemasi, "Fellini's *Casanova*: The Final Nights," *American Film* 1 (1976), 8–16; or De Santi and Monti, eds., *Saggi e documenti sopra "Il Casanova" di Federico Fellini*. Two excellent but different analyses of the film are: Millicent Marcus, "Fellini's *Casanova*: Portrait of the Artist," *Quarterly Review of Film Studies* 5 (1980), 19–34; and Joseph Markulin, "Plot and Character in Fellini's *Casanova*: Beyond *Satyricon*," *Italian Quarterly* 23 (1982), 65–74. On *Orchestra Rehearsal*, see two interviews with Fellini: "In chiave di Fellini," *Panorama*, 17 October 1978, pp. 168–85; and "L'Italia suonata di Fellini," *Euro*, June 1978, pp. 50–57. The original manuscript for *Orchestra Rehearsal* may be consulted in Indiana University's Lilly Library. For *The City of Women*, see Gideon Bachmann, "Federico Fellini: 'The Cinema Seen as a Woman . . . ,'" *Film Quarterly* 34 (1980–81), 2–9; and the stupendous photographic reproductions of work on the set in Monti, ed., *Bottega Fellini: "La città delle donne"—progetto, lavorazione, film*.
7. Leo Janos, "The New Fellini: Venice on Ice," *Time*, 17 May 1976, p. 77.
8. For a consideration of Visconti's last works, see Di Giusti, *I film di Luchino Visconti*, pp. 138–52.

9. For critical comment on Antonioni's Chinese documentary and *The Passenger*, see section IX.A of the bibliography, especially Biarese and Tassone, *I film di Michelangelo Antonioni*, pp. 146–56; and Chatman, *Antonioni or, The Surface of the World*, pp. 168–202. On the Chinese documentary, see also Umberto Eco, "De Interpretatione, or the Difficulty of Being Marco Polo," *Film Quarterly* 30 (1977), 8–12.

10. In addition to the bibliography on De Sica listed in section IX.O, see the film's source, Giorgio Bassani, *The Garden of the Finzi-Continis*, trans. William Weaver (New York: Harcourt, 1977).

11. For Rosi, see the bibliography in IX.EE, especially Bolzoni, *I film di Francesco Rosi*, as well as Michalczyk, *The Italian Political Filmmakers*, pp. 19–63; the best discussion of *Christ Stopped at Eboli* is in Marcus, *Italian Film in the Light of Neorealism*, pp. 339–59.

12. In the 1970s, Volonté emerged as the most important actor in the genre of the political film, working with Rosi, the Taviani brothers, Montaldo, Petri, and others; for an interview with him, see "Gian Maria Volonté Talks about Cinema and Politics," *Cinéaste* 7 (1975), 10–13.

13. Cited in MacBean, *Film and Revolution*, p. 269. For bibliography on Petri, see section IX.BB; in addition, see Michalczyk, *The Italian Political Filmmakers*, pp. 210–34; and Marcus, *Italian Film in the Light of Neorealism*, pp. 263–82.

14. MacBean, *Film and Revolution*. p. 272.

15. For a discussion of Bellocchio's last works, see Michalczyk, *The Italian Political Filmmakers*, pp. 149–81; and an interview in Tassone, *Parla il cinema italiano*, 2:9–44.

16. For scripts and the most recent criticism on the Taviani brothers, see the bibliography in section IX.HH that includes the English translation of the book by Gavino Ledda that inspired the film *Padre Padrone*.

17. For Olmi, see section IX.Y of the bibliography, as well as a lengthy interview in Tassone, *Parla il cinema italiano*, 2:179–220.

CHAPTER 10

1. In addition to the critical works and screenplays listed in section IX.J of the bibliography, see an excellent interview in Tassone, *Parla il cinema italiano*, 2:105–42.

2. Henry Giroux, "The Challenge of Neo-Fascist Culture," *Cinéaste* 6 (1975), 31–32; a companion article, equally violently opposed to *The Night Porter*, is Ruth McCormick's "Fascism à la Mode or Radical Chic?" *Cinéaste* 6 (1975), 31, 33–34, which not only sees the film as a neo-Fascist work but also drags out the old Stalinist chestnut that once defined Fascism as the "open, blatant, unabashedly repressive dictatorship of the bourgeoisie" (p. 34)—a formula that no serious scholar of *Italian* Fascism accepts any longer.

3. Teresa De Lauretis, "The Case of *The Night Porter*: A Woman's Film?" *Film Quarterly* 30 (1976–77), 35.
4. See Cavani's introduction to *Il portiere di notte*, p. viii and passim.
5. De Lauretis, "The Case of *The Night Porter*," p. 35.
6. See section IX.KK of the bibliography. In spite of the numerous monographs and screenplays published in Italy on various directors since the appearance of the first edition of this book, Lina Wertmüller remains unstudied in her native country with a serious work of criticism. In partial compensation for this critical neglect, Ms. Wertmüller has been named in 1988 to the post of commissioner to assist in the reorganization of Rome's Centro Sperimentale di Cinematografia.
7. Cited in Tassone, *Parla il cinema italiano*, 2:129–30.
8. An excellent treatment of Wertmüller's origins in the Italian comic tradition is William and Joan Magretta, "Lina Wertmüller and the Tradition of Italian Carnivalesque Comedy," *Genre* 12 (1979), 25–43.
9. For an analysis of sex and politics in *Mimi* or *Love and Anarchy*, see: Peter Biskind, "Lina Wertmüller: The Politics of Private Life," *Film Quarterly* 28 (1974–75), 10–16; or Marcus, *Italian Film in the Light of Neorealism*, pp. 313–38.
10. Wertmüller, *The Screenplays of Lina Wertmüller*, p. 194.
11. For once, I agree with John Simon, "Wertmüller's *Seven Beauties*—Call It a Masterpiece," *New York* 9 (2 February 1976), 24–31. The most important attack upon the film is Bruno Bettelheim's puzzling argument that *Seven Beauties* provides a "justification for accepting the world that produced concentration camps," in "Reflections: Surviving," *New Yorker* 52 (1976), 31–36, 38–39, 42–52; Bettelheim's unconvincing argument is effectively rebutted by Robert Boyers, "Politics & History: Pathways in European Film," *Salmagundi* 38–39 (1977), 50–79.
12. Wertmüller, *The Screenplays of Lina Wertmüller*, p. 325.
13. For recent critical comment on Scola's works, see section IX.GG of the bibliography.
14. For specific comment on *We All Loved Each Other Very Much*, see: Peter Bondanella, "La comédie 'métacinématographique' d'Ettore Scola," *CinémAction* 42 (1987), 91–99; Ben Lawton, "Italian Neorealism: A Mirror Construction of Reality," *Film Criticism* 3 (1979), 21–22; or Marcus, *Italian Film in the Light of Neorealism*, pp. 391–421.
15. Cited by Gili, *Le cinéma italien*, pp. 303–4.
16. Critical comment on these figures is somewhat limited: see sections IX.C, IX.X and IX.II of the bibliography for works on Avati, Moretti, and Troisi; in addition, see the general works in section III.E. In my opinion, only Avati and Moretti have matured into major talents since the publication of the first edition of this book, and both directors are deserving of far more attention (and far wider distribution of their works) than has occurred to date.

17. For Zeffirelli, see section IX.MM of the bibliography (of particular interest is the director's very interesting autobiography).
18. For Montaldo's *Marco Polo*, see section IX.W of the bibliography.

CHAPTER 11

1. The best general guides to Italian cinema since the publication of the first edition of this book are to be found in two catalogues published by Florence's Mediateca Regionale Toscana: Andrea Vannini, ed., *1975/1985: le strane occasioni del cinema italiano—i registi e i film*; and Maresa D'Arcangelo and Giovanni M. Rossi, eds., *1975/1985: gli anni maledetti del cinema italiano*. Together, the two reference works provide an exhaustive listing of Italian film production during the past decade, with particular attention to inaccessible information on younger directors or actors.
2. For the script of the film, including important critical statements, see *E la nave va*, eds. Federico Fellini and Tonino Guerra. The most important critical comment on the work is to be found in Tullio Kezich, *Fellini*, pp. 484–501; Raffaele Monti and Pier Marco De Santi, eds., *L'invenzione consapevole: disegni e materiali di Federico Fellini per il film "E la nave va"*; a series of articles in Gilles Ciment, ed., *Federico Fellini*; and in Hollis Alpert, *Fellini: A Life*, pp. 276–94. The Lilly Library Fellini Archive at Indiana University contains the original manuscript of the *soggetto* or story idea for this film.
3. See Ornella Volta, "Une analyse," and "Entretiens avec Federico Fellini," in Gilles Ciment, ed., *Federico Fellini*, pp. 138–41 and 150–55, and Gérard Legrand, "La soprano et le rhinocéros," in *ibid.*, pp. 146–49, for excellent discussions of the metacinematic aspect of *And the Ship Sails On*, to which this discussion is indebted.
4. For the scripts of these two works, see: Federico Fellini, *Ginger e Fred*, ed. Mimo Guerrini; and Federico Fellini, *Block-Notes di un regista*. The second volume also contains a number of scenarios for films Fellini considered but decided not to make. The Lilly Library Fellini Archive at Indiana University holds the original manuscript of *Ginger and Fred* as well as an early version of *Interview*.
5. Even though Fellini has made a number of films for television as well as several television commercials, such excursions into the mass media have always reflected Fellini's personal style rather than that typical of ordinary television programming. As he noted in an important statement on television, "In television one must see everything with clarity. The expressive operation of which I was speaking, basic to the cinema, is not required, is not possible in television, nor is it even appreciated. Therefore, in television the image has an illustrative character. It is an illustration, not an expression.

Rossellini was correct, then, when he understood immediately that the most direct method of communicating—and the best means of employing television—was to produce illustrated instructions—that is, a kind of lecture with slides which are emphasized from time to time by a simple editing" (cited from Federico Fellini, "Fellini on Television: A *Director's Notebook* and *The Clowns*," in Peter Bondanella, ed., *Federico Fellini: Essays in Criticism*, p. *14*).

6. Cited by Dario Zanelli, "*Intervista:* un film 'in diretta' dalla città del Cinema," in *Nel mondo di Federico*, p. 12 (author's translation).

7. For a detailed analysis of this point of view (with a juxtaposition of *Interview* and *Fellini: A Director's Notebook*), see Olivier Curchod, "J'écris *Paludes*," in Gilles Ciment, ed., *Fellini*, pp. 168–72, to which this discussion is indebted.

8. For an interesting discussion of this aspect of the film by its scriptwriter, see Gianfranco Angelucci, "Un'intervista tutta da vedere," *Intermedia Journal* 1, #5 (1987), 36–39, 41.

9. Cited from Federico Fellini, *Block-notes di un regista*, p. 182 (author's translation).

10. Cited by Gianfranco Angelucci in "Un'intervista tutta da vedere," p. 41 (author's translation).

11. Marcus, *Italian Film in the Light of Neorealism*, p. 372. The discussion on *The Night of the Shooting Stars* in this work (pp. 360–90) is the most interesting treatment of the film. For other examinations of the Tavianis' most recent films, see books by De Santi, Ferrucci, and Orto in section IX. HH of the bibliography.

12. The term is Millicent Marcus's in *Italian Film in the Light of Neorealism*, p. 369. For a survey of America's role in the postwar Italian cinema (including a consideration of *The Night of the Shooting Stars* in this context), see Peter Bondanella, "America and the Post-War Italian Cinema," *Rivista di studi italiani* 2 (1984), 106–25.

13. Paolo and Vittorio Taviani, *Good Morning, Babylon*, p. 80; for the most detailed discussion of this film, see Riccardo Ferrucci, ed., *La Bottega Taviani: un viaggio nel cinema da San Miniato a Hollywood*.

14. For Leone's *Once upon a Time in America*, see the spectacular photographic album *"C'era una volta in America": un film di Sergio Leone—Photographic Memories*, ed. Marcello Garofalo, or Oreste De Fornari, *Tutti i film di Sergio Leone*; for Bertolucci's *The Last Emperor*, see Edward Behr, *The Last Emperor*; Pu Yi, *From Emperor to Citizen*; and especially Enzo Ungari and Donald Ranvaud, eds., *Scene madri di Bernardo Bertolucci*.

15. In terms of record awards, Bertolucci's *Last Emperor* trails behind only a few films: *Ben Hur* (1959) with eleven Oscars; *West Side Story* (1961) with ten Oscars; it stands in third place for total awards with the legendary *Gone with the Wind* (1939) and with *Gigi* (1958). The awards Bertolucci's film received

were given for the best picture, direction, adaptation, photography, sound, editing, original music, set design, and costumes. Only two other Italian directors have received more than a single Oscar (De Sica and Fellini), but their awards were in the foreign film category.

16. Cited in "C'era una volta la mia America," *Radio corriere TV* 65, #6 (1988), p. 54 (author's translation); the same article serves as a preface to the collection of photographs edited by Marcello Garofalo.

17. Oreste De Fornari, *Tutti i film di Sergio Leone*, p. 110 (author's translation).

18. Cited in Tony Rayns, "Bertolucci in Beijing," *Sight and Sound* 57 (1986–87), 39.

19. Cited by Tony Rayns, "Model Citizen: Bernardo Bertolucci on Location in China," *Film Comment* 23 (1987), 36.

20. Tiziano Terzani, "Quanta ingenuità!: Bertolucci, é solo propaganda," *La Repubblica* (16 October 1987), p. 28.

21. For an excellent discussion of the characteristics of "art-film narration," deriving from techniques developed in European cinema in the late 1950s and the 1960s, especially the creation of a discontinuous narrative by means of flashbacks and flashforwards, see David Bordwell's *Narration in the Fiction Film*, pp. 74-98, 205-33.

22. Cited by Richard Corliss in "Signor Oscar," *Time* (25 April 1988), p. 40. Besides Bertolucci's record number of Oscars, the astonishing success of *The Last Emperor* in America may also be gauged by the fact that both the cover picture of this issue of *Time* and Corliss's cover story were devoted to Bertolucci's achievement.

23. For the most recent considerations of Scola's work, see Pier Marco De Santi and Rossano Vittori, *I film di Ettore Scola*; and Peter Bondanella, "La comédie 'métacinématographique' d'Ettore Scola," in Michel Serceau, ed., *La comédie italienne de Don Camillo à Berlusconi, CinémAction* 42 (1987), 91–99.

24. Cited by De Santi and Vittori, *I film di Ettore Scola*, pp. 158–59.

25. For the most recent critical work on Monicelli, see Stefano Della Casa, *Mario Monicelli*, a book that views *Let's Hope It's a Girl* in a surprisingly negative fashion.

26. For discussion of this film, see the recent studies by Chatman or Biarese and Tassone in section IX.A of the bibliography, as well as Gideon Bachmann's "A Love of Today: An Interview with Michelangelo Antonioni," *Film Quarterly* 36 (1983), 1–4.

27. For critical comment on Carpi's work, see Aldo Tassone, *Parla il cinema italiano*, 2:85–106.

28. For the available critical books on Avati and Moretti, see: Paolo Romano and Roberto Tirapelle, eds., *Il cinema di Pupi Avati*; Flavio De Bernardinis, *Nanni Moretti*; and Memmo Giovannini, et. al., *Nanni Moretti*.

29. I am grateful to Franco Mariotti of Cinecittà for providing me with these figures from the Ministero del turismo e dello spettacolo (the figure for 1987 is an estimated figure based upon projections from past years).

30. For information on ticket sales, the structure of the circuit, and its lack of quality equipment, see the articles "Luce in sala!" *Ciak si gira* 4, #5 (May 1988), 46–49; and "Inchiesta: lo stato delle sale," *Ciak si gira* 4, #6 (June 1988), 66–73 and 4, #7 (July 1988), 66–71.

A Selected Bibliography
on the Italian Cinema

The following bibliography includes only the most important items, usually books, anthologies, and scripts. Many brief articles have been omitted, although they may be cited in the footnotes.

I. REFERENCE

Ferraù, Alessandro, ed. *Annuario del cinema italiano 1987–1988*. Rome: Fusa Editrice, 1987.
Filmlexicon degli autori e delle opere. 9 vols. Rome: Edizioni di Bianco e Nero, 1958, 1974.
Reggiani, Stefano. *Dizionario del postdivismo: 101 attori italiani del cinema e della TV*. Turin: Edizioni RAI, 1985.
Rifilato, Gabriele, ed. *Cineteca d'autore*. Rome: Gallo Editore, 1986 [videocassettes available *in Italy*].
Rondolino, Gianni, ed. *Catalogo Bolaffi del cinema italiano 1945/1955*. Turin: Bolaffi, 1967.
———. *Catalogo Bolaffi del cinema italiano 1956/1965*. Turin: Bolaffi, 1967.
———. *Catalogo Bolaffi del cinema italiano 1966/1975*. Turin: Bolaffi, 1975.
———. *Catalogo Bolaffi del cinema italiano 1975/1976*. Turin: Bolaffi, 1976.
———. *Catalogo Bolaffi del cinema italiano 1976/1977*. Turin: Bolaffi, 1977.
———. *Catalogo Bolaffi del cinema italiano 1977/1978*. Turin: Bolaffi, 1978.
———. *Catalogo Bolaffi del cinema italiano 1978/1979*. Turin: Bolaffi, 1979.
———. *Catalogo Bolaffi del cinema italiano 1979/1980*. Turin: Bolaffi, 1980.
———. *Dizionario del cinema italiano 1945–1969*. Turin: Einaudi, 1969.
Schedario cinematografico. 8 vols. Rome: Centro dello spettacolo e della communicazione sociale, 1972.

447

Video Film in TV. 4th ed. Rome: Newcom Publications, 1987 [videocassettes available *in Italy*].

II.   BACKGROUNDS TO ITALIAN CINEMATIC CULTURE:
TWENTIETH-CENTURY ITALIAN HISTORY, CULTURE, AND
LITERATURE

Barzini, Luigi. *The Italians.* New York: Atheneum, 1964.
Bondanella, Peter, and Julia Conaway. *Dictionary of Italian Literature.* Westport, CT: Greenwood Press, 1979.
Caesar, Michael, and Peter Hainsworth, eds. *Writers & Society in Contemporary Italy: A Collection of Essays.* New York: St. Martin's Press, 1984.
Calvino, Italo. "Major Currents in Italian Fiction Today," *Italian Quarterly* 4 (1960), 3–15.
———. *The Path to the Nest of Spiders.* Trans. Archibald Colquhoun. New York: Ecco Press, 1976.
Cannistraro, Philip V., ed. *Historical Dictionary of Fascist Italy.* Westport, CT: Greenwood Press, 1982.
Coppa, Frank J., ed. *Dictionary of Modern Italian History.* Westport, CT: Greenwood Press, 1985.
Haycraft, John. *Italian Labyrinth: Italy in the 1980s.* London: Secker & Warburg, 1985.
Heiney, Donald. *America in Modern Italian Literature.* New Brunswick, NJ: Rutgers University Press, 1964.
———. *Three Italian Novelists: Moravia, Pavese, Vittorini.* Ann Arbor, MI: University of Michigan Press, 1968.
Jeannet, Angela, and Louise Barnett, eds. and trans. *New World Journeys: Contemporary Italian Writers and the Experience of America.* Westport, CT: Greenwood Press, 1977.
Kogan, Norman. *A Political History of Italy: The Postwar Years.* New York: Praeger, 1983.
Mack Smith, Denis. *Italy: A Modern History.* Ann Arbor, MI: University of Michigan Press, 1969.
———. *Mussolini.* New York: Knopf, 1982.
Pavese, Cesare. *American Literature: Essays and Opinions.* Trans. Edwin Fussell. Berkeley: University of California Press, 1970.
Praz, Mario. "Hemingway in Italy." In Roger Asselineau, ed., *The Literary Reputation of Hemingway in Europe,* pp. 93–125. New York: New York University Press, 1965.
Ruland, Richard. *America in Modern European Fiction: From Image to Metaphor.* New Brunswick, NJ: Rutgers University Press, 1976.

Spagnoletti, Giacinto. *La letteratura italiana del nostro secolo.* 3 vols. Milan: Mondadori, 1985.

Spotts, Frederic, and Theodore Wieser. *Italy: A Difficult Democracy—a Survey of Italian Politics.* Cambridge: Cambridge University Press, 1986.

III. GENERAL HISTORIES OF ITALIAN CINEMA

A. COMPREHENSIVE STUDIES

Bernardini, Aldo, and Jean A. Gili, eds. *Le cinéma italien de "La prise de Rome" (1905) à "Rome, ville ouverte" (1945).* Paris: Éditions du Centre Pompidou, 1986.

Bertetto, Paolo. *Il piú brutto del mondo: il cinema italiano oggi.* Milan: Bompiani, 1982.

Bondanella, Peter. "America and the Post-War Italian Cinema," *Rivista di studi italiani* 2 (1984), 106–25.

———. "Course File: Italian Cinema from Neorealism to the Present," *The American Film Institute Education Newsletter* 6 (1983), 4–10; reprinted in *College Course Files,* ed. Patricia Erens (University Film and Video Association, Monograph no. 5, 1986), pp. 104–109.

———. *Italian Cinema: From Neorealism to the Present.* 1st ed. New York: Frederick Ungar Publishers, 1983.

———. "Italy." In William Luhr, ed. *World Cinema Since 1945,* pp. 349–79. New York: Frederick Ungar Publishers, 1987.

Brunetta, Gian Piero. *Storia del cinema italiano 1895–1945.* Rome: Editori Riuniti, 1979.

———. *Storia del cinema italiano dal 1945 agli anni ottanta.* Rome: Editori Riuniti, 1982.

Buache, Freddy. *Le cinéma italien 1945–1979.* Lausanne: Éditions L'Age d'Homme, 1979.

Carpi, Fabio. *Cinema italiano del dopoguerra.* Milan: Schwarz, 1966.

Jaratt, Vernon. *The Italian Cinema.* New York: Arno Press, 1972 [original ed., 1951].

Leprohon, Pierre. *The Italian Cinema.* Trans. Roger Greaves and Oliver Stallybrass. London: Secker & Warburg, 1972 [rev. ed. of original French edition—Paris: Éditions Séghers, 1966].

Liehm, Mira. *Passion and Defiance: Film in Italy from 1942 to the Present.* Berkeley: University of California Press, 1984.

Livolsi, Marino, ed. *Schermi e ombre: gli italiani e il cinema del dopoguerra.* Florence: La Nuova Italia, 1988.

Lizzani, Carlo. *Il cinema italiano, 1895–1979*. 2 vols. Rome: Editori Riuniti, 1979. 2nd ed. published as *Il cinema italiano dalle origini agli anni ottanta*. Rome: Editori Riuniti, 1982.

Spinazzola, Vittorio. *Cinema e pubblico: lo spettacolo filmico in Italia 1945–1960*. Milan: Bompiani, 1974.

Torri, Bruno. *Cinema italiano: dalla realtà alle metafore*. Palermo: Palumbo Editore, 1973.

Turconi, Davide, and Antonio Sacchi, eds. *Bianconero rosso e verde: immagini del cinema italiano 1910–1980*. Florence: La Casa Usher, 1983.

B.   THE SILENT ERA

Barbina, Alfredo, ed. *Sperduti nel buio*. Turin: Nuova ERI, 1987.

Bernardini, Aldo. *Cinema muto italiano: ambiente, spettacoli e spettatori 1896/1904*. Bari: Laterza, 1980.

———. *Cinema muto italiano: arte, divismo e mercato 1910–1914*. Rome: Laterza, 1982.

———. *Cinema muto italiano: industria e organizzazione dello spettacolo 1905–1909*. Rome: Laterza, 1981.

———, and Flavia De Lucis, eds. *C'era il cinema: L'Italia al cinema tra Otto e Novecento (Reggio Emilio 1886–1915)*. Modena: Edizioni Panini, 1983.

Carillo, Massimo. *Tra le quinte del cinematografo: cinema, cultura e società in Italia 1900–1937*. Bari: Edizioni Dedalo, 1987.

Flint, R. W., ed. and trans. *Marinetti: Selected Writings*. New York: Noonday Press, 1972.

Kirby, Michael. *Futurist Performances*. New York: Dutton, 1971.

Martinelli, Vittorio, ed. *Il cinema muto italiano: i film degli anni venti / 1921–1922. Bianco e nero* 42, #1–3 (1981).

———. *Il cinema muto italiano: i film degli anni venti / 1923–1931. Bianco e nero* 42, #4–6 (1981).

———. *Il cinema muto italiano: i film del dopoguerra / 1919. Bianco e nero* 41, #1–3 (1980).

———. *Il cinema muto italiano: i film del dopoguerra / 1920. Bianco e nero* 41, #4–6 (1980).

Paolella, Roberto. *Storia del cinema muto*. Naples: Giannini, 1956.

Redi, Riccardo. *Ti parlerò . . . d'amore: cinema italiano fra muto e sonoro*. Turin: Edizioni ERI, 1986.

Verdone, Mario. *Cinema e letteratura del futurismo*. Rome: Edizioni di Bianco e Nero, 1968.

———, ed. *Poemi e scenari cinematografici d'avanguardia*. Rome: Officina Edizioni, 1975.

C. SOUND AND THE FASCIST ERA

Aprà, Adriano, and Patrizia Pistagnesi, eds. *The Fabulous Thirties: Italian Cinema 1929–1944.* Milan: Electra International, 1979.

Bernagozzi, Giampaolo. *Il mito dell'immagine.* Bologna: Editrice CLUEB, 1983.

Brancalini, Romano. *Celebri e dannati—Osvaldo Valenti e Luisa Freda: storia e tragedia di due divi del regime.* Milan: Longanesi, 1985.

Brunetta, Gian Piero. *Cinema italiano tra le due guerre: fascismo e politica cinematografica.* Milan: Mursia, 1975.

Carabba, Claudio. *Il cinema del ventennio nero.* Florence: Vallecchi, 1974.

Cardillo, Massimo. *Il duce in moviola: politica e divismo nei cinegiornali e documentari "Luce."* Bari: Edizioni Dedalo, 1983.

Gili, Jean A. *L'Italie de Mussolini et son cinéma.* Paris: Henri Veyrier, 1985.

———. *Stato fascista e cinematografia: repressione e promozione.* Rome: Bulzoni Editore, 1981.

Hay, James. *Popular Film Culture in Fascist Italy: The Passing of the Rex.* Bloomington: Indiana University Press, 1987.

Landy, Marcia. *Fascism in Film: The Italian Commercial Cinema, 1931–1943.* Princeton: Princeton University Press, 1986.

Laura, Ernesto G. *L'immagine bugiarda: mass-media e spettacolo nella Repubblica di Salò (1943–1945).* Rome: ANCCI, 1987.

Mancini, Elaine. *Struggles of the Italian Film Industry During Fascism, 1930–1935.* Ann Arbor, MI: University of Michigan Research Press, 1985.

Mida, Massimo, and Lorenzo Quaglietti, eds. *Dai telefoni bianchi al neorealismo.* Rome: Laterza, 1980.

Nuovi materiali sul cinema italiano 1929–1943. 2 vols. Ancona: Mostra sul cinema italiano, 1976.

Redi, Riccardo, ed. *Cinema italiano sotto il fascismo.* Venice: Marsilio Editori, 1979.

Savio, Francesco. *Ma l'amore no: realismo, formalismo, propaganda e telefoni bianchi nel cinema italiano di regime 1930–1943.* Milan: Sonzogno, 1975.

D. NEOREALISM AND ITS HERITAGE: 1945 TO 1968

Aprà, Adriano, and Claudio Carabba, eds. *Neorealismo d'appendice—per un dibattito sul cinema popolare: il caso Matarazzo.* Florence: Guaraldi Editore, 1976.

Aristarco, Guido. *Antologia di "Cinema nuovo": 1952–1958.* Florence: Guaraldi Editore, 1975.

———. *Sciolti dal giuramento: il dibattito critico-ideologico sul cinema negli anni Cinquanta.* Bari: Edizioni Dedalo, 1981.

Armes, Roy. *Patterns of Realism: A Study of Italian Neo-Realism*. Cranbury, NJ: A. S. Barnes, 1971.

Bernagozzi, Giampaolo. *Il cinema corto: il documentario nella vita italiana 1945–1980*. Florence: La Casa Usher, 1980.

Canziani, Alfonso, and Cristina Bragaglia. *La stagione neorealista*. Bologna: Cooperativa Libraria Universitaria Editrice, 1976.

Debreczeni, François, and Heinz Steinberg, eds. *Le néorealisme italien: bilan de la critique*. Paris: Études Cinématographiques, nos. 32–35, 1964.

Falaschi, Giovanni, ed. *Realtà e retorica: la letteratura del neorealismo italiano*. Florence: G. D'Anna, 1977.

Faldini, Franca, and Goffredo Fofi, eds. *L'avventurosa storia del cinema italiano raccontata dai suoi protagonisti 1935–1959*. Milan: Feltrinelli, 1979.

———. *L'avventurosa storia del cinema italiano raccontata dai suoi protagonisti 1960–1969*. Milan: Feltrinelli, 1981.

Ferrero, Adelio, Giovanna Grignaffini, and Leonardo Quaresima. *Il cinema italiano degli anni '60*. Florence: Guaraldi Editore, 1977.

Ferretti, Gian Carlo, ed. *Introduzione al neorealismo*. Rome: Editori Riuniti, 1977.

Kolker, Robert Phillip. *The Altering Eye: Contemporary International Cinema*. New York: Oxford University Press, 1983.

Marcus, Millicent. *Italian Film in the Light of Neorealism*. Princeton: Princeton University Press, 1986.

Materiali sul cinema italiano degli anni '50. Pesaro: Mostra Internazionale del Nuovo Cinema, 1978.

Miccichè, Lino, ed. *Il neorealismo cinematografico italiano*. Venice: Marsilio Editori, 1975.

Olivieri, Angelo. *L'imperatore in platea: i grandi del cinema italiano dal "Marc'Aurelio" allo schermo*. Bari: Edizioni Dedalo, 1986.

Overbey, David, ed. *Springtime in Italy: A Reader in Neorealism*. Hamden, CT: Archon Books, 1979.

Pellizzari, Lorenzo, ed. *Cineromanzo: il cinema italiano 1945–1953*. Milan: Longanesi, 1978.

Pintus, Pietro. *Storia e film: trent'anni di cinema italiano (1945–1975)*. Rome: Bulzoni Editore, 1980.

Taylor, John Russell. *Cinema Eye, Cinema Ear*. New York: Hill and Wang, 1964.

Tinazzi, Giorgio, ed. *Il cinema italiano degli anni '50*. Venice: Marsilio Editori, 1979.

———, and Marina Zancan, eds. *Cinema e letteratura del neorealismo*. Venice: Marsilio Editori, 1983.

Venti anni di cinema italiano nei saggi di ventotto autori. Rome: Sindacato nazionale giornalisti cinematografici italiani editore, 1965.

Vitzizzai, Elisabetta Chicco, ed. *Il neorealismo: antifascismo e popolo nella letteratura dagli anni trenta agli anni cinquanta*. Turin: Paravia, 1977.

Williams, Christopher, ed. *Realism and the Cinema: A Reader.* London: Routledge & Kegan Paul, 1980.

E. ITALIAN CINEMA FROM 1968 TO THE PRESENT

Attolini, Vito. *Sotto il segno del film (cinema italiano 1968/1976).* Bari: Mario Adda Editore, 1983.
D'Arcangelo, Maresa, and Giovanni M. Rossi, eds. *1975/1985: gli anni maledetti del cinema italiano.* Florence: Mediateca Regionale Toscana, 1986.
Faldini, Franca, and Goffredo Fofi, eds. *Il cinema italiano d'oggi 1970–1984 raccontato dai suoi protagonisti.* Milan: Mondadori, 1984.
Miccichè, Lino, ed. *Cinema italiano degli anni '70: cronache 1969–78.* Venice: Marsilio Editori, 1980.
——. *Il cinema italiano degli anni '60.* Venice: Marsilio Editori, 1975.
Montini, Franco, ed. *Una generazione in cinema: esordi ed esordienti italiani 1975–1988.* Venice: Marsilio Editori, 1988.
——. *I novissimi: gli esordienti nel cinema italiano degli anni '80.* Turin: Nuova ERI, 1988.
Morabito, Mimmo, ed. *Nostri autori prossimo venturi.* Florence: Mediateca Regionale Toscana, 1987.
Vannini, Andrea, ed. *1975/1985: le strane occasioni del cinema italiano—i registi e i film.* Florence: Mediateca Regionale Toscana, 1987.
Witcombe, Roger T. *The New Italian Cinema.* New York: Oxford University Press, 1982.

IV. THEMATIC OR GENERIC STUDIES

A. LITERATURE AND ITALIAN CINEMA

Attolini, Vito. *Dal romanzo al set: cinema italiano dalle origini ad oggi.* Bari: Edizioni Dedalo, 1988.
Brunetta, Gian Piero, ed. *Letteratura e cinema.* Bologna: Zanichelli, 1976.
D'avack, Massino. *Cinema e letteratura.* Rome: CanEsi, 1964.
Geduld, Harry, ed. *Authors on Film.* Bloomington: Indiana University Press, 1972.
Guidorizzi, Ernesto. *La narrativa italiana e il cinema.* Florence: Sansoni, 1973.
Horton, Andrew S., and Joan Magretta, eds. *Modern European Filmmakers and the Art of Adaptation.* New York: Frederick Ungar Publishers, 1981.
Lauretta, Enzo, ed. *Pirandello e il cinema.* Agrigento: Atti del Centro Nazionale di Studi Pirandelliani, 1978.

McDougal, Stuart Y., ed. *Made into Movies: From Literature to Film*. New York: Holt, Rinehart & Winston, 1985.
Vannini, Andrea, ed. *Vasco Pratolini e il cinema*. Florence: Edizioni La Bottega del Cinema, 1987.

B.   SEX AND CENSORSHIP

Argentieri, Mino. *La censura nel cinema italiano*. Rome: Editori Riuniti, 1974.
Baragli, Enrico, S. J. *Cinema cattolico: documenti della S. Sede sul cinema*. Rome: Città Nuova Editrice, 1965.
Boarini, Vittorio, ed. *Erotismo, eversione, merce*. Bologna: Cappelli, 1974.
Carrano, Patrizia. *Malafemmina: la donna nel cinema italiano*. Florence: Guaraldi Editore, 1977.
Fantuzzi, Virgilio. *Cinema sacro e profano*. Rome: Edizioni "La civiltà cattolica," 1983.
Grazzini, Giovanni. *Eva dopo Eva: la donna nel cinema italiano dagli anni Sessanta a oggi*. Rome: Laterza, 1980.
Grossini, Giancarlo. *120 film di Sodoma: analisi del cinema pornografico*. Bari: Edizioni Dedalo, 1982.
Massaro, Gianni. *L'occhio impuro: cinema, censura e moralizzatori nell'Italia degli Anni Settanta*. Milan: Sugar, 1976.
Mellen, Joan. *Women and their Sexuality in the New Film*. New York: Horizon Press, 1973.
Pastore, Sergio. *Proibitissimo: la censura nel tempo*. Naples: Adriano Gallina Editore, 1980.
Turroni, Giuseppe. *Viaggio nel corpo: la commedia erotica nel cinema italiano*. Milan: Moizzi Editore, 1979.
Tyler, Parker. *Screening the Sexes: Homosexuality in the Movies*. New York: Doubleday, 1973.

C.   ITALIAN FILM COMEDY

Aprà, Adriano, and Patrizia Pistagnesi, eds. *Comedy, Italian Style 1950–1980*. Turin: Edizioni RAI, 1986.
d'Amico, Masolino. *La commedia all'italiana: il cinema comico in Italia dal 1945 al 1975*. Milan: Mondadori, 1985.
Gili, Jean A. *Arrivano i mostri: i volti della commedia italiana*. Bologna: Cappelli, 1980.
———. *La comédie italienne*. Paris: Henri Veyrier, 1983.
Laura, Ernesto G. *Comedy Italian Style*. Rome: ANICA, n.d.
———. *Italian History Comedy Style*. Rome: ANICA, n.d.

Mast, Gerald. *The Comic Mind: Comedy and the Movies*. Indianapolis: Bobbs-Merrill, 1973.
Salizzato, Claver, and Vito Zagarrio, eds. *Effetto commedia: teoria, generi, paesaggi della commedia cinematografica*. Rome: Di Giacomo Editore, 1985.
Serceau, Michel, ed. *La comédie italienne de Don Camillo à Berlusconi*. *Ciném-Action*, 42 (1987).

D.   POLITICAL AND HISTORICAL THEMES AND GENRES

Argentieri, Mino, and Angelo Turchini. *Cinema e vita contadina: "Il mondo degli ultimi" di Gian Butturini*. Bari: Edizioni Dedalo, 1984.
Bondanella, Peter. *The Eternal City: Roman Images in the Modern World*. Chapel Hill: The University of North Carolina Press, 1987.
Brunetta, Gian Piero, et al., eds. *La cinepresa e la storia: fascismo, antifascismo, guerra e resistenza nel cinema italiano*. Milan: Edizioni scolastiche Bruno Mondadori, 1985.
Cammarota, Domenico. *Il cinema peplum*. Rome: Fanucci Editore, 1987.
Elley, Derek. *The Epic Film: Myth and History*. London: Routledge & Kegan Paul, 1984.
Farassino, Alberto, and Tatti Sanguineti, eds. *Gli uomini forti*. Milan: Mazzotta, 1983.
Freda, Riccardo. *Divoratori di celluloide: 50 anni di memorie cinematografiche e non*. Rome: Il Formichiere, 1981.
Gili, Jean A., ed. *Fascisme et résistance dans le cinéma italien (1922–1968)*. Paris: Études Cinématographiques, nos. 82–83, 1970.
Gori, Gianfranco. *Patria diva: la storia d'Italia nei film del ventennio*. Florence: La Casa Usher, 1988.
———, ed. *Passato ridotto: gli anni del dibattito su cinema e storia*. Florence: La Casa Usher, 1982.
Michalczyk, John J. *The Italian Political Filmmakers*. Rutherford, NJ: Fairleigh Dickinson University Press, 1986.
Solomon, Jon. *The Ancient World in the Cinema*. Cranbury, NJ: A. S. Barnes, 1978.
Sorlin, Pierre. *The Film in History: Restaging the Past*. Oxford: Basil Blackwell, 1980.
Zanotto, Piero, and Fiorello Zangrando. *L'Italia di cartone*. Padua: Livia Editrice, 1973.

E.   THE ITALIAN WESTERN

Ferrini, Franco, ed. *L'antiwestern e il caso Leone*. Rome: Bianco e Nero, 1971.
Frayling, Christopher. *Spaghetti Westerns: Cowboys and Europeans from Karl May*

to Sergio Leone. London: Routledge & Kegan Paul, 1981.
Moscati, Massimo. *Western all'italiana: guida ai 407 film, ai registi, agli attori*.
    Milan: Pan Editrice, 1978.
Nachbar, Jack, ed. *Focus on the Western*. Englewood Cliffs, NJ: Prentice-Hall,
    1974.
Roth, Lane. *Film Semiotics, Metz, and Leone's Trilogy*. New York: Garland, 1983.
Staig, Laurence, and Tony Williams. *Italian Western: The Opera of Violence*.
    London: Lorrimer, 1975.

F.   MISCELLANEOUS TOPICS

Arosio, Mario, Giuseppe Cereda, and Franca Iseppi. *Cinema e cattolici in Italia*.
    Milan: Editrice Massimo, 1974.
Giuliani, Gianna. *Le striscie interiori: cinema italiano e psicanalisi*. Rome:
    Bulzoni, 1980.
Ruggeri, Giovanni, and Mario Guarino. *Berlusconi: inchiesta sul signor TV*.
    Rome: Editori Riuniti, 1987.
Spot in Italy: 30 anni di pubblicità televisiva italiana. Turin: Edizioni ERI, 1987.

V.   STUDIES OF INDIVIDUAL ACTORS

Bernardini, Aldo. *Nino Manfredi*. Rome: Gremese Editore, 1979.
————, and Claudio G. Fava. *Ugo Tognazzi*. Rome: Gremese Editore, 1978; 1985
    (2nd ed.).
Caldiron, Orio. *Totò*. Rome: Gremese Editore, 1980.
Cammarota, Domenico. *Il cinema di Totò*. Rome: Fanucci Editore, 1986.
Carrano, Patrizia. *La Magnani*. Milan: Rizzoli, 1986 [preface by Federico Fel-
    lini].
Degiovanni, Bernard. *Vittorio Gassman*. Paris: Éditions PAC, 1980.
Delli Colli, Laura. *Monica Vitti*. Rome: Gremese Editore, 1987.
Detassis, Piera, and Mario Sesti, eds. *Bellissimi—generazioni di attori a confronto:
    L' "ultima onda" del cinema italiano e la grande tradizione del dopoguerra*.
    Ancona: Il Lavoro Editoriale, 1987.
Faldini, Franca, and Goffredo Fofi. *Totò: l'uomo e la maschera*. Milan: Felltrinelli,
    1977; *Totò*. 2nd rev. ed. Naples: Tullio Pironti Editore, 1987.
Fava, Claudio G. *Alberto Sordi*. Rome: Gremese Editore, 1979.
————, and Matilde Hochkofler. *Marcello Mastroianni*. Rome: Gremese Editore,
    1980.
Gambetti, Giacomo. *Vittorio Gassman*. Rome: Gremese Editore, 1982.
Gassman, Vittorio. *Un grande avvenire dietro le spalle: vita, amori e miracoli di un
    mattatore narrati da lui stesso*. Milan: Longanesi, 1981.

Hochkofler, Matilde. *Anna Magnani*. Rome: Gremese Editore, 1984.

Kezich, Tullio, ed. *Giulietta Masina (La Chaplin Mujer): Entrevista realizada por Tullio Kezich*. Valencia: Fernando Torres, 1985.

Laura, Ernesto G. *Alida Valli*. Rome: Gremese Editore, 1979.

Masi, Stefano, and Enrico Lancia. *Sophia Loren*. Rome: Gremese Editore, 1985.

Ponzi, Maurizio. *Gina Lollobrigida*. Rome: Gremese Editore, 1982.

Pruzzo, Pierro, and Enrico Lancia. *Amadeo Nazzari*. Rome: Gremese Editore, 1983.

VI. ECONOMIC OR SOCIOLOGICAL ANALYSES OF ITALIAN CINEMA (INCLUDING DISCUSSIONS OF GOVERNMENTAL INSTITUTIONS RELATED TO THE ITALIAN FILM INDUSTRY)

Alloway, Lawrence. *The Venice Biennale 1895–1968: From Salon to Goldfish Bowl*. Greenwich, CT: New York Graphic Society, 1968.

Aprà, Adriano, Giuseppe Ghigi, and Patrizia Pistagnesi, eds. *Cinquant'anni di cinema a Venezia*. Venice: Edizioni RAI, 1982.

Barlozzetti, Guido, et al., eds. *Modi di produzione del cinema italiano: La Titanus*. Rome: Di Giacomo Editore, 1985.

Bernardini, Aldo, and Vittorio Martinelli, eds. *Titanus: la storia e tutti i film di una grande casa di produzione*. Milan: Coliseum Editore, 1986.

Bizzari, Libero. *Il cinema italiano: industria, mercato, pubblico*. Rome: Edizioni Gulliver, 1987.

———, and Liberto Solaroli. *L'industria cinematografica italiana*. Florence: Parenti Editore, 1958.

Campari, Roberto. *Hollywood—Cinecittà: il racconto che cambia*. Milan: Feltrinelli, 1980.

Chiarini, Luigi. *Un leone e altri animali: cinema e contestazione alla Mostra di Venezia 1968*. Milan: Sugar Editore, 1969.

Contaldo, Francesco, and Franco Fanelli. *L'affare cinema: multinazionali, produttori, e politici nella crisi del cinema italiano*. Milan: Feltrinelli, 1979.

Del Buono, Oreste, and Lietta Tornabuoni, eds. *Era Cinecittà: vita, morte e miracoli di una fabbrica di film*. Milan: Bompiani, 1979.

Della Fornace, Luciana. *Il film in Italia dalla ideazione alla proiezione: strutture e processi dell'industria cinematografica*. Rome: Bulzoni, 1978.

Di Monte, Ezio, et al., eds. *La città del cinema (produzione e lavoro nel cinema italiano 1930/1970)*. Rome: Editrice R. Napoleone, 1979.

Farassino, Alberto, and Tatti Sanguineti. *Lux Film: Esthètique et système d'un studio italien*. Locarno: Éditions du Festival international du Film de Locarno, 1984.

Freddi, Luigi. *Il cinema*. 2 vols. Rome: L'Arnia, 1949.

Grassi, Giovanna, ed. *L'altro schermo: libro bianco sui cineclub, le sale d'essai e i punti di diffusione cinematografica alternativa.* Venice: Marsilio Editori, 1978.

Huaco, George A. *The Sociology of Film Art.* New York: Basic Books, 1965.

Ivaldi, Nedo. *La prima volta a Venezia: mezzo secolo di Mostra del cinema nei ricordi della critica.* Padua: Edizioni Studio Tesi, 1982.

Kaufman, Hank, and Gene Lerner. *Hollywood sul Tevere.* Milan: Sperling & Kupfer Editori, 1982.

Laura, Ernesto G., ed. *Tutti i film di Venezia 1932–1984.* 2 vols. Venice: La Biennale, 1985.

Magrelli, Enrico, ed. *Sull'industria cinematografica italiana.* Venice: Marsilio Editori, 1986.

Mariotti, Franco, ed. *I cinquant'anni di Cinecittà.* Rome: Ente autonomo di gestione per il cinema, 1989.

Monicelli, Mino, ed. *Cinema italiano: ma cos'è questa crisi?* Bari: Laterza, 1979.

Quaglietti, Lorenzo. *Storia economico-politica del cinema italiano 1945–1980.* Rome: Editori Riuniti, 1980.

Redi, Riccardo, and Claudio Camerini, eds. *Cinecittà 1: industria e mercato nel cinema italiano tra le due guerre.* Venice: Marsilio Editori, 1985.

Savio, Francesco. *Cinecittà anni trenta: parlano 116 protagonisti del secondo cinema italiano (1930–1943).* 3 vols. Rome: Bulzoni, 1979.

Sorlin, Pierre. *Sociologia del cinema.* Trans. Luca Baldini. Milan: Garzanti, 1979; trans. of original French ed. of 1977.

Vivere il cinema: cinquant'anni del Centro Sperimentale di Cinematografia. Rome: Presidenza del Consiglio dei Ministri, 1987.

VII.   FILM THEORY AND FILM CRITICISM

A.   FILM THEORY

Andrew, J. Dudley. *Concepts in Film Theory.* New York: Oxford University Press, 1984.

————. *The Major Film Theories: An Introduction.* New York: Oxford University Press, 1976.

Aristarco, Guido. *Il dissolvimento della ragione: discorso sul cinema.* Milan: Feltrinelli, 1965.

————. *Il mito dell'attore: come l'industria della star produce il sex symbol.* Bari: Edizioni Dedalo, 1983.

————. *Marx, le cinéma et la critique du film.* Paris: Études Cinématographiques, nos. 88–92, 1972.

————. *Storia delle teoriche del film.* Turin: Einaudi, 1951.

Barbaro, Umberto. *L'arte dell'attore.* Rome: Bianco e Nero Editore, 1950.

————. *Film: soggetto e sceneggiatura*. Rome: Edizioni Bianco e Nero, 1939.

————. *Il film e il risarcimento marxista dell'arte*. Rome: Editori Riuniti, 1974.

————. *Neorealismo e realismo*. Ed. Gian Piero Brunetta. 2 vols. Rome: Editori Riuniti, 1976.

Bazin, André. *Qu'est-ce que le cinéma?—IV. Une esthétique de la Réalité: le néo-réalisme*. Paris: Éditions du Cerf, 1962.

————. *What Is Cinema? Part Two*. Berkeley: University of California Press, 1971.

Bettetini, Gianfranco. *L'indice del realismo*. Milan: Bompiani, 1971.

————. *The Language and Technique of the Film*. The Hague: Mouton, 1973.

Bordwell, David. *Narration in the Fiction Film*. Madison, WI: University of Wisconsin Press, 1985.

Branigan, Edward. *Point of View in the Cinema: A Theory of Narration and Subjectivity in Classical Film*. Berlin: Mouton Publishers, 1984.

Bruno, Edoardo, ed. *Teorie e prassi del cinema in Italia 1950–1970*. Milan: Mazzota Editore, 1972.

————, ed. *Teorie del realismo*. Rome: Bulzoni Editore, 1977.

Casetti, Francesco. *Teorie del cinema del dopoguerra a oggi*. Milan: Espresso Strumenti, 1978.

Chiarini, Luigi. *Cinema e film: storia e problemi*. Rome: Bulzoni, 1972.

————. *Cinema quinto potere*. Bari: Laterza, 1954.

————. *Il film nella battaglia delle idee*. Rome: Fratelli Bocca, 1954.

De Lauretis, Teresa. "Semiotics, Theory, and Social Practice: A Critical History of Italian Semiotics." *Cine-Tracts* 2, #1 (1978), 1–14.

Eco, Umberto. "On the Contribution of Film to Semiotics." *Quarterly Review of Film Studies* 2, #1 (1977), 1–14.

————. "Towards a Semiotic Inquiry into the Television Message." *Working Papers in Cultural Studies* 3 (1972), 103–22.

Gambetti, Giacomo. *Zavattini mago e tecnico*. Rome: Ente dello spettacolo Editore, 1986.

MacCann, Richard, ed. *Film: A Montage of Theories*. New York: Dutton, 1966.

Mast, Gerald, and Marshall Cohen, eds. *Film Theory and Criticism: Introductory Readings*. 2nd ed. New York: Oxford University Press, 1979.

Nichols, Bill, ed. *Movies and Methods*. 2 vols. Berkeley: University of California Press, 1976, 1985.

Pasinetti, Francesco. *L'arte del cinematografo: articoli e saggi teorici*. Venice: Marsilio Editori, 1980.

Pasolini, Pier Paolo. "The Catholic Irrationalism of Fellini." *Film Criticism* 9, #1 (1984), 63–73.

————. "The Cinema of Poetry." *Cahiers du Cinéma in English* 6 (1966), 34–43 [also printed in Nichols, *Movies and Methods*, vol. 1].

————. "Cinematic and Literary Stylistic Features." *Film Culture* 24 (1962), 42–43.

————. *Empirismo eretico*. Milan: Garzanti, 1972.

————. *Heretical Empiricism*. Ed. Louise K. Barnett and trans. Ben Lawton and Louise K. Barnett. Bloomington: Indiana University Press, 1988.

————. "The Pesaro Papers." *Cinim* 3 (1969), 6–11.

————. "Pier Paolo Pasolini: An Epical-Religious View of the World." *Film Quarterly* 18 (1965), 31–45.

————. "The Scenario as a Structure Designed to Become Another Structure." *Wide Angle* 2, #1 (1978), 40–47.

Rosen, Philip, ed. *Narrative, Apparatus, Ideology: A Film Theory Reader.* New York: Columbia University Press, 1986.

Stam, Robert. *Reflexivity in Film and Literature: From Don Quixote to Jean-Luc Godard.* Ann Arbor, MI: University of Michigan Research Press, 1985.

B.   FILM CRITICS AND FILM CRITICISM IN ITALY (EXCLUSIVE OF THEORY)

Aristarco, Guido. *Neorealismo e nuova critica cinematografica: cinematografia e vita nazionale negli anni quaranta e cinquanta: tra rotture e tradizioni.* Florence: Nuova Guaraldi Editrice, 1980.

Bianca, Pividori, ed. *Critica italiana primo tempo: 1926–1934.* Rome: Studi monografici di Bianco e Nero, 1973.

Bolzoni, Francesco, ed. *Critici e autori: complici e/o avversari?* Venice: Marsilio Editori, 1976.

Brunetta, Gian Piero. *Umberto Barbaro e l'idea del neorealismo (1930–1943).* Padua: Liviana Editrice, 1969.

De Marchi, Bruno, ed. *La critica cinematografica in Italia: rilievi sul campo.* Venice: Marsilio Editori, 1977.

De Santis, Giuseppe. *Verso il neorealismo: un critico cinematografico degli anni quaranta.* Ed. Callisto Cosulich. Rome: Bulzoni Editore, 1982.

Flaiano, Ennio. *Lettere d'amore al cinema*. Milan: Rizzoli, 1978.

————. *Un film alla settimana*. Ed. Tullio Kezich. Rome: Bulzoni Editore, 1988.

Fofi, Goffredo. *Capire con il cinema*. Milan: Feltrinelli, 1977.

————. *Il cinema italiano: servi e padroni*. Milan: Feltrinelli, 1971.

Furno, Mariella, and Renzo Renzi, eds. *Il neorealismo nel fascismo: Giuseppe De Santis e la critica cinematografica 1941–1943.* Bologna: Edizioni della Tipografia Compositori, 1984.

Grazzini, Giovanni. *Il cinemondo: dieci anni di film, 1976–1986.* 11 vols. Rome: Laterza, 1987.

Hiller, Jim, ed. *Cahiers du Cinéma—the 1950s: Neo-Realism, Hollywood, New Wave.* Cambridge, MA.: Harvard University Press, 1985.

Kezich, Tullio. *Il cento film: un anno al cinema 1977–1978.* Milan: Edizioni Il Formichiere, 1978.

————. *Il dolce cinema*. Milan: Bompiani, 1978.

————. *Il filmottanta: cinque anni al cinema 1982–1986.* Milan: Mondadori, 1986.

————. *Il millefilm: dieci anni al cinema 1967–1977.* 2 vols. Milan: Edizioni Il Formichiere, 1978.

————. *Il nuovissimo millefilm: cinque anni al cinema 1977–1982.* Milan: Mondadori, 1983.

Moravia, Alberto. *Al cinema: centoquarantotto film d'autore.* Milan: Bompiani, 1975.

Renzi, Renzo. *Il fascismo involontario e altri scritti.* Bologna: Cappelli, 1975.

————. *La sala buia: diario di un disamore.* Bologna: Cappelli, 1978.

————. *Da Starace ad Antonioni: diario critico di un ex balilla.* Padua: Marsilio Editori, 1964.

VIII. COLLECTIONS OF INTERVIEWS WITH DIRECTORS

Garibaldi, Andrea, Roberto Giannarelli, and Guido Giusti, eds. *Qui comincia l'avventura del signor. . . : Dall'anonimato al successo ventitre protagonisti del cinema italiano raccontano.* Florence: La Casa Usher, 1984.

Geduld, Harry, ed. *Film Makers on Film Making.* Bloomington: Indiana University Press, 1967.

Georgakas, Dan, and Lenny Rubenstein, eds. *The Cinéaste Interviews on the Art and Politics of the Cinema.* Chicago: Lake View Press, 1983.

Gili, Jean, ed. *Le cinéma italien.* Paris: Union Générale d'Éditions, 1978.

Samuels, Charles Thomas, ed. *Encountering Directors.* New York: Putnam's, 1972.

Sarris, Andrew, ed. *Interviews with Film Directors.* New York: Avon, 1969.

Tassone, Aldo, ed. *Parla il cinema italiano.* 2 vols. Milan: Edizioni il Formichiere, 1979–1980.

IX. MAJOR ITALIAN DIRECTORS: CRITICAL WORKS AND SCRIPTS

A. MICHELANGELO ANTONIONI

Antonioni, Michelangelo. *"L'Avventura": A Film by Michelangelo Antonioni.* Ed. George Amberg. New York: Grove Press, 1969.

————. *Blow-Up.* New York: Frederick Ungar Publishers, 1971.

————. *Chung Kuo Cina.* Ed. Lorenzo Cucco. Turin: Einaudi, 1974.

————. *Il deserto rosso.* Ed. Carlo Di Carlo. Bologna: Cappelli, 1978.

————. *"L'eclisse" di Michelangelo Antonioni.* Ed. John Francis Lane. Bologna: Cappelli, 1962.

————. *Identificazione di una donna.* Ed. Aldo Tassone. Turin: Einaudi, 1983.
————. *Il mistero di Oberwald.* Ed. Gianni Massironi. Turin: Edizioni RAI, 1981.
————. *The Passenger.* Eds. Mark Peploe, Peter Wollen, and Michelangelo Antonioni. New York: Grove Press, 1975.
————. *Il primo Antonioni.* Ed. Carlo Di Carlo. Bologna: Cappelli, 1973 [Italian scripts for *Gente del Po, N. U., L'amorosa menzogna, Superstizione, I vinti, La signora senza camelie,* and *Cronaca di un amore*].
————. *Professione: reporter.* Ed. Carlo Di Carlo. Bologna: Cappelli, 1975.
————. *Screenplays of Michelangelo Antonioni.* New York: Orion Press, 1963 [English scripts for *L'avventura, Il grido, La notte,* and *L'eclisse*].
————. *Sei film.* Turin: Einaudi, 1964 [*Le amiche, Il grido, L'avventura, La notte, L'eclisse, Il deserto rosso* plus a preface by Antonioni].
————. *Tecnicamente dolce.* Ed. Aldo Tassone. Turin: Einaudi, 1976.
————. *That Bowling Alley on the Tiber: Tales of a Director.* Trans. William Arrowsmith. New York: Oxford University Press, 1986.
————. *"Zabriskie Point" di Michelangelo Antonioni.* Bologna: Cappelli, 1970.
Aristarco, Guido. *Su Antonioni: materiali per un'analisi critica.* Rome: La Zattera di Babele, 1988.
Biarese, Cesare, and Aldo Tassone. *I film di Michelangelo Antonioni.* Rome: Gremese Editore, 1985.
Cameron, Ian, and Robin Wood. *Antonioni.* London: Studio Vista, 1968.
Chatman, Seymour. *Antonioni or, The Surface of the World.* Berkeley: University of California Press, 1985.
Di Carlo, Carlo, ed. *Michelangelo Antonioni.* Rome: Edizioni di Bianco e Nero, 1964.
————, ed. *Michelangelo Antonioni 1942–1965.* Rome: Ente autonomo di gestione per il cinema, 1988.
Estève, Michele, ed. *Michelangelo Antonioni: l'homme et l'objet.* Paris: Études Cinématographiques, nos. 36–37, 1964.
Huss, Roy, ed. *Focus on "Blow-Up."* Englewood Cliffs, NJ: Prentice-Hall, 1971.
Leprohon, Pierre. *Michelangelo Antonioni.* 4th ed. Paris: Éditions Séghers, 1969.
————. *Michelangelo Antonioni: An Introduction.* Trans. Scott Sullivan. New York: Simon and Schuster, 1963 [translation of an early version of the original French edition].
Lyons, Robert J. *Michelangelo Antonioni's Neo-Realism: A World View.* New York: Arno Press, 1976.
Mancini, Michele, and Giuseppe Perrella, eds. *Architetture della visione/Architecture in Vision.* 2 vols. Rome: Coneditor, 1985.
Michelangelo Antonioni: identificazione di un autore. 2 vols. Parma: Pratiche, 1983, 1985.

Perry, Ted, and Raymond Prieto. *Michelangelo Antonioni: A Guide to References and Resources*. Boston: G. K. Hall, 1986.

Tinazzi, Giorgio. *Michelangelo Antonioni*. Florence: La Nuova Italia, 1974.

Trebbi, Fernando. *Il testo e lo squardo: antitesi, circolarità, incrociamento in "Professione: reporter": saggio su Michelangelo Antonioni*. Bologna: Pàtron Editore, 1976.

B. DARIO ARGENTO

Giovanni, Fabio. *Dario Argento: il brivido, il sangue, il thrilling*. Bari: Edizioni Dedalo, 1986.

Pugliese, Roberto. *Dario Argento*. Florence: La Nuova Italia, 1987.

C. PUPI AVATI

Maraldi, Antonio, ed. *Pupi Avati: cinema e televisione*. Gambettola: Centro Cinema Città di Cesena, 1980.

Romano, Paolo, and Roberto Tirapelle, eds. *Il cinema di Pupi Avati*. Verona: Sequenze, 1987.

D. MARCO BELLOCCHIO

Bellocchio, Marco. *China Is Near*. Ed. Tommaso Chiaretti. New York: Orion Press, 1969.

————. *Marcia trionfale*. Ed. Anna Maria Tatò. Turin: Einaudi, 1976.

————. *"Nel nome del padre" di Marco Bellocchio*. Ed. Goffredo Fofi. Bologna: Cappelli, 1971.

————. *"I pugni in tasca": un film di Marco Bellocchio*. Milan: Garzanti, 1967.

————. *Salto nel vuoto*. Eds. Alberto Barbera, Gianni Volpi, and Massimo Fagioli. Milan: Feltrinelli, 1981.

Bernardi, Sandro. *Marco Bellocchio*. Florence: La Nuova Italia, 1978.

Lodato, Nuccio. *Marco Bellocchio*. Milan: Moizzi Editore, 1977.

E. BERNARDO BERTOLUCCI

Alley, Robert. *Last Tango in Paris*. New York: Dell, 1972.

Behr, Edward. *The Last Emperor*. London: Futura, 1987.

Bertolucci, Bernardo. *Bernardo Bertolucci's "Last Tango in Paris."* New York:

Delta, 1973 [includes essays by Pauline Kael and Norman Mailer].
————. *Ultimo tango a Parigi*. Turin: Einaudi, 1973.
————, Franco Arcalli, and Giuseppe Bertolucci. *Novecento: atto primo* and *Novecento: atto secondo*. 2 vols. Turin: Einaudi, 1973.
Carroll, Kent E., ed. *Closeup: "Last Tango in Paris."* New York: Grove Press, 1973.
Casetti, Francesco. *Bernardo Bertolucci*. Florence: La Nuova Italia, 1978.
Di Giovanni, Norman Thomas. 1900. New York: Dell, 1976.
Estève, Michel, ed. *Bernardo Bertolucci*. Paris: Études Cinématographiques, nos. 122–26, 1979.
Kline, T. Jefferson. *Bertolucci's Dream Loom: A Psychoanalytic Study of Cinema*. Amherst, MA: University of Massachusetts Press, 1987.
Kolker, Robert Phillip. *Bernardo Bertolucci*. New York: Oxford University Press, 1985.
Ungari, Enzo, and Donald Ranvaud, eds. *Scene madri di Bernardo Bertolucci*. 2nd rev. ed. Milan: Ubulibri, 1987.
Yi, Pu. *From Emperor to Citizen*. Beijing: Foreign Languages Press, 1964.

F.   ALESSANDRO BLASETTI

Aprà, Adriano, and Riccardo Redi, eds. *"Sole": soggetto, sceneggiatura, note per la realizzazione*. Rome: Di Giacomo Editore, 1985.
Blasetti, Alessandro. *Il cinema che ho vissuto*. Ed. Franco Prono. Bari: Edizioni Dedalo, 1982.
————. *Scritti sul cinema*. Ed. Adriano Aprà. Venice: Marsilio Editori, 1982.
Salizzato, Claver, and Vito Zagarrio, eds. *"La corono di ferro": un modo di produzione italiano*. Rome: Di Giacomo Editore, 1985.

G.   MAURO BOLOGNINI

Brancati, Vitaliano. *Bell'Antonio*. Trans. Stanley Hochmann. New York: Frederick Ungar Publishers, 1978.
di Montezemola, Vittorio Cordero, ed. *Bolognini*. Rome: Istituto Poligrafico dello Stato, 1977.

H.   MARIO CAMERINI

Germani, Sergio Grmek. *Mario Camerini*. Florence: La Nuova Italia, 1980.

I. RENATO CASTELLANI

Castellani, Renato. *"Giulietta e Romeo" di Renato Castellani*. Ed. Stelio Martini. Bologna: Cappelli, 1956.
————. *Quattro soggetti*. Rome: Centro Cattolico Cinematografico, 1983.
Trassati, Sergio. *Renato Castellani*. Florence: La Nuova Italia, 1984.

J. LILIANA CAVANI

Cavani, Liliana. *"Milarepa" di Liliana Cavani*. Ed. Italo Moscati. Bologna: Cappelli, 1974.
————. *Il portiere di notte*. Turin: Einaudi, 1975.
————, and Enrico Medioli. *Oltre la porta*. Turin: Einaudi, 1982.
————, and Italo Moscati. *Lettere dall'interno: racconto per un film su Simone Weil*. Turin: Einaudi, 1974.
Tiso, Ciriaco. *Liliana Cavani*. Florence: La Nuova Italia, 1975.

K. LUIGI COMENCINI

Comencini, Luigi. *"Tutti a Casa": un film di Dino De Laurentis*. Rome: Salvatore Sciascia Editore, 1960.
Gili, Jean A. *Luigi Comencini*. Paris: Edilig, 1981.
Pirro, Ugo, and Luigi Comencini. *Delitto d'amore*. Milan: Vangelista Editore, 1974.
Trionfera, Claudio. *Italian Directors: Luigi Comencini*. Rome: ANICA, n.d.

L. VITTORIO COTTAFAVI

Rondolino, Gianni. *Vittorio Cottafavi: cinema e televisione*. Bologna: Cappelli, 1980.

M. GIUSEPPE DE SANTIS

Camerino, Vincenzo, ed. *Il cinema di Giuseppe De Santis*. Lecce: Elle Edizioni, 1982.
Cinema & Cinema 9, #30 (1982) [special De Santis issue].
De Santis, Giuseppe. *"Riso amaro": un film diretto da Giuseppe De Santis*. Ed. Carlo Lizzani. Rome: Officina Edizioni, 1978.

————. *Verso il neorealismo: un critico cinematografico degli anni quaranta.* Ed. Callisto Cosulich. Rome: Bulzoni Editore, 1982.

Farassino, Alberto. *Giuseppe De Santis.* Milan: Moizzi Editore, 1978.

Masi, Stefano. *Giuseppe De Santis.* Florence: La Nuova Italia, 1981.

Parisi, Antonio. *Il cinema di Giuseppe De Santis tra passione e ideologia.* Rome: Cadmo Editore, 1983.

N.   VITTORIO DE SETA

De Seta, Vittorio. *"Un uomo a metà" di Vittorio De Seta: analisi di un film in costruzione.* Ed. Filippo De Sanctis. Bologna: Cappelli, 1966.

O.   VITTORIO DE SICA

Agel, Henri. *Vittorio De Sica.* Paris: Éditions Universitaires, 1964.

Bartolini, Luigi. *Bicycle Thieves.* Trans. C. J. Richards. New York: Macmillan, 1950.

Bolzoni, Francesco. *Quando De Sica era Mister Brown.* Turin: Edizioni ERI, 1985.

Caldiron, Orio, ed. *Vittorio De Sica. Bianco e Nero* 36, nos. 9–12 (1975) [special De Sica issue with bibliography].

Darretta, John. *Vittorio De Sica: A Guide to References and Resources.* Boston: G. K. Hall, 1983.

De Sica, Vittorio. *The Bicycle Thief.* New York: Simon and Schuster, 1968.

————. *Lettere dal set.* Eds. Emi De Sica and Giancarlo Governi. Milan: Sugar Edizioni, 1987.

————. *Miracle in Milan.* Baltimore: Penguin, 1969.

Leprohon, Pierre. *Vittorio De Sica.* Paris: Éditions Séghers, 1966.

Mercader, Maria. *La mia vita con Vittorio De Sica.* Milan: Mondadori, 1978.

Pecori, Franco. *Vittorio De Sica.* Florence: La Nuova Italia, 1980.

P.   FEDERICO FELLINI

Agel, Genevière. *Les chemins de Fellini.* Paris: Éditions du Cerf, 1956.

Alpert, Hollis. *Fellini: A Life.* New York: Atheneum, 1986.

Benderson, Albert E. *Critical Approaches to Federico Fellini's "8½."* New York: Arno Press, 1974.

Benevelli, Elio. *Analisi di una messa in scena: Freud e Lacan nel "Casanova" di Fellini.* Bari: Dedali Libri, 1979.

Betti, Liliana. *Fellini: An Intimate Portrait.* Trans. Joachim Neugroschel. Boston: Little, Brown, 1979.

———, ed. *Federico A. C.: disegni per il "Satyricon" di Federico Fellini.* Milan: Edizioni Libri, 1970.

———, and Gianfranco Angelucci, eds. *Casanova rendez-vous con Federico Fellini.* Milan: Bompiani, 1975.

———, and Oreste Del Buono, eds. *Federcord: disegni per "Amarcord" di Federico Fellini.* Milan: Edizioni Libri, 1974.

Bìspurri, Ennio. *Federico Fellini: il sentimento latino della vita.* Rome: Editrice Il Ventaglio, 1981.

Bondanella, Peter, ed. *Federico Fellini: Essays in Criticism.* New York: Oxford University Press, 1978.

Boyer, Deena. *The Two Hundred Days of "8½."* New York: Garland, 1978.

Budgen, Suzanne. *Fellini.* London: British Film Institute, 1966.

Burke, Frank. *Federico Fellini: "Variety Lights" to "La Dolce Vita."* Boston: Twayne, 1984.

Cianfarani, Carmine, ed. *Federico Fellini: Leone d'Oro, Venezia 1985.* Rome: ANICA, 1985.

Ciment, Gilles, ed. *Federico Fellini.* Paris: Éditions Rivages, 1988.

Costello, Donald. *Fellini's Road.* Notre Dame, IN: University of Notre Dame Press, 1983.

de Miro, Ester, and Mario Guaraldi, eds. *Fellini della memoria.* Florence: La Casa Usher, 1983.

De Santi, Pier Marco. *I disegni di Fellini.* Rome: Laterza, 1982.

———, and Raffaele Monti, eds. *Saggi e documenti sopra "Il Casanova" di Federico Fellini.* Pisa: Quaderni dell'Istituto di storia dell'arte dell'Università di Pisa, 1978.

Estève, Michel, ed. *Federico Fellini: aux sources de l'imaginaire.* Paris: Études Cinématographiques, nos. 127–130, 1981.

———, ed. *Federico Fellini: "8½."* Paris: Études Cinématographiques, nos. 28–29, 1963.

Fava, Claudio G., and Aldo Viganò. *I film di Federico Fellini.* 2nd ed. Rome: Gremese Editore, 1987. English edition: *The Films of Federico Fellini.* Trans. Shula Curto. Secaucus, NJ: Citadel Press, 1985 [translation of first Italian edition of 1981].

Fellini, Federico. *Block–notes di un regista.* Milan: Longanesi, 1988.

———. *Casanova.* Eds. Federico Fellini and Bernardino Zapponi. Turin: Einaudi, 1977.

———. *La città delle donne.* Milan: Garzanti, 1980.

———. *I clowns.* Ed. by Renzo Renzi. Bologna: Cappelli, 1970; reprint, 1988.

———. *La Dolce Vita.* New York: Ballantine, 1961.

———. *La dolce vita.* Milan: Garzanti, 1981.

————. *Early Screenplays: "Variety Lights" and "The White Sheik."* New York: Grossman, 1971.

————. *"8½": Federico Fellini, Director.* Ed. Charles Affron. New Brunswick, NJ: Rutgers University Press, 1987.

————. *E la nave va.* Eds. Federico Fellini and Tonino Guerra. Milan: Longanesi, 1983.

————. *Fare un film.* Turin: Einaudi, 1980.

————. *Fellini on Fellini.* Eds. Anna Keel and Christian Strich. London: Eyre Methuen, 1976.

————. *Fellini Satyricon.* Ed. Dario Zanelli, Bologna: Cappelli, 1969.

————. *Fellini's Casanova.* Ed. Bernardino Zapponi. New York: Dell, 1977.

————. *Fellini's Satyricon.* Ed. Dario Zanelli. New York: Ballantine, 1970.

————. *Fellini TV: "Block–notes di un regista" / "I clowns."* Ed. Renzo Renzi. Bologna: Cappelli, 1972.

————. *Il film "Amarcord."* Eds. Gianfranco Angelucci and Liliana Betti. Bologna: Cappelli, 1974.

————. *Ginger e Fred.* Ed. Mimo Guerrini. Milan: Longanesi, 1986.

————. *Intervista sul cinema.* Ed. Giovanni Grazzini. Rome: Laterza, 1983. English edition: *Comments on Film.* Trans. Joseph Henry. Fresno: The Press of California State College at Fresno, 1988.

————. *Juliet of the Spirits.* Ed. Tullio Kezich. New York: Orion Press, 1965.

————. *La mia Rimini.* Bologna: Cappelli, 1987.

————. *"Moraldo in the City" & "A Journey with Anita."* Ed. and trans. John C. Stubbs. Urbana: University of Illinois Press, 1983.

————. *Le notti di Cabiria.* Milan: Garzanti, 1981.

————. *"8½" di Federico Fellini.* Ed. Camilla Cederna. Bologna: Cappelli, 1965.

————. *Il primo Fellini: "Lo sceicco bianco," "I vitelloni," "La strada," "Il bidone."* Ed. Renzo Renzi. Bologna: Cappelli, 1969.

————. *Prova d'orchestra.* Milan: Garzanti, 1980.

————. *Quattro film.* Intro. by Italo Calvino. Turin: Einaudi, 1974.

————. *Un regista a Cinecittà.* Milan: Mondadori, 1988.

————. *"Roma" di Federico Fellini.* Ed. Bernardino Zapponi. Bologna: Cappelli, 1972.

————. *Lo sceicco bianco.* Milan: Garzanti, 1980.

————. *La Strada.* Eds. François-Regis Bastide, Juliette Caputo, and Chris Marker. Paris: Éditions du Seuil, 1955.

————. *La Strada. L'Avant-Scène du Cinéma* 102 (April 1970), 7–51.

————. *"La Strada": Federico Fellini, Director.* Eds. Peter Bondanella and Manuela Gieri. New Brunswick, NJ: Rutgers University Press, 1987.

————. *"La strada": sceneggiatura originale di Federico Fellini e Tullio Pinelli.* Rome: Edizioni Bianco e Nero, 1955.

————. *Three Screenplays: "I Vitelloni," "Il Bidone," "The Temptations of Dr. Antonio."* New York: Grossman, 1970.

Grau, Jordi. *Fellini desde Barcelona*. Barcelona: Ambit Servicios Editoriales, 1985.
Hughes, Eileen Lanouette. *On the Set of "Fellini Satyricon": A Behind-the-Scenes Diary*. New York: Morrow, 1971.
Ketcham, Charles B. *Federico Fellini: The Search for a New Mythology*. New York: Paulist Press, 1976.
Kezich, Tullio. *Fellini*. Milan: Camunia Editrice, 1987.
————. *Il dolce cinema*. Milan: Bompiani, 1978.
Mollica, Vincenzo, ed. *Scenari: il fumetto e il cinema di Fellini*. Montepulciano: Editori del grifo, 1984.
Monti, Raffaele, ed. *Bottega Fellini: "La città delle donne"—progetto, lavorazione, film*. Rome: De Luca, 1981.
————, and Pier Marco De Santi, eds. *L'invenzione consapevole: disegni e materiali di Federico Fellini per il film "E la nave va."* Florence: Artificio, 1984.
Murray, Edward. *Fellini the Artist*. 2nd ed. New York: Frederick Ungar Publishers, 1985.
Pecori, Franco. *Federico Fellini*. Florence: La Nuova Italia, 1974.
Perry, Ted. *Filmguide to "8½."* Bloomington: Indiana University Press, 1975.
Prats, A. J. *The Autonomous Image: Cinematic Narration & Humanism*. Lexington: The University Press of Kentucky, 1981.
Price, Barbara Anne and Theodore. *Federico Fellini: An Annotated International Bibliography*. Metuchen, NJ: The Scarecrow Press, 1978.
Rondi, Brunello. *Il cinema di Fellini*. Rome: Edizioni di Bianco e Nero, 1965.
Rosenthal, Stuart. *The Cinema of Federico Fellini*. New York: A. S. Barnes, 1976.
Salachas, Gilbert. *Federico Fellini: An Investigation into His Films and Philosophy*. Trans. Rosalie Siegel. New York: Crown, 1969 [translation of original 1963 French edition].
Solmi, Angelo. *Fellini*. London: Merlin Press, 1967.
Strich, Christian, ed. *Fellini's Faces*. New York: Holt, Rinehart & Winston, 1982.
————, ed. *Fellini's Films: The Four Hundred Most Memorable Stills from Federico Fellini's Fifteen and a Half Films*. New York: Putnam's, 1977.
Stubbs, John C. *Federico Fellini: A Guide to References and Resources*. Boston: G. K. Hall, 1978.
Zanelli, Dario. *Nel mondo di Federico*. Preface by Federico Fellini. Turin: Nuova Edizioni ERI RAI, 1987.
Zanzotto, Andrea. *Filò: per il "Casanova" di Fellini*. Milan: Mondadori, 1988.

Q.   MARCO FERRERI

Accialini, Fulvio, and Lucia Coluccelli. *Marco Ferreri*. Milan: Edizioni il Formichiere, 1979.
Ferreri, Marco. *Chiedo asilo*. Ed. Maurizio Grande. Milan: Feltrinelli, 1980.

————. *L'ultima donna*. Ed. Anna Maria Tatò. Turin: Einaudi, 1976.
Grande, Maurizio. *Marco Ferreri*. Florence: La Nuova Italia, 1974.

R.   PIETRO GERMI

Attolini, Vito. *Il cinema di Pietro Germi*. Leece: Elle Edizioni, 1986.
Germi, Pietro. *"L'uomo di paglia" di Pietro Germi*. Ed. Fausto Montesanti.
    Bologna: Cappelli, 1958.

S.   ALBERTO LATTUADA

Bruno, Edoardo. *Italian Directors: Alberto Lattuada*. Rome: ANICA, n.d.
Camerini, Claudio. *Alberto Lattuada*. Florence: La Nuova Italia, 1981.
Cosulich, Callisto. *I film di Alberto Lattuada*. Rome: Gremese Editore, 1985.
Lattuada, Alberto. *"La steppa" di Alberto Lattuada*. Ed. Franco Calderoni.
    Bologna: Cappelli, 1962.
Oldoini, Enrico. *A proposito di "Così come sei": dall'idea al film*. Bologna:
    Cappelli, 1978.
Turroni, Giuseppe. *Alberto Lattuada*. Milan: Moizzi Editore, 1977.

T.   SERGIO LEONE

Cèbe, Gilles. *Sergio Leone*. Paris: Henri Veyrier, 1983.
Cumbow, Robert C. *Once upon a Time: The Films of Sergio Leone*. Metuchen, NJ:
    The Scarecrow Press, 1987.
De Fornari, Oreste. *Sergio Leone*. Milan: Moizzi Editore, 1977.
————. *Tutti i film di Sergio Leone*. Milan: Ubulibri, 1984.
Frayling, Christopher. *Spaghetti Westerns: Cowboys and Europeans from Karl May
    to Sergio Leone*. London: Routledge & Kegan Paul, 1981.
Gabutti, Diego. *C'era una volta in America*. Milan: Rizzoli, 1984.
Leone, Sergio. *"C'era una volta in America": un film di Sergio Leone—Pho-
    tographic Memories*. Ed. Marcello Garofalo. Rome: Editalia, 1988.
————. *Per un pugno di dollari*. Ed. Luca Verdone. Bologna: Cappelli, 1979.
Roth, Lane. *Film Semiotics, Metz, and Leone's Trilogy*. New York: Garland, 1983.

U.   CARLO LIZZANI

Lizzani, Carlo. *"Fontamara" dal romanzo di Ignazio Silone*. Turin: Edizioni ERI,
    1980.

————. *"L'oro di Roma" di Carlo Lizzani*. Ed. Giovanni Vento. Bologna: Cappelli, 1961.
————. *"Il processo di Verona" di Carlo Lizzani*. Ed. Antonio Savignano. Bologna: Cappelli, 1963.

V.   MARIO MONICELLI

Borghini, Fabrizio. *Mario Monicelli: cinquant'anni di cinema*. Pisa: Edizioni Master, 1985.
Della Casa, Stefano. *Mario Monicelli*. Florence: La Nuova Italia, 1986.
Monicelli, Mario. *L'arte della commedia*. Ed. Lorenzo Codelli. Bari: Edizioni Dedalo, 1986.
————. *"I compagni" di Mario Monicelli*. Ed. Pio Baldelli. Bologna: Cappelli, 1963.

W.   GIULIANO MONTALDO

Miles, Keith, and David Butler. *Marco Polo*. New York: Dell, 1982.
Montaldo, Giuliano, and Vincenzo Labella. *"Marco Polo": come nasce un film*. Turin: Edizioni RAI, 1980.

X.   NANNI MORETTI

De Bernardinis, Flavio. *Nanni Moretti*. Florence: La Nuova Italia, 1987.
Giovannini, Memmo, Enrico Magrelli, and Mario Sesti. *Nanni Moretti*. Naples: Edizioni scientifiche italiane, 1986.

Y.   ERMANNO OLMI

Aprà, Adriano, ed. *Il cinema di Ermanno Olmi*. Parma: Incontri Cinematografici Monticelli Terme—Parma, 1979.
Dillon, Jeanne. *Ermanno Olmi*. Florence: La Nuova Italia, 1985.
Kezich, Tullio, and Piero Maccarinelli, eds. *Da Roth a Olmi: "La leggenda del santo bevitore."* Siena: Nuova Immagine Cinema, 1988.
Olmi, Ermanno. *L'albero degli zoccoli*. Ed. Giacomo Gambetti. Turin: Edizioni RAI, 1980.
————. *"E venne un uomo": un film di Ermanno Olmi*. Eds. Giacomo Gambetti and Claudio Sorgi. Milan: Garzanti, 1965.

Tabanelli, Giorgio. *Ermanno Olmi: nascita del documentario poetico.* Rome: Bulzoni, 1987.

Z.   PIER PAOLO PASOLINI

Bertini, Antonio. *Teoria e tecnica del film in Pasolini.* Rome: Bulzoni, 1979.
Boccaccio, Giovanni. *The Decameron: A Norton Critical Edition.* Eds. and trans. Mark Musa and Peter Bondanella. New York: Norton, 1977.
De Giusti, Luciano. *I film di Pier Paolo Pasolini.* Rome: Gremese Editore, 1983.
Duflot, Jean, ed. *Entretiens avec Pier Paolo Pasolini.* Paris: Éditions Pierre Belfond, 1970.
Estève, Michel, ed. *Pier Paolo Pasolini: un "cinéma de poésie."* Paris: Études Cinématographiques, nos. 112–14, 1977.
————, ed. *Pier Paolo Pasolini: le mythe et le sacré.* Études Cinématographiques, nos. 109–11, 1976.
Ferrero, Adelio. *Il cinema di Pier Paolo Pasolini.* Milan: Mondadori, 1978.
Gervais, Marc. *Pier Paolo Pasolini.* Paris: Éditions Séghers, 1973.
Luzi, Alfredo, and Luigi Martellini, eds. *Pier Paolo Pasolini.* Urbino: Argalia Editore, 1973.
Pasolini, Pier Paolo. *"Edipo re": un film di Pier Paolo Pasolini.* Milan: Garzanti, 1967.
————. *Empirismo eretico.* Milan: Garzanti, 1972.
————. *Heretical Empiricism.* Ed. Louise K. Barnett and trans. by Ben Lawton and Louise K. Barnett. Bloomington: Indiana University Press, 1988.
————. *"Medea": un film di Pier Paolo Pasolini.* Milan: Garzanti, 1970.
————. *Oedipus Rex.* Trans. John Matthews. New York: Frederick Ungar, 1971.
————. *Poems.* Trans. Norman MacAfee. New York: Vintage, 1982.
————. *The Ragazzi.* Trans. Emile Capouya. New York: Grove Press, 1968.
————. *Teorema.* Milan: Garzanti, 1968.
————. *Trilogia della vita.* Ed. Giorgio Gattei. Milan: Mondadori, 1987.
————. *Uccellacci e uccellini.* Milan: Garzanti, 1975.
————. *Il vangelo secondo Matteo.* Milan: Garzanti, 1964.
————. *A Violent Life.* Trans. William Weaver. London: Jonathan Cape, 1968.
Petraglia, Sandro. *Pier Paolo Pasolini.* Florence: La Nuova Italia, 1974.
Quintavalle, Uberto Paolo. *Giornate di Sodoma: ritratto di Pasolini e del suo ultimo film.* Milan: Sugar, 1976.
Siciliano, Enzo. *Pasolini: A Biography.* Trans. John Shepley. New York: Random House, 1982.
Snyder, Stephen. *Pier Paolo Pasolini.* Boston: Twayne, 1980.
Stack, Oswald, ed. *Pasolini on Pasolini.* Bloomington: Indiana University Press, 1970.
Willemen, Paul, ed. *Pier Paolo Pasolini.* London: British Film Institute, 1977.

AA.   GIOVANNI PASTRONE

Radicati, Roberto, and Ruggero Rossi, eds. *"Cabiria": visione storica del III secolo a. c.* Turin: Museo Nazionale del Cinema, 1977.
Usai, Paolo Cherchi. *Giovanni Pastrone*. Florence: La Nuova Italia, 1985.

BB.   ELIO PETRI

Gili, Jean A., ed. *Elio Petri*. Nice: Faculté des Lettres et Sciences Humaines, 1974.
Rossi, Alfredo. *Elio Petri*. Florence: La Nuova Italia, 1979.

CC.   GILLO PONTECORVO

Ghirelli, Massino. *Gillo Pontecorvo*. Florence: La Nuova Italia, 1978.
Mellen, Joan. *Filmguide to "The Battle of Algiers."* Bloomington: Indiana University Press, 1973.
Pontecorvo, Gillo. *Gillo Pontecorvo's "The Battle of Algiers."* Ed. Piernico Solinas. New York: Scribner's, 1973.

DD.   DINO RISI

Bellumori, Cinzia. *Dino Risi*. Rome: ANICA, n.d.
Viganò, Aldo. *Dino Risi*. Milan: Moizzi Editore, 1977.

EE.   FRANCESCO ROSI

Bolzoni, Francesco. *I film di Francesco Rosi*. Rome: Gremese Editore, 1986.
Gili, Jean A., ed. *Francesco Rosi: Cinéma et pouvoir.* Paris: Éditions du Cerf, 1976.
Rosi, Francesco. *Salvatore Giuliano*. Ed. Tullio Kezich. Rome: Edizioni FA, 1961.
———. *"Uomini contro" di Francesco Rosi*. Ed. Callisto Cosulich. Bologna: Cappelli, 1970.
———, and Eugenio Scalfari. *"Il caso Mattei": un corsaro al servizio della repubblica*. Bologna: Cappelli, 1972.
Zambetti, Sandro. *Francesco Rosi*. Florence: La Nuova Italia, 1976.

FF.   ROBERTO ROSSELLINI

Aprà, Adriano, ed. *Rosselliniana: bibliografia internazionale, dossier "Paisà."* Rome: Di Giacomo Editore, 1987.
Baldelli, Pio. *Roberto Rossellini: i suoi film (1936–1972) e la filmografia completa.* Rome: Edizioni Samonà e Savelli, 1972.
Baudy, Leo, and Morris Dickstein, eds. *Great Film Directors: A Critical Anthology.* New York: Oxford University Press, 1978.
Brunette, Peter. *Roberto Rossellini.* New York: Oxford University Press, 1987.
Bruno, Edoardo, ed. *R. R. Roberto Rossellini.* Rome: Bulzoni Editore, 1979.
Guarner, José Luis. *Roberto Rossellini.* Trans. Elisabeth Cameron. New York: Praeger, 1970.
MacBean, James Roy. *Film and Revolution.* Bloomington: Indiana University Press, 1975.
Masi, Stefano, and Enrico Lancia. *I film di Roberto Rossellini.* Rome: Gremese Editore, 1987.
Pirro, Ugo. *Celluloide.* Milan: Rizzoli, 1983.
Roberto Rossellini. Rome: Ente autonomo di gestione per il cinema, 1987.
Rondolino, Gianni. *Roberto Rossellini.* Florence: La Nuova Italia, 1974.
Rossellini, Roberto. *Era notte a Roma.* Ed. Renzo Renzi. Bologna: Cappelli, 1960.
———. *Il mio metodo.* Ed. Adriano Aprà. Venice: Marsilio Editori, 1987.
———. *Quasi un'autobiografia.* Ed. Stefano Roncoroni. Milan: Mondadori, 1987. French edition: *Fragments d'une autobiographie.* Paris: Éditions Ramsay, 1987.
———. *La trilogia della guerra.* Ed. Stefano Roncoroni. Bologna: Cappelli, 1972.
———. *The War Trilogy.* Ed. Stefano Roncoroni. New York: Grossman, 1973.
Serceau, Michel. *Roberto Rossellini.* Paris: Éditions du Cerf, 1986.
Trasatti, Sergio. *Rossellini e la televisione.* Rome: La Rassegna Editrice, 1978.
Verdone, Mario. *Roberto Rossellini.* Paris: Éditions Séghers, 1963.

GG.   ETTORE SCOLA

Bondanella, Peter. "La comédie 'métacinématographique' d'Ettore Scola." In Michel Serceau, ed., *La comédie italienne de Don Camillo à Berlusconi.* *CinémAction* 42 (1987), 91–99.
De Santi, Pier Marco, and Rossano Vittori. *I film di Ettore Scola.* Rome: Gremese Editore, 1987.
Marinucci, Vincio. *Ettore Scola.* Rome: ANICA, n.d.
Scola, Ettore. *Una giornata particolare.* Milan: Longanesi, 1977.

HH. PAOLO AND VITTORIO TAVIANI

Accialini, Fulvio, and Lucia Coluccelli. *Paolo e Vittorio Taviani*. Florence: La Nuova Italia, 1979.
Aristarco, Guido. *Sotto il segno dello scorpione: il cinema dei fratelli Taviani*. Florence: Casa Editrice G. D'Anna, 1977.
Cooperativa Nuovi Quaderni, eds. *Cinema e utopia: i fratelli Taviani, ovvero il significato dell'esagerazione*. Parma: Nuovi Quaderni, 1974.
De Poli, Marco. *Paolo e Vittorio Taviani*. Milan: Moizzi Editore, 1977.
De Santi, Pier Marco. *I film di Paolo e Vittorio Taviani*. Rome: Gremese Editore, 1988.
Ferrucci, Riccardo, ed. *La bottega Taviani: un viaggio nel cinema da San Miniato a Hollywood*. Florence: La Casa Usher, 1987.
Ledda, Gavino. *Padre Padrone: The Education of a Shepherd*. Trans. George Salmanazar. New York: Urizen Books, 1979.
Orto, Nuccio. *La notte dei desideri: il cinema dei fratelli Taviani*. Palermo: Sellerio Editore, 1987.
Paolo & Vittorio Taviani: Leone d'Oro, Venezia 1986. Rome: ANICA, 1986.
Taviani, Paolo and Vittorio. *Padre padrone*. Bologna: Cappelli, 1977.
———. *San Michele aveva un gallo—Allonsanfan*. Bologna: Cappelli, 1974.
———. *Sotto il segno dello Scorpione—Il prato*. Turin: ERI, 1981.
———, with the collaboration of Tonino Guerra. *Good Morning, Babylon*. London: Faber & Faber, 1987.

II. MASSIMO TROISI

Troisi, Massimo, and Anna Pavignano. *Ricomincio da tre: sceneggiatura dal film*. Milan: Feltrinelli, 1981.

JJ. LUCHINO VISCONTI

Aristarco, Guido. *Su Visconti: materiali per un'analisi critica*. Rome: La Zattera di Babele, 1986.
Baldelli, Pio. *Luchino Visconti*. Milan: Mazzotta Editore, 1973; rev. ed. 1982.
Bencivenni, Alessandro. *Luchino Visconti*. Florence: La Nuova Italia, 1983.
De Giusti, Luciano. *I film di Luchino Visconti*. Rome: Gremese Editore, 1985.
Estève, Michel, ed. *Luchino Visconti: L'histoire et l'esthétique*. Paris: Études Cinématographiques, nos. 26–27, 1963.
Ferrera, Giuseppe. *Luchino Visconti*. Paris: Éditions Séghers, 1970.
Ferrero, Adelio, ed. *Visconti: il cinema*. Modena: Stampa Cooptip, 1977.

Mancini, Elaine. *Luchino Visconti: A Guide to References and Resources*. Boston: G. K. Hall, 1986.

Nowell-Smith, Geoffrey. *Visconti*. 2nd ed. New York: Viking, 1973.

Renzi, Renzo, and Caterina d'Amico de Carvalho, eds. *Visconti: il mio teatro*. 2 vols. Bologna: Cappelli, 1979.

Rondolini, Gianni. *Luchino Visconti*. Turin: UTET, 1981.

Schifano, Laurence. *Luchino Visconti: Les feux de la passion*. Paris: Perrin, 1987.

Servadio, Gaia. *Luchino Visconti: A Biography*. New York: Franklin Watts, 1983.

Simon, John. *Movies into Film*. New York: Dial Press, 1971.

Stirling, Monica. *A Screen of Time: A Study of Luchino Visconti*. New York: Harcourt Brace Jovanovich, 1979.

Tonetti, Claretta. *Luchino Visconti*. Boston: Twayne, 1983.

Villien, Bruno. *Visconti*. Barcelona: Calmann-Lévy, 1986 [in French].

Visconti, Luchino. *Bellissima*. Ed. Enzo Ungari. Bologna: Cappelli, 1977.

―――. *Boccaccio '70*. Eds. Carlo Di Carlo and Gaio Fratini. Bologna: Cappelli, 1962.

―――. *"La caduta degli dei (Götterdämmerung)" di Luchino Visconti*. Ed. Renzo Renzi. Bologna: Cappelli, 1969.

―――. *Il film "Il gattopardo" e la regia di Luchino Visconti*. Ed. Renzo Renzi. Bologna: Cappelli, 1963.

―――. *Gruppo di famiglia in un interno*. Ed. Renzo Renzi. Bologna: Cappelli, 1975.

―――. *"Ludwig" di Luchino Visconti*. Ed. Renzo Renzi. Bologna: Cappelli, 1973.

―――. *"Morte a Venezia" di Luchino Visconti*. Ed. Renzo Renzi. Bologna: Cappelli, 1971.

―――. *"Le notti bianche" di Luchino Visconti*. Ed. Renzo Renzi. Bologna: Cappelli, 1957.

―――. *Ossessione*. Ed. Enzo Ungari. Bologna: Cappelli, 1977.

―――. *"Rocco e i suoi fratelli" di Luchino Visconti*. Eds. Guido Aristarco and Gaetano Carancini. Bologna: Cappelli, 1960.

―――. *"Senso" di Luchino Visconti*. Ed. G. B. Cavallaro. Bologna: Cappelli, 1955.

―――. *La terra trema*. Ed. Enzo Ungari. Bologna: Cappelli, 1977.

―――. *Three Screenplays: "White Nights," "Rocco and His Brothers," "The Job."* Trans. Judith Green. New York: Orion Press, 1970.

―――. *Two Screenplays: "La Terra Trema," "Senso."* Trans. Judith Green. New York: Orion Press, 1970.

―――. *Vaghe stelle dell'orsa*. Ed. Renzo Renzi. Bologna: Cappelli, 1965.

―――, and Suso Cecchi d'Amico. *Alla ricerca del tempo perduto*. Milan: Mondadori, 1986.

KK.   LINA WERTMÜLLER

Ferlita, Ernest, and John R. May. *The Parables of Lina Wertmüller.* New York: Paulist Press, 1977.
Prats, A. J. *The Autonomous Image: Cinematic Narration & Humanism.* Lexington: The University Press of Kentucky, 1981.
Wertmüller, Lina. *The Head of Alvise.* New York: Morrow, 1982.
———. *The Screenplays of Lina Wertmüller.* Trans. Steven Wagner. New York: Quadrangle, 1977.

LL.   LUIGI ZAMPA

Zampa, Luigi. *Il primo giro di manovella: il romanzo sull'ambiente del cinema.* Rome: Trevi Editore, 1980.

MM.   FRANCO ZEFFIRELLI

Zeffirelli, Franco. *Il mio Gesù.* Milan: Sperling & Kupfer, 1977.
———. *Zeffirelli: An Autobiography.* New York: Weidenfeld & Nicolson, 1986.

X.   ITALIAN CAMERAMEN, SCRIPTWRITERS, MUSICIANS, AND SPECIAL EFFECTS TECHNICIANS

Amidei, Sergio. *Soggetti cinematografici.* Ed. Lorenzo Codelli. Gorizia: Comune di Gorizia, 1985.
Bertelli, Gian Carlo, and Pier Marco De Santi, eds. *Omaggio a Flaiano.* Pisa: Giardini, 1987.
De Santi, Pier Marco. *La musica di Nino Rota.* Rome: Laterza, 1983.
———, ed. *Omaggio a Nino Rota.* Pisa: Assessorato per gli Istituti Culturali del Comune di Pistoia, 1981.
Flaiano, Ennio. *Un film alla settimana.* Ed. Tullio Kezich. Rome: Bulzoni Editore, 1988.
Masi, Stefano. *Nel buio della moviola: introduzione alla storia del montaggio.* L'Aquila: La Lanterna Magica, 1985.
———. *Storie della luce.* L'Aquila: La Lanterna Magica, 1985.
Pellizzari, Lorenzo, ed. *Carlo Rambaldi e gli effetti speciali.* San Marino: AIEP Editore, 1987.
Prédal, René. *La photo de cinéma suivi d'un dictionnaire de cent chefs opérateurs.* Paris: Éditions du Cerf, 1985.

Questerbert, Marie-Christine. *Les scénaristes italiens*. Lausanne: 5 Continents-Hatier, 1988.

Tonino Guerra. Rimini: Maggioli Editore, 1985.

Tonti, Aldo. *Odore di cinema*. Florence: Vallecchi Editore, 1964.

Zavattini, Cesare. *Basta con i soggetti!* Ed. Roberta Mazzoni. Milan: Bompiani, 1979.

―――. *Diario cinematografico*. Ed. Valentina Fortichiari. Milan: Bompiani, 1979.

―――. *"I misteri di Roma" di Cesare Zavattini*. Ed. Francesco Bolzoni. Bologna: Cappelli, 1963.

―――. *Neorealismo ecc*. Ed. Mino Argentieri. Milan: Bompiani, 1979.

―――. *Opere*. Ed. Renato Barilli. Milan: Bompiani, 1974.

―――. *Una, cento, mille lettere*. Ed. Silvana Cirillo. Milan: Bompiani, 1988.

―――. *Zavattini: Sequences from a Cinematic Life*. Trans. William Weaver. Englewood Cliffs, NJ: Prentice-Hall, 1970.

Rental Information for
16-mm Prints and Videocassettes

This information on rental or purchase sources for 16-mm prints of Italian films and videocassettes has been checked for accuracy as carefully as possible. The reader is warned, however, that addresses, telephone numbers, and the holdings of individual companies (especially insofar as video material is concerned) change constantly. In addition to the current catalogues of the individual companies, the best single reference work, in large measure the basis of the present list, is to be found in James L. Limbacher, ed., *Feature Films: A Directory of Feature Films on 16mm and Videotape Available for Rental, Sale, and Lease* (New York: R. R. Bowker, 1985), 8th or subsequent editions.

I. Rental and or Purchase Sources

BUD

Budget Films
4590 Santa Monica Blvd.
Los Angeles, California 90029
(213) 660-0187

CG

Cinema Guild
1667 Broadway, Suite 802
New York, New York 10019
(212) 246-5522

CIV

Cinema Five
1585 Broadway
New York, New York 10036
(212) 975-0550

COR

Corinth Films
410 East 62th Street
New York, New York 10021
(212) 421-4770

FAC

Facets Multimedia, Inc.
1517 West Fullerton Avenue
Chicago, Illinois 60614
(800) 331-6197
(Videocassettes only)

FES

Festival Films
2841 Irving Avenue
South Minneapolis, Minnesota 55408
(612) 870-4744

FI

Films, Inc.
733 Wilmette Avenue, Suite 202
Wilmette, Illinois 60091
(800) 323-1406

IMAGES

Images Film
300 Phillips Park Road
Mamaroneck, New York 10543
(914) 381-2993

IVY

Ivy Films
165 West 46th Street
New York, New York 10036
(212) 382-0111

KI

Kino, International

250 West 57th Street
New York, New York 10019
(212) 586-8720

KP

Kit Parker Films
1245 Tenth Street
Monterey, California 93940
(800) 538-5838

L

The Liberty Company
695 West Seventh Street
Plainfield, New Jersey 07060
(201) 757-1450

MOMA

The Museum of Modern Art
Circulation Director
Department of Film
11 West 53rd Street
New York, New York 10019
(212) 956-4207

NL

New Line Cinema
575 Eighth Avenue
New York, New York 10023
(212) 674-7460

NY

New Yorker Films
16 West 61st Street
New York, New York 10023
(212) 247-6110

RI

Reel Images
P. O. Box C
Sandy Hook, Connecticut 06482
(203) 426-2574

SP

Speedimpex
44–45 39th Street
Long Island City, New York 11109
(718) 392-7477
(Videocassettes only, most in the
original Italian without subtitles)

SW

Swank Motion Pictures
201 Jefferson Avenue
St. Louis, Missouri 63166
(800) 325-3344

TIF

Tamarelle's International Films
110 Cohasset Stage Road
Chico, California 95926
(800) 356-3577
(Videocassettes only)

TWF

Trans-World Films
332 South Michigan Avenue
Chicago, Illinois 60604
(312) 922-1530

TWY

Twyman Films
4700 Wadsworth Road
P. O. Box 605
Dayton, Ohio 45414
(513) 276-5941

WFC

Wholesome Film Center
20 Melrose Street
Boston, Massachusetts 02116
(617) 426-0155

CWL

Clem Williams Films
2240 Noblestown Road
Pittsburgh, Pennsylvania 15205
(800) 245-1146

II. Selected Italian Films Listed by Director and Coded to Distributors

Videocassettes of Italian films sold or rented by the two main sources in the United States (FAC or TIF) are naturally in the format suitable for American VHS video recorders. Since many of the users of this book may also wish to obtain the original *Italian* videotapes and may have access to a video recorder capable of playing videocassettes in the European format (PAL), videocassettes available in this format in Italy have been indicated with an asterisk (*). Specific information as to the distributors of such videocassettes in Italy may be obtained from the two publications dedicated to Italian videotapes listed in section I of the bibliography.

GIANFRANCO ANGELUCCI
Honey   FAC

MICHELANGELO ANTONIONI
L'Avventura   FAC, FI, TIF
Blow-Up   FAC, FI, *
The Eclipse   FAC, MOMA, WFC, *
Identification of a Woman   SP, *
The Lady without Camellias   CG
Love in the City   BUD, FAC, L,
   NYF, TIF
La Notte   NYF
The Passenger   FAC, FI
Red Desert   FAC, FI, SP, TIF, *
Story of a Love Affair   NYF
Zabriskie Point   FAC, FI, TIF, *

DARIO ARGENTO
The Bird with the Crystal
   Plumage   BUD, *
The Cat O'Nine Tails   TWF, *
Deep Red   FI, *
Suspira   FI, *

PUPI AVATI
Christmas Present   *
The Employees   *
Graduation Party   *

MARIO BAVA
Baron Blood   SW
Black Sabbath   BUD, IVY
Hercules in the Haunted World   BUD
Planet of the Vampires   FI

MARCO BELLOCCHIO
China Is Near   COR, TIF
The Devil in the Flesh   *
The Eyes, the Mouth   FAC, SW, TIF
Fists in the Pockets   KP
Henry IV   FAC, TIF
In the Name of the Father   NYF

BERNARDO BERTOLUCCI
Before the Revolution   FAC, NYF
The Conformist   FAC, FI
The Grim Reaper   FAC
The Last Emperor   FAC, SW, TIF, *
Last Tango in Paris   FAC, FI, *
Luna   FI, TWY
The Making of 1900   FI, L
1900   FAC, FI
Partner   FAC, NYF
The Spider's Stratagem   NYF
The Tragedy of a Ridiculous
   Man   SW

ALESSANDRO BLASETTI
1860   MOMA, *
Ettore Fieramosca   SP, *
Fabiola   BUD, *
The Iron Crown*
The Jester's Supper   SP, *
The Old Guard   *

MAURO BOLOGNINI
Bell'Antonio   FI
La Grande Bourgeoise   FAC

BRUNO BOZZETTO
Allegro Non Troppo FAC, NLC, TIF
Mr. Rossi Looks for Happiness TIF
Mr. Rossi's Vacation TIF

TINTO BRASS
Caligula FAC, *
La chiave TIF, *
Miranda *

FRANCO BRUSATI
Bread and Chocolate CIV, SP
To Forget Venice FAC, FI, SP, TIF, *

MARIO CAIANO
The Terror of Rome against the Son of Hercules FAC

MARIO CAMERINI
Ulysses TIF, *

GIORGIO CAPITANI
Lobster for Breakfast FAC, TIF, *

FABIO CARPI
Basileus Quartet CIV, FAC

RENATO CASTELLANI
Romeo and Juliet BUD, FI, KP, SP, TIF, CWF

LILIANA CAVANI
The Berlin Affair TIF, *
Beyond Good and Evil FI, *
Galileo SW, *

The Night Porter FAC, SP, TIF, *
The Skin SP, *

E. B. CLUCHER (English pseudonym for ENZO BARBONE)
They Call Me Trinity FI
Trinity Is Still My Name FI

LUIGI COMENCINI
Bread, Love, and Fantasy *
Bread, Love, and Jealousy *
Till Marriage Do Us Part CIV, TIF
Traffic Jam *
Turn Around, Eugene! *

SERGIO CORBUCCI
Django *

VITTORIO COTTAFAVI
Hercules and the Captive Women BUD
Legions of the Nile FI

GIUSEPPE DE SANTIS
Bitter Rice NYF
Italiano Brava Gente FI, *

VITTORIO DE SETA
Bandits of Orgosolo FAC

VITTORIO DE SICA
The Bicycle Thief COR, FAC, FI, TIF, *
Boccaccio '70 FAC, SP, *
A Brief Vacation FI

The Children Are Watching Us   FAC
The Garden of the Finzi-
   Continis   CIV, FAC, SP, TIF
The Gold of Naples   FAC, KP,*
Marriage Italian Style   FI,*
Miracle in Milan   FAC, FI,*
The Roof   BUD, FAC, KP, TIF
Shoeshine   FAC, FI,*
Teresa Venerdì   CG, FAC, SP, TIF
Two Women   FAC, FI, TIF
Umberto D   FAC, FI, TIF
Yesterday, Today and Tomorrow   FI,*

FEDERICO FELLINI
Amarcord   FAC, FI, SP, TIF,*
And the Ship Sails On   FAC, SW,
   TIF
Boccaccio '70   FAC, SP,*
Ciao Federico!   FAC
The City of Women   NYF, SP, TIF,*
The Clowns   FAC, FI, TIF
Director's Notebook   FI, IMAGES,
   TWY
La Dolce Vita   FAC, FI, SP, TIF,*
8½   COR, FAC, SP, TIF,*
Fellini Satyricon   FAC, FI, TIF,*
Fellini's Casanova   SW, CWF
Fellini's Roma   FI
Ginger and Fred   FAC, FI, TIF,*
Juliet of the Spirits   FAC, FI, SP,*
Love in the City   FAC, NYF, TIF
The Nights of Cabiria   FAC, FI,
   TIF,*
Orchestra Rehearsal   NYF
Spirits of the Dead   BUD, FI,*
La Strada   FAC, FI, TIF
The Swindle   IVY
Variety Lights   FAC, NYF
I Vitelloni   COR, FAC, SP, TIF,*
The White Sheik   FAC, NYF, SP,
   TIF,*

MARCO FERRERI
The Ape Woman   FI
Don't Touch the White Woman   *
La Grande Bouffe   *
The Last Woman   COR,*
L'udienza   FAC, TIF
Tales of Ordinary Madness   FAC, TIF

PIETRO FRANCISCI
Hercules   FAC, CWF
Hercules Unchained   FAC, CWF

RICCARDO FREDA
The Horrible Dr. Hitchcock   IVY

CARMINE GALLONE
Scipio Africanus *

PIETRO GERMI
Alfredo, Alfredo   FI, SP,*
Divorce Italian Style *
In the Name of the Law *
Seduced and Abandoned   FAC, KP,
   TIF

ENRICO GUAZZONI
Quo Vadis?   FAC, MOMA

ALBERTO LATTUADA
The Bandit *
The Cricket   FAC, TIF
Love in the City   FAC, NYF, TIF
Mafioso   FI,*
La Mandragola *
Stay As You Are   FAC, NLC, TIF
Variety Lights   FAC, NYF

GABRIELE LAVIA
Scandalous Gilda *

SERGIO LEONE
The Colossus of Rhodes   FI
Duck, You Sucker!   FI, *
A Fistful of Dollars   FAC, FI
For a Few Dollars More   FAC, FI, *
The Good, the Bad, and the
   Ugly   FAC, FI, TIF, *
Once upon a Time in America   FAC,
   SW, *
Once upon a Time in the West   FAC,
   FI, *

NANNI LOY
Cafe Express   FAC
Head of the Family   FAC
Where's Piccone?   FAC, KI, TIF

LUIGI MAGNI
In the Name of the Pope King   FAC,
   KI, SP, TIF, *

FRANCESCO MASELLI
Love in the City   BUD, FAC, L,
   NYF, TIF

MARIO MONICELLI
Amici miei   SP, TIF, *
Big Deal on Madonna Street   FAC,
   NYF, *
Boccaccio '70   FAC, SP, *
The Great War *
Let's Hope It's a Girl *
The Organizer   BUD, IMAGES
The Passionate Thief   FAC

Totò Looks for a House *
A Very Petit Bourgeois *
Viva Italia!   CIV
We Want the Colonels! *

GIULIANO MONTALDO
Sacco and Vanzetti   BUD, FAC, FI,
   TWY

NANNI MORETTI
Bianca *
Ecco Bombo   FI
The Mass Is Over   FI, *

MAURIZIO NICHETTI
Ratataplan *

ERMANNO OLMI
The Fiancés   KP
A Man Named John   FI
The Sound of Trumpets   FI
The Tree of the Wooden Clogs   NYF, *

PIER PAOLO PASOLINI
Accattone   FI
The Arabian Nights   FAC, *
The Canterbury Tales   FAC, FI, *
The Decameron   FAC, FI, *
The Gospel According to St.
   Matthew   COR, FAC, FI, KP,
   TIF, *
Hawks and Sparrows   KI, *
Mamma Roma   SP, *
Medea   FAC, NLC, TIF, *
Notes for an African Orestes   CG
Oedipus Rex   FAC, KI, *
Pig Pen   NLC

Rogopag   FI
Salò   FI,*
Teorema   BUD, FAC, KI,*
Whoever Says the Truth Shall Die: A
   Film on Pier Paolo Pasolini
   (director, Philo Bregstein) FAC

GIOVANNI PASTRONE
Cabiria   FAC, MOMA

ELIO PETRI
Investigation of a Citizen above
   Suspicion   COR, SW
The Tenth Victim   FI, TIF,*
The Working Class Goes to
   Heaven   NLC,*

GILLO PONTECORVO
The Battle of Algiers   FAC, FI, TIF,*
Burn!   FAC, FI,*
Kapo   FI,*

DINO RISI
Bread, Love, and . . .   *
The Easy Life   *
How Funny Can Sex Be?   TIF
Love in the City   BUD, L, NYF, TIF
The Monsters   *

FRANCESCO ROSI
Carmen   FAC, SW,*
Christ Stopped at Eboli   FAC, TIF
Excellent Cadavers   *
Hands Over the City   *
Lucky Luciano   FAC, FI, TIF
The Mattei Case   *
Salvatore Giuliano   SW
Three Brothers   CIV, FAC, SP, TIF,*

ROBERTO ROSSELLINI
The Age of the Medici   FAC, FI
Augustine of Hippo   FAC
Blaise Pascal   FAC
Era Notte a Roma   FI
Europe '51   FAC
Fear   FAC, FI
The Flowers of St. Francis   FAC,*
Garibaldi   L,*
General Della Rovere   FAC, NYF,
   TIF
Germany, Year Zero   FAC, FI, SP,
   TIF,*
The Machine to Kill Bad People   FI
The Messiah   FAC, *
The Miracle   FAC, TIF
Open City   BUD, COR, FAC, FI,
   IMAGES, KP, L, TIF,*
Paisan   BUD, FAC, FI, IMAGES,
   TIF,*
The Rise to Power of Louis XIV   FAC,
   FI, MOMA, TIF
Rogopag   FI
Socrates   NYF
Stromboli   BUD, FAC, FI, KP, L,
   TIF
Vanina Vanini   COR, FAC
Voyage to Italy   FAC, FI, IMAGES,
   TIF

SALVATORE SAMPERI
Ernesto   FAC
Malicious   FAC,*
Submission   FAC

ETTORE SCOLA
Le Bal   CIV, FAC, TIF,*
Dirty, Mean and Nasty (Down and
   Dirty)   FAC, NLC, TIF,*
A Drama of Jealousy and Other
   Things   SW, TWY

The Family FAC, NY,*
Macaroni FAC, FI, TIF,*
La Nuit de Varennes FAC, SW, TIF,*
Passion of Love FAC, SP, TIF,*
A Special Day CIV, FAC, TIF,*
We All Loved Each Other Very Much CIV, FAC, TIF
Will Our Heroes Succeed in Locating Their Friend Mysteriously Disappeared in Africa? *

PAOLO AND VITTORIO TAVIANI
Allonsanfan FAC, KI, TIF
Good Morning, Babylon FAC, KI
Kaos FI,*
The Meadow NYF
The Night of the Shooting Stars FAC, FI, SP, TIF,*
Padre Padrone CIV, FAC, TIF

CINZIA TH TORRINI
Game of Chance *
Hotel Colonial *

MASSIMO TROISI
I'm Starting from Three *

TONINO VALERII
My Name Is Nobody FAC, SP, SW, TWY, CWF,*

CARLO VERDONE
Acqua e sapone FAC,*

MARCO VICARIO
The Sensual Man FAC, TIF
Wifemistress FI, TIF

LUCHINO VISCONTI
Bellissima CG, FAC, TIF,*

Boccaccio '70 FAC, SP,*
Conversation Piece FAC, NLC
The Damned FAC, SW, TIF, TWY
Death in Venice FAC, SW, TIF,*
The Innocent FAC, FI,*
The Leopard FI,*
Ludwig FI,*
Obsession FAC, TIF,*
Rocco and His Brothers COR, FAC,*
Sandra COR
Senso (The Wanton Countess) COR, FAC, NYF,*
The Stranger FI
La Terra Trema FAC, FI,*

LINA WERTMÜLLER
All Screwed Up NLC, TIF
Bell Starr Story FAC
Blood Feud TIF
Joke of Destiny FAC, TIF
The Lizards (I basilischi) SP,*
Love and Anarchy CIV, FAC, TIF,*
A Night Full of Rain FI, SW, TWY
The Seduction of Mimi FAC, NLC, TIF,*
Seven Beauties CIV, FAC, SP, TIF
Sotto Sotto FAC, SP, SW, TIF,*
Summer-Night (with Greek Profile, Almond Eyes, and Scent of Basil) FAC, TIF
Swept Away CIV, FAC, SP, TIF

FRANCO ZEFFIRELLI
Brother Sun, Sister Moon FAC, FI,*
The Champ FI,*
Endless Love SW
Jesus of Nazareth TIF,*
Othello TIF
Romeo and Juliet FI, TIF
The Taming of the Shrew SW, TWY,*
La Traviata FAC, SW, TIF

Index